CHAMPIONS (CONTINUED ON BACK END PAPER)

W	D	Away L	F	A	Pts	Goal Average	No of Players	Ever Present
8	3	0	35	8	19	3.36	18	2
7	2	2	30	18	16	3.23	19	3
5	1	5	24	17	11	2.86	21	3
8	0	5	38	25	16	3.57	15	2
9	2	4	42	19	20	3.33	15	3
7	4	4	35	29	18	2.80	24	1
8	3	4	29	23	19	2.66	16	2
6	4	5	31	28	16	2.60	17	2
11	2	2	37	22	24	2.43	17	4
8	4	3	29	17	20	1.86	23	1
4	5	8	18	27	13	2.23	24	1
10	2	5	32	17	22	2.26	21	2
7	5	5	23	22	19	1.73	18	3
7	3	7	18	21	17	1.47	19	1
7	1	9	23	29	15	1.58	23	3
6	4	7	14	18	16	1.41	22	2
9	1	7	31	21	19	2.11	21	nil
9	2	8	30	31	20	2.07	21	1
4	6	9	23	34	14	1.94	27	nil
8	5	6	38	29	21	2.13	25	nil
10	4	5	33	21	24	1.71	25	1
6	5	8	22	23	17	2.21	18	nil
8	4	7	25	22	20	1.89	26	nil
7	3	9	25	33	17	1.57	21	nil
11	2	6	39	26	24	2.26	22	1
6	7	6	27	27	19	2.05	21	1
11	3	5	32	18	25	2.00	24	nil
11	3	7	39	26	25	2.47	18	1
6	10	5	23	20	22	1.88	23	1
7	9	5	20	21	23	1.50	22	2
9	5	7	20	18	23	1.66	19	3
8	6	7	25	24	22	1.42	22	1
11	8	2	38	18	30	1.64	22	nil
9	5	7	42	43	23	2.19	24	nil
6	5	10	32	38	17	2.28	21	3
9	5	7	42	38	23	2.42	24	2
3	7	11	31	46	13	2.04	22	4
11	4	6	49	37	26	2.50	22	1

THE GUINNESS BOOK OF
SOCCER
FACTS & FEATS
2nd Edition

THE GUINNESS BOOK OF
SOCCER
FACTS & FEATS
2nd Edition

By Jack Rollin

GUINNESS SUPERLATIVES LIMITED
2 CECIL COURT, LONDON ROAD, ENFIELD, MIDDLESEX

ACKNOWLEDGEMENTS
The author wishes to acknowledge the
following sources: Maurice Golesworthy, The
Encyclopaedia of Association Football; C. R.
Williamson; Rothmans Football Yearbooks;
FIFA News; World Soccer; also the following
assistance: Lionel Francis and Margaret
Millership.

© **Jack Rollin and Guinness Superlatives
    Ltd 1979**
Editorial: Peter Matthews Stan Greenberg
Alex Reid and David Roberts
Artwork: Eddie Botchway Don Roberts and
Pat Gibbon
Design and layout: David Roberts
Picture research: Beverley Waites
Index: Anna Pavord

Published in Great Britain by
Guinness Superlatives Ltd
2 Cecil Court London Road Enfield Middlesex

ISBN 0 85112 203 5
'Guinness' is a registered trade mark of
Arthur Guinness Son & Co Ltd
Colour separation by
Newsele Litho Ltd, London and Milan

Printed and bound in Great Britain by
Butler and Tanner, Ltd, Frome
Typeset by Redwood Burn Ltd, Trowbridge

Contents

Introduction

The second edition of the *Guinness Book of Soccer Facts and Feats* provides not only an extension to the information which was featured in the first edition but treads further fresh ground in many different areas. Thus while more territory is covered and in some depth, the vital, original links with basic facts and figures are maintained.

Even with the material which has remained constant there have been additions here and there as well as a different view of a familiar subject. For example whereas the first edition had a comparison of the League champions since the initial Football League season in 1888–89, now the F.A. Cup which was featured in highlights previously, comes under the same type of scrutiny from 1871–72.

Similarly the Football League and Scottish League club directories have been redesigned and in the case of the latter provided with extra information.

Then while the first edition included the leading scorers in the four English divisions since the war, now those who figured between the wars are featured and for the First Division alone all those dating back to the start of the competition in 1888–89.

Charts feature the growth in the membership of countries belonging to the world governing body FIFA since 1904 and a map of the world with the latest statistics concerning teams, players and referees, which again updates the previous book. And on the eve of the European Cup's 25th anniversary there is a graph showing trends in attendances and goalscoring.

The rivalry between Manchester City and Manchester United and similarly the Glasgow pair Celtic and Rangers can also be found as can further players who have made a century of international appearances.

Among the entirely new sections is an A to Z of all Football League and Scottish League clubs with one main story for each, varying from high peaks to low ebbs and also the serious to the amusing. In fact covering the many and varied facets of the game.

An analysis of last season's domestic football in Europe in an easy to read form provides a comprehensive look at the Continental game and there are new entries in the Miscellany which proved to be one of the most popular features in the first edition. Moreover an increased pictorial content and a more economical use of text reflects the expansion of this second edition.

MILESTONES

THE LAWS OF THE GAME AS THEY STOOD IN 1872

1. The maximum length of ground shall be 200 yards, the maximum breadth shall be 100 yards, the length and breadth shall be marked off with flags; and the goal shall be upright posts, 8 yards apart, with a tape across them, 8 feet from the ground.

2. The winners of the toss shall have the choice of goals. The game shall be commenced by a place kick from the centre of the ground by the side losing the toss, the other side shall not approach within 10 yards of the ball until it is kicked off.

3. After a goal is won the losing side shall kick off, and goals shall be changed. In the event, however, of no goal having fallen to either party at the lapse of half the allotted time, ends shall then be changed. After the change of ends at half-time, ends shall not again be changed.

4. A goal shall be won when the ball passes between the goal posts under the tape, not being thrown, knocked on, or carried. The ball hitting one or other of the goal or boundary posts rebounding into play is considered in play.

5. When the ball is in touch, the first player who touches it shall throw it from the point on the boundary line where it left the ground, in a direction at right angles with the boundary line, to a distance of at least six yards, and it shall not be in play until it shall have touched the ground and the player throwing it in shall not play it until it shall have touched the ground and the player throwing it in shall not play it until it has been played by another player.

6. When a player has kicked the ball, any one of the same side who is nearer to the opponent's goal-line is out of play, and may not touch the ball himself nor in any way whatever prevent any other player from doing so until the ball has been played, unless there are at least three of his opponents between him and their own goal; but no player is out of play when the ball is kicked from behind the goal-line.

7. No player shall carry or knock on the ball; nor shall any player handle the ball under any pretence whatever. In the event of any infringement of this rule, a free kick shall be forfeited to the opposite side from the spot where the infringement took place, but in no case shall a goal be scored from such free kick.

8. Neither tripping nor hacking shall be allowed, and no player shall use his hands to hold or push his adversary, nor charge him from behind.

9. A player shall not throw the ball nor pass it to another except in the case of the goalkeeper, who shall be allowed to use his hands for the protection of his goal.

10. No player shall take the ball from the ground with his hands while it is in play under any pretence whatever.

11. No player shall wear any nails, except such as have their heads driven in flush with the leather, iron plates, or gutta percha on the soles or heels of his boots.

1848 The first rules drawn up at Cambridge University.

1855* Sheffield, the oldest soccer club still in existence, founded.

1862 Notts County, the oldest Football League club, founded.

1863 Football Association formed in London on 26 October.

---

* The date of Sheffield's foundation was given as 1855 in the Sheffield City Almanack (1902). And in the issue of the *Sheffield Telegraph* dated 29 September 1954 an article quoted H. B. Willey, a previous Secretary of the club, as follows: 'I used to have the Minute Book for 1855 but it was borrowed and never returned.'

1865 Tape to be stretched across the goals 8 ft from the ground.

1866 Offside rule altered to allow a player to be onside when three of opposing team are nearer their own goal-line.
Fair catch rule omitted.

1867 Queen's Park, the oldest Scottish club, founded.

1869 Kick-out rule altered and goal-kicks introduced.

1871 Start of the F.A. Cup. Goalkeepers first mentioned in laws.

1872 First official international, between Scotland and England at Glasgow.
The Wanderers win the F.A. Cup final.
Corner kick introduced.

1873 Scottish F.A. formed and the start of the Scottish Cup.

Preston North End 1888–89 : Back Row (non-players) left to right : Right Hon. R. W. Hanbury, Sir W. E. M. Tomlinson, Mr. Sudell. Middle Row : G. Drummond, R. Howarth, D. Russell, R. Holmes, J. Graham, Dr. Mills-Roberts. Front Row : J. Gordon, J. Ross, J. Goodall, F. Dewhurst, S. Thomson.

1874   Umpires first mentioned in laws.
        Shinguards introduced.
1875   The cross-bar replaces tape on the goal-posts.
1876   F.A. of Wales formed.
        The first international between Scotland and Wales.
1877   The London Association and the Sheffield Association agree to use the same rules.
        A player may be charged by an opponent if he is facing his own goal.
1878   Referees use a whistle for the first time.
1879   First international between England and Wales.
        Cliftonville, the oldest Irish club, founded.
1880   Irish F.A. formed and the start of the Irish Cup.
1882   Ireland's first internationals with Wales and England.
        International Football Association Board set up.
        Two-handed throw-in introduced.
1883   First international between Scotland and Ireland.
        The first British International Championship.
1885   Professionalism legalised in England.
        Arbroath beat Bon Accord 36–0 in Scottish Cup; still a record score for an official first-class match.

1886   International caps first awarded.
1888   Football League formed.
1889   Preston North End achieve the League and F.A. Cup 'double'.
1890   Irish League formed.
        First hat-trick in the F.A. Cup Final, by Blackburn's William Townley.
        Goal nets invented.
        Scottish League formed.
1891   Referees and linesmen replace umpires.
        Introduction of the penalty kick.
1892   Penalty taker must not play the ball twice.
        Extra time allowed for taking a penalty.
        Goal nets used in F.A. Cup Final for the first time.
        Division Two of the Football League formed.
1893   Scotland adopts professionalism.
1894   First F.A. Amateur Cup final.
        Division Two of Scottish League formed.
        Referee given complete control of the game. Unnecessary for players in future to appeal to him for a decision.
        Goalkeeper can only be charged when playing the ball or obstructing an opponent.

Alf Common and the spectre of inflationary transfer fees in 1905 after his move from Sunderland to Middlesbrough with the hope that the ghostly clutches of the Second Division would be banished at the same time. The spiral has continued unabated.

1895 F.A. Cup stolen from a Birmingham shop window. It was never recovered.
Goalposts and cross-bars must not exceed 5 in. in width.
Player taking throw-in must stand on touch-line.

1897 Aston Villa win both the League and the F.A. Cup.
The Corinthians tour South America.
The word 'intentional' introduced into the law on handling.

1898 Players' Union first formed.

1899 Promotion and relegation first used in the Football League, replacing Test Matches.

1901 Tottenham Hotspur win the F.A. Cup while members of the Southern League.

1902 Terracing collapses during the Scotland–England match at Ibrox Park, killing 25.

1904 FIFA formed in Paris, on 21 May.

1905 First £1,000 transfer. Alf Common moves from Sunderland to Middlesbrough.
First international in South America, between Argentina and Uruguay.
England joins FIFA.

1907 Amateur F.A. formed. Players' Union (now Professional Footballers' Association (PFA) re-formed.

1908 England play in Vienna, their first international against a foreign side.
The first Olympic soccer tournament in London, won by the United Kingdom.

1910 Scotland, Wales and Ireland join FIFA.

1912 Goalkeeper not permitted to handle ball outside his own penalty area.

1913 Defending players not to approach within ten yards of ball at a free-kick.

1914 Defending players not to approach within ten yards of ball at corner kick.

1916 The South American Championship first held.

1920 Division Three (Southern Section) of the Football League formed.
Players cannot be offside at a throw-in.

1921 Division Three (Northern Section) formed.

1922 Promotion and relegation introduced in the Scottish League.

1923 First F.A. Cup final at Wembley: Bolton beat West Ham before a record crowd.

1924 A goal may be scored direct from a corner kick.

1925 Offside law changed to require two instead of three defenders between attacker and goal.
Player taking throw-in must have both feet on touch-line.

THE FIRST WELSH VICTORY IN THE ENGLISH CUP: A DRAMATIC FINAL.

THE GREATEST FOOTBALL MATCH OF THE YEAR AS SEEN FROM THE AIR: THE STADIUM AT WEMBLEY, PACKED WITH A MIGHTY CONCOURSE OF 90,000 SPECTATORS, DURING THE FINAL FOR THE FOOTBALL ASSOCIATION CUP, BETWEEN CARDIFF CITY AND WOOLWICH ARSENAL, PLAYED BEFORE THE KING.

THE KING JOINS IN COMMUNITY SINGING BY THE ASSEMBLED SPECTATORS: HIS MAJESTY (CENTRE) WITH LORD DERBY (NEXT TO RIGHT); AND MR. AND MRS. WINSTON CHURCHILL (STANDING TOGETHER BEHIND THE KING).

THE ONE AND ONLY GOAL, KICKED BY FERGUSON (LEFT), THAT GAVE CARDIFF THE VICTORY: LEWIS, THE ARSENAL GOAL-KEEPER (KNEELING) UNLUCKILY KNOCKS THE BALL THROUGH THE POSTS IN TRYING TO SAVE.

1926 Huddersfield Town achieve the first hat-trick of League Championships.
1927 Cardiff City take the F.A. Cup out of England for the first time.
Mitropa Cup begins.
J. C. Clegg, President of the F.A., knighted.
1928 British associations leave FIFA over broken-time payments to amateurs.
First £10,000 transfer: David Jack goes from Bolton to Arsenal.
Dixie Dean scores 60 goals for Everton in Division One, a Football League record.
1929 England lose 4–3 to Spain in Madrid, their first defeat on the continent.
Goalkeeper compelled to stand still on his goal-line at penalty-kick.
1930 Uruguay win the first World Cup, in Montevideo, Uruguay.
F. J. Wall, secretary of the F.A., knighted.
1931 Goalkeeper permitted to carry ball four steps instead of two.
Instead of free-kick after a foul throw-in it reverts to opposing side.
Scotland lose 5–0 to Austria in Vienna, their first defeat on the continent.

Hector Castro (just to left of right-hand upright) known as "El Manco" (one-arm) scores Uruguay's fourth goal in the 1930 World Cup Final against Argentina in Montevideo. They won 4–2. (Popperfoto)

1933 Numbers worn for the first time in the F.A. Cup Final.
1934 Italy win the second World Cup, in Rome, Italy.
1935 Arsenal equal Huddersfield's hat-trick of League Championships.
Arsenal centre-forward Ted Drake scores seven goals against Aston Villa at Villa Park, a Division One record.
1936 Defending players not permitted to tap the ball into goalkeeper's hands from a goal-kick.
Luton centre-forward Joe Payne scores 10 goals against Bristol Rovers, a Football League record.
Dixie Dean overhauls Steve Bloomer's 352 goals in the Football League.
1937 A record crowd of 149,547 watch the Scotland v England match at Hampden Park.
Defending players not permitted to tap the ball into goalkeeper's hands from free-kick inside penalty area.
Weight of ball increased from 13–15 oz. to 14–16 oz.
Arc of circle ten yards radius from penalty spot to be drawn outside penalty area.
1938 Italy retain the World Cup, in Paris, France.
Laws of the game rewritten.
Scotland's Jimmy McGrory retires, having scored 550 goals in first-class football, a British record.
1946 British associations rejoin FIFA.
The Burnden Park tragedy: 33 killed and

over 400 injured during an F.A. Cup tie between Bolton and Stoke.

1949 Aircraft carrying Italian champions Torino crashes at Superga near Turin, killing all on board.

England are beaten 2–0 by Republic of Ireland at Goodison Park, so losing their unbeaten home record against sides outside the home countries.

Rangers win the first 'treble' – Scottish League, Scottish Cup and League Cup.

S. F. Rous, secretary of the F.A., knighted.

1950 Uruguay win the fourth World Cup, in Rio de Janeiro, Brazil.

England, entering for the first time, lose 1–0 to USA.

Scotland's unbeaten home record against foreign opposition ends in a 1–0 defeat by Austria at Hampden Park.

1951 Obstruction included as an offence punishable by indirect free-kick.

Studs must project three-quarters of an inch instead of half an inch.

1952 Billy Wright overhauls Bob Crompton's record of 42 caps.

Newcastle United retain the F.A. Cup, the first club to do so in the 20th century.

England lose their unbeaten home record against continental opposition, going down 6–3 to Hungary at Wembley.

1954 West Germany win the fifth World Cup in Berne, Switzerland.

England suffer their heaviest international defeat, beaten 7–1 by Hungary at Budapest.

The Union of European Football Associations (UEFA) formed.

Ball not to be changed during the game unless authorised by the referee.

1955 European Cup of the Champions and Inter-Cities Fairs Cup started.

1956 Real Madrid win the European Cup.

First floodlit match in the Football League: Portsmouth v Newcastle United on 22 February.

1957 George Young retires with a record 53 Scottish caps.

John Charles of Leeds United becomes the first British player to be transferred to a foreign club (Juventus, Italy).

1958 Manchester United lose eight players in the Munich air disaster on 6 February.

Brazil win the sixth World Cup, in Stockholm, Sweden.

Sunderland, continuously in Division One, relegated.

Football League re-organisation: Division Three and Division Four started.

1959 Billy Wright plays his 100th game for England, against Scotland, and retires at the end of the season with a world record 105 appearances.

1960 USSR win the first European Nations Cup, in Paris, France.

Real Madrid win the European Cup for the fifth consecutive time.

1961 Sir Stanley Rous becomes President of FIFA.

Tottenham Hotspur win the League and Cup, the first 'double' of the 20th century.

The Professional Football Association (PFA) succeed in achieving the abolition of the maximum wage.

Fiorentina win the first European Cup-Winners Cup.

1962 Brazil retain the seventh World Cup in Santiago, Chile.

Denis Law is transferred from Torino to Manchester United, the first transfer over £100,000 paid by a British club.

1963 The centenary of the F.A. England beat the Rest of the World 2–1, at Wembley.

The Football League's 'retain and transfer' system declared illegal.

Tottenham Hotspur win the European Cup-Winners Cup, the first British success in Europe.

1964 Spain win the European Nations' Cup, in Madrid, Spain.

More than 300 killed and 500 injured in

The Brazilian team's lap of honour after their triumph in winning the 1958 World Cup in Stockholm, Sweden beating the host nation 5–2. (Popperfoto)

rioting during an Olympic qualifying game between Peru and Argentina at Lima, Peru.

Jimmy Dickinson (Portsmouth) becomes the first player to make 700 Football League appearances.

1965 Stanley Matthews becomes the first footballer to be knighted.

Arthur Rowley retires having scored a record 434 Football League goals.

The Football League agree to substitutes for one injured player.

1966 England win the eighth World Cup, at Wembley.

The Football League allow substitutes for any reason.

1967 Alf Ramsey, England's team manager, knighted.

Celtic become the first Scottish club to win the European Cup.

1968 Italy win the European Football Championship, in Rome, Italy.

A world record transfer: Pietro Anastasi moves from Varese to Juventus for £440,000.

Manchester United win the European Cup: Matt Busby knighted.

Leeds United become the first British club to win the Fairs Cup.

1969 Leeds win the Football League Championship with a record 67 points.

1970 Brazil win the ninth World Cup, in Mexico City and win the Jules Rimet Trophy outright.

The aftermath of the Ibrox Park disaster when 66 people were killed in January 1971. (Syndication International)

Bobby Moore (right) with Jackie Charlton celebrate the 1966 World Cup success with the Jules Rimet trophy after beating West Germany 4–2. (Popperfoto)

Bobby Charlton wins his 106th England cap in the quarter-finals to overhaul Billy Wright's record.

The first £200,000 transfer in Britain: Martin Peters moves from West Ham to Tottenham Hotspur.

1971 Britain's worst-ever crowd disaster: 66 killed at a match between Rangers and Celtic and Ibrox Park.

Arsenal achieve the League and Cup 'double'.

Barcelona win the Fairs Cup outright (to be replaced by the UEFA Cup) after beating the holders Leeds United 2–1.

1972 Tottenham Hotspur defeat Wolverhampton Wanderers in the first all-British European final, the UEFA Cup.

West Germany win the European Football Championship, in Brussels, Belgium.

1973 Ajax win the European Cup for the third consecutive time.

Bobby Moore makes his 108th appearance for England, a new record.

Johan Cruyff becomes the first £1 million transfer, moving from Ajax to Barcelona for £922,300.

1974 Joao Havelange of Brazil replaces Sir Stanley Rous as President of FIFA.

West Germany win the tenth World Cup in Munich, West Germany.

Denis Law makes his 55th appearance for Scotland, a new record.

Denis Law in acrobatic mood on the day of his 55th and final appearance for Scotland against Zaire in the 1974 World Cup. (Syndication International)

1975   Leeds United banned from competing in Europe for any of two seasons in the next four, after their fans rioted at the European Cup final in Paris.
Terry Paine overhauls Jimmy Dickinson's record of 764 League games.

1976   Bayern Munich win the European Cup for the third consecutive time.
Czechoslovakia win the European Football Championship in Belgrade, Yugoslavia, beating West Germany.
Pat Jennings makes his 60th appearance for Northern Ireland, a new record.
The Football League abandon 'goal average', introducing 'goal difference'.
Liverpool win their ninth League title, overhauling Arsenal's record.

1977   Liverpool win their 10th League title as well as the European Cup.

Kevin Keegan transferred from Liverpool to SV Hamburg for £500,000, the highest fee involving a British club.
Kenny Dalglish transferred from Celtic to Liverpool for £440,000, a record fee between British clubs.
First World Youth Cup, held in Tunisia and won by USSR.

1978   Liverpool retain the European Cup.
Nottingham Forest the only Football League club not a limited company win their first Championship title. Forest also win the League Cup.
Ipswich Town become the 40th different team to win the F.A. Cup.
Kenny Dalglish makes his 56th appearance for Scotland to overhaul Denis Law's record.
Argentina win the eleventh World Cup in Buenos Aires, Argentina.

1979   David Mills transferred from Middlesbrough to West Bromwich Albion for

David Mills (right) signs for West Bromwich Albion
accompanied by his new manager Ron Atkinson.
(Syndication International)

£516,000, a record fee between British clubs.

Trevor Francis, transferred from Birmingham City to Nottingham Forest for £1 million, breaks the record for a single transfer involving British clubs.

Phil Parkes transferred from Queen's Park Rangers to West Ham United for £565,000 establishes a new record fee for a goalkeeper. (See transfers under Miscellaneous)

Manchester City pay £750,000 for Mick Robinson the Preston North End striker.

Laurie Cunningham the West Bromwich Albion and England winger signs for Real Madrid in a £900,000 move.

Right : Phil Parkes the most expensive goalkeeper following
his transfer from Queen's Park Rangers to West Ham United.
(Syndication International)

League Club Stories

Aberdeen, whose Scottish Cup Final with Celtic at Hampden Park on 24 April 1937 attracted 146,433 spectators for the biggest attendance in Britain for any match outside an international, became the first club in the country to possess an all-seated stadium. On 5 August 1978 a 24,000 capacity new-look Pittodrie Stadium was officially opened for a friendly with Tottenham Hotspur. The attendance that day was 18,000.

Airdrieonians were unbeaten in home Scottish League, Division One matches from 23 September 1922 to 5 December 1925. During this period they finished runners-up in four successive seasons and also won the Scottish Cup in 1924, beating Hibernian 2–0. However, the nearest they came to the championship was in 1924–25 when they finished three points behind Rangers, the third time they had been runners-up to this team, while the following season they were second to Celtic.

Albion Rovers reached the Scottish Cup Final in 1919–20 after beating Rangers 2–0. The club had moved from Whifflet in Lanarkshire to their new ground at Cliftonhill Park, Coatbridge and played their first game there on Christmas Day just three months before the semi-final with Rangers. They held Rangers twice to draws, the first of which saw James Gordon miss a penalty for Rangers. In the final Albion were narrowly beaten 3–2 by Kilmarnock.

Aldershot were forced to seek re-election to Division Four at the end of the 1958–59 season but established two records during the campaign. On 13 September Gateshead, making their first appearance at Aldershot, were beaten 8–1 in the club's highest League win and at Hartlepool on 25 October Albert Mundy scored in six seconds after the kick-off for Aldershot, who won 3–0. At the time Aldershot were second from the bottom with only Gateshead beneath them.

Alloa Athletic were the first club to win promotion in the Scottish League. In the 1921–22 season they became champions of Division Two with 60 points from 38 matches. Only one team was promoted to Division One which was reduced in size from 22 to 20 by the relegation of three teams.

Alloa were relegated the following season when two up and two down was introduced between the two divisions. The club also suffered when finishing runners-up in the 1938–39 season. The 1939–40 programme was abandoned after five matches because of the Second World War. When a return to the peacetime formula was resumed in 1946–47, drastic re-organisation of the Scottish League left the top division reduced from 20 teams to 16 and the lower one from 18 to 14 and there was no Division A place for Alloa.

Arbroath are the oldest club north of the Forth and in 1884 beat Rangers 2–1 in a Scottish Cup tie. Rangers protested over the size of the pitch sending a telegram to the Scottish F.A. which read: 'Beaten on a back green.' The referee said that measured along the goal-line, the field was over the minimum but measured at right angles it was 49 yards and 1 foot. The appeal was upheld and the tie ordered to be replayed. Arbroath were ordered to add over two feet and make their pitch square. The protest was dismissed but Rangers appealed against the decision. Rangers won on the extended pitch.

After weeks of negotiating with the London Passenger Transport Board, Herbert Chapman, the **Arsenal** manager, was successful in persuading them to rename Gillespie Road Underground station. From 5 November 1932 it became known as Arsenal.

Aston Villa have won the F.A. Cup on a record seven occasions. But their experience when they first entered the competition in 1879–80 was rather strange. In the first round they were drawn away to Stafford Road Railway Works, the leading Wolverhampton club at the time. Villa drew 1–1 and beat them 3–2 in the replay at Perry Barr. They were drawn against Oxford University in the second round but for some unaccountable reason scratched from the competition. While the Varsity were formidable at the time and Villa might have been in awe of them, it seems more probable that their Birmingham Senior Cup tie with Birmingham carried more weight at the time and they won this trophy that season.

The phrase "All Change" had a different meaning when Gillespie Road Underground Station became Arsenal.

Ayr United provided both full-backs, John Smith and Phil McCloy, for the Scottish team against England at Wembley on 12 April 1924. They played their part in a 1–1 draw and in the corresponding match on 4 April 1925 at Hampden Park, McCloy made his second appearance for Scotland in a 2–0 victory.

In the 1945–46 season the F.A. Cup was played on the two-legged system. **Barnsley** were drawn to play Newcastle at St. James' Park and United won this first leg 4–2 before 60,384 spectators. The second leg was on the following Wednesday and local collieries in the Barnsley area put up the following notice: 'In order that management may have knowledge of the numbers intending to be absent on Wednesday afternoon, will those whose relatives are to be buried on that day please apply by Tuesday for permission to attend.' There were 27,000 'funerals' and Barnsley honoured their dead by winning 3–0, even though they missed a penalty, and Newcastle's cup hopes were killed off.

Berwick Rangers are the only English club in the Scottish League. Their ground at Shielfield Park, Tweedmouth, Berwick-on-Tweed, is situated in England. On 28 January 1967 a record crowd of 13,365 was attracted to it to see Glasgow Rangers beaten 1–0 by Berwick through a goal by Sammy Reid. It was Rangers' first failure to get past that stage of the competition for 30 years. Berwick's player-manager was Jock Wallace who subsequently became manager of Rangers and took them to another treble of League Championship, League Cup and Scottish Cup successes in the 1977–78 season.

Birmingham City hold at least one goalscoring record. They are the only side to have scored double figures in as many as five Football League matches. In the 1892–93 season, when still known as Small Heath, they beat Walsall Town 12–0 at Small Heath. The following season they defeated Ardwick 10–2 again at home, and in March 1901 Blackpool came to Muntz Street, Small Heath, to be beaten 10–1. In April 1903 there was another 12–0 victory, this time over Doncaster Rovers, and the fifth of these double-figure scores came at St. Andrew's in January 1915 when Glossop were beaten 11–1. All five games were in Division Two. In that victory against Glossop, whose only goal was scored by the famous amateur international (later sporting journalist) Ivan Sharpe, there were two four-minute spells in each of which Birmingham scored four goals. Inside-left Jimmy Windridge hit five and centre-forward A. W. Smith obtained four.

James Forrest of **Blackburn Rovers** was the first professional to assist England against Scotland. It

James Forrest of Blackburn Rovers and England, the first professional to play for England against Scotland.

was on 21 March 1885 and Forrest had already played for England in their three previous international matches. Scotland protested about his inclusion and the England team manager made him wear a different jersey which was white but a closer fit than the others. Forrest received £1 for playing for England. His wages were £1 a week from Blackburn so that week they stopped his wages. He did, however, later become a director of the club.

In October 1927 **Blackpool** sent representatives to Nelson to sign Jimmy Hampson. They discovered he had gone to the cinema and persuaded the manager there to flash the following message on the screen: 'Will Jimmy Hampson please call at the manager's office immediately!' He was duly signed there.

John William Sutcliffe was born in 1868 near Halifax, but was brought up in the rugby stronghold of Bradford. At 17 he was playing for Bradford's first XV at full-back but two years later he joined Heckmondwike only for that club to fall foul of the professionalism which was to lead to the formation of the Rugby League code.

Sutcliffe was then persuaded to join **Bolton Wanderers** in September 1889 and in his first match under the new code was tried at centre-forward in the reserves against Accrington reserves. An opportunity arrived for Sutcliffe to attempt a shot at goal and Dick Horne the Accrington

goalkeeper saved from him. But Sutcliffe following up seized Horne, lifted him up and stood him on his head in the mud. Both players (including the up-ended Horne) and crowd were convulsed with laughter and Sutcliffe, crestfallen, 'slunk back to the centre a sadder and wiser footballer'. Sutcliffe was later used at full-back but eventually he was put into goal.

So successful was he that he not only became Bolton's first choice playing in the Cup Final in 1894, but made five appearances for England. He completed his career with Millwall, Manchester United, Plymouth Argyle and Southend United and later coached in Holland before becoming Bradford City's trainer.

An all-round sportsman, he had played for England at Rugby v New Zealand in 1889, ran with Padiham in his youth, skated, bicycled, boxed and played billiards and even topped the batting averages in Bolton League cricket.

John William Sutcliffe of Bolton Wanderers who overcame some initial problems in the game.

On 2 September 1939 **Bournemouth** beat Northampton Town 10–0 at Dean Court. It was the only occasion in the club's history that they had reached double figures in a League game. Unfortunately war was declared the following day and the score was not officially recognised.

Bradford City have the oldest club ground attendance record of any Football League club still in the competition. On 11 March 1911 their fourth round tie with Burnley attracted 39,146 spectators. City won 1–0 and went on to win the Cup beating Newcastle United 1–0 in a replay at Old Trafford after a goalless draw at Crystal Palace. They also finished fifth in Division One, their highest position in their history and level on points with the third and fourth placed teams but with an inferior goal average.

Brechin City reached the sixth round of the Scottish Cup in the 1955–56 season but only after being taken to four matches by non-League Peebles in the fourth round. The original game at Glebe Park ended in a 1–1 draw. Brechin drew 4–4 at Peebles in the replay after extra time. The second replay at Easter Road ended 0–0 after extra time but at Tannadice Park, Dundee, Brechin finally won 6–2. Then in the fifth round Brechin were held to a 1–1 draw at home by Arbroath before winning the replay 3–2 on their opponents' ground. Partick beat Brechin 3–1 at Firhill in the sixth round.

When **Brentford** arrived at Swansea to fulfill a Third Division (Southern Section) fixture on 29 April 1922 they found themselves three men short. Three players had missed their connection at Cardiff and had to complete the journey by road. The start was delayed but eventually Brentford had to take to the field two short with player-manager Archie Mitchell, normally a centre-half and who was not in the side, in goal. Swansea took the lead after five minutes and at half-time the missing players arrived to complete Brentford's full complement. Brentford still lost 1–0.

Brighton and Hove Albion scored 68 League goals in their 42 Division Three (Southern Section) matches during the 1933–34 season and finished an undistinguished tenth. Their top goalscorer was Oliver Brown with 12 goals, but in only eight matches.

In the 1962–63 season **Bristol City's** total of goals scored in Division Three was only four short of the club's all-time record of 104 scored in 1926–27 when they won promotion to Division Two. Yet, despite scoring a century, they could finish no higher than 14th. That is the lowest position of any century scorers in Football League history.

Bristol City's free-scoring forward line in 1962–63 was Alec Tait, Brian Clark, John Atyeo, Bobby Williams and Jantzen Derrick. Clark was top scorer with 23 Division Three goals. Their victories included a 6–3 win over Southend United, a 5–1 win at Bradford P.A., another by the same score at Northampton. The problem was their defence which conceded 92 goals.

The first footballer to be specially flown to a match in this country was an amateur and the enterprising club that chartered a plane for his flight was not one of the more fashionable clubs but **Bristol Rovers** who were at the time still in Division Three (Southern Section). After playing their first three matches of the 1932–33 season, Rovers were in such desperate straits through injuries that they had difficulty in assembling a team for their mid-week home game with Southend United on 7 September. It was obvious to their Manager, Captain Prince-Cox, that he would need the services of amateur centre-forward Vivian Gibbins. However, arranging for him to attend a mid-week game was not easy as he was a London School-teacher and in those days the authorities were not flexible over time off.

Not to be denied, Captain Prince-Cox decided upon the idea of flying Gibbins from Romford Aerodrome to Filton, but as he was told that 1½ hours would be needed for the flight unless an especially fast aircraft was obtained then even this would present a tight schedule, for Gibbins had to be at Eastville in time for a 6.15 pm kick-off.

As it happened Gibbins, a full and amateur cap for England, landed at Filton within half an hour of kick-off time and suffering no air sickness helped Bristol Rovers win 3–1.

Burnley's initial entry into the F.A. Cup in the 1885–86 season brought them into conflict with the early problems of professionalism. They were barred from playing their professionals in the first match with Darwen Old Wanderers and were forced to field their entire reserve side. Darwen won 11–0.

George Ross captained **Bury** from left-half in both their successful F.A. Cup winning teams of 1900 and 1903. Born in Morayshire he had come to Lanarkshire at an early age and linked up with Bury at 16. He stayed for 20 years until 1906 and shortly after he had established himself, an early reference in the club's minutes showed appreciation of his services: 'Resolved that the pay of George Ross be increased from three to four shillings (20p) per week.'

On 7 October 1978 **Cambridge United** won their first home Division Two match beating Preston North End 1–0. Their goalscorer was Tom

Finney, an Irish international with the same name as Preston's most capped player, Tom Finney, an English international who made 76 appearances for his country and set up a club record of 187 League goals for them between 1946 and 1960.

Three seasons before they defeated Arsenal to become the only team to take the F.A. Cup out of England, **Cardiff City** succeeded in beating Arsenal on three successive Saturdays, twice in Division One and once in the F.A. Cup: 19 January 1924 (A) 2–1; 26 January (H) 4–0 and in the second round of the cup 2 February (H) 1–0.

The following month Cardiff players captained the respective teams when Wales met Scotland at Ninian Park on 16 February. Jimmy Blair led the visitors and Fred Keenor the home side. A year later Cardiff supplied international players for three countries on the same day, 28 February 1925: Jimmy Nelson for Scotland at right-back; Tom Farquharson in goal for Ireland and five players for Wales: Willie Davies, Jack Nicholls and Harold Beadles in the forward line, Fred Keenor at centre-half and Edgar Thomas, an amateur and captain of the club's Combination side, at left-half.

Two weeks earlier at Tynecastle on 14 February, City supplied four of the five forwards for Wales against Scotland: Willie Davies, Nicholls, Len Davies and Beadles. In spite of their absence and also that of Keenor and Nelson (for Scotland), Cardiff fulfilled a Division One fixture that day at home to Notts County and drew 1–1. That season City had 11 internationals on their staff.

Ivor Broadis who was one of the youngest player-managers with Carlisle United after the last war. (Popperfoto)

Ivor Broadis, a war-time bomber pilot, was appointed player-manager of **Carlisle United** in August 1946 at the age of 23, having only had experience in war-time football as an amateur for Tottenham Hotspur and Millwall. He transferred himself to Sunderland in 1949 for £18,000. Later he played for Manchester City and Newcastle United before returning to Carlisle for another spell as player-manager between 1955 and 1959 before ending his career with Queen of the South in 1960. He made 14 appearances for England as an inside-forward.

In the 1925 Scottish Cup Final Dundee led **Celtic** by a single goal with seven minutes remaining. Patsy Gallagher, known as the 'Mighty Atom', started a solo run for Celtic from the edge of his own penalty area, beating one opponent after another. Close to the Dundee goal he was brought down in a heavy tackle, but reacting quickly he somersaulted backwards with the ball held firmly between his feet and carried it into the net from which he had to be disentangled. But the goal counted and Celtic then won the match with a Jimmy McGrory header two minutes from time.

In 1919 **Charlton Athletic's** ground was hewn out of a chalk pit, hence its name of The Valley. There were no stands or dressing rooms and players used a room over a nearby fish shop in East Street behind a public house called 'The Lads of the Village'. The fishmonger was a keen supporter of the club and frequently attended matches with a haddock nailed to a stick which he waved during play. This is probably the derivation of the club's nickname of the Haddicks.

Chelsea were involved in a match of 11 goals with Manchester United at Stamford Bridge on 16 October 1954. They were ahead only once at 2–1 and were 3–2 behind at half-time. But they pulled back from being 5–2 down to be just 6–5 behind with 12 minutes remaining. Chelsea lost but had the consolation of winning the championship later in the season.

After the United match, Chelsea's manager Ted Drake, told his scout, Jimmy Thompson, on the telephone that it had been one of the finest matches he had seen. Thompson replied that he had been elsewhere watching the finest prospect he had ever seen – Jimmy Greaves.

At the end of the 1974–75 season **Chester** were promoted from Division Four by having .03 of a better goal average than Lincoln City after both had finished with 57 points. It was the first time Chester had been promoted since their election to

Division Three (Northern Section) in 1931 and they were the last of the Football League clubs in membership during 1974–75 to win promotion since the competition started. Chester conceded only nine goals at home in 23 matches.

Chesterfield have been renowned for the excellent quality of the goalkeepers they have produced and one of them, Ray Middleton, made 277 consecutive Football League appearances with the club and Derby County. If war-time Football League (North) matches in the 1945–46 season are added then his run totalled 319. He had 210 successive peace-time League games for Chesterfield before being transferred to Derby County where he added another 67 before being left out of their side on 17 January 1953. Middleton had joined Chesterfield in 1937 and later became a J.P., an honour bestowed on him for services with youth clubs in the district. During the war when working as a miner he insured his hands for £2,000.

In the 1909–10 season **Clyde** reached the final of the Scottish Cup, having disposed of both previous season's finalists, Rangers and Celtic. Their final opponents were Dundee and with three minutes remaining Clyde led by two goals only for the Tayside team to equalise before the final whistle. The replay produced a goalless draw but the third meeting went to Dundee by the odd goal in three. Clyde had to wait 29 years before they won the Cup.

In 1967 **Clydebank** had the assistance of Ayrton Ignaccio, a coloured Brazilian who had played for Celtic and Reims in France. In a match at Forfar it was so cold that he had to be substituted 15 minutes from the end of play.

Colchester United appointed a secretary one day in 1963 and sacked him the next when some of his claims to experience failed to pass examination.

Christmas Day 1919 was a double celebration for **Coventry City** despite the fact that they were beaten 3–2 by Stoke. The reason for joy was that the two goals scored were the first the side had been able to achieve in Division Two for nearly three months.

On 4 October 1919 Coventry City had been beaten 2–1 at home by Leicester City. There followed 11 Division Two games without a single goal before this dismal run was broken; this is a Football League record. Despite their poor scoring record, only 35 goals achieved in 42 matches, Coventry just managed to avoid relegation that season. It is still recorded, however, as one of the most difficult seasons in the club's history. This is emphasised by the fact that they needed to call upon no less than 44 players to complete their League programme, which is a Football League record for the highest number of players used by a club in a single season.

Soon after Christmas, with the team stuck firmly at the bottom of the table, they dipped deeply into their coffers and came up with £1,500 to secure the transfer of Dick Parker from Sunderland. It was largely due to this player's efforts that they avoided relegation for he ended the season as their top scorer with nine goals.

Cowdenbeath finished runners-up in the Scottish League, Division Two in the 1921–22 season but were not promoted as only one club went up that season. After becoming champions of the same division in 1938–39 with 60 points from 34 matches the abandoned programme, when war came, robbed them of promotion through League reorganisation in 1946. But they did spend ten seasons in Division One between 1924 and 1934 and Willie Devlin was twice top scorer in Scottish League games with 33 and 40 goals respectively in their first two seasons in the division.

Crewe Alexandra have never reached the F.A. Cup Final but can claim to have had two former players who refereed the match. Aaron Scragg was in charge of the 1899 final and Jackie Pearson, who made one international appearance for England against Ireland in 1892, was referee of the 1911 game.

Crystal Palace won a cup tie at Goodison Park, Everton 6–0 in the 1921–22 season. Just promoted the season before as champions of Division Three (Southern Section) they completely harassed and hustled Everton out of the game. A contemporary report said that 'Everton were outplayed in every position except at outside-left, and that exception was due to the painful fact that Harrison never saw the ball.' Palace goalkeeper Jack Alderson spent most of the game eating oranges.

Darlington won the championship of Division Three (Northern Section) in the 1924–25 season with the team under the managership of Jack English which cost only £80 in transfer fees. That entire amount was paid out for one player, centre-forward David Brown from Kilmarnock, and he was Darlington's leading scorer with 39 League goals, a club record. Between 1923 and 1926 Brown scored 74 for the club in the Northern Section.

Alec Grant was probably the lowest paid professional footballer of all time *pro rata* when **Derby County** retained him at wages of 3d (1¼p) a week in the 1947–48 season. This goalkeeper was at the time, however, as a schoolmaster taking examinations he had missed during the war and agreed to this 'nominal' fee so that he could play when studies permitted. A former Bury and Aldershot goalkeeper he later played for Newport County and Leeds United.

Doncaster Rovers created several club and Football League records in the 1946–47 season: 72 points; 33 wins including 18 away; only three defeats; an intact defensive record in 20 matches and 42 goals for Clarrie Jordan at centre-forward. The following season they were relegated.

Dumbarton claim to have been the first team to win the Scottish Cup using the modern formation (2–3–5). In 1883 they beat Vale of Leven 2–1 after a 2–2 draw. Their side included four contemporary internationals and four more who later gained such honours. The goalkeeper James McAulay made eight appearances for Scotland finishing on the winning side in each one.

Albert Juliussen scored 13 goals for **Dundee** in two successive Scottish Division B matches in the 1946–47 season. At Alloa on 8 March 1947 he scored six in a 10–0 win and on 22 March he scored seven at home to Dunfermline Athletic in another 10–0 win. Juliussen scored 30 goals in 15 League games that season for Dundee who finished champions of Division B and won promotion to Division A by scoring 113 goals in 26 matches.

Dundee United were formed as Dundee Hibernians in 1910 and entered the Scottish League Division Two. But at the end of the 1921–22 season they withdrew. Efforts were made to revive the club and they attempted to change the name of the club to Dundee City. But Dundee F.C., which had been formed in 1893 and whose ground was on the other side of the same Tannadice Street in Dundee, objected to the new proposal claiming that as the oldest club in the area they should be entitled to the name of City if they so desired. The Scottish Football Association upheld Dundee's case and Dundee Hibernians became Dundee United.

Andy Wilson had two seasons with **Dunfermline Athletic** after the First World War before returning to his original club, Middlesbrough, in 1921. At the time Dunfermline were not members of the Scottish League. Wilson made 12 successive appearances for Scotland, six of them while with Dunfermline, and scored 13 goals. He later played for Chelsea and after retiring became a bowls champion.

When **East Fife** reached the Scottish Cup Final in 1938 with a shoe-string staff they were so badly hit by injuries that they had to sign two players expressly for the purpose of appearing in the tie. Danny McKerrall, a Falkirk reserve, was signed as East Fife had no other outside-left. Against Kilmarnock they drew 1–1. For the replay East Fife were forced to make another change, signing John Harvey from Hearts to replace injured left-half David Herd. But they won 4–2 after extra time with McKerrall, who scored twice, and Harvey thus winning medals in their first cup games for the club.

East Stirlingshire won the championship of Division Two in the 1931–32 season with 55 points from 38 matches, but by only 0.057 of a goal better than St. Johnstone, against whom they suffered their only home defeat by 1–0.

On the last day of the 1927–28 season Dixie Dean, with 57 League goals, needed three more to overhaul the existing individual goalscoring record in the Football League. Arsenal were the opponents at Goodison and they scored first. Dean equalised

Dixie Dean celebrated his record breaking season of goalscoring in a manner fitting his reputation. (Syndication International)

and with a penalty added his second, only for **Everton** to concede an own goal. But three minutes from the end Dean scored his third for a new record, Everton won the match 3–2 and the League Championship.

In the 1923–34 season **Exeter City** completed 13 successive away matches without scoring a goal. In their 42 Division Three (Southern Section) matches that season they managed just 37 goals, the lowest in the Division and matched only by Queen's Park Rangers. But while Exeter finished 16th with 37 points, Rangers were bottom with 31.

Falkirk reversed the tradition of Scottish clubs selling their players to England when they paid £5,000 for the services of inside-forward Syd Puddefoot in February 1922. Born in West Ham he had joined United from Limehouse Town during the 1912–13 season and actually rejoined the Hammers from Blackburn Rovers after Falkirk had transferred him back to England in February 1925. With Blackburn he twice appeared for England and won an F.A. Cup winners' medal in 1928.

The 'Royals' watch Forfar Athletic . . .

Syd Puddefoot who was one of the first English players to find fame north of the border. (Popperfoto)

In 1923 the Duke (later to become King George VI) and Duchess of York accompanied by the Earl and Countess of Strathmore attended **Forfar Athletic's** match with Albion Rovers. The Strathmore estate at Glamis was close by and the nobility were regular visitors to Station Park during this era.

In the 1931–32 season **Fulham** became champions of Division Three (Southern Section) scoring a club record 111 goals. Of this total newly-signed centre-forward Frank Newton scored 41, an individual record for them as well. He had previously scored 86 goals in 94 League games for Stockport County who had obtained him from Barnsley. But earlier in his life he had been at various times in the Army, Royal Navy, Merchant Navy, Calcutta Police and East India Railway. He was born in Quebec . . . Durham.

Fred Fox was selected to play for England against France in May 1925 while a **Gillingham** player, but by the time the match was played he had been transferred to Millwall. A goalkeeper, he actually only appeared in the first half in Paris on 21 May before being kicked in the face. Billy Walker took over in goal in the second half but England still won 3–2 with ten men.

Pat Glover established three individual records for **Grimsby Town** as their most prolific aggregate scorer, top marksman in one season and the player who made more international appearances while with them than anyone else. Born in Swansea this centre-forward signed for Grimsby at the age of 17 in 1930 and succeeded Ernie Coleman when he was transferred to Arsenal in 1932. In the 1933–34 season Glover scored a record 42 League goals and helped the club to promotion to Division One. At the start of the 1937–38 season a knee injury seriously affected his career and in May 1939 he was transferred to Plymouth Argyle for whom he briefly appeared before prematurely retiring. His total of League goals for Grimsby was 182 and he made seven international appearances for Wales.

Howard Matthews had been a Football League goalkeeper for 20 years when **Halifax Town** signed him in 1928. Beginning his career outside the League with Burton United he joined Oldham Athletic in 1908 and stayed with them until moving to Port Vale in 1926. Coventry secured his services in the close season of 1928 but he moved to Halifax shortly afterwards, making 33 appearances in the 1928–29 season and a further seven in 1929–30, despite the fact that he had been born in Tredegar in November 1884.

David Wilson scored 246 goals for **Hamilton Academicals** between 1928 and 1939. In the 1936–37 season he finished as top scorer in the Scottish League, Division One with 34 goals. Wilson was an Englishman born at Hepburn-on-Tyne.

On 27 November 1916 a doomed German Zeppelin, caught in the glare of searchlights and in flames from the fire of a persistent Royal Flying Corps pilot's armoury, jettisoned its remaining bombs as it made for the sea. Two of them shattered the main stand at **Hartlepool United's** ground. After the war the club claimed £2,500 compensation from the German government. The claim was relentlessly pressed by correspondence, but the only tangible reply was another bomb on the ground in the Second World War.

Bill Walsh's eight goals for **Hearts** in a 15–0 victory over King's Park in the second round of the Scottish Cup on 13 February 1937, is worth recalling not only because it is one of the finest individual efforts in this competition, but also because it was achieved by one of a comparatively small number of Englishmen to have been successful as goalscorers North of the border.

Walsh was born at Blackpool and developed with South Shore Wednesday in the local league. He was rejected by Bolton Wanderers before Oldham Athletic signed him in the 1933–34 season. In 1935–36 he created a record for that club (since beaten) by netting 32 League goals in

the season and that summer he was transferred to Hearts. He only stayed there a little over a season however, before returning to England and joining Millwall with whom he remained until the outbreak of the war.

Hereford United won promotion to Division Three at the end of the 1972–73 season, their first in the Football League. Despite winning only two of their first 14 matches they were unbeaten in their next 14 and lost only two of their last 14 to finish runners-up.

Hibernian were founded by Irishmen in Edinburgh in 1875. In September of that year the Edinburgh Association was formed but Hibs were refused admission on the grounds that they were too rough. They applied to the Scottish Football Association but were also turned down and their entry money refunded. They tried again the following year, backed by a petition and were reluctantly admitted, though entry to the Scottish Cup was refused at first. But when Hibs won the Cup in 1887 it so stimulated interest among Irish Catholics in Glasgow that it led to the formation of the Celtic.

Jimmy Glazzard headed five goals for **Huddersfield Town** in their Division Two match against Everton during the 1952–53 season. All five came from centres by left-winger Vic Metcalfe. Huddersfield won 8–2 at Leeds Road.

Jimmy Glazzard, an unusual event on 7 April 1953.

In the 1929–30 season **Hull City** defeated Plymouth Argyle (A) 4–3, Blackpool (H) 3–1, Manchester City (A) 2–1 and Newcastle United (H) 1–0 after a 1–1 draw (A) to earn a place in the F.A. Cup semi-final and a tie against Arsenal. Hull's side that season included Sam Weaver, Dally Duncan and Ronnie Starling, all of whom went on to win international honours elsewhere. The side managed to draw 2–2 with Arsenal at Elland Road, Leeds and only lost the replay by a single goal at Villa Park to the eventual winners. Yet at the end of the season they were relegated to Division Three (Northern Section) because of inferior goal average to two other clubs.

When **Ipswich Town** reached the 1978 F.A. Cup Final at Wembley it was not the first time they had played at the Empire Stadium. On 13 October 1928 before their entry into the Football League nearly ten years later, their Southern Amateur League fixture with Ealing Association was played at Wembley Stadium instead of at nearby Corfton Road where the pitch was declared unfit. Ipswich won 4–0 in front of a 1,200 crowd.

When **Kilmarnock** won the Scottish League Championship in the 1964–65 season for the first time in their history, everything depended on the last match. In it they defeated Hearts 3–2 to take the title by 0.04 of a goal from Hearts.

The 1962–63 season was badly interrupted by postponements caused by extreme weather conditions, but indirectly it might have changed **Leeds United's** appalling run of misery in the F.A. Cup. Their third round tie with Middlesbrough was rearranged twelve times but when it was eventually played Leeds won 2–0 at Ayresome Park and thus ended a sequence which had seen them lose every F.A. Cup tie they had played since the 1951–52 season.

On 20 October 1928 **Leicester City** were playing Portsmouth in a Division One Match. Arthur Chandler, the City centre-forward, had scored five goals when five swans flew over the ground at Filbert Street. Shortly afterwards a sixth swan crossed and Chandler soon added his sixth. Leicester won 10–0, their record score. Between 1923 and 1935 Chandler scored a club record 262 League goals for the club.

Andy Graver was three times signed by **Lincoln City** and on each occasion he cost less money than when he had been transferred. He originally cost £3,000 when signed in September 1950 from Newcastle United. In his second season Lincoln

Andy Graver the centre-forward who became a source of goalscoring importance to Lincoln City as well as means of helping to balance the club's budget. (Popperfoto)

won promotion to Division Two. In December 1954 he was transferred to Leicester City for £30,000, but returned in the following June for £11,000. He left again in November 1955 for Stoke City at £12,000 who sold him to Boston United for £4,000 in September 1957. Graver's third spell started in October 1958 when Lincoln obtained his services from Boston for only £1,500. And although his active career with them ended in 1961 he made a fourth appearance in 1964 as the club's youth team coach.

Ephraim Longworth and Donald McKinlay were full-back partners at **Liverpool** from 1910 to 1928. Bolton born, Longworth made 341 League appearances having started his career with Bolton Wanderers before moving to Leyton. He played five times for England in full internationals and was the first Liverpool player to captain England. McKinlay, a Scot, had arrived the season before and remained for 20 years appearing in 389 League matches. The two appeared in the club's 1914 beaten Cup Final side and won championship medals in successive seasons, 1921–22 and 1922–23.

Luton Town were the first professional club in the South of England. The club's minute books confirmed on 15 December 1890 that 'It was resolved that 5 shillings (25p) per week be offered to the brothers F. and H. Whitby and Reed' and on 10 August 1891 a minute was passed after the players Saunders, Wright, Hoy, Deacon, Burley, Cheshire, F. and H. Whitby had taken part in a meeting specially called for the purpose 'that the players be allowed 2/6d (12½p) per week for matches played at home, 6d (2½p) extra for out matches, while time lost before 12.00 am to be made up to them on reasonable terms.' Luton's first 'gate' on 5 September 1891 was £3 and one penny.

Manchester City valued Northampton Town's outside-right, Maurice Dunkley, so much that they transferred three players in an exchange deal to obtain his signature in 1938; right-half Keillor McCullough, centre-forward Fred Tilson and outside left Charlie Rodger. Dunkley was unable to save City from relegation from Division One or help them back in the 1938–39 season. But in 1946–47 the first season after the war he was the regular outside-right when City won the championship of Division Two before returning to his original club, Kettering Town.

In the latter stages of the 1933–34 season **Manchester United** were in danger of being relegated to Division Three (Northern Section). In an attempt to change their fortunes they changed their colours to a design of cherry hoops on white. On 5 May 1934 the last match was at Millwall who were second from bottom with one point more than United. United won 2–0 and Millwall went down. The old colours re-appeared at the beginning of the following season.

While members of the Midland League, and three seasons before their election to Division Three (Southern Section) in 1931, **Mansfield Town** reached the fourth round of the F.A. Cup. Their run of success in the competition began in the fourth qualifying round but they needed to win a replay 2–0 against Ardsley after a 2–2 draw before beating Shirebrook, also of the Midland League, 4–2 away in the first round proper. In round two they won 2–1 at Barrow and were drawn at Molineux against Wolverhampton Wanderers, then in Division Two, in the third round. Mansfield's weekly wage bill was £37 and they trained on eggs and milk. But they had sufficient energy to beat Wolves by the only goal. Their reward was yet another away match at Highbury against Arsenal before a 45,000 crowd. Mansfield had an early break when awarded a penalty but captain Chris Staniforth missed it and Arsenal eventually won 2–0.

Mansfield were runaway Midland League champions that season and played 50 League games in that competition.

Ferranti Thistle, founded in 1943, gained admission to the Scottish League Division Two in 1974 and were promptly informed that since their name had commercial connections they would have to change it before they could be allowed to compete. They then became **Meadowbank Thistle** and since their ground was unsuitable for League football they switched to the Meadowbank Stadium, opened for the 1970 Commonwealth Games where the 16,000 capacity enclosure is not open completely for football as only the 7,500 seats in the main stand are used for matches.

In the 1973–74 season **Middlesbrough** finished 15 points ahead of their nearest rivals, Luton Town, in Division Two, the biggest margin ever produced by a team winning the championship of any division in the Football League. Middlesbrough had a run of 24 unbeaten matches after losing 2–0 at home to Fulham on 1 September and before being beaten 5–1 at Nottingham Forest on 2 February. In 15 of their home matches they kept a clean sheet.

On 13 November 1948 **Millwall** were playing in an away Division Three (Southern Section) match at Fellows Park against Walsall. They had taken a 1–0 lead when their goalkeeper Malcolm Finlayson was kicked in the face and had to go to hospital to receive stitches in the wound. In his absence Millwall put centre-forward Jimmy Constantine in goal.

Finlayson accompanied by a director returned from hospital in the second half, when Millwall were then losing 3–1, to find the gates shut. Despite trying to attract someone's attention they were unable to gain admission. Finlayson had to climb over a gate to get in and still dazed by his injury nearly made for the wrong end. But he resumed in goal and within 12 minutes Millwall had made the score 4–3 in their own favour. Walsall equalised through Norman Male a full-back who had had to go on the wing himself after an ankle injury and who had scored his team's third goal as well.

Millwall made it 5–4, Walsall drew level again but in the 86th minute John Short completed his hat-trick for Millwall to make the score 6–5. However in the dying seconds Walsall hit the crossbar. A crowd of 9,604 watched one of the most exciting matches ever seen at the ground and Millwall's win was the only away success that Saturday outside Division One.

Montrose have had only two players who have achieved full international honours and both of them appeared in the same match for Scotland. George Brown was at right-back and Alexander Keillor at inside-left in the Scottish team against Northern Ireland in Belfast on 19 March 1892. Keillor, who scored the first goal in a 3–2 win, had been capped once previously with Montrose and subsequently joined Dundee where he made four more international appearances.

In the 1966–67 season **Morton** set up three records for the Scottish League, Division Two, with the most wins (33), most points (69) and best defensive record (20 goals conceded), in winning the championship. In 1963–64 when they had previously won this title they achieved two club records, with their highest aggregate of 135 League goals and an individual scoring record by Allan McGraw of 41 goals.

Bob Ferrier was the highest-scoring winger in Scottish football. An outside-left he joined **Motherwell** from Petershill and between 1919 and 1937 he made 626 Scottish League appearances and scored 256 goals including a record 32 for a winger in the 1929–30 season in 37 League matches. He was an Englishman born in Sheffield.

In the 1952 F.A. Cup Final **Newcastle United** fielded international players from five different countries: Jackie Milburn (England), Bobby Mitchell and Frank Brennan (Scotland), Billy Foulkes (Wales), Alf McMichael (Northern Ireland) and George Robledo (Chile). United beat Arsenal 1–0 with a goal from Robledo.

Tudor Martin spent only one season with **Newport County** but finished it as their top goalscorer in 1929–30 with 34 League goals in Division Three (Southern Section). He made an appearance for Wales against Ireland on 1 February 1930, though it coincided with Ireland's biggest win against the Welsh by seven clear goals. Signed from West Bromwich Albion he was transferred to Wolverhampton Wanderers and in 1931 Newport were not re-elected because of being involved in an illegal lottery. They were also refused entry in the F.A. Cup for 1931–32 but were re-elected to the Southern Section in 1932.

Northampton Town became the first team to reach Division One from Division Four. After winning promotion from Division Four in 1961 they spent two seasons in each of Divisions Three and Two before moving into Division One in 1965. Four of their players, Mike Everitt, Terry Branston, Derek Leck and Barry Lines went through all four divisions with them. Northampton remained only for that season in the top division and went straight back to Division Four by 1968 after suffering relegation in successive seasons.

In October 1967 **Norwich City** made history by signing Gerry Howshall for £25,000 from West Bromwich Albion in the full blaze of publicity at the Supporters Club's annual dinner. Ten years previously the local newspaper had had to chip in to assist in the payment of the players' wages.

The official history of **Nottingham Forest** Football Club records that in the years immediately following the Second World War on first team match days at the City Ground, a jackdaw boarded a Nottingham Corporation bus at Council House Square and alighted at Trent Bridge from whence he flew to the City Ground.

The bird that fancied Nottingham Forest . . .

Notts County had to endure twelve years without an F.A. Cup victory over another Football League club. After beating Tranmere Rovers 2–0 in the third round on 4 January 1958 they did not defeat League opposition in the competition again until beating Port Vale 1–0 on 21 November 1970 in the first round. Yet in 1894 they had been the first club from Division Two to win the trophy.

In 1971 **Oldham Athletic** won the one and only Ford Motor Company Sporting League award in which one point was awarded for each goal scored at home, two for away goals but five points were deducted for each player cautioned by the referee and ten for each one sent off. The entire 92 Football League clubs competed for this honour and Oldham received £50,000 as well as all eight monthly prizes of £2,500. Their total points balance at the end of the season was 97. And they were also promoted after finishing in third place in Division Four.

On 7 February 1925 Albert Pape the Clapton **Orient** centre-forward travelled with his side to play against Manchester United in a Division Two match at Old Trafford. Just before the match he was transferred to United, the move being sanctioned by telephone agreement with the Football League. United won 4–2.

Oxford United were the first club from Division Four to reach the sixth round of the F.A. Cup. In the fifth round they defeated Blackburn Rovers, then the leaders in Division One, 3–1 at Manor Road. Oxford lost 2–1 in the next round on 29 February 1964 to Preston North End but a new ground attendance record of 22,730 was established.

In the 1921 Scottish Cup Final **Partick Thistle** had to field a side lacking four regular players all on the injured list. The match had been switched to Celtic Park and the Scottish F.A. doubled the price of admission from one to two shillings (10p). As a result only 28,000 turned up. The only goal of the game came when Jimmy Bowie the Rangers left-half was off the field putting on a new pair of shorts having had his original pair partly ripped in a tackle. In his absence Partick right-winger John Blair hit a speculative shot which deceived Willie Robb.

On 26 January 1974 **Peterborough United** were sponsored, by Brierley's, for £5,000 for an F.A. Cup tie against Leeds United. At the time it was the largest single sponsorship ever obtained in soccer. But Leeds won 4–1.

Welshman Moses Russell, known as 'Dan', was prematurely bald to such an extent that when **Plymouth Argyle** were interested in signing him, Secretary-Manager Bob Jack asked to see his birth certificate before they committed themselves. A full-back signed from Merthyr Town in 1914 he made 376 appearances until 1929 when he joined Thames. Born in New Tredegar he added 20 appearances for Wales while with Plymouth to the three he had had with Merthyr.

The spats of **Portsmouth** manager Jack Tinn became famous in their 1939 F.A. Cup run, but it was Fred Worrall, the Pompey winger, who had to fasten them on match days throughout the club's success that year. He became tired of the ritual but Tinn always insisted. Yet Worrall had his own superstition and he played with a sixpence (2½p) in his boot and a miniature horseshoe in his pocket.

Fred Worrall (left) and Manager Jack Tinn (extreme right).

In the 1885–86 F.A. Cup competition Burslem **Port Vale**, as they were then known, reached the fifth round without playing a match. In the third round they had a walkover when their opponents, Leek, scratched from the competition. In the fourth they received a bye and in the fifth they scratched themselves after a drawn match with Brentwood.

Preston North End achieved the record score in an F.A. Cup tie when they beat Hyde United 26–0 in the first round on 15 October 1887.

Yet their experience in their previous tournaments had been diverse. In 1883–84 they beat Great Lever (H) 4–1 and Eagley (H) 9–1 before drawing with Upton Park (H) 1–1. But the club was then disqualified for professionalism.

Upton Park lodged a protest against the validity of their opponents, alleging that they were professionals. The protest was upheld and Preston were expelled from the competition and did not even enter the following season.

In 1885–86 Preston began by beating Astley Bridge (H) 11–3 and then defeated Bolton Wanderers (A) 3–2.

New rules had been added to the F.A. Cup during the close season when professionalism was recognised. One said: 'Professionals shall be allowed to compete in all Cups provided they are qualified as follows: in cup matches by birth or residence for two years past within six miles of the ground or headquarters of the club for whom they play.'

But Bolton protested that Preston's Geordie Drummond had been working in his native Scotland during this qualifying period. It was upheld but the ironic sequel was that Wanderers' Jack Powell had been working in Ruabon, Wales, and they, too, were disqualified.

But while Powell's career at Bolton ended and he joined Newton Heath (later Manchester United), Drummond remained at Preston to play his part in their subsequent successes.

Signed in 1883 this outstanding utility player, who once dribbled through the entire Corinthians team to score, made his first appearance in the September, and was in their side which finished as runners-up in the F.A. Cup in 1888 and the winning team a year later. Subsequently he played for Liverpool before coming back to Preston as trainer.

Preston reached double figures in another F.A. Cup match when they defeated Reading 18–0 in the first round on 27 January 1894.

In the 1940–41 Football League War Cup, a competition decided over two legs, Preston beat Arsenal 2–1 at Blackburn after a 1–1 draw at Wembley. During the competition they had beaten Tranmere Rovers (H) 12–0 and (A) 8–1.

On 2 October 1919 **Queen of the South** were due to play the Celtic 'A' side at Palmerston Park in a friendly. Celtic failed to arrive and Queens played a junior select team instead. But the juniors refused to play the second half because of some dispute about payment.

Queen's Park were an established and renowned amateur club when they finally entered the Scottish League, Division One in 1900. They had won the Scottish Cup ten times and finished as runners-up twice as well as twice being beaten finalists in the F.A. Cup in 1884 and 1885. Yet in 1922 they became the first club relegated in Scottish League history.

Queen's Park Rangers have had more grounds than any Football League club past or present. In all they have used twelve different sites: Welford's Fields; London Scottish Ground, Brondesbury; Home Farm; Kensal Rise Green; Gun Club, Wormwood Scrubs; Kilburn Cricket Ground; Kensal Rise Athletic Ground; Latimer Road, Notting Hill; Agricultural Society, Park Royal; Park Royal Ground; Loftus Road and White City. There have been three periods at Loftus Road including the present one from 1963 after a season at the White City. In fact in their earlier spell at the White City they had their record attendance on 9 January 1932 for an F.A. Cup third round tie against Leeds United when 41,097 watched their 3–1 victory.

Raith Rovers can claim to be one of the few clubs who have been shipwrecked. In 1920 their voyage to the Canary Islands, where they were to undertake a tour, was interrupted by a violent storm, although mercifully all hands survived the drama.

All at sea with Raith Rovers . . .

Rangers achieved the first treble in Scottish football in the 1948–49 season, winning the Division One title and losing only one home match, defeating Clyde 4–1 in the Scottish Cup Final and beating Raith Rovers 2–0 in the League Cup Final.

Reading reached the semi-final of the F.A. Cup in the 1926–27 season. But they started in unconvincing style, being held at home by Weymouth in a 4–4 draw. The replay was also at Reading by arrangement between the two sides and this time Reading won 5–0. In the second round they beat Southend United 3–2 at home before a marathon third round against Manchester United. In the original game at Elm Park, Reading drew 1–1 despite finishing with nine men, having lost Dougall with a broken leg and McConnell dismissed. The tie developed into a battle of attrition and another 2–2 draw followed at Old Trafford before Reading won the third game 2–1 at Villa Park.

In the fourth round Reading accounted for Portsmouth 3–1 and in the fifth Brentford 1–0 both matches being at home, the latter watched on 19 February 1927 by 33,042 spectators. The sixth round produced a 3–1 win at Swansea but further Welsh opposition from Cardiff City, the eventual winners, ended their run when they defeated Reading 3–0 at Wolverhampton.

Rochdale finished runners-up to Wolverhampton Wanderers in Division Three (Northern Section) during the 1923–24 season. The 26 goals they conceded was the second best ever in the section. They were undefeated at home and let in only eight goals including a run of seven matches on their own ground without conceding one at all. They also had a run of 20 successive League matches without defeat. Though Wolves finished one point above them, Rochdale had the satisfaction of holding them twice to goalless draws.

Rotherham United finished level on points with both champions Birmingham City and runners-up Luton Town in the 1954–55 season but missed promotion on goal average, despite scoring more goals and winning more matches than either of the promoted pair in Division Two.

Alex McLaren made five appearances in goal for Scotland during his five seasons with **St. Johnstone** before moving to Leicester City in 1933. Born locally in Perth, his games for Scotland included matches against Norway, Germany and Holland in the summer tour of 1929 which are the most overlooked international fixtures of Scotland's history even though the results were respectively 7–3, 1–1 and 2–0 for the Scots.

One of the most outstanding individual feats achieved by a single player against Rangers was by David Lindsay for **St. Mirren** at Paisley on 9 January 1904 in a Scottish League, Division One match. Rangers led 2–1 at half-time but in the second half a referee of apparently easy persuasion awarded four penalties, three of them to St. Mirren. Right-winger Lindsay converted the three given to St. Mirren and he also added another goal to help his side win 5–4.

Scunthorpe United were one of four clubs elected to the Football League in June 1950 when the competitors were increased from 88 clubs to 92. At the first vote the Lincolnshire team could not even make second place of the two Northern clubs to be elected, but as the vote ended in a tie between Workington and Wigan Athletic, a completely new vote was taken. This time Scunthorpe and Wigan tied, but at the third vote Scunthorpe were voted in. At the time they were without a manager.

Joe Shaw appeared in a club record number of 629 League matches for **Sheffield United** between August 1948 and 1966 chiefly at wing-half or centre-half. The nearest he came to achieving international honours for England was in the five test matches played against Australia in the summer of 1951.

Joe Shaw a consistent player, unlucky not to be awarded full international honours, during his lengthy service with Sheffield United as a half-back. (Syndication International)

"Take away that . . . . cup."

Oliver Cromwell presented the first cup which **Sheffield Wednesday** won. On 15 February 1868 Wednesday beat the Garrick Club in the final of the Cromwell Cup, a trophy offered by Oliver Cromwell, the stage-manager of the Alexandra Theatre.

Shrewsbury Town reached the sixth round of the F.A. Cup for the first time in the 1978–79 season beating Mansfield Town (A) 2–0; Doncaster Rovers (A) 3–0; Cambridge United (H) 3–1 and then Manchester City (H) 2–0. In the fifth round at Aldershot the scores were level at 1–1 with a minute remaining. Aldershot scored only for Shrewsbury to equalise at 2–2 twenty seconds from the final whistle. Shrewsbury won the replay 3–1 after extra time. In the sixth round Shrewsbury drew 1–1 away to Wolverhampton Wanderers but lost the replay 3–1 at Gay Meadow.

Shrewsbury Town's longest F.A. Cup run in 1978–79 included victory over Manchester City. Here Paul Maguire (right) challenges Paul Futcher for possession. (Syndication International)

Since the formation of the Football League in 1888 **Southampton** can claim to have made more appearances in the latter stages of the F.A. Cup than any other club before entering the League. They reached the last eight in 1899, 1905, 1906 and 1908, the semi-finals in 1898 and the finals of 1900 and 1902.

In the 1921–22 season top scorer for **Southend United** in Division Three (Southern Section) matches was left-back Jimmy Evans with ten goals all of them from the penalty spot. He made three appearances for Wales that season and a fourth in 1922–23.

In November 1951 **Stenhousemuir** staged the first floodlit football match in Scotland when they played Hibernian in a friendly. It was also one of the first under lights to be held anywhere in Britain at the time of the revival of floodlighting after early attempts in the previous century.

Stirling Albion were formed in 1945. They joined the Eastern League and in the 1946–47 season won the Scottish League Division 'C'. They entered Division 'B' the following season finishing eighth and in 1948–49 were runners-up on goal average from the champions Raith Rovers. Promotion to Division 'A' was achieved but they suffered immediate relegation. Further instant promotion, relegation and promotion again then followed but after surviving another season in Division 'A', they managed only 6 points in 30 matches during 1954–55 and finished bottom again only to be spared relegation when two more clubs were added to the top division.

Stockport County can claim to have scored as many goals in one match as they had spectators in another game. Thirteen people attended their Division Two match with Leicester City on 7 May 1921. The game was played at Old Trafford, Manchester, as County's ground was under suspension.

Thirteen years later they beat Halifax Town 13–0 in a Division Three (Northern Section) match on 6 January 1934 on their own Edgeley Park ground. At half-time the score was 2–0 and the goals came thus: Hill (8 mins), Hill (14), Lythgoe (50, Hill (51), Vincent (53, penalty), Foulkes (57), Downes (59), Stevenson (61), Downes (65), Downes (66), Lythgoe (80), Stevenson (86) and Downes (88).

At the end of the 1942–43 season **Stoke City's** retained list of 48 professionals included no fewer than 44 who were locally born. Only a handful were still able to assist the club at the time because of wartime conditions. In fact when the war began, like other clubs, Stoke were left with only three professionals, though another 22 were in the Territorial Army and became available later on.

Stranraer's ground at Stair Park situated on the shores of Loch Ryan is on the same latitude as Newcastle and nearer to Ireland than Glasgow. But few other Scottish clubs can claim to have 10 per cent of their local inhabitants attending matches with a 1,250 crowd inside.

After Raich Carter the **Sunderland** captain received the F.A. Cup from the Queen in 1937 at Wembley he had to clutch the trophy with one arm and hold the stand which had come away from it with his other hand. Meanwhile the Queen was still trying to hand him his cup-winners' medal. He was rescued from his predicament by his colleague Alec Hall who relieved him of the stand. Sunderland had beaten Preston North End 3–1.

"Ironside of the Vetch Field."

Wilf Milne, the **Swansea Town (now City)** left-back played in 500 League matches for the club before scoring his first goal. Born Wallsend, Northumberland, he was signed from Walker Celtic in 1919 and played for 18 seasons making a club record 585 League appearances.

The highest score made in their first League match by a Football League club still in membership in the 1978–79 season, was 9–1 by **Swindon Town** against Luton Town on 28 August 1920 in a Division Three (Southern Section) game. Four of their goals were scored by Harold Fleming whose association with the club only came about because of a breakdown in health.

It forced him to take an outdoor occupation and since he had played in local football there he asked Swindon for a trial in October 1907 at 20. After an outing on the left-wing he was signed and within two years he had become an England cap at inside-right, even though his club was still outside the League. Twice they reached the F.A. Cup semi-finals, in 1910 and 1912, when members of the Southern League. Fleming was first capped against Scotland in April 1909 and won his last

against the Scots five years later, scoring his ninth goal in 11 matches. He retired in 1924.

Torquay United began the 1931–32 season with only 15 players. Their early matches were played with the handicap of many injuries and they lost 7–0 at Crystal Palace and 10–2 at Fulham. They even lost 6–3 at home to Watford, and their only point in four games was in a 1–1 home draw with Bournemouth. When they were due to travel to Mansfield for their fifth game manager Frank Womack found he could only muster 10 players and two of these were not fully fit, so at the last moment he contacted one of the previous season's players and registered him just before setting off for Mansfield. They won 4–2.

Tottenham Hotspur were an ambitious and successful Southern League club in 1908 when they left that competition and applied for membership of Division Two of the Football League. Unfortunately they failed to become elected and the Southern would not have them back. Luckily Stoke resigned from Division Two and another election was held. Three times Spurs tied with Lincoln City, but the Management Committee gave a casting vote in Spurs' favour and, as the club won promotion in their first season, their faith was apparently justified.

In the 1952–53 season **Tranmere Rovers** were drawn at home to Tottenham Hotspur in the third round of the F.A. Cup. A first half goal by Lloyd Iceton put Rovers into a half-time lead and inspired by the individual skill of veteran Cyril Done deserved to restrict Spurs to just an equaliser. But in the replay Spurs won 9–1 at White Hart Lane on 14 January 1953 for Rovers' heaviest defeat in their history.

On 14 January 1933 Arsenal were on their way to the championship of Division One. But in a third round F.A. Cup tie at **Walsall** they were beaten by second half goals, one from Gilbert Alsop and another, a penalty, from Bill Sheppard, after Arsenal defender, Tommy Black, had been sent off. In the fourth round Walsall lost by two clear goals away to Manchester City.

Billy Lane scored three goals in three minutes for **Watford** against Clapton Orient on 12 December 1933 in a Division Three (Southern Section) match. Watford won 6–0 and it was their highest score in the League during the season in which they finished 15th while Orient were four places above them. Lane was not Watford's top scorer that

season but the following season he scored 35 League and Cup goals to equal a club record.

In October 1907 an outside-left named Tommy Dilly left **West Bromwich Albion** to join Derby County. Dilly was a Scot from Arbroath and he was to be the last of his countrymen to play for West Bromwich Albion for 30 years. The spell was not broken until October 1937 when the Albion signed Glasgow-born winger or inside-forward George Dudley from Vono Sports. He had previously played for Albion Rovers.

George was joined at the Hawthorns in August 1944 by his younger brother Jimmy. George left for Banbury Spencer in 1946 but Jimmy continued to give Albion excellent service until moving to Walsall in December 1959.

In **West Ham United's** first year under their present title in 1900, two of their players were right-back Syd King and outside-left Charlie Paynter. Injury prematurely ended the careers of both but they remained with the club. King was secretary-manager from 1901 to 1932 while Paynter became assistant trainer in 1902, trainer in 1912, team manager in 1932 and secretary-manager during the Second World War before retiring in 1950.

Wolverhampton Wanderers scored a century of goals in each of four successive seasons. In 1957–58

Jimmy Murray who achieved a century of goals in the halcyon days of Wolverhampton Wanderers during the 1950s. (Colorsport)

they finished as League Champions in Division One and scored 103 goals. They retained their full title the following season when they scored 110. In 1959–60 they finished runners-up and achieved 106 goals and though they slipped to third the next season they still managed to obtain 103. Of these 422 goals, Jimmy Murray scored 102.

Wigan Athletic had a crowd of 13,871 against Sheffield Wednesday in a second round F.A. Cup tie at Springfield Park on 17 December 1977, the biggest in the round that season, while still outside the League. They also drew 10,142 for the visit of Bury in the first round of the competition on 25 November 1978, their first as members of Division Four. But the same day Barnsley had 10,433 for the visit of Worksop; Watford 11,551 for Dagenham and Portsmouth 13,338 for Northampton Town.

Wimbledon reached the fourth round of the F.A. Cup in the 1974–75 season after winning at Burnley in the previous round, the first in the competition by a non-League club on a Division One ground for 54 years. Wimbledon then held Leeds United to a goalless draw at Elland Road before losing the replay at Crystal palace by an own goal. In 1976–77 they held Middlesbrough to a draw at Plough Lane and only lost the replay through a penalty goal.

Wrexham were probably the first club in Wales to adopt three half-backs and one of the earliest to do so anywhere in Britain. It happened in the first Welsh Cup Final in 1878 against Druids. Charles Murless, J.P., the Wrexham captain noticed that his two centre-forwards were getting in each other's way and told one to drop back to became a centre-half. Wrexham won 1–0 but the Welsh F.A. provided neither cup nor medals for the occasion.

York City won their first Football League match on 31 August 1929 away to Wigan Borough by two clear goals. Their first goal in the competition was credited to Reg Stockhill a 15-year-old English schoolboy international making his first and only appearance in the first team that season. Stockhill made one more appearance in the 1930–31 season and subsequently joined Scarborough. But from here he was transferred to Arsenal and then Derby County before returning to York during the war.

LEAGUE POINTS

Most points in a single season
Liverpool achieved 68 points in 42 Division One matches in 1978–79. They lost only four games and conceded 16 goals, the lowest for League Champions in a 42-match programme. Unbeaten at home, they dropped only two points to Leeds United and Everton. Liverpool were eight points ahead and achieved their 30th and last win at Elland Road in their 11th title on 17th May 1979, by 3–0 against Leeds who had held the previous record of 67 points in 1968–69.

Tottenham Hotspur achieved 70 points in 42 Division Two matches in 1919–20. They won their first seven matches and only suffered their initial defeat in the thirteenth at Bury on 8 November. They were also unbeaten at home where only two visitors escaped with a point. Tottenham failed to score in only two matches from a total of 102 goals.

Aston Villa achieved 70 points in 46 Division Three matches in 1971–72. Their most successful spell came from mid-January to mid-March when an unbeaten run produced 19 points out of a possible 22. Their 32 wins was also a record for the division, with 20 of these coming at home.

Nottingham Forest achieved 70 points in 46 Division Three (Southern) matches in 1950–51. Their 110 goals established a club record, while the 30 wins was also a record for the division. Wally Ardron set up a club record with 36 goals.

Bristol City also achieved 70 points in 46 Division Three (Southern) matches in 1954–55. They were champions, nine points ahead of Leyton Orient. Of their 101 goals, John Atyeo scored 28 and Jimmy Rogers 25. City also set up a record of 30 wins for the division. Yet Orient had led the division in mid-season.

Doncaster Rovers achieved 72 points in 42 Division Three (Northern) matches in 1946–47. They completed the double of home and away wins over twelve of their rivals. Five players between them collected 109 of the club's 123 League goals, with Clarrie Jordan top scorer with 42. Two other division records were achieved with 33 wins and only three defeats.

Lincoln City achieved 74 points in 46 Division Four matches in 1975–76. They also set up a record of 32 wins and only four defeats. They had two unbeaten runs of 14 matches; the first from mid-October to the end of the season. Their 111 goals was the first three-figure total in the League since 1966–67. Only once however did the side reach as many as six goals.

Fewest points in a single season
Leeds United achieved only 18 points in 42 Division One matches 1946–47. Six matches were won, all at home, and only one draw was achieved away and that to Brentford, the side who were relegated with Leeds but had achieved seven more points than United.

Queen's Park Rangers achieved only 18 points in 42 Division One matches in 1968–69. They had won promotion from Division Two for the first time the previous season. During the 1968–69 term they equalled their heaviest defeat when beaten 8–1 by Manchester United on 19 March 1969. Their four wins all came at home and only three points were derived away. They finished 12 points beneath the second from bottom club Leicester City.

Glossop only achieved 18 points in 34 Division One matches in 1899–1900. It was their only season in the division and they won just four matches. The club resigned from the League in 1919.

Notts County achieved only 18 points in 34 Division One matches in 1904–05. They won only five matches but despite finishing bottom were re-elected to Division One on its extension to 20 clubs.

Woolwich Arsenal achieved only 18 points in 38 Division One matches in 1912–13. They won only three matches. They did not win promotion to Division One but were elected to it on the extension to 22 clubs in 1919.

Doncaster Rovers achieved only eight points in 34 matches in Division Two in 1904–05. Their nearest rivals were 12 points away. They were not re-elected. Originally they gained admission in 1901 but dropped out two years later only to be re-elected in 1904. Subsequently they returned to the League as members of Division Three (Northern) in 1923.

Loughborough Town achieved only eight points in 34 Division Two matches in 1899–1900. They won only one match and were not re-elected. They conceded 100 goals. Yet the previous season they had beaten Darwen 10–0 for their highest scoring victory.

Rochdale achieved only 21 points in 46 Division Three matches in 1973–74. They won only twice, including once away in September. In February a home match with Cambridge United attracted only 450 spectators.

Merthyr Town achieved only 21 points in 42 Division Three (Southern) matches in 1924–25 and equalled this figure in 1929–30. They won eight matches in the former season suffering 29 defeats but only six in the latter when they conceded a record 135 goals and were not re-elected.

Queen's Park Rangers achieved only 21 points in 42 matches in Division Three (Southern) in 1925–26. They had to apply for re-election for the second time in three years. Their nearest rivals were Charlton Athletic and Exeter City, 14 points above them.

Rochdale achieved only 11 points in 40 matches in Division Three (Northern) in 1931–32. They suffered 33 defeats, including 17 in succession. They also suffered a record 13 consecutive home defeats after beating New Brighton 3–2 on 7 November 1931. Wigan Borough's withdrawal from the League meant only 40 matches were played that season.

Workington achieved only 19 points in 46 matches in Division Four in 1976–77. Only two points came from their last 13 games and 102 goals were conceded. They finished bottom six points behind their nearest rivals and were not re-elected.

LEAGUE GOALS

Fewest goals conceded in single season
Liverpool conceded only 16 goals in 42 Division One matches in 1978–79. Goalkeeper Ray Clemence, who played in every match, was beaten three times on one occasion away to Aston Villa on 16th April 1979 in a 3–1 defeat, but did not let more than one goal past him in any other game. On 28 occasions he kept a clean sheet, including 17 times at home where just four goals were conceded. Liverpool were champions eight points ahead of Nottingham Forest who had shared with them the previous lowest-goals total of 24. Liverpool achieved 85 goals themselves, the highest by the League champions since 1967–68. They conceded only seven goals in the last 21 games.

Manchester United conceded only 23 goals in 42 Division Two matches in 1924–25. Only a late revival in which they took as many points in their last six matches as they had achieved in the pre-vious 11, enabled them to gain promotion in second place. Significantly they drew their last match at Barnsley 0–0.

Southampton conceded 21 goals in 42 Division Three (Southern) matches in 1921–22. They were champions and promoted but with two matches remaining Plymouth Argyle had led them by four points. However, while Southampton won twice, Plymouth lost their last two games and were edged out on goal average.

Port Vale conceded 21 goals in 46 Division Three (Northern) matches in 1953–54. The three games they lost also established a record for fewest defeats. Only five goals were conceded at home in four matches. Port Vale kept a clean sheet in 30 games overall. And in winning the championship they had an 11 point lead over runners-up Barnsley.

Bristol Rovers conceded 33 goals in 46 Division Three matches in 1973–74. Though they were top after completing their programme, Oldham Athletic overtook them and York City were level on 61 points with an inferior goal average. Rovers had managed only 12 points from their last 12 matches after 42 from the first 27 games.

Peterborough United conceded 33 goals in 46 Division Three matches in 1977–78. Seven of these came in two matches at the end of the season and cost them promotion as they finished fourth, with an inferior goal difference to Preston North End.

Gillingham conceded 30 goals in 46 Division Four matches in 1963–64. They were champions on goal average despite the fact that they scored only 59 goals, one more than Carlisle United had actually conceded. Carlisle scored 113 themselves but Gillingham were divisional champions by .018 of a goal.

Fewest goals scored in single season

Leicester City scored only 26 goals in 42 Division One matches in 1977–78. Three goals on one occasion was their highest total. They failed to score at all in 23 matches. They finished bottom, with an inferior goal difference to Newcastle United and ten points beneath the third relegated club West Ham United.

Watford scored only 24 goals in 42 Division Two matches in 1971–72. They also failed to score more than two goals in any one match and did not score at all in 23. In the second half of the season they achieved only six goals in 21 matches.

Crystal Palace scored only 33 goals in 42 Division Three (Southern) matches in 1950–51. Though they reached four goals on two occasions, they failed to score at all in 24 games.

Crewe Alexandra scored only 32 goals in 42 Division Three (Northern) matches in 1923–24. They did however manage to achieve 27 points, two more than the bottom two clubs.

Stockport County scored only 27 goals in 46 Division Three matches in 1969–70. Three goals on one occasion was their highest total. They failed to score at all in 25 matches. They finished bottom, seven points beneath their nearest rivals Barrow.

Bradford (Park Avenue) scored only 30 goals in 46 Division Four matches in 1967–68. They did not score more than two goals in any one match and failed to score at all in 22. They won four matches and drew 15 but finished bottom, eight points beneath their nearest rivals Workington.

Workington scored only 30 goals in 46 Division Four matches in 1975–76. Three goals on one occasion was their highest score. In fact five goals came in their last two matches, their only two away wins of the season. They failed to score at all in 23 matches and finished bottom.

Most goals scored in single season (Team)

Aston Villa scored 128 goals in 42 Division One matches during 1930–31. They scored in every home match and failed in only three away. Eighty-six goals came at home and in 20 games four goals or more were recorded. At Villa Park, Middlesbrough were beaten 8–1; Manchester United 7–0; Huddersfield Town 6–1 and Arsenal 5–1. Villa also won 6–1 at Huddersfield and 4–0 at Birmingham. Top scorer was Pongo Waring with 49 goals, while Eric Houghton had 30. Yet Villa could only finish runners-up, seven points behind Arsenal.

Middlesbrough scored 122 goals in 42 Division Two matches during 1926–27. On three occasions they scored seven goals: against Portsmouth and Swansea at home and also at Grimsby, while they managed six on two other occasions. Portsmouth in fact finished eight points behind them but were also promoted. Yet Middlesbrough took only one point and scored just one goal in their first four League matches. In the fourth they brought in George Camsell who ended the season as their top scorer with 59 goals. His total included eight hat-tricks.

George Camsell the Middlesbrough centre-forward who was introduced to notable effect in 1926–27. (Popperfoto)

Millwall scored 127 goals in 42 Division Three (Southern) matches in 1927–28. Unbeaten at home where they dropped only two points, Millwall also won 11 times away and finished ten points ahead of second placed Northampton Town. Millwall achieved 9–1 wins against Torquay United and Coventry City as well as scoring seven goals once and six on four occasions including once away. However, they themselves were also beaten 5–0 and 6–1 away.

Bradford City scored 128 goals in 42 Division Three (Northern) matches in 1928–29. They managed double figures in their opening League game at home to Rotherham United whom they defeated 11–1, in what proved to be the club's record victory. Promotion was not decided until the last match of the season, however, with Stockport County finishing one point behind them. Top scorer Albert Whitehurst, secured during the season, was leading scorer with 24 goals in only 15

matches, including seven in succession against Tranmere Rovers on 6 March 1929 in an 8–0 win.

City not only habitually scored more goals than the opposition but they were so often in total command that they prevented their opponents from scoring. In one run of five League games during March that season they reached a total of 29 goals without reply in this sequence: 8–0, 8–0, 5–0, 5–0 and 3–0. Indeed, around this period this astonishing team netted 43 goals in 12 games during which they conceded only two goals and not more than one in a particular game. Yet the club had faced liquidation at the end of the previous season and was almost wound up.

Queen's Park Rangers scored 111 goals in 46 Division Three matches in 1961–62. But they could finish no higher than fourth and Bournemouth who were third edged them out on goal average despite scoring 42 goals fewer.

Peterborough United scored 134 goals in 46 Division Four matches in 1960–61. Seven goals were reached twice, six on four occasions including once away at Stockport, who were ironically the only side to prevent Peterborough from scoring at home during the season. Terry Bly was top scorer with 52 league goals, a record for the division. The second best supported team in the division at home with an average of 14,222, Peterborough produced the highest support away with 12,182 on average in their first season in the Football League.

Most goals against in single season (Team)
Blackpool conceded 125 goals in 42 Division One matches during 1930–31. Their heaviest defeat, 10–1, a club record, was against Huddersfield Town on 13 December 1930. Seven goals were conceded on three occasions, including at home to Leeds United in a 7–3 defeat. But Blackpool escaped relegation by one point, finishing above Leeds. The previous season they had won promotion as Division Two champions with record points and goals.

Darwen conceded 141 goals in 34 Division Two matches during 1898–99. It proved the last season in the club's eventful eight season League history and they suffered three 10–0 defeats away, gathering only nine points from a possible 68 and were not re-elected.

Merthyr Town conceded 135 goals in 42 Division Three (Southern) matches in 1929–30. They were bottom, nine points beneath their nearest rivals. Coventry City still have the cheque they received as their share of the receipts from a midweek match at Merthyr's Penydarren Park in April 1930 which amounted to 18s 4d (92p). Merthyr were not re-elected in what was their third plea for re-admission. Between September 1922 and September 1925 they had created a Football League record with a run of 61 away games without a win. And in 1924–25 they suffered 29 defeats overall in 42 matches, a record for the division.

Nelson conceded 136 goals in 42 Division Three (Northern) matches in 1927–28. These included conceding nine goals in one match, eight in another and seven in a third. But they had had their own scoring successes earlier. In 1924–25 they scored seven on two occasions, while in their most prolific season 1926–27 a total of 104 goals included two more scores of seven. In 1925–26 they also scored seven goals in successive games.

Accrington Stanley conceded 123 goals in 46 Division Three matches in 1959–60. But only once did they concede as many as six goals. And they took more points (14) from away matches than at home.

Hartlepool United conceded 109 goals in 46 Division Four matches in 1959–60. Seven goals were conceded once and six on two occasions.

LEAGUE WINS

Most wins in single season
Tottenham Hotspur won 31 of their 42 Division One matches in 1960–61. They finished eight points ahead of Sheffield Wednesday to win the championship with 66 points. Of their 115 goals all but 14 were from their most regularly called upon five forwards. The same season they achieved the League and Cup double, the third team to accomplish the feat. Only four other sides have scored more goals in the history of Division One.

Tottenham Hotspur also won 32 of their 42 Division Two matches in 1919–20. Nineteen of these came from home wins but it was a 3–1 win at Stoke on 10 April that ensured the club of winning the championship.

Plymouth Argyle won 30 of their 42 Division Three (Southern) matches in 1929–30. They had finished as runners-up six times in succession during the previous eight seasons. But not until the 19th match did they lose and their total of 68 points was a club record. Yet they had started the season £6,000 in debt.

Millwall won 30 of their 42 Division Three (Southern) matches in 1927–28. Nineteen of these came from home wins where only two points were dropped in drawn matches.

Cardiff City won 30 of their 42 Division Three (Southern) matches in 1946–47. Eighteen of these came from home wins where just three points were dropped in drawn matches. Only 11 goals were conceded at home.

Nottingham Forest won 30 of their 46 Division Three (Southern) matches in 1950–51. Sixteen of these came from home wins. Only six matches were lost overall and ten drawn. The club also achieved a record 70 points and a record total of 110 goals. Thirty-two points were contributed from away matches.

Bristol City also won 30 of their 46 Division Three (Southern) matches in 1954–55. Thirteen came from away wins. The club also achieved a record 70 points.

Doncaster Rovers won 33 of their 42 Division Three (Northern) matches in 1946–47. They won 18 away matches, taking 37 points, lost only three times overall and established a record 72 points.

Aston Villa won 32 of their 46 Division Three matches in 1971–72. Twenty matches were won at home including 11 consecutively between October and March.

Lincoln City won 32 of their 46 Division Four matches in 1975–76. Twenty-one of these came from home wins. Only two points were dropped in drawn games on their own ground. The club also set records for most wins, most points and fewest defeats in a season in the division.

Record home wins in single season
Brentford won all 21 games in Division Three (Southern) in 1929–30.

Record away wins in single season
Doncaster won 18 of 21 games in Division Three (Northern) in 1946–47.

Most drawn games in single season
Norwich City drew 23 of their 42 Division One matches in 1978–79. They finished 16th in the division, drawing 10 times at home and 13 away in gaining 37 points. In 1978–79 Carlisle United had equalled the previous record of 22 drawn games in Division Three which had been held by three clubs: Tranmere Rovers in Division Three in

1970–71; Aldershot in Division Four in 1971–72 and Chester in Division Three in 1977–78. Carlisle had finished 6th, compared with Tranmere (18th), Aldershot (17th) and Chester (5th).

LEAGUE DEFEATS

Most defeats in single season
Leeds United suffered 30 defeats in 42 Division One matches in 1946–47. Ten came from home matches and 20 away. Only six matches were won all at home.

Blackburn Rovers suffered 30 defeats in 42 Division One matches in 1965–66. Fourteen came from home matches and 16 away. Eight matches were won and they included 6–1 and 5–0 wins at home and 4–1 and 3–0 successes away.

Tranmere Rovers suffered 31 defeats in 42 Division Two matches in 1938–39. They finished 14 points beneath their nearest rivals and picked up only one point from away games.

Newport County suffered 31 defeats in 46 Division Three Matches in 1961–62. Twelve of these came from home matches. Their heaviest defeat was 8–1 at Notts County.

Merthyr Town suffered 29 defeats in 42 Division Three (Southern) matches in 1924–25. Their 21 points was a record low for the division.

Rochdale suffered 33 defeats in 40 Division Three (Northern) matches in 1931–32. Only 11 points were taken, including just one away from home. 135 goals were conceded and their nearest rivals were 13 points above them.

Workington suffered 32 defeats in 46 Division Four matches in 1975–76. Fourteen of these came from home matches and only 21 points were achieved. The record would have been worse but for the club recording their only two away wins in the last two games of the season.

Fewest defeats in single season
Preston North End went through 22 Division One matches in 1888–89 without a defeat. Only four points were dropped, including just one at home to Aston Villa on 10 November, the runners-up who finished 11 points behind them.

Leeds United suffered only two defeats in 42 Division One matches in 1968–69. These occurred on 28 September at Manchester City when they lost 3–1 and at Burnley on 19 October when they were beaten 5–1. After this defeat Leeds had a run of 28 undefeated matches until the end of the season.

Liverpool went through 28 Division Two matches without defeat in 1893–94. They won 22 and drew six of their matches. They then won their test match for promotion and drew the first two games of the following season to establish a run of 31 matches without defeat.

Burnley suffered only two defeats in 30 Division Two matches in 1897–98. They won 20 and drew eight of their games. Included among the 80 goals they scored was a 9–3 victory over Loughborough Town.

Bristol City suffered only two defeats in 38 Division Two matches in 1905–06. They won 30 and drew six of their matches. Thirty-one of their points came from away matches which produced 13 wins and five draws. They also won 14 consecutive League matches.

Leeds United suffered only three defeats in 42 Division Two matches in 1963–64. They won 24 matches which was one fewer than runners-up Sunderland who finished two points below them.

Queen's Park Rangers suffered five defeats in 46 Division Three matches in 1966–67. They won 26 and drew 15 of their matches. They finished 12 points ahead of runners-up Middlesbrough and scored 103 goals while conceding only 38. The same season they won the League Cup.

Southampton suffered only four defeats in 42 Division Three (Southern) matches in 1921–22. They conceded just 21 goals, a record for the division. Their 61 points was also a club record. Among their wins was an 8–0 success over Northampton Town. However they won 23 matches, two fewer than Plymouth Argyle who finished as runners-up on goal average behind them.

Plymouth Argyle suffered only four defeats in 42 Division Three (Southern) matches in 1929–30. Their 68 points was a club record. They conceded only 38 goals and won 30 of their matches.

Port Vale suffered only three defeats in 46 Division Three (Northern) matches in 1953–54. They won 26 matches and drew 17. Both figures were better than those of any of their rivals and they finished 11 points ahead of Barnsley the runners-up.

Doncaster Rovers suffered only three defeats in 42 Division Three (Northern) matches in 1946–47. Of their record 33 wins, 18 came away and they established a record of 72 points as well.

Wolverhampton Wanderers suffered only three defeats in 42 Division Three (Northern) matches in 1923–24. Twenty-four matches were won, one fewer than achieved by the runners-up Rochdale who finished a point behind. Fifteen matches were drawn by Wolves and only 27 goals conceded, one more than Rochdale.

Lincoln City suffered only four defeats in 46 Division Four matches in 1975–76. They won 32 matches, achieved a record 74 points and scored 111 goals.

Fewest wins in single season
Stoke achieved only three wins in 22 Division One matches in 1889–90. They finished bottom with 10 points, only two fewer than the previous season when they had won only four matches. They failed to gain re-election but subsequently returned to the League in 1891 when it was extended to 14 clubs.

Woolwich Arsenal achieved only three wins in 38 Division One matches in 1912–13. They also amassed just 18 points. They scored only 26 goals, finished bottom and were relegated to the Second Division.

Loughborough Town achieved only one win in 34 Division Two matches in 1899–1900. They drew six games but finished bottcm, 10 points beneath their nearest rivals Luton Town. They scored only 18 goals and conceded 100. They failed to gain re-election.

Merthyr Town achieved six wins in 42 Division Three (Northern) matches in 1929–30. They drew nine but finished bottom nine points behind Gillingham.

Rochdale achieved four wins in 40 Division Three (Northern) matches in 1931–32. They suffered 33 defeats, including 17 in succession, as well as a record 13 consecutive home defeats.

Rochdale achieved only two wins in 46 Division Three matches in 1973–74. They played the last 22 matches without a win and achieved only nine points from them in drawn games.

Southport achieved only three wins in 46 matches in Division Four in 1976–77. But they managed to finish six points above the bottom club Workington.

SEQUENCES

After losing 1–0 at Leeds United's Elland Road ground on 19 November 1977, Nottingham Forest completed 42 Division One matches without defeat until losing 2–0 at Anfield against Liverpool on 9 December 1978. They drew 21 and won the other 21 matches. On 30 September 1978 their 2–1 win at Aston Villa had equalled Leeds United's record of 34 matches without defeat, established in the 1968–69 and 1969–70 seasons.

Leeds United were undefeated in the first 29 matches of the 1973–74 season before losing 3–2 at Stoke City on 23 February 1974. This is a Football League record from the start of the season.

Liverpool were unbeaten in all 28 matches (winning 22, drawing 6) in Division Two during the 1893–94 season. They also won their 29th match, the extra 'Test Match' (used to decide promotion and relegation between the top two divisions) and the first two matches of the 1894–95 season in Division One before losing 2–1 to Aston Villa on 8 September 1894. In all there had been 31 games without defeat. They were the first club to win the Division Two championship without losing.

Millwall were undefeated in the first 19 matches of the 1959–60 season in Division Four. They also hold the Football League record for the longest home run without defeat. After losing their last match of 1963–64 season at The Den they were unbeaten in 59 consecutive League games on their own ground before losing 2–1 to Plymouth Argyle on 14 January 1967.

Winning Sequences
Bristol City won 14 successive Division Two matches in the 1905–06 season, an achievement which was equalled by Preston North End in 1950–51.

Tottenham Hotspur won 11 successive Division One matches from the start of 1960–61. They also achieved eight consecutive away wins and a total of 16 throughout the season.

Huddersfield Town completed 18 Division One matches without defeat between 15 November 1924 and 14 November 1925, winning 12 and drawing six.

Losing Sequences

Crewe Alexandra went 30 Division Three (Northern) matches in the 1956–57 season without a win. After defeating Scunthorpe United 2–1 on 19 September they did not achieve victory again until 13 April when they beat Bradford City 1–0. Crewe finished bottom with 21 points and were forced to seek re-election.

Manchester United lost their first 12 matches in Division One during the 1930–31 season. The first win was 2–0 against Birmingham at Old Trafford on 1 November 1930. They did not recover from this disastrous start and finished bottom with 22 points, nine points behind their nearest rivals.

Rochdale lost 17 successive Division Three (Northern) matches in 1931–32. After defeating New Brighton 3–2 on 7 November 1931 they had to wait until drawing 1–1 with the same opposition on 9 March 1932. Rochdale finished bottom with only 11 points from 40 matches only, as Wigan Borough had resigned.

Nelson played 24 away matches in Division Three (Northern) without achieving a point. Their 1–1 draw with Halifax Town on 29 March 1930 had been their last away from home because they failed to gain re-election at the end of the 1930–31 season.

Merthyr played 61 away matches in Division Three (Southern) without a win between September 1922 and September 1925. In the 1922–23 season they still finished 17th, were 11th the following season and 13th in 1923–24. But in 1924–25 they were bottom with 21 points.

LEAGUE INFORMATION

Whatever happened to those clubs who dropped out of the Football League? Some became extinct while others struggled on in minor competitions. Some were subsequently revived by new clubs who use the name of their predecessor in the League but have really no connection with them.

One of the first clubs to drop out for ever was **Accrington** in 1893. They had been among the Football League's original members in 1888, which says much for their status as a leading professional club at that time. They managed to survive for four seasons, but in the 1892–93 season finished next to bottom, and with the introduction of Division Two and Test matches they were relegated. Before the new season opened they resigned.

In fact they very soon went out of existence and were succeeded as the town's leading club by Accrington Stanley who subsequently competed in the Lancashire Combination and moved to Peel Park. The Stanley was quite a different club from the former League members but they eventually suffered the same fate.

Accrington Stanley became members of the new Division Three (Northern Section) in 1921, generally finding it a struggle until March 1962 when they resigned. The following year they were compulsorily wound up in the High Court when they were unable to pay their debts. Their ground was sold to the Lancashire County Council.

It should be added that in 1968 a new club using the name Accrington Stanley was formed and is currently playing in the Lancashire Combination.

Another club that dropped out of the League in 1893 was **Bootle,** founded as early as 1877, which had been one of the most enterprising clubs in the Liverpool area. Playing at Marsh Lane, Bootle, they had vied with Everton in a bid to become the most powerful member of the Liverpool F.A., but while Everton prospered, Bootle had only one season in Division Two of the Football League and then ceased to exist.

In the 1890s the brewing town of Burton was well represented in top class football with two clubs in Division Two of the Football League, **Burton Swifts** and **Burton Wanderers**. For a while they were reasonably well supported and in the 1895–96 season the Wanderers had an especially successful season. They were fourth, only four points behind the champions Liverpool. A year later, however, both clubs were struggling and had to apply for re-election.

The Swifts were successful but the Wanderers failed to obtain enough support and dropped out until 1901 when they amalgamated with the Swifts under the new title of Burton United. Their situation did not improve, however, and after having to apply for re-election three times in succession they were finally rejected in 1907. They struggled on for a few seasons in the Birmingham and District League but then split up. The more modern Burton Albion club has no connection with them.

Darwen is a club with a lengthy history and soon after they were founded by a group of mill workers in about 1875 they became one of the first clubs in the country to adopt professionalism. Elected to the Football League in 1891 they dropped into Division Two the following season, regained Division One status at the first attempt but then fell back into Division Two again. In 1899 they were bottom and failed to gain re-election, but the club has since continued in the Lancashire Combination and more recently in the Cheshire

Clubs no longer in membership with the Football League and Scottish League are still recalled through the club programmes which have become collectors items since the teams disappeared from those competitions.

County League. At their peak Darwen reached the semi-finals of the F.A. Cup in 1881.

Gainsborough Trinity is another club that has survived to this day despite losing Football League status. Founded around 1890 they were playing in the Midland League when elected to Division Two of the Football League in 1896, but except for 1904–05, when they were sixth, they were generally in the lower half of the table, and after finishing bottom in 1911–12 lost their place to Lincoln City. They were for many years one of the best known clubs in the Midland League, but have more recently transferred to the Northern Premier League.

Glossop North End had a longer run in the League than any of the clubs mentioned so far – 17 seasons from 1898 to 1915 when the First World War brought an end to League Football. In fact Glossop did not actually resign until 1919 when peace-time football was about to recommence.

Loughborough Town was another club that did not survive rejection by the Football League. They were members of the Midland League before being elected to Division Two in 1895, but they had two or three disastrous seasons, winning only one game in 1899–1900, and were thrown out. They continued for a while in the Midland League but were eventually superseded by Loughborough College.

The career of the **Middlesbrough Ironopolis** was brief. Founded in 1889 they played in the Northern League. In 1892 it was decided to combine with the older Middlesbrough club and apply for election to the Football League, but when this bid failed the amalgamation was dissolved. The following year Ironopolis gained entry on their own, but by the end of their first season in Division Two they were in such dire financial straits that they folded up, leaving the way clear for the other Middlesbrough club to carry on as the town's principal combination.

New Brighton Tower had a brief stay in the Football League before the First World War but has never been heard of since. There is no connection between them and the New Brighton club founded in 1921.

New Brighton Tower was backed by a Greek millionaire, M. Yberamboo, and were elected to Division Two in 1898 when it was increased from 16 to 18 members. They survived well enough for three seasons, but in 1901 they rather surprisingly resigned. Finance was not as freely forthcoming as had been expected. Two years later they went out of business.

The Cheshire club, **Northwich Victoria,** which is still in existence in the Northern Premier League, had only two seasons in Division Two of the Football League, 1892–93 and 1893–94, but in that time they introduced to League football one of the most outstanding outside rights of all time, Billy Meredith.

There have been several more who have dropped out since. When the new Division Three was formed out of the old Southern League in 1920 and the new Northern Section came into being a year later, several clubs were introduced to League football who have since had to drop out. Among the earliest were **Aberdare Athletic, Ashington, Durham City, Merthyr Town, Nelson, Stalybridge Celtic** and **Wigan Borough,** none of which remained in membership after 1931. The last to depart being Wigan Borough who resigned in October 1931. They disbanded almost immediately and have no connection with Wigan Athletic.

The only other club that dropped out permanently during the period between the two world wars was **Thames,** who played at West Ham Greyhound Stadium. Founded in 1928 they had played in the Southern League before displacing Merthyr Town in Division Three (Southern Section) in 1930. They finished 20th in their first season and 22nd in the next. It was enough—they did not even bother to seek re-election and were immediately disbanded.

Most of the other clubs just mentioned have survived to this day with the exception of Aberdare Athletic and Merthyr Town. The Merthyr Tydfil club was reformed after the Second World War and has no connection with its predecessor.

Of the more recent clubs to drop out, **Bradford Park Avenue** were wound up in April 1974 and **Barrow, Southport, Workington** and **Gateshead** are in the Northern Premier League (although the latter has been completely reconstituted).

It was not until the Football League's initial season in 1888–89 had been under way that it was agreed to award two points for a win and one for a draw. In fact the idea of adopting this system was not unanimously accepted for there was a strong body of opinion that only wins should count for points and draws should be entirely ignored. In the end the present system was adopted by six votes to four.

At the same time it was also decided that there should eventually be a second division and a system of four up and four down, but with the Management Committee retaining the right to require the clubs to compete against each other to decide superiority.

This system, under which games were known as 'Test matches', did in fact come into force at the end of the 1892–93 season, the first of Division Two, but it was for three clubs from either division and not four.

Thus in 1893 Notts County and Accrington (14th and 15th respectively) were relegated after Notts County had lost 3–2 to Darwen (3rd in Division Two), and Accrington lost 1–0 to Sheffield United (2nd in Division Two).

The bottom club in Division One – Newton Heath (Manchester United) were relegated because they were beaten 5–2 by Division Two's top club, Small Heath (Birmingham) after a 1–1 draw.

After three seasons it was decided to reduce the number of teams competing in this end of season promotion and relegation struggle to two from each division, but the number of games was increased with each team having to play their opposite number from the other division both at home and away. This system was played in 1897–98, but the results were ignored when it was subsequently decided to increase each division by two clubs, and Blackburn Rovers, who should have been relegated as a result of the Test matches were re-elected.

Since then there has been automatic promotion and relegation of two up and two down between the divisions. This was increased to four up and down between Divisions Three and Four when the latter was formed in 1958, and also to three up and down between the first three divisions from 1973.

When Division Three was split into Northern and Southern sections there were continual arguments as to which played the better class of football. The last two representative games played between these sections did not clear up the argument, but as the details appear in few record books they are well worth recording here.

On 2 April 1957, Division Three North and South met at Stockport and the North won 2–1. Holden and Ackerman scored for the winners and Langman for the South.

North:– Gray (Gateshead); Brown (Workington), Cahill (Barrow); Hunter (Accrington S.), Greener (Darlington), Hutchinson (Chesterfield); Finney, K. (Stockport Co.), Broadis (Carlisle United), Ackerman (Carlisle United), Holden (Stockport Co.), Cripsey (Hull City).

South:– Pickering (Northampton Town), Jardine (Millwall), Fisher (Colchester United), Wilson (Brighton), Parker (Southampton), Elsworthy (Ipswich Town), Hellawell (Q.P.R.), Dorman (Walsall), Langman, N. (Plymouth Argyle), Mills (Torquay United), Cutler (Bournemouth).

In the next and final game between these two representative sides at Selhurst Park on 30 October 1957, the result was a draw 2–2. The scorers were Steele 2 (South), Luke and Tomlinson (North).

South:– Springett (Q.P.R.), Bannister (Shrewsbury Town), Sherwood (Newport County), Veitch (Millwall), Harvey (Exeter City), Wilson (Brighton); Harrison (Crystal Palace), Shepherd (Millwall), Hollis (Southend United), Steele (Port Vale), Wright (Colchester United).

North:– McLaren (Bury), Robertson (Bury), Feasey (Hull City), Bertolini (Workington), Taylor (Southport), Crowe (Mansfield Town), Tomlinson (Chesterfield), Broadis (Carlisle United), Stewart (Accrington S.), Holden (Stockport Co.), Luke (Hartlepool).

With clubs from Division Three complaining about the lack of Cup football, the Football League decided to give them a competition of their own in 1933. There were to be two knock-out competitions played in mid-week, one for the Northern Section and one for the Southern Section.

Had it not been for the war there might have been an answer to the argument about which was the superior section, for in 1939 the League decided that the competition, which had not been

the success it had hoped, would be cut down to games between the second and third clubs in each section with the winners competing for gold medals in a North v. South Final. By the time peace-time football was resumed this idea had been abandoned.

Southern Section winners
1933–34 **Exeter City**
1934–35 **Bristol Rovers**
1935–36 **Coventry City**
1936–37 *****Watford and Millwall**
1937–38 **Reading**
Northern Section winners
1933–34 **Darlington**
1934–35 **Stockport County**
1935–36 **Chester**
1936–37 **Chester**
1937–38 **Southport**
1938–39 **Bradford City**

* After playing two drawn games Watford and Millwall were pronounced joint winners.

The 1939 Final of the Southern Section Cup was never played.

Some interesting scores in these competitions include – 1933–34: Exeter City 11, Crystal Palace 6; Bournemouth & Boscombe 7, Bristol City 1; 1934–35: Chesterfield 8, Mansfield Town 1; 1936–37: Luton Town 2, Notts County 4; Watford 8, Notts County 3 (this game had to be held over until the beginning of the next season); Doncaster Rovers 7, Lincoln City 2.

Exeter City's remarkable 11–6 victory over Crystal Palace was one of the first games played in the Southern Section Cup in 1933–34 and still remains to this day among the highest scoring aggregates in a game under the auspices of the Football League. It was played at St. James's Park on 24 January 1934, and only one of the Exeter City forward line failed to score, Harold Houghton. Centre-forward Fred Whitlow (formerly with Charlton Athletic) scored six goals for the City, whose other scorers were Wrightson (2), Hurst (2), Scott.

Jack Beby (formerly with Leicester City and Bristol Rovers) was the suffering Palace goalkeeper that day, and their scorers were Fyfe (2), Thompson, Dawes (3).

After such a remarkable start nothing could halt Exeter and they went on to become the first holders of the Southern Section Cup by beating Watford 4–2, Coventry 1–0 (after a 1–1 draw),

Brighton 4–3 (after two draws 1–1, 1–1), and Torquay United 1–0 in the Final at Plymouth.

Mention of Albert Dawes, who had only recently joined Palace from Northampton Town, is a reminder of the fact that the Selhurst Park club had two of their greatest goalscorers on their books that season, Dawes and Peter Simpson. Dawes took over when Simpson, who had created the club's scoring record with 46 in 1930–31, was having trouble with fluid on the knee.

In that record-breaking 1930–31 campaign Simpson had scored six in a 7–2 victory over Exeter City in Division Three (Southern Section), so Whitlow was taking revenge in the Cup match previously mentioned. Dawes scored 38 goals in his best season for the Palace, 1935–36, but his finest individual effort was five goals in a 6–1 victory over Cardiff City during the previous campaign. Simpson scored 154 goals for the Palace between 1930 and 1936, and that is still a record for the club. Dawes obtained a total of 91.

LEAGUE RECORDS

Darwen went through their entire Division Two programme in 1896–97 without a drawn game. The Lancashire club's record that season was P30 W14 L16. That was the last occasion in Football League history that a club completed a season without drawing a single game.

Four clubs have won the Championship of the Second and First Divisions in successive seasons: Liverpool 1904–05 and 1905–06; Everton 1930–31 and 1931–32; Tottenham Hotspur 1949–50 and 1950–51; and Ipswich Town 1960–61 and 1961–62.

Such consistency over two seasons is quite remarkable and maybe only those clubs who have won the League Championship in successive seasons can claim an even greater achievement.

The story of Liverpool and Everton during the period mentioned is particularly interesting because both have staged astonishing recoveries, each having been relegated from Division One only the season before winning the Division Two title. Several other clubs have done this, of course, but none of them went on to win the League title in their first season back in the senior division.

Liverpool did not make their rapid recovery through wholesale changes, indeed six of their players retained their first team places throughout the three seasons in question – full-backs Billy Dunlop and 'Knocker' West; half-backs Maurice Parry and Alex Raisbeck, and forwards Alec Raybould and Jack Cox. Six others played throughout the period although not so regularly in the League side.

Everton had four men holding their first team places more or less regularly throughout the three seasons under review – full-back Warney Cresswell and forwards Ted Critchley, Dixie Dean and Jimmy Stein. Indeed, Dean scored 105 League goals over this period. There were, in fact, 14 players who made appearances for them in each of the three seasons.

Sunderland enjoyed the best run of victories for a Football League Championship winning team. Perhaps a little surprisingly it was nearly 90 years ago in the 1891–92 season and the record created in that campaign has never been equalled by any other League title-winning side.

The Sunderland side of 1891–92 was the combination that was known as the 'Team of all Talents'. It was predominantly a Scottish team and their Manager, Tom Watson, used to tell some exciting stories of his 'raids' across the border to snatch local stars from the Scottish clubs, much to the disgust of their supporters.

The record that Sunderland created that season, was that of winning 13 matches in a row. After losing 3–1 at Blackburn on 7 November, Sunderland did not drop a single point until 9 April when they were beaten 1–0 away to Notts County. Outstanding in this side were goalkeeper Ned Doig who did not miss a single game, full-back Donald Gow, half-backs Hugh Wilson and Johnny Auld, and forwards Jimmy Hannah and Jimmy Millar, who were all Scottish internationals. They were led by Jock Campbell, the most dangerous centre-forward of his day. The only Englishman in the League side was Tom Porteous, a full-back who had played for his country in the previous season. He generally had the honour of captaining this remarkable combination.

The following season Sunderland again won the Championship with only one or two changes in the side and were the first team to score 100 goals in a League season. In fact it was not until after the First World War that a century of goals was exceeded in Division One. Sunderland were runners-up the next year but won the title again in 1894–95, three championships in four years.

TOP SCORER IN THE FIRST DIVISION FROM THE BEGINNING*

Season	Leading scorer	Team	Goals
1888–89	John Goodall	Preston N.E.	21
1889–90	Jimmy Ross	Preston N.E.	24
1890–91	Jack Southworth	Blackburn Rovers	26
1891–92	John Campbell	Sunderland	32
1892–93	John Campbell	Sunderland	31
1893–94	Jack Southworth	Everton	27
1894–95	John Campbell	Sunderland	22
1895–96	Johnny Campbell	Aston Villa	20
	Steve Bloomer	Derby County	20
1896–97	Steve Bloomer	Derby County	22
1897–98	Fred Wheldon	Aston Villa	21
1898–99	Steve Bloomer	Derby County	23
1899–1900	Bill Garratt	Aston Villa	27
1900–01	Steve Bloomer	Derby County	24
1901–02	James Settle	Everton	18
	Fred Priest	Sheffield Utd	18
1902–03	Alec Raybould	Liverpool	31
1903–04	Steve Bloomer	Derby County	20
1904–05	Arthur Brown	Sheffield Utd	23
1905–06	Bullet Jones	Birmingham	26
	Albert Shepherd	Bolton W.	26
1906–07	Alec Young	Everton	30
1907–08	Enoch West	Nottingham F.	27
1908–09	Bert Freeman	Everton	38
1909–10	John Parkinson	Liverpool	29
1910–11	Albert Shepherd	Newcastle Utd	25
1911–12	Harold Hampton	Aston Villa	25
	Dave McLean	Sheffield Wed.	25
	George Holley	Sunderland	25
1912–13	Dave McLean	Sheffield Wed.	30
1913–14	George Elliott	Middlesbrough	31
1914–15	Bobby Parker	Everton	35

* Goalscorers in the earliest seasons are difficult to check as match reports often did not trouble to mention the actual scorers.
See the first edition of *The Guinness Book of Soccer*, Facts and Feats for leading goalscorers 1946–1978.

Leading League Goalscorers 1919–39 Division One

Season	Leading scorer	Team	Goals
1919–20	Fred Morris	W.B.A.	37
1920–21	Joe Smith	Bolton W.	38
1921–22	Andy Wilson	Middlesbrough	31
1922–23	Charlie Buchan	Sunderland	30
1923–24	Wilf Chadwick	Everton	28
1924–25	Fred Roberts	Manchester City	31
1925–26	Ted Harper	Blackburn Rovers	43
1926–27	Jimmy Trotter	Sheffield Wed.	37
1927–28	Dixie Dean	Everton	60
1928–29	Dave Halliday	Sunderland	43
1929–30	Vic Watson	West Ham Utd.	41
1930–31	Pongo Waring	Aston Villa	49
1931–32	Dixie Dean	Everton	44
1932–33	Jack Bowers	Derby County	35
1933–34	Jack Bowers	Derby County	35
1934–35	Ted Drake	Arsenal	42
1935–36	Ginger Richardson	W.B.A.	39
1936–37	Freddie Steele	Stoke City	33
1937–38	Tommy Lawton	Everton	38
1938–39	Tommy Lawton	Everton	35

Division Two

Season	Leading Scorer	Team	Goals
1919–20	Sam Taylor	Huddersfield Town	35
1920–21	Syd Puddefoot	Huddersfield Town	29
1921–22	Jimmy Broad	Stoke City	25
1922–23	Harry Bedford	Blackpool	32
1923–24	Harry Bedford	Blackpool	34
1924–25	Arthur Chandler	Leicester City	33
1925–26	Bob Turnbull	Chelsea	39
1926–27	George Camsell	Middlesbrough	59
1927–28	Jimmy Cookson	W.B.A.	38
1928–29	Jimmy Hampson	Blackpool	40
1929–30	Jimmy Hampson	Blackpool	45
1930–31	Dixie Dean	Everton	39
1931–32	Cyril Pearce	Swansea Town	35
1932–33	Ted Harper	Preston N.E.	37
1933–34	Pat Glover	Grimsby Town	42
1934–35	Jack Milsom	Bolton W.	31
1935–36	Jock Dodds	Sheffield Utd	34
	Bob Finan	Blackpool	34
1936–37	Jack Bowers	Leicester City	33
1937–38	George Henson	Bradford P.A.	27
1938–39	Hugh Billington	Luton Town	28

Division Three (South)

Season	Leading scorer	Team	Goals
1920–21	John Connor	Crystal Palace	28
	Ernie Simms	Luton Town	28
	George Whitworth	Northampton Town	28
1921–22	Frank Richardson	Plymouth Argyle	31
1922–23	Fred Pagnam	Watford	30
1923–24	Billy Haines	Portsmouth	28
1924–25	Jack Fowler	Swansea Town	28
1925–26	Jack Cock	Plymouth Argyle	32
1926–27	Harry Morris	Swindon Town	47
1927–28	Harry Morris	Swindon Town	38
1928–29	Andrew Rennie	Luton Town	43
1929–30	George Goddard	Q.P.R.	37
1930–31	Peter Simpson	Crystal Palace	46
1931–32	Clarrie Bourton	Coventry City	49
1932–33	Clarrie Bourton	Coventry City	40
1933–34	Cyril Pearce	Charlton Athletic	26
1934–35	Ralph Allen	Charlton Athletic	32
1935–36	Albert Dawes	Crystal Palace	38
1936–37	Joe Payne	Luton Town	55
1937–38	Harry Crawshaw	Mansfield Town	25
1938–39	Ben Morton	Swindon Town	28

Division Three (North)

Season	Leading scorer	Team	Goals
1921–22	Jim Carmichael	Grimsby Town	37
1922–23	George Beel	Chesterfield	23
	Jim Carmichael	Grimsby Town	23
1923–24	David Brown	Darlington	27
1924–25	David Brown	Darlington	39
1925–26	Jimmy Cookson	Chesterfield	44
1926–27	Albert Whitehurst	Rochdale	44
1927–28	Joe Smith	Stockport County	38
1928–29	Jimmy McConnell	Carlisle United	43
1929–30	Frank Newton	Stockport County	36
1930–31	Jimmy McConnell	Carlisle United	37
1931–32	Alan Hall	Lincoln City	42
1932–33	Bill McNaughton	Hull City	39
1933–34	Alf Lythgoe	Stockport County	46
1934–35	Gilbert Alsop	Walsall	40
1935–36	Bunny Bell	Tranmere Rovers	33
1936–37	Ted Harston	Mansfield Town	55
1937–38	John Roberts	Port Vale	28
1938–39	Sam Hunt	Carlisle United	32

Nottingham Forest's managerial
duo: Brian Clough and Peter
Taylor (Syndication International)

Trevor Francis, Nottingham
Forest's £1 million signing from
Birmingham City. (Provincial
Sports Photography)

Peter Shilton, the Nottingham Forest and England goalkeeper. (Syndication International)

Kenny Burns of Nottingham Forest with the trophy he won from the Football Writers Association in 1978. (Syndication International)

Action from the Wrexham v Blyth Spartans
F.A. Cup tie in 1977-78 when the non-league
club reached the fifth round, but were beaten
after a replay at Newcastle. (Syndication
International)

Ted MacDougall joined Bournemouth from
Southampton during the 1978-79 season but
continued his goalscoring feats which made
him the most prolific scoring Scot of players
still active in the Football League. (Syndication
International)

Above: The victorious Ipswich Town team with the F.A. Cup after their first win at Wembley in 1978 against Arsenal. (Syndication International)

A model of the proposed complex which will include a new ground for Millwall F.C. in South London. (Sporting Pictures)

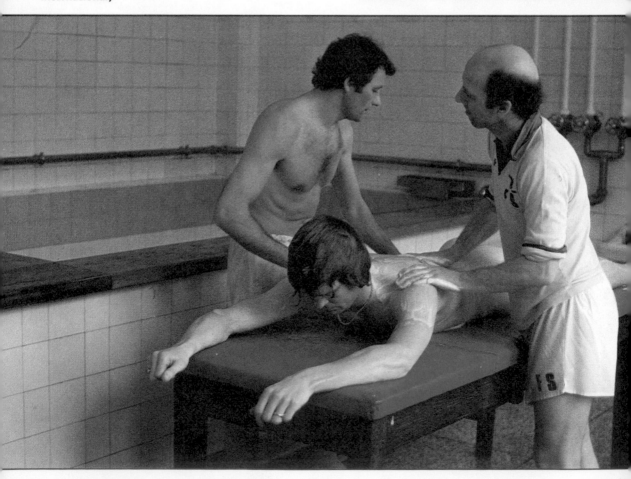

Above: Tracksuited Ron Greenwood, the England Manager who has been revitalising the outlook for the national team. (Syndication International)

Below: Tottenham Hotspur players training at White Hart Lane with indications of the worst of the elements which affected the 1978-79 programme. (Sporting Pictures)

Above: A view of the Manchester United ground at Old Trafford, Manchester. (Sporting Pictures)

Left: Willie Young, Fred Street (physiotherapist) and Terry Neill (Manager) in the Arsenal treatment room. (Sporting Pictures)

Kenny Dalglish scores the only goal of the 1978 European Cup Final for Liverpool against FC Bruges. (Syndication International)

Rangers pose for a team group. During the 1977-78 season they achieved a treble of successes: the League Championship, Scottish F.A. Cup and Scottish League Cup. (Syndication International)

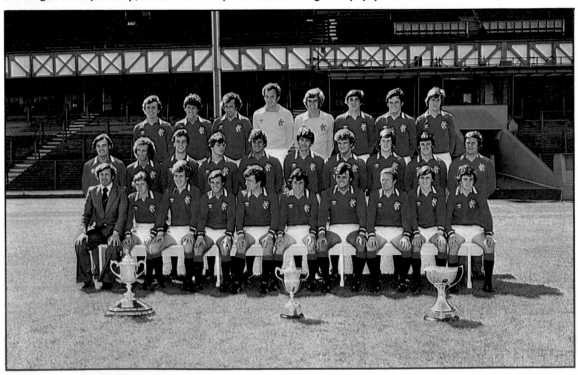

MANCHESTER DERBY MATCHES

The rivalry between the two Manchester teams dates back in terms of League football to before the turn of the century. During the 1978–79 season the game at Maine Road saw Sammy McIlroy (centre) of United dashing between City players Dave Watson (left) and Colin Bell. (Manchester Evening News)

Manchester City v. Manchester United
City founded in 1887 as Ardwick F.C. becoming Manchester City in 1894.

In League matches the results of City's home matches with their score first:

Season	Score	Season	Score
1894–95	2–5	1951–52	1–2
1895–96	2–1	1952–53	2–1
1896–97	0–0	1953–54	2–0
1897–98	0–1	1954–55	3–2
1898–99	4–0	1955–56	1–0
1902–03	0–2	1956–57	2–4
1906–07	3–0	1957–58	2–2
1907–08	0–0	1958–59	1–1
1908–09	1–2	1959–60	3–0
1910–11	1–1	1960–61	1–3
1911–12	0–0	1961–62	0–2
1912–13	0–2	1962–63	1–1
1913–14	0–2	1966–67	1–1
1914–15	1–1	1967–68	1–2
1919–20	3–3	1968–69	0–0
1920–21	3–0	1969–70	4–0
1921–22	4–1	1970–71	3–4
1925–26	1–1	1971–72	3–3
1928–29	2–2	1972–73	3–0
1929–30	0–1	1973–74	0–0
1930–31	4–1	1975–76	2–2
1936–37	1–0	1976–77	1–3
1947–48	0–0	1977–78	3–1
1948–49	0–0	1978–79	0–3
1949–50	1–2		

Manchester United v. Manchester City
United founded in 1878 as Newton Heath, becoming Manchester United in 1902.

In League matches the results of United's home matches with their score first:

Season	Score	Season	Score
1894–95	4–1	1951–52	1–1
1895–96	1–1	1952–53	1–1
1896–97	2–1	1953–54	1–1
1897–98	1–1	1954–55	0–5
1898–99	3–0	1955–56	2–1
1902–03	1–1	1956–57	2–0
1906–07	1–1	1957–58	4–1
1907–08	3–1	1958–59	4–1
1908–09	3–1	1959–60	0–0
1910–11	2–1	1960–61	5–1
1911–12	0–0	1961–62	3–2
1912–13	0–1	1962–63	2–3
1913–14	0–1	1966–67	1–0
1914–15	0–0	1967–68	1–3
1919–20	1–0	1968–69	0–1
1920–21	1–1	1969–70	1–2
1921–22	3–1	1970–71	1–4
1925–26	1–6	1971–72	1–3
1928–29	1–2	1972–73	0–0
1929–30	1–3	1973–74	0–1
1930–31	1–3	1975–76	2–0
1936–37	3–2	1976–77	3–1
1947–48	1–1	1977–78	2–2
1948–49	0–0	1978–79	1–0
1949–50	2–1		

Overall record

CITY	**29 wins**
UNITED	**36 wins**
DRAWN	**33**
TOTAL	**98**

FOOTBALL LEAGUE CUP
1960~79

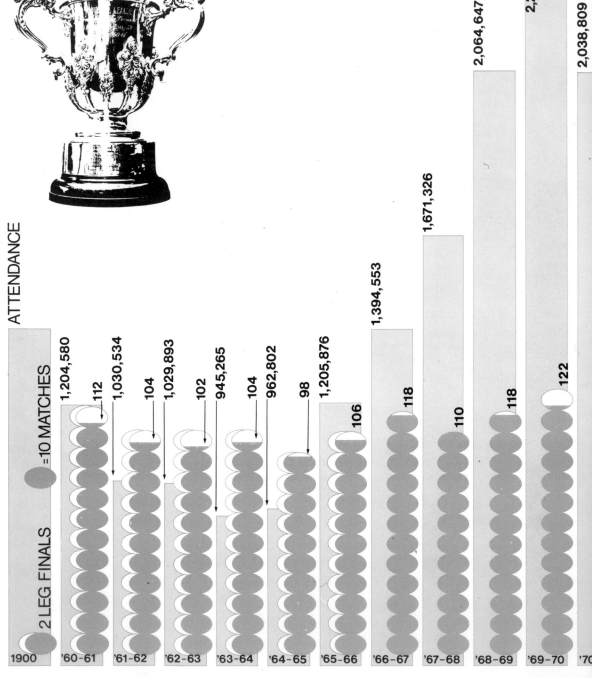

ATTENDANCE

● =10 MATCHES

2 LEG FINALS

Year	Attendance	Matches
1900		
'60-61	1,204,580	112
'61-62	1,030,534	104
'62-63	1,029,893	102
'63-64	945,265	104
'64-65	962,802	98
'65-66	1,205,876	106
'66-67	1,394,553	118
'67-68	1,671,326	110
'68-69	2,064,647	118
'69-70	2,299,819	122
'70-	2,038,809	

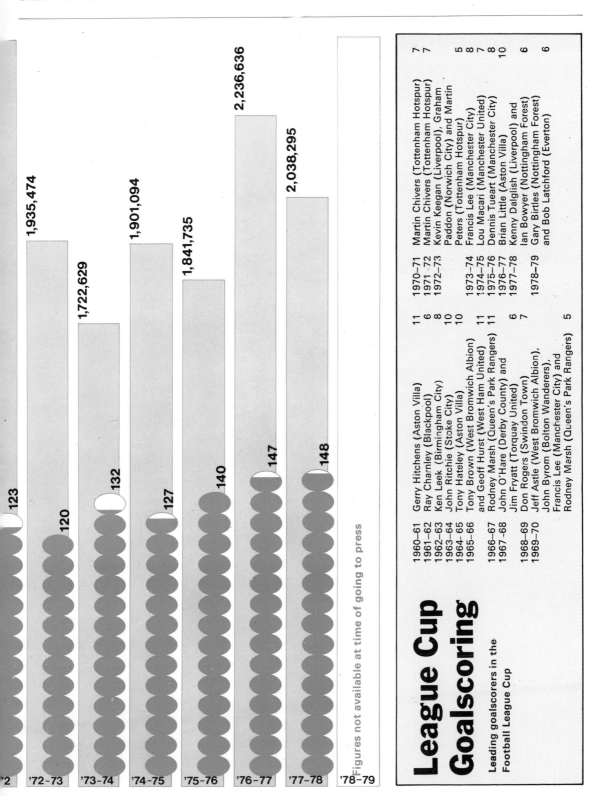

1,935,474
1,722,629
1,901,094
1,841,735
2,236,636
2,038,295

123
120
132
127
140
147
148

'2 '72–73 '73–74 '74–75 '75–76 '76–77 '77–78 '78–79

Figures not available at time of going to press

League Cup Goalscoring

Leading goalscorers in the Football League Cup

Season	Scorer	Goals
1960–61	Gerry Hitchens (Aston Villa)	11
1961–62	Ray Charnley (Blackpool)	6
1962–63	Ken Leek (Birmingham City)	8
1963–64	John Ritchie (Stoke City)	10
1964–65	Tony Hateley (Aston Villa)	10
1965–66	Tony Brown (West Bromwich Albion) and Geoff Hurst (West Ham United)	11
1966–67	Rodney Marsh (Queen's Park Rangers)	11
1967–68	John O'Hare (Derby County) and Jim Fryatt (Torquay United)	6
1968–69	Don Rogers (Swindon Town)	7
1969–70	Jeff Astle (West Bromwich Albion), John Byrom (Bolton Wanderers), Francis Lee (Manchester City) and Rodney Marsh (Queen's Park Rangers)	5
1970–71	Martin Chivers (Tottenham Hotspur)	7
1971–72	Martin Chivers (Tottenham Hotspur)	7
1972–73	Kevin Keegan (Liverpool), Graham Paddon (Norwich City) and Martin Peters (Tottenham Hotspur)	5
1973–74	Francis Lee (Manchester City)	8
1974–75	Lou Macari (Manchester United)	7
1975–76	Dennis Tueart (Manchester City)	8
1976–77	Brian Little (Aston Villa)	10
1977–78	Kenny Dalglish (Liverpool) and Ian Bowyer (Nottingham Forest)	6
1978–79	Gary Birtles (Nottingham Forest) and Bob Latchford (Everton)	6

Football League Club directory

Ground	Capacity & Record	League career		Honours (domestic) League	Cup

ALDERSHOT (1926) Red, blue, white trim/white

Ground	Capacity & Record	League career		Honours (domestic) League	Cup
Recreation Ground High Street Aldershot GU11 1TW 117 × 76 yd	16,000 19,138 v Carlisle FA Cup 4th Rd replay, 28 January 1970	1932–58 Div. 3(S) 1958–73 Div. 4 1973–76 Div. 3	1976–　Div. 4	Highest placing 8th Div. 3 1974	FA Cup never past 5th Rd League Cup never past 2nd Rd

ARSENAL (1886) Red, white sleeves/white

Ground	Capacity & Record	League career		Honours (domestic) League	Cup
Arsenal Stadium Highbury London N5 110 × 71 yd	60,000 73,295 v Sunderland Div. 1 9 March 1935	1893–1904 Div. 2 1904–13 Div. 1 1913–15 Div. 2 1919–　Div. 1		Div. 1 Champions 1931, 1933, 1934, 1935, 1938, 1948, 1953, 1971 Runners-up 1926, 1932, 1973, Div. 2 runners-up 1904	FA Cup winners 1930, 1936, 1950, 1971, 1979 Runners-up 1927, 1932, 1952, 1972, 1978 League Cup runners-up 1968, 1969

ASTON VILLA (1874) Claret, blue sleeves/white

Ground	Capacity & Record	League career		Honours (domestic) League	Cup
Villa Park Trinity Road Birmingham B6 6HE 115 × 75 yd	53,000 76,588 v Derby Co FA Cup 6th Rd 2 March 1946	1888 (founder member of League) 1936–38 Div. 2 1938–59 Div. 1 1959–60 Div. 2 1960–67 Div. 1	1967–70 Div. 2 1970–72 Div. 3 1972–75 Div. 2 1975–　Div. 1	Div. 1 Champions 1894, 1896, 1897, 1899, 1900, 1910, Runners-up 1889, 1903, 1908, 1911, 1913, 1914, 1931, 1933 Div. 2 Champions 1938, 1960 Runners-up 1975 Div. 3 Champions 1972	FA Cup winners 1887, 1895, 1897, 1905, 1913, 1920, 1957 (a record) Runners-up 1892, 1924 League Cup winners 1961, 1975, 1977 Runners-up 1963, 1971

BARNSLEY (1887) Red/white

Ground	Capacity & Record	League career		Honours (domestic) League	Cup
Oakwell Ground Grove Street Barnsley 111 × 75 yd	38,500 40,255 v Stoke City FA Cup 5th Rd 15 February 1936	1898 elected to Div. 2 1932–34 Div. 3(N) 1934–38 Div. 2 1938–39 Div. 3(N) 1946–53 Div. 2 1953–55 Div. 3(N)	1955–59 Div. 2 1959–65 Div. 3 1965–68 Div. 4 1968–72 Div. 3 1972–79 Div. 4 1979–　Div. 3	Div. 3(N) Champions 1934, 1939, 1955 Runners-up 1954 Div. 4 runners-up 1968	FA Cup winners 1912 Runners-up 1910 League Cup never past 3rd Rd

BIRMINGHAM CITY (1875) Blue, white trim/white, blue trim

Ground	Capacity & Record	League career		Honours (domestic) League	Cup
St Andrews Birmingham B9 4NH 115 × 75 yd	51,000 66,844 v Everton FA Cup 5th Rd 11 February 1939	1892–94 Div. 2 1894–96 Div. 1 1896–1901 Div. 2 1901–02 Div. 1 1902–03 Div. 2 1903–08 Div. 1 1908–21 Div. 2 1921–39 Div. 1	1946–48 Div. 2 1948–50 Div. 1 1950–55 Div. 2 1955–65 Div. 1 1965–72 Div. 2 1972–79 Div. 1 1979–　Div. 2	Div. 2 Champions 1893, 1921, 1948, 1955 Runners-up 1894, 1901, 1903, 1972	FA Cup runners-up 1931, 1956 League Cup winners 1963

Most League Points	Goals	Record win	Player highest number of goals Aggregate	Player highest number of goals Individual	Most League appearances	Most capped player
						ALDERSHOT
57, Div. 4 1978–79	83, Div. 4 1963–64	8–1 v Gateshead Div. 4 13 September 1958	Jack Howarth 171, 1965–71, 1972–77	John Dungworth 26 Div. 4 1978–79	Len Walker 450, 1964—76	Peter Scott, 1, N. Ireland 1979
						ARSENAL
66, Div. 1 1930–31	127, Div. 1 1930–31	12–0 v Loughborough T. Div. 2 12 March 1900	Cliff Bastin 150, 1930–47	Ted Drake 42 Div. 1 1934–35	George Armstrong 500, 1960–77	Pat Rice 48, N. Ireland 1968–79
						ASTON VILLA
70, Div. 3 1971–72	128, Div. 1 1930–31	13–0 v Wednesbury Old Athletic FA Cup 1st Rd 1886	Harry Hampton 213, 1904–20 Billy Walker 213, 1919–34	Pongo Waring 49 Div. 1 1930–31	Charlie Aitken 560, 1961–76	Peter McParland 33, N. Ireland 1954–61
						BARNSLEY
67, Div. 3(N) 1938–39	118, Div. 3(N) 1933–34	9–0 v Loughborough T Div. 2 28 January 1899 Accrington Stanley Div. 3(N) 3 February 1934	Ernest Hine 123, 1921–26, 1934–38	Cecil McCormack 33 Div. 2 1950–51	Barry Murphy 514, 1962–78	Eddie McMorran 9, N. Ireland 1950–52
						BIRMINGHAM CITY
59, Div. 2 1947–48	103, Div. 2 1893–94	12–0 v Walsall Town Swifts Div. 2 17 December 1892 Doncaster Rovers Div. 2 11 April 1903	Joe Bradford 249, 1920–35	Joe Bradford 29 Div. 1 1927–28	Gil Merrick 486, 1946–60	Malcolm Page 27, Wales 1971–79

Ground	Capacity & Record	League career	Honours (domestic) League	Cup

BLACKBURN ROVERS (1875) Blue-white halves/white

| Ewood Park Blackburn BB2 4JF 116 × 72 yd | 34,000 61,783 v Bolton W FA Cup 6th Rd 2 March 1929 | 1888 (founder member of League) 1936–39 Div. 2 1946–47 Div. 1 1947–57 Div. 2 1957–66 Div. 1 | 1966–71 Div. 2 1971–75 Div. 3 1975–79 Div. 2 1979– Div. 3 | Div. 1 Champions 1912, 1914 Div. 2 Champions 1939 Runners-up 1958 Div. 3 Champions 1975 | FA Cup winners 1884, 1885, 1886, 1890, 1891, 1928 Runners-up 1882, 1960 League Cup semi-finalists 1962 |

BLACKPOOL (1887) Tangerine, white trim/white

| Bloomfield Road Blackpool FY1 6JJ 111 × 73 yd | 29,540 39,118 v Manchester U Div. 1 19 April 1952 | 1896 elected to Div. 2 1899 failed re-election 1900 re-elected 1900–30 Div. 2 1930–33 Div. 1 | 1933–37 Div. 2 1937–67 Div. 1 1967–70 Div. 2 1970–71 Div. 1 1971–78 Div. 2 1978– Div. 3 | Div. 1 runners-up 1956 Div. 2 Champions 1930 Runners-up 1937, 1970 | FA Cup winners 1953 Runners-up 1948, 1951 League Cup semi-finalists 1962 |

BOLTON WANDERERS (1874) White/navy blue

| Burnden Park Bolton BL3 2QR 113 × 76 yd | 43,000 69,912 v Manchester C FA Cup 5th Rd 18 February 1933 | 1888 (founder member of League) 1899–1900 Div. 2 1900–03 Div. 1 1903–05 Div. 2 1905–08 Div. 1 1908–09 Div. 2 1909–10 Div. 1 | 1910–11 Div. 2 1911–33 Div. 1 1933–35 Div. 2 1935–64 Div. 1 1964–71 Div. 2 1971–73 Div. 3 1973–78 Div. 2 1978– Div. 1 | Div. 2 Champions 1909, 1978 Runners-up 1900, 1905, 1911, 1935 Div. 3 Champions 1973 | FA Cup winners 1923, 1926, 1929, 1958 Runners-up 1894, 1904, 1953 League Cup semi-finalists 1977 |

AFC BOURNEMOUTH (1899) Red white trim/white

| Dean Court Ground Bournemouth Dorset 115 × 75 yd | 22,000 28,799 v Manchester U FA Cup 6th Rd 2 March 1957 | 1923 elected to Div. 3(S) 1970–71 Div. 4 1971–75 Div. 3 1975– Div. 4 | | Div. 3(S) runners-up 1948 Div. 4 runners-up 1971 | FA Cup never past 6th Rd League Cup never past 4th Rd |

BRADFORD CITY (1903) White with maroon and amber trim/white

| Valley Parade Ground Bradford BD8 7DY 110 × 76 yd | 23,469 39,146 v Burnley FA Cup 4th Rd 11 March 1911 | 1903 elected to Div. 2 1908–22 Div. 1 1922–27 Div. 2 1927–29 Div. 3(N) 1929–37 Div. 2 | 1937–61 Div. 3 1961–69 Div. 3 1969–72 Div. 3 1972–77 Div. 4 1977–78 Div. 3 1978– Div. 4 | Div. 2 Champions 1908 Div. 3(N) Champions 1929 | FA Cup winners 1911 League Cup never past 5th Rd |

BRENTFORD (1889) Red-white stripes/black

| Griffin Park Braemar Road Brentford Middlesex TW8 0NT 114 × 75 yd | 37,000 39,626 v Preston NE FA Cup 6th Rd 5 March 1938 | 1920 (founder member of Div. 3) 1921–33 Div. 3(S) 1933–35 Div. 2 1935–47 Div. 1 1947–54 Div. 2 1954–62 Div. 3 | 1962–63 Div. 4 1963–66 Div. 3 1966–72 Div. 4 1972–73 Div. 3 1973–78 Div. 4 1978– Div. 3 | Div. 2 Champions 1935 Div. 3(S) Champions 1933 Runners-up 1930, 1958 Div. 4 Champions 1963 | FA Cup never past 6th Rd League Cup never past 3rd Rd |

Most League Points	Goals	Record win	Player highest number of goals Aggregate	Individual	Most League appearances	Most capped player

BLACKBURN ROVERS

Most League Points	Goals	Record win	Aggregate	Individual	Most League appearances	Most capped player
60, Div. 3 1974–75	114, Div. 2 1954–55	11–0 v Rossendale United FA Cup 1884–85	Tommy Briggs 140, 1952–58	Ted Harper 43 Div. 1 1925–26	Ronnie Clayton 580, 1950–69	Bob Crompton 41, England 1902–14

BLACKPOOL

58, Div. 2 1929–30 & 1967–68	98, Div. 2 1929–30	10–0 v Lanerossi Vicenza Anglo-Italian tournament 10 June 1972	Jimmy Hampson 247, 1927–38	Jimmy Hampson 45 Div. 2 1929–30	Jimmy Armfield 568, 1952–71	Jimmy Armfield 43, England 1959–66

BOLTON WANDERERS

61, Div. 3 1972–73	96, Div. 2 1934–35	13–0 v Sheffield United FA Cup 2nd Rd 1 February 1890	Nat Lofthouse 255, 1946–61	Joe Smith 38 Div. 1 1920–21	Eddie Hopkinson 519, 1956–70	Nat Lofthouse 33 England 1951–58

AFC BOURNEMOUTH

62, Div. 3 1971–72	88, Div. 3(S) 1956–57	11–0 v Margate FA Cup 1st Rd 20 November 1971	Ron Eyre 202, 1924–33	Ted MacDougall 42 Div. 4 1970–71	Ray Bumstead 412, 1958–70	Tommy Godwin 4, Eire 1956–58

BRADFORD CITY

63, Div. 3(N) 1928–29	128, Div. 3(N) 1928–29	11–1 v Rotherham United Div. 3(N) 25 August 1928	Frank O'Rourke 88, 1906–13	David Layne 34 Div. 4 1961–62	Ian Cooper 443, 1965–77	Harry Hampton 9, N. Ireland 1911–14

BRENTFORD

62, Div. 3(S) 1932–33 Div. 4 1962–63	98, Div. 4 1962–63	9–0 v Wrexham Div. 3 15 October 1963	Jim Towers 153, 1954–61	Jack Holliday 36 Div. 3(S) 1932–33	Ken Coote 514, 1949–64	Idris Hopkins 12, Wales 1934–39

Ground	Capacity & Record	League career	Honours (domestic) League	Cup

BRIGHTON & HOVE ALBION (1900) Blue-white stripes/blue

Ground	Capacity & Record	League career	Honours (domestic) League	Cup
The Goldstone Ground Old Shoreham Road Hove, Sussex BN3 7DE 112 × 75 yd	36,000 36,747 v Fulham Div. 2 27 December 1958	1920 (founder member of Div. 3) 1921–58 Div. 3(S) 1958–62 Div. 2 1962–63 Div. 3 1963–65 Div. 4	1965–72 Div. 3 1972–73 Div. 2 1973–77 Div. 3 1977–79 Div. 2 1979– Div. 1	Div. 2 Runners-up 1979 Div. 3(S) Champions 1958 Runners-up 1954, 1956 Div. 3 runners-up 1972, 1977 Div. 4 Champions 1965	FA Cup never past 5th Rd League Cup never past 5th Rd

BRISTOL CITY (1894) Red/white

| Ashton Gate
Bristol
BS3 2EJ
115 × 75 yd | 30,868
43,335 v
Preston NE
FA Cup 5th Rd
16 February 1935 | 1901 elected
to Div. 2
1906–11 Div. 1
1911–22 Div. 2
1922–23 Div. 3(S)
1923–24 Div. 2
1924–27 Div. 3(S) | 1927–32 Div. 2
1932–55 Div.3(S)
1955–60 Div. 2
1960–65 Div. 3
1965–76 Div. 2
1976–   Div. 1 | Div. 1 runners-up
1907
Div. 2 champions
1906
Runners-up 1976
Div. 3(S)
Champions 1923,
1927, 1955
Runners-up 1938
Div. 3 runners-up
1965 | FA Cup
runners-up
1909
League Cup
semi-finalists
1971 |

BRISTOL ROVERS (1883) Blue-white quarters/white

| Bristol Stadium
Eastville
Bristol BS5 6NN
110 × 70 yd | 39,333
38,472 v
Preston NE
FA Cup 4th Rd
30 January 1960 | 1920 (founder
member of Div. 3)
1921–53 Div. 3(S)
1953–62 Div. 2 | 1962–74 Div. 3
1974–   Div. 2 | Div. 3(S)
Champions 1953
Div. 3 runners-up
1974 | FA Cup never
past 6th Rd
League Cup
never past
5th Rd |

BURNLEY (1882) Claret/Blue

| Turf Moor
Burnley
BB10 4BX
115 × 73 yd | 38,000
54,775 v
Huddersfield T
FA Cup 3rd Rd
23 February 1924 | 1888 (founder
member of
League)
1897–98 Div. 2
1898–1900 Div. 1
1900–13 Div. 2
1913–30 Div. 1 | 1930–47 Div. 2
1947–71 Div. 1
1971–73 Div. 2
1973–76 Div. 1
1976–   Div. 2 | Div. 1 Champions
1921, 1960
Runners-up
1920, 1962
Div. 2 Champions
1898, 1973
Runners-up
1913, 1947 | FA Cup winners
1914
Runners-up
1947, 1962
League Cup
semi-finalists
1961, 1969 |

BURY (1885) White/royal blue

| Gigg Lane
Bury
BL9 9HR
112 × 72 yd | 35,000
35,000 v
Bolton W
FA Cup 3rd Rd
9 January 1960 | 1894 elected
to Div. 2
1895–1912 Div. 1
1912–24 Div. 2
1924–29 Div. 1
1929–57 Div. 2
1957–61 Div. 3 | 1961–67 Div. 2
1967–68 Div. 3
1968–69 Div. 2
1969–71 Div. 3
1971–74 Div. 4
1974–   Div. 3 | Div. 2 Champions
1895
Runners-up
1924
Div. 3 Champions
1961
Runners-up
1968 | FA Cup winners
1900, 1903
League Cup
semi-finalists
1963 |

CAMBRIDGE UNITED (1919) Black-amber stripes/black

| Abbey Stadium
Newmarket Road
Cambridge
115 × 75 yd | 12,000
14,000 v
Chelsea
Friendly
1 May 1970 | 1970 elected
to Div. 4
1973–74 Div. 3
1974–77 Div. 4 | 1977–78 Div. 3
1978–   Div. 2 | Div. 4 Champions
1977
Div. 3 runners-up
1978 | FA Cup never
past 3rd Rd
League Cup
never past
2nd Rd |

Most League Points	Goals	Record win	Player highest number of goals Aggregate	Individual	Most League appearances	Most capped player
BRIGHTON & HOVE ALBION						
65, Div. 3(S) 1955–56 Div. 3 1971–72	112, Div. 3(S) 1955–56	10–1 v Wisbech FA Cup 1st Rd 13 November 1965	Tommy Cook 113, 1922–29	Peter Ward 32 Div. 3 1976–77	Tug Wilson 509, 1922–36	Jack Jenkins 8, Wales 1924–26
BRISTOL CITY						
70, Div. 3(S) 1954–55	104, Div. 3(S) 1926–27	11–0 v Chichester FA Cup 1st Rd 5 November 1960	John Atyeo 315, 1951–66	Don Clark 36 Div. 3(S) 1946–47	John Atyeo 597, 1951–66	Billy Wedlock 26, England 1907–14
BRISTOL ROVERS						
64, Div. 3(S) 1952–53	92, Div. 3(S) 1952–53	7–0 Swansea T Div. 2 2 Oct. 1954 Brighton & HA Div. 3(S) 29 Nov. 1952 Shrewsbury T Div. 3, 21 Mar. 1964	Geoff Bradford 245, 1949–64	Geoff Bradford 33 Div. 3(S) 1952–53	Stuart Taylor 524, 1966–79	Matt O'Mahoney 6, Eire ; 1, N Ireland 1938–39
BURNLEY						
62, Div. 2 1972–73	102, Div. 1 1960–61	9–0 v Darwen Div. 1 9 January 1892 Crystal Palace FA Cup 2nd Rd replay 1908–09 New Brighton FA Cup 4th Rd 26 January 1957	George Beel 178, 1923–32	George Beel 35 Div. 1 1927–28	Jerry Dawson 530, 1906–29	Jimmy McIlroy 52, N. Ireland 1951–63
BURY						
68, Div. 3 1960–61	108, Div. 3 1960–61	12–1 v Stockton FA Cup 1st Rd replay 1896–97	Norman Bullock 124, 1920–35	Norman Bullock 31 Div. 1 1925–26	Norman Bullock 506, 1920–35	Bill Gorman 11, Eire 1936–38
CAMBRIDGE UNITED						
65, Div. 4 1976–77	87, Div. 4 1976–77	6–0 v Darlington Div. 4 18 September 1971	Alan Biley 63, 1975–79	Alan Biley 21 Div. 3 1977–78	Terry Eades 248, 1970–77	None

Ground	Capacity & Record	League career		Honours (domestic) League	Cup

CARDIFF CITY (1899) Blue with yellow and white trim/blue

Ground	Capacity & Record	League career		Honours League	Cup
Ninian Park Cardiff CF1 8SX 112 × 76 yd	20,805 57,800 v Arsenal Div. 1 22 April 1953	1920 elected to Div. 2 1921–29 Div. 1 1929–31 Div. 2 1931–47 Div. 3(S) 1947–52 Div. 2 1952–57 Div. 1	1957–60 Div. 2 1960–62 Div. 1 1962–75 Div. 2 1975–76 Div. 3 1976– Div. 2	Div. 1 runners-up 1924 Div. 2 runners-up 1921, 1952, 1960 Div. 3(S) Champions 1947 Div. 3 runners-up 1976	FA Cup winners 1927 Runners-up 1925 League Cup semi-finalists 1966

CARLISLE UNITED (1904) Blue/white

Ground	Capacity & Record	League career		Honours League	Cup
Brunton Park Carlisle CA1 1LL 117 × 78 yd	28,000 27,500 v Birmingham C FA Cup 3rd Rd 5 January 1957 and Middlesbrough FA Cup 5th Rd 7 February 1970	1928 elected to Div. 3(N) 1958–62 Div. 4 1962–63 Div. 3 1963–64 Div. 4 1964–65 Div. 3	1965–74 Div. 2 1974–75 Div. 1 1975–77 Div. 2 1977– Div. 3	Promoted to Div. 1 1974 Div. 3 Champions 1965 Div. 4 runners-up 1964	FA Cup never past 6th Rd League Cup semi-finalists 1970

CHARLTON ATHLETIC (1905) Red/white

Ground	Capacity & Record	League career		Honours League	Cup
The Valley Floyd Road Charlton London SE7 8AW 114 × 78 yd	66,000 75,031 v Aston Villa FA Cup 5th Rd 12 February 1938	1921 elected to Div. 3(S) 1929–33 Div. 2 1933–35 Div. 3(S) 1935–36 Div. 2	1936–57 Div. 1 1957–72 Div. 2 1972–75 Div. 3 1975– Div. 2	Div. 1 runners-up 1937 Div. 2 runners-up 1936 Div. 3(S) Champions 1929, 1935	FA Cup winners 1947 Runners-up 1946 League Cup never past 4th Rd

CHELSEA (1905) Blue/blue

Ground	Capacity & Record	League career		Honours League	Cup
Stamford Bridge London SW6 114 × 71 yd	60,000 82,905 v Arsenal Div. 1 12 October 1935	1905 elected to Div. 2 1907–10 Div. 1 1910–12 Div. 2 1912–24 Div. 1 1924–30 Div. 2	1930–62 Div. 1 1962–63 Div. 2 1963–75 Div. 1 1975–77 Div. 2 1977–79 Div. 1 1979– Div. 2	Div. 1 Champions 1955 Div. 2 runners-up 1907, 1912, 1930, 1963, 1977	FA Cup winners 1970 Runners-up 1915, 1967 League Cup winners 1965 Runners-up 1972

CHESTER (1884) Blue-white stripes/blue

Ground	Capacity & Record	League career		Honours League	Cup
The Stadium Sealand Road Chester CH1 4LW 114 × 76 yd	20,000 20,500 v Chelsea FA Cup 3rd Rd replay 16 January 1952	1931 elected to Div. 3(N) 1958–75 Div. 4 1975– Div. 3		Div. 3(N) runners-up 1936	FA Cup never past 5th Rd League Cup semi-finalists 1975

CHESTERFIELD (1866) Blue/white

Ground	Capacity & Record	League career		Honours League	Cup
Recreation Ground Chesterfield 114 × 72 yd	28,500 30,968 v Newcastle U Div. 2 7 April 1939	1899 elected to Div. 2 1909 failed re-election 1921 elected to Div. 3(N) 1931–33 Div. 2	1933–36 Div. 3(N) 1936–51 Div. 2 1951–58 Div. 3(N) 1958–61 Div. 3 1961–70 Div. 4 1970– Div. 3	Div. 3(N) Champions 1931, 1936 Runners-up 1934 Div. 4 Champions 1970	FA Cup never past 5th Rd League Cup never past 4th Rd

Most League Points	Goals	Record win	Player highest number of goals		Most League appearances	Most capped player
			Aggregate	Individual		
						CARDIFF CITY
66, Div. 3(S) 1946–47	93, Div. 3(S) 1946–47	9–2 v Thames Div. 3(S) 6 February 1932	Len Davies 127, 1921–29	Stan Richards 31 Div. 3(S) 1946–47	Tom Farquharson 445, 1922–35	Alf Sherwood 39, Wales 1946–56
						CARLISLE UNITED
62, Div. 3(N) 1950–51	113, Div. 4 1963–64	8–0 v Hartlepool United Div. 3(N) 1 September 1928 Scunthorpe United Div. 3(N) 25 December 1952	Jimmy McConnell 126, 1928–32	Jimmy McConnell 42 Div. 3(N) 1928–29	Alan Ross 466, 1963–79	Eric Welsh 4, N Ireland 1966–67
						CHARLTON ATHLETIC
61, Div. 3(S) 1934–35	107, Div. 2 1957–58	8–1 Middlesbrough Div. 1 12 September 1953	Stuart Leary 153, 1953–62	Ralph Allen 32 Div. 3(S) 1934–35	Sam Bartram 583, 1934–56	John Hewie 19, Scotland 1956–60
						CHELSEA
57, Div. 2 1906–07	98, Div. 1 1960–61	13–0 v Jeunesse Hautcharage Cup-Winners' Cup 1st Rd 29 September 1971	Bobby Tambling 164, 1958–70	Jimmy Greaves 41 Div. 1 1960–61	Ron Harris 616, 1962–79	Eddie McCreadie 23, Scotland 1965–69
						CHESTER
56, Div. 3(N) 1946–47 Div. 4 1964–65	119, Div. 4 1964–65	12–0 v York City Div. 3(N) 1 February 1936	Gary Talbot 83, 1963–67 1968–70	Dick Yates 36 Div. 3(N) 1946–47	Ray Gill 408, 1951–62	Bill Lewis 9, Wales 1894–96
						CHESTERFIELD
64, Div. 4 1969–70	102, Div. 3(N) 1930–31	10–0 v Glossop North End Div. 2 17 January 1903	Herbert Munday 112, 1899–1909	Jimmy Cookson 44 Div. 3(N) 1925–26	Dave Blakey 613, 1948–67	Walter McMillen 4, N Ireland 1937–38

Ground	Capacity & Record	League career		Honours (domestic) League	Cup

COLCHESTER UNITED (1937) Blue-white stripes/blue

Ground	Capacity & Record	League career		Honours (domestic) League	Cup
Layer Road Ground Colchester 110 × 71 yd	16,150 19,072 v Reading FA Cup 1st Rd 27 November 1948	1950 elected to Div. 3(S) 1958–61 Div. 3 1961–62 Div. 4 1962–65 Div. 3 1965–66 Div. 4	1966–68 Div. 3 1968–74 Div. 4 1974–76 Div. 3 1976–77 Div. 4 1977– Div. 3	Div. 4 runners-up 1962	FA Cup never past 6th Rd League Cup never past 5th Rd

COVENTRY CITY (1883) Sky blue/sky blue

Ground	Capacity & Record	League career		Honours (domestic) League	Cup
Highfield Road Coventry 110 × 75 yd	48,000 51,457 v Wolverhampton W Div. 2 29 April 1967	1919 elected to Div. 2 1925–26 Div. 3(N) 1926–36 Div. 3(S) 1936–52 Div. 2 1952–58 Div. 3(S)	1958–59 Div. 4 1959–64 Div. 3 1964–67 Div. 2 1967– Div. 1	Div. 2 Champions 1967 Div. 3 Champions 1964 Div. 3(S) Champions 1936 Runners-up 1934 Div. 4 runners-up 1959	FA Cup never past 6th Rd League Cup never past 5th Rd

CREWE ALEXANDRA (1877) Red/white

Ground	Capacity & Record	League career		Honours (domestic) League	Cup
Football Ground Gresty Road Crewe 113 × 75 yd	17,000 20,000 v Tottenham H FA Cup 4th Rd 30 January 1960	1892 (founder member of Div. 2) 1896 failed re-election 1921 re-elected to Div. 3(N)	1958–63 Div. 4 1963–64 Div. 3 1964–68 Div. 4 1968–69 Div. 3 1969– Div. 4	Highest placing 10th Div. 2 1893	FA Cup semi-finalists 1888 League Cup never past 3rd Rd

CRYSTAL PALACE (1905) White with red diagonal band/white

Ground	Capacity & Record	League career		Honours (domestic) League	Cup
Selhurst Park London SE25 6PU 110 × 75 yd	51,000 51,801 v Burnley Div. 2 11 May 1979	1920 (founder member of Div. 3) 1921–25 Div. 2 1925–58 Div. 3(S) 1958–61 Div. 4 1961–64 Div. 3	1964–69 Div. 2 1969–73 Div. 1 1973–74 Div. 2 1974–77 Div. 3 1977–79 Div. 2 1979– Div. 1	Div. 2 Champions 1979 runners-up 1969 Div. 3 runners-up 1964 Div. 3(S) Champions 1921 Runners-up 1929, 1931, 1939 Div. 4 Runners-up 1961	FA Cup semi-finalists 1976 League Cup never past 5th Rd

DARLINGTON (1883) White with red trim/black

Ground	Capacity & Record	League career		Honours (domestic) League	Cup
Feethams Ground Darlington 110 × 74 yd	20,000 21,023 v Bolton W League Cup 3rd Rd 14 November 1960	1921 (founder member of Div. 3(N)) 1925–27 Div. 2 1927–58 Div. 3(N)	1958–66 Div. 4 1966–67 Div. 3 1967– Div. 4	Div. 3(N) Champions 1925 Runners-up 1922 Div. 4 runners-up 1966	FA Cup never past 5th Rd League Cup never past 5th Rd

DERBY COUNTY (1884) White/blue

Ground	Capacity & Record	League career		Honours (domestic) League	Cup
Baseball Ground Shaftesbury Crescent Derby DE3 8NB 110 × 71 yd	38,500 41,826 v Tottenham H Div. 1 20 September 1969	1888 (founder member of League) 1907–12 Div. 2 1912–14 Div. 1 1914–15 Div. 2 1915–21 Div. 1	1921–26 Div. 2 1926–53 Div. 1 1953–55 Div. 2 1955–57 Div. 3(N) 1957–69 Div. 2 1969– Div. 1	Div. 1 Champions 1972, 1975 Runners-up 1896, 1930, 1936 Div. 2 Champions 1912, 1915, 1969 Runners-up 1926 Div. 3(N) Champions 1957 Runners-up 1956	FA Cup winners 1946 Runners-up 1898, 1899, 1903 League Cup semi-finalists 1968

Most League Points	Goals	Record win	Player highest number of goals Aggregate	Individual	Most League appearances	Most capped player
						COLCHESTER UNITED
60, Div. 4 1973–74	104, Div. 4 1961–62	9–1 v Bradford City Div. 4 30 September 1961	Martyn King 131, 1959–65	Bobby Hunt 37 Div. 4 1961–62	Peter Wright 421, 1952–64	None
						COVENTRY CITY
60, Div. 4 1958–59 Div. 3 1963–64	108, Div. 3(S) 1931–32	9–0 v Bristol City Div. 3(S) 28 April 1934	Clarrie Bourton 171, 1931–37	Clarrie Bourton 49 Div. 3(S) 1931–32	George Curtis 486, 1956–70	Dave Clements 21, N Ireland 1965–71
						CREWE ALEXANDRA
59, Div. 4 1962–63	95, Div. 3(N) 1931–32	8–0 v Rotherham United Div. 3(N) 1 October 1932	Bert Swindells 126, 1928–37	Terry Harkin 34 Div. 4 1964–65	Tommy Lowry 436, 1966–67	Bill Lewis 12, Wales 1890–92
						CRYSTAL PALACE
64, Div. 4 1960–61	110, Div. 4 1960–61	9–0 v Barrow Div. 4 10 October 1959	Peter Simpson 154, 1930–36	Peter Simpson 46 Div. 3(S) 1930–31	Terry Long 432, 1956–69	Ian Evans 13, Wales 1975–77
						DARLINGTON
59, Div. 4 1965–66	108, Div. 3(N) 1929–30	9–2 v Lincoln City Div. 3(N) 7 January 1928	David Brown 74, 1923–26	David Brown 39 Div. 3(N) 1924–25	Ron Greener 442, 1955–68	None
						DERBY COUNTY
63, Div. 2 1968–69 Div. 3(N) 1955–56, 1956–57	111, Div. 3(N) 1956–57	12–0 v Finn Harps UEFA Cup 3rd Rd First leg 15 September 1976	Steve Bloomer 291, 1892–1906 1910–14	Jack Bowers 37 Div. 1 1930–31 Ray Straw 37 Div. 3(N) 1956–57	Jack Parry 478, 1949–66	Roy McFarland 28, England 1971–76

Ground	Capacity & Record	League career		Honours (domestic) League	Cup

DONCASTER ROVERS (1879) Red/white

Belle Vue Ground Doncaster 118 × 79 yd	30,000 37,149 v Hull City Div. 3(N) 2 October 1948	1901 elected to Div. 2 1903 failed re-election 1904 re-elected 1905 failed re-election 1923 re-elected to Div. 3(N) 1935–37 Div. 2	1937–47 Div. 3(N) 1947–48 Div. 2 1948–50 Div. 3(N) 1950–58 Div. 2 1958–59 Div. 3 1959–66 Div. 4 1966–67 Div. 3 1967–69 Div. 4 1969–71 Div. 3 1971– Div. 4	Div. 3(N) Champions 1935, 1947, 1950 Runners-up 1938, 1939 Div. 4 Champions 1966, 1969	FA Cup never past 5th Rd League Cup never past 5th Rd

EVERTON (1878) Blue/white

Goodison Park Liverpool L4 4EL 112 × 78 yd	58,000 78,299 v Liverpool Div. 1 18 September 1948	1888 (founder member of League) 1930–31 Div. 2 1931–51 Div. 1 1951–54 Div. 2 1954– Div. 1	Div. 1 Champions 1891, 1915, 1928, 1932, 1939, 1963, 1970 Runners-up 1890, 1895, 1902, 1905, 1909, 1912 Div. 2 Champions 1931 Runners-up 1954	FA Cup winners 1906, 1933, 1966 Runners-up 1893 1897, 1907, 1968 League Cup runners-up 1977

EXETER CITY (1904) White/white

St James Park Exeter 114 × 73 yd	16,500 20,984 v Sunderland FA Cup 6th Rd replay 4 March 1931	1920 elected to Div. 3 1921–58 Div. 3(S) 1958–64 Div. 4 1964–66 Div. 3	1966–77 Div. 4 1977– Div. 3	Div. 3(S) runners-up 1933 Div. 4 runners-up 1977	FA Cup never past 6th Rd League Cup never past 4th Rd

FULHAM (1880) White/black

Craven Cottage Stevenage Road Fulham London SW6 110 × 75 yd	42,000 49,335 v Millwall Div. 2 8 October 1938	1907 elected to Div. 2 1928–32 Div. 3(S) 1932–49 Div. 2 1949–52 Div. 1 1952–59 Div. 2	1959–68 Div. 1 1968–69 Div. 2 1969–71 Div. 3 1971– Div. 2	Div. 2 Champions 1949 Runners-up 1959 Div. 3(S) Champions 1932 Div. 3 runners-up 1971	FA Cup runners-up 1975 League Cup never past 5th Rd

GILLINGHAM (1893) Blue/white

Prestfield Stadium Gillingham 114 × 75 yd	22,000 23,002 v QPR FA Cup 3rd Rd 10 January 1948	1920 (founder member of Div. 3) 1921 Div. 3(S) 1938 failed re-election 1950 re-elected to Div. 3(S)	1958–64 Div. 4 1964–71 Div. 3 1971–74 Div. 4 1974– Div. 3	Div. 4 Champions 1964 Runners-up 1974	FA Cup never past 5th Rd League Cup never past 4th Rd

Most League Points	Goals	Record win	Player highest number of goals		Most League appearances	Most capped player
			Aggregate	Individual		
			DONCASTER ROVERS			
72, Div. 3(N) 1946–47	123, Div. 3(N) 1946–47	10–0 v Darlington Div. 4 25 January 1964	Tom Keetley 180, 1923–29	Clarrie Jordan 42 Div. 3(N) 1946–47	Fred Emery 406, 1925–36	Len Graham 14, N Ireland 1951–58
			EVERTON			
66, Div. 1 1969–70	121, Div. 2 1930–31	11–2 v Derby County FA Cup 1st Rd 1889–90	Dixie Dean 349, 1925–37	Dixie Dean 60 Div. 1 1927–28	Ted Sagar 465, 1929–53	Alan Ball 39, England 1966–71
			EXETER CITY			
62, Div. 4 1976–77	88, Div. 3(S) 1932–33	8–1 v Coventry City Div. 3(S) 4 December 1926 Aldershot Div. 3(S) 4 May 1935	Alan Banks 105, 1963–66, 1967–73	Fred Whitlow 34 Div. 3(S) 1932–33	Arnold Mitchell 495, 1952–66	Dermot Curtis 1, Eire 1963
			FULHAM			
60, Div. 2 1958–59 Div. 3 1970–71	111, Div. 3(S) 1931–32	10–1 v Ipswich Town Div. 1 26 December 1963	Bedford Jezzard 154, 1948–56	Frank Newton 41 Div. 3(S) 1931–32	Johnny Haynes 598, 1952–70	Johnny Haynes 56, England 1954–62
			GILLINGHAM			
62, Div. 4 1973–74	90, Div. 4 1973–74	10–1 v Gorleston FA Cup 1st Rd 16 November 1957	Brian Yeo 135, 1963–75	Ernie Morgan 31 Div. 3(S) 1954–55 Brian Yeo 31 Div. 4 1973–74	John Simpson 571, 1957–72	Fred Fox 1, England 1925 Damien Richardson 1, Eire 1973

Ground	Capacity & Record	League career		Honours (domestic) League	Cup

GRIMSBY TOWN (1878) Black-white stripes/black

Ground	Capacity & Record	League career		Honours (domestic) League	Cup
Blundell Park Cleethorpes South Humberside DN35 7PY 111 × 74 yd	24,000 31,657 v Wolverhampton W FA Cup 5th Rd 20 February 1937	1892 (founder member of Div. 2) 1901–03 Div. 1 1903–10 Div. 2 1910 failed re-election 1911 re-elected to Div. 2 1920–21 Div. 3 1921–26 Div. 3(N) 1926–29 Div. 2 1929–32 Div. 1	1932–34 Div. 2 1934–48 Div. 1 1948–51 Div. 2 1951–56 Div. 3(N) 1956–59 Div. 2 1959–62 Div. 3 1962–64 Div. 2 1964–68 Div. 3 1968–72 Div. 4 1972–77 Div. 3 1977–79 Div. 4 1979– Div. 3	Div. 2 Champions 1901, 1934 Runners-up 1929 Div. 3(N) Champions 1926, 1956 Runners-up 1952 Div. 3 runners-up 1962 Div. 4 Champions 1972 Runners-up 1979	FA Cup semi-finalists 1936, 1939 League Cup never past 5th Rd

HALIFAX TOWN (1911) Royal blue with white trim/white

Ground	Capacity & Record	League career		Honours (domestic) League	Cup
Shay Ground Halifax HX1 2YS 110 × 70 yd	25,000 36,885 v Tottenham H FA Cup 5th Rd 14 February 1953	1921 (founder member of Div. 3(N)) 1958–63 Div. 3 1963–69 Div. 4	1969–76 Div. 3 1976– Div. 4	Div. 3(N) runners-up 1935 Div. 4 runners-up 1969	FA Cup never past 5th Rd League Cup never past 4th Rd

HARTLEPOOL UNITED (1908) Blue/white

Ground	Capacity & Record	League career		Honours (domestic) League	Cup
The Victoria Ground Hartlepool 113 × 77 yd	16,000 17,426 v Manchester U FA Cup 3rd Rd 5 January 1957	1921 (founder member of Div. 3(N)) 1958–68 Div. 4	1968–69 Div. 3 1969– Div. 4	Div. 3 (N) runners-up 1957	FA Cup never past 4th Rd League Cup never past 5th Rd

HEREFORD UNITED (1924) White with black and red trim/black

Ground	Capacity & Record	League career		Honours (domestic) League	Cup
Edgar Street Hereford 111 × 80 yd	17,500 18,114 v Sheffield W FA Cup 3rd Rd 4 January 1958	1972 elected to Div. 4 1973–76 Div. 3 1976–77 Div. 2	1977–78 Div. 3 1978– Div. 4	Div. 3 Champions 1976 Div. 4 runners-up 1973	FA Cup never past 4th Rd League Cup never past 3rd Rd

HUDDERSFIELD TOWN (1908) Blue-white stripes/white

Ground	Capacity & Record	League career		Honours (domestic) League	Cup
Leeds Road Huddersfield HD1 6PE 115 × 75 yd	48,000 67,037 v Arsenal FA Cup 6th Rd 27 February 1932	1910 elected to Div. 2 1920–52 Div. 1 1952–53 Div. 2 1953–56 Div. 1 1956–70 Div. 2	1970–72 Div. 1 1972–73 Div. 2 1973–75 Div. 3 1975– Div. 4	Div. 1 Champions 1924, 1925, 1926 Runners-up 1927, 1928, 1934 Div. 2 Champions 1970 Runners-up 1920, 1953	FA Cup winners 1922 Runners-up 1920, 1928, 1930, 1938 League Cup semi-finalists 1968

Most League Points	Goals	Record win	Player highest number of goals		Most League appearances	Most capped player
			Aggregate	Individual		
						GRIMSBY TOWN
68, Div. 3(N) 1955–56	103, Div. 2 1933–34	9–2 v Darwen Div. 2 15 April 1899	Pat Glover 182, 1930–39	Pat Glover 42 Div. 2 1933–34	Keith Jobling 448, 1953–69	Pat Glover 7, Wales 1931–39
						HALIFAX TOWN
57, Div. 4 1968–69	83, Div. 3(N) 1957–58	7–0 v Bishop Auckland FA Cup 2nd Rd replay 10 January 1967	Ernest Dixon 129, 1922–30	Albert Valentine 34 Div. 3(N) 1934–35	John Pickering 367, 1965–74	None
						HARTLEPOOL UNITED
60, Div. 4 1967–68	90, Div. 3(N) 1956–57	10–1 v Barrow Div. 4 4 April 1959	Ken Johnson 98, 1949–64	William Robinson 28 Div. 3(N) 1927–28	Wattie Moore 448, 1948–64	Ambrose Fogarty 1, Eire 1964
						HEREFORD UNITED
63, Div. 3 1975–76	86, Div. 3 1975–76	11–0 v Thynnes FA Cup 1947–48	Dixie McNeil 85, 1974–77	Dixie McNeil 35 Div. 3 1975–76	Steve Emery 198, 1973–79	Brian Evans 1, Wales 1973
						HUDDERSFIELD TOWN
64, Div. 2 1919–20	97, Div. 2 1919–20	10–1 v Blackpool Div. 1 13 December 1930	George Brown 142, 1921–29	Sam Taylor 35 Div. 2 1919–20 George Brown 35 Div. 1 1925–26	Billy Smith 520, 1914–34	Jimmy Nicholson 31, N Ireland 1965–71

Ground	Capacity & Record	League career		Honours (domestic) League	Cup

HULL CITY (1904) Black-amber stripes/black

Ground	Capacity & Record	League career		Honours (domestic) League	Cup
Boothferry Park Hull HU4 6EU 112 × 75 yd	42,000 55,019 v Manchester U FA Cup 6th Rd 26 February 1949	1905 elected to Div. 2 1930–33 Div. 3(N) 1933–36 Div. 2 1936–49 Div. 3(N) 1949–56 Div. 2 1956–58 Div. 3(N)	1958–59 Div. 3 1959–60 Div. 2 1960–66 Div. 3 1966–78 Div. 2 1978– Div. 3	Div. 3(N) Champions 1933, 1949 Div. 3 Champions 1966 Runners-up 1959	FA Cup semi-finalists 1930 League Cup never past 4th Rd

IPSWICH TOWN (1887) Blue/white

Ground	Capacity & Record	League career		Honours (domestic) League	Cup
Portman Road Ipswich Suffolk IP1 2DA 112 × 72 yd	32,000 38,010 v Leeds United FA Cup 6th Rd 8 March 1975	1938 elected to Div. 3(S) 1954–55 Div. 2 1955–57 Div. 3(S) 1957–61 Div. 2	1961–64 Div. 1 1964–68 Div. 2 1968– Div. 1	Div. 1 Champions 1962 Div. 2 Champions 1961, 1968 Div. 3(S) Champions 1954, 1957	FA Cup winners 1978 League Cup never past 5th Rd

LEEDS UNITED (1919) White/white

Ground	Capacity & Record	League career		Honours (domestic) League	Cup
Elland Road Leeds LS11 0ES 117 × 76 yd	50,000 57,892 v Sunderland FA Cup 5th Rd replay 15 March 1967	1920 elected to Div. 2 1924–27 Div. 1 1927–28 Div. 2 1928–31 Div. 1 1931–32 Div. 2	1932–47 Div. 1 1947–56 Div. 2 1956–60 Div. 1 1960–64 Div. 2 1964– Div. 1	Div. 1 Champions 1969, 1974 Runners-up 1965, 1966, 1970, 1971, 1972 Div. 2 Champions 1924, 1964 Runners-up 1928, 1932, 1956	FA Cup winners 1972 Runners-up 1965, 1970, 1973 League Cup winners 1968

LEICESTER CITY (1884) Blue/white

Ground	Capacity & Record	League career		Honours (domestic) League	Cup
City Stadium Filbert Street Leicester 112 × 75 yd	34,000 47,298 v Tottenham H FA Cup 5th Rd 18 February 1928	1894 elected to Div. 2 1908–09 Div. 1 1909–25 Div. 2 1925–35 Div. 1 1935–37 Div. 2 1937–39 Div. 1	1946–54 Div. 2 1954–55 Div. 1 1955–57 Div. 2 1957–69 Div. 1 1969–71 Div. 2 1971–78 Div. 1 1978– Div. 2	Div. 1 runners-up 1929 Div. 2 Champions 1925, 1937, 1954, 1957, 1971 Runners-up 1908	FA Cup runners-up 1949, 1961, 1963, 1969 League Cup winners 1964 Runners-up 1965

LINCOLN CITY (1883) Red-white stripes/black

Ground	Capacity & Record	League career		Honours (domestic) League	Cup
Sincil Bank Lincoln 110 × 75 yd	25,300 23,196 v Derby Co League Cup 4th Rd 15 November 1967	1892 (founder member of Div. 2) 1908 failed re-election 1909 re-elected 1911 failed re-election 1912 re-elected 1920 failed re-election 1921 re-elected	1921–32 Div. 3(N) 1932–34 Div. 2 1934–48 Div. 3(N) 1948–49 Div. 2 1949–52 Div. 3(N) 1952–61 Div. 3 1961–62 Div. 3 1962–76 Div. 4 1976–79 Div. 3 1979– Div. 4	Div. 3(N) Champions 1932, 1948, 1952 Runners-up 1928, 1931, 1937 Div. 4 Champions 1976	FA Cup never past 5th Rd (equivalent) League Cup never past 4th Rd

Most League Points	Goals	Record win	Player highest number of goals Aggregate	Individual	Most League appearances	Most capped player

HULL CITY

Most League Points	Goals	Record win	Aggregate	Individual	Most League appearances	Most capped player
69, Div. 3 1965–66	109, Div. 3 1965–66	11–1 v Carlisle United Div. 3(N) 14 January 1939	Chris Chilton 195, 1960–71	Bill McNaughton 39 Div. 3(N) 1932–33	Andy Davidson 511, 1947–67	Terry Neill 15, N Ireland 1970–73

IPSWICH TOWN

Most League Points	Goals	Record win	Aggregate	Individual	Most League appearances	Most capped player
64, Div. 3(S) 1953–54 1955–56	106, Div. 3(S) 1955–65	10–0 v Floriana (Malta) Euro. Cup 1st Rd 25 September 1962	Ray Crawford 203, 1958–63, 1966–69	Ted Phillips 41 Div. 3(S) 1956–57	Mick Mills 469, 1966–79	Allan Hunter 45, N Ireland 1972–79

LEEDS UNITED

Most League Points	Goals	Record win	Aggregate	Individual	Most League appearances	Most capped player
67, Div. 1 1968–69	98, Div. 2 1927–28	10–0 v Lyn Oslo (Norway) Euro. Cup 1st Rd First leg 17 September 1969	John Charles 154, 1948–57, 1962	John Charles 42 Div. 2 1953–54	Jack Charlton 629, 1953–73	Billy Bremner 54, Scotland 1965–75

LEICESTER CITY

Most League Points	Goals	Record win	Aggregate	Individual	Most League appearances	Most capped player
61, Div. 2 1956–57	109, Div. 2 1956–57	10–0 v Portsmouth Div. 1 20 October 1928	Arthur Chandler 262, 1923–35	Arthur Rowley 44 Div. 2 1956–57	Adam Black 530, 1919–35	Gordon Banks 37, England 1963–66

LINCOLN CITY

Most League Points	Goals	Record win	Aggregate	Individual	Most League appearances	Most capped player
74, Div. 4 1975–76	121, Div. 3(N) 1951–52	11–1 v Crewe Alexandra Div. 3(N) 29 September 1951	Andy Graver 144, 1950–55, 1958–61	Allan Hall 42 Div. 3(N) 1931–32	Tony Emery 402, 1946–59	David Pugh 3, Wales,1900–01 Con Moulson 3, Eire 1936–37 George Moulson 3, Eire 1948

Ground	Capacity & Record	League career		Honours (domestic) League	Cup

LIVERPOOL (1892) Red/red

| Anfield Road Liverpool 4 110 × 75 yd | 56,318 61,905 v Wolverhampton W FA Cup 4th Rd 2 February 1952 | 1893 elected to Div. 2 1894–95 Div. 1 1895–96 Div. 2 1896–1904 Div. 1 | 1904–05 Div. 2 1905–54 Div. 1 1954–62 Div. 2 1962– Div. 1 | Div. 1 Champions 1901, 1906, 1922, 1923, 1947, 1964, 1966, 1973, 1976, 1977, 1979 (record) Runners-up 1899, 1910, 1969, 1974, 1975, 1978 Div. 2 Champions 1894, 1896, 1905, 1962 | FA Cup winners 1965, 1974 Runners-up 1914, 1950, 1971, 1977 League Cup runners-up 1978 |

LUTON TOWN (1885) Orange with navy blue and white trim/navy blue

| 70-72 Kenilworth Road Luton 112 × 72 yd | 25,000 30,069 v Blackpool FA Cup 6th Rd replay 4 March 1959 | 1897 elected to Div. 2 1900 failed re-election 1920 elected to Div. 3 1921–37 Div. 3(S) 1937–55 Div. 2 1955–60 Div. 1 | 1960–63 Div. 2 1963–65 Div. 3 1965–68 Div. 4 1968–70 Div. 3 1970–74 Div. 2 1974–75 Div. 1 1975– Div. 2 | Div. 2 runners-up 1955, 1974 Div. 3 runners-up 1970 Div. 4 Champions 1968 Div. 3(S) Champions 1937 Runners-up 1936 | FA Cup runners-up 1959 League Cup never past 5th Rd |

MANCHESTER CITY (1887) Sky blue/sky blue

| Maine Road Moss Side Manchester M14 7WN 119 × 79 yd | 52,500 84,569 v Stoke City FA Cup 6th Rd 3 March 1934 | 1892 elected to Div. 2 as Ardwick FC 1894 elected to Div. 2 as Manchester C 1899–1902 Div. 1 1902–03 Div. 2 1903–09 Div. 1 1909–10 Div. 2 | 1910–26 Div. 1 1926–28 Div. 2 1928–38 Div. 1 1938–47 Div. 2 1947–50 Div. 1 1950–51 Div. 2 1951–63 Div. 1 1963–66 Div. 2 1966– Div. 1 | Div. 1 Champions 1937, 1968 Runners-up 1904, 1921, 1977 Div. 2 Champions 1899, 1903, 1910, 1928, 1947, 1966 Runners-up 1896, 1951 | FA Cup winners 1904, 1934, 1956, 1969 Runners-up 1926, 1933, 1955 League Cup winners 1970, 1976 Runners-up 1974 |

MANCHESTER UNITED (1878) Red/white

| Old Trafford Manchester M16 0RA 116 × 76 yd | 60,500 70,504 v Aston Villa Div. 1 27 December 1920 | 1892 elected to Div. 1 as Newton Heath. Changed name 1902 1894–1906 Div. 2 1906–22 Div. 1 1922–25 Div. 2 1925–31 Div. 1 | 1931–36 Div. 2 1936–37 Div. 1 1937–38 Div. 2 1938–74 Div. 1 1974–75 Div. 2 1975– Div. 1 | Div. 1 Champions 1908, 1911, 1952, 1956, 1957, 1965, 1967 Runners-up 1947, 1948, 1949, 1951, 1959, 1964, 1968 Div. 2 Champions 1936, 1975 Runners-up 1897, 1906, 1925, 1938 | FA Cup winners 1909, 1948, 1963, 1977 Runners-up 1957, 1958, 1976, 1979 League Cup semi-finalists 1970, 1971, 1975 |

Most League Points	Goals	Record win	Player highest number of goals Aggregate	Individual	Most League appearances	Most capped player
						LIVERPOOL
68, Div. 1 1978–79	106, Div. 2 1895–96	11–0 v Stromsgodset (Norway) Cup-Winners' Cup 17 September 1974	Roger Hunt 245, 1959–69	Roger Hunt 41 Div. 2 1961–62	Ian Callaghan 640, 1960–78	Emlyn Hughes 59, England 1970–79
						LUTON TOWN
66, Div. 4 1967–68	103, Div. 3(S) 1936–37	12–0 v Bristol Rovers Div. 3(S) 13 April 1936	Gordon Turner 243, 1949–64	Joe Payne 55 Div. 3(S) 1936–37	Bob Morton 494, 1948–64	George Cummins 19, Eire 1953–61
						MANCHESTER CITY
62, Div. 2 1946–47	108, Div. 2 1926–27	11–3 v Lincoln City Div. 2 23 March 1895	Tommy Johnson 158, 1919–30	Tommy Johnson 38 Div. 1 1928–29	Alan Oakes 565, 1959–76	Colin Bell 48, England 1968–75
						MANCHESTER UNITED
64, Div. 1 1956–57	103, Div. 1 1956–57, 1958–59	10–0 v Anderlecht (Belgium) European Cup Prelim Rd 26 September 1956	Bobby Charlton 198, 1956–73	Dennis Viollet 32 Div. 1 1959–60	Bobby Charlton 606, 1956–73	Bobby Charlton 106, England 1958–70

Ground	Capacity & Record	League career		Honours (domestic) League	Cup

MANSFIELD TOWN (1905) Amber/blue

Field Mill Ground	23,500 ·	1931 elected	1963–72 Div. 3	Div. 3 Champions	FA Cup never
Quarry Lane	24,467 v	to Div. 3(S)	1972–75 Div. 4	1977	past 6th Rd
Mansfield	Nottingham F	1932–37 Div. 3(N)	1975–77 Div. 3	Div. 4 Champions	League Cup
115 × 72 yd	FA Cup 3rd Rd	1937–47 Div. 3(S)	1977–78 Div. 2	1975	never past
	10 January 1953	1947–58 Div. 3(N)	1978– Div. 3	Div 3(N)	5th Rd
		1958–60 Div. 3		Runners-up 1951	
		1960–63 Div. 4			

MIDDLESBROUGH (1876) Red with white trim/red

Ayresome Park	42,000	1899 elected to	1929–54 Div. 1	Div. 2 Champions	FA Cup never
Middlesbrough	53,596 v	Div. 2	1954–66 Div. 2	1927, 1929, 1974	past 6th Rd
Teesside	Newcastle U	1902–24 Div. 1	1966–67 Div. 3	Runners-up 1902	League Cup
115 × 75 yd	Div. 1	1924–27 Div. 2	1967–74 Div. 2	Div. 3 runners-up	semi-finalists
	27 December 1949	1927–28 Div. 1	1974– Div. 1	1967	1976
		1928–29 Div. 2			

MILLWALL (1885) Blue/white

The Den	32,000	1920 (founder	1962–64 Div. 3	Div. 3(S)	FA Cup
Cold Blow Lane	48,672 v	members of Div. 3)	1964–65 Div. 4	Champions	semi-finalists
London SE14 5RH	Derby Co	1921 Div. 3(S)	1965–66 Div. 3	1928, 1938	1900, 1903, 1937
112 × 74 yd	FA Cup 5th Rd	1928–34 Div. 2	1966–75 Div. 2	Div. 3 runners-up	League Cup
	20 February 1937	1934–38 Div. 3(S)	1975–76 Div. 3	1966	never past
		1938–48 Div. 2	1976– Div. 2	Div. 4 Champions	5th Rd
		1948–58 Div. 3(S)		1962	
		1958–62 Div. 4		Runners-up 1965	

NEWCASTLE UNITED (1882) Black-white stripes/black

St James' Park	40,480	1893 elected	1961–65 Div. 2	Div. 1 Champions	FA Cup winners
Newcastle-upon-Tyne	68,386 v	to Div. 2	1965–78 Div. 1	1905, 1907, 1909,	1910, 1924, 1932,
NE1 4ST	Chelsea Div. 1	1898–1934 Div. 1	1978– Div. 2	1927	1951, 1952, 1955
115 × 75 yd	3 September 1930	1934–48 Div. 2		Div. 2 Champions	Runners-up
		1948–61 Div. 1		1965	1905, 1906, 1908,
				Runners-up	1911, 1974
				1898, 1948	League Cup
					runners-up 1976

NEWPORT COUNTY (1912) Sky blue-white stripes/sky blue

Somerton Park	22,060	1920 (founder	1932–39 Div. 3(S)	Div. 3(S)	FA Cup never
Newport	24,268 v	member of Div. 3)	1946–47 Div. 2	Champions 1939	past 5th Rd
Mon	Cardiff City	1921 Div. 3(S)	1947–58 Div. 3(S)		League Cup
112 × 78 yd	Div. 3(S)	1931 dropped out	1958–62 Div. 3		never past
	16 October 1937	of League	1962– Div. 4		3rd Rd
		1932 re-elected			

Most League Points	Goals	Record win	Player highest number of goals Aggregate	Individual	Most League appearances	Most capped player

MANSFIELD TOWN

Most League Points	Goals	Record win	Aggregate	Individual	Most League appearances	Most capped player
68, Div. 4 1974–75	108, Div. 4 1962–63	9–2 v Rotherham United Div. 3(N) 27 December 1932 Hounslow Town replay 5 November 1962	Harry Johnson 104, 1931–36	Ted Harston 55 Div. 3(N) 1936–37	Don Bradley 417, 1949–62	None

MIDDLESBROUGH

65, Div. 2 1973–74	122, Div. 2 1926–27	9–0 v Brighton & HA Div. 2 23 August 1958	George Camsell 326, 1925–39	George Camsell 59 Div. 2 1926–27	Tim Williamson 563, 1902–23	Wilf Mannion 26, England 1946–51

MILLWALL

65, Div. 3(S) 1927–28 Div. 3 1965–66	127, Div. 3(S) 1927–28	9–1 v Torquay United Div. 3(S) 29 August 1927 Coventry City Div. 3(S) 19 November 1927	Derek Possee 79, 1967–73	Richard Parker 37 Div. 3(S) 1926–27	Barry Kitchener 489, 1967–79	Eamonn Dunphy 22, Eire 1966–71

NEWCASTLE UNITED

57, Div. 2 1964–65	98, Div. 1 1951–52	13–0 v Newport County Div. 2 5 October 1946	Jackie Milburn 178, 1946–57	Hughie Gallacher 36 Div. 1 1926–27	Jim Lawrence 432, 1904–22	Alf McMichael 40, N Ireland 1949–60

NEWPORT COUNTY

56, Div. 4 1972–73	85, Div. 4 1964–65	10–0 v Merthyr Town Div. 3(S) 10 April 1930	Reg Parker 99, 1948–54	Tudor Martin 34 Div. 3(S) 1929–30	Ray Wilcox 530, 1946–60	(All for Wales) Fred Cook 2 1925 Jack Nicholls 2 1924 Alf Sherwood 2 1956 Bill Thomas 2 1930 Harold Williams 2 1949

Ground	Capacity & Record	League career		Honours (domestic) League	Cup

NORTHAMPTON TOWN (1897) White with claret trim/white

County Ground Abington Avenue Northampton NN1 4PS 120 × 75 yd	20,000 24,523 v Fulham Div. 1 23 April 1966	1920 (founder member of Div. 3) 1921 Div. 3(S) 1958–61 Div. 4 1961–63 Div. 3 1963–65 Div. 2 1965–66 Div. 1	1966–67 Div. 2 1967–68 Div. 3 1968–76 Div. 4 1976–77 Div. 3 1977– Div. 4	Div. 2 runners-up 1965 Div. 3 Champions 1963 Div. 3(S) runners-up 1928, 1950 Div. 4 runners-up 1976	FA Cup never past 5th Rd League Cup never past 5th Rd

NORWICH CITY (1905) Yellow/green

Carrow Road Norwich NR1 1JE 114 × 74 yd	32,000 43,984 v Leicester City FA Cup 6th Rd 30 March 1963	1920 (founder member of Div. 3) 1921 Div. 3(S) 1934–39 Div. 2 1946–58 Div. 3(S)	1958–60 Div. 3 1960–72 Div. 2 1972–74 Div. 1 1974–75 Div. 2 1975– Div. 1	Div. 2 Champions 1972 Div. 3(S) Champions 1934 Div. 3 runners-up 1960	FA Cup semi-finalists 1959 League Cup winners 1962 Runners-up 1973, 1975

NOTTINGHAM FOREST (1865) Red/white

City Ground Nottingham NG2 5FJ 115 × 78 yd	41,930 49,945 v Manchester U Div. 1 28 October 1967	1892 elected to Div. 1 1906 Div. 2 1907 Div. 1 1911–22 Div. 2 1922–25 Div. 1 1925–49 Div. 2	1949–51 Div. 3(S) 1951–57 Div. 2 1957–72 Div. 1 1972–77 Div. 2 1977– Div. 1	Div. 1 Champions 1978, Runners-up 1967, 1979 Div. 2 Champions 1907, 1922 Runners-up 1957 Div. 3(S) Champions 1951	FA Cup winners 1898, 1959 League Cup winners 1978, 1979

NOTTS COUNTY (1862) Black-white stripes/black

County Ground Meadow Lane Nottingham NG2 3HJ 117 × 76 yd	40,000 47,310 v York City FA Cup 6th Rd 12 March 1955	1888 (founder member of League) 1893–97 Div. 2 1897–1913 Div. 1 1913–14 Div. 2 1914–20 Div. 1 1920–23 Div. 2 1923–26 Div. 1 1926–30 Div. 2	1930–31 Div. 3(S) 1931–35 Div. 2 1935–50 Div. 3(S) 1950–58 Div. 2 1958–59 Div. 3 1959–60 Div. 4 1960–64 Div. 3 1964–71 Div. 4 1971–73 Div. 3 1973– Div. 2	Div. 2 Champions 1897, 1914, 1923 Runners-up 1895 Div. 3(S) Champions 1931, 1950 Runners-up 1937 Div. 4 Champions 1971 Runners-up 1960	FA Cup winners 1894 Runners-up 1891 League Cup never past 5th Rd

OLDHAM ATHLETIC (1894) Blue/white

Boundary Park Oldham 110 × 74 yd	30,000 47,671 v Sheffield W FA Cup 4th Rd 25 January 1930	1907 elected to Div. 2 1910–23 Div. 1 1923–35 Div. 2 1935–53 Div. 3(N) 1953–54 Div. 2 1954–58 Div. 3(N)	1958–63 Div. 4 1963–69 Div. 3 1969–71 Div. 4 1971–74 Div. 3 1974– Div. 2	Div. 1 runners-up 1915 Div. 2 runners-up 1910 Div. 3(N) Champions 1953 Div. 3 Champions 1974 Div. 4 runners-up 1963	FA Cup semi-finalists 1913 League Cup never past 3rd Rd

Most League Points	Goals	Record win	Player highest number of goals Aggregate	Individual	Most League appearances	Most capped player

NORTHAMPTON TOWN

Most League Points	Goals	Record win	Player highest number of goals Aggregate	Individual	Most League appearances	Most capped player
68, Div. 4 1975–76	109, Div. 3 1962–63 Div. 3(S) 1952–53	10–0 v Walsall Div. 3(S) 5 November 1927	Jack English 135, 1947–60	Cliff Holton 36 Div. 3 1961–62	Tommy Fowler 521, 1946–61	E Lloyd Davies 12, Wales 1908–14

NORWICH CITY

Most League Points	Goals	Record win	Player highest number of goals Aggregate	Individual	Most League appearances	Most capped player
64, Div. 3(S) 1950–51	99 Div. 3(S) 1952–53	10–2 v Coventry City Div. 3(S) 15 March 1930	Johnny Gavin 122, 1945–54, 1955–58	Ralph Hunt 31 Div. 3(S) 1955–56	Ron Ashman 590, 1947–64	Ted MacDougall 7, Scotland 1975

NOTTINGHAM FOREST

Most League Points	Goals	Record win	Player highest number of goals Aggregate	Individual	Most League appearances	Most capped player
70, Div. 3(S) 1950–51	110, Div. 3(S) 1950–51	14–0 v Clapton FA Cup 1st Rd 1890–91	Grenville Morris 199, 1898–1913	Wally Ardron 36 Div. 3(S) 1950–51	Bob McKinlay 614, 1951–70	Martin O'Neill 29, N Ireland 1972–79

NOTTS COUNTY

Most League Points	Goals	Record win	Player highest number of goals Aggregate	Individual	Most League appearances	Most capped player
69, Div. 4 1970–71	107, Div. 4 1959–60	15–0 v Thornhill United FA Cup 1st Rd 24 October 1885	Les Bradd 125, 1967–78	Tom Keetley 39 Div. 3(S) 1930–31	Albert Iremonger 564, 1904–26	Bill Fallon 7, Eire 1934–38

OLDHAM ATHLETIC

Most League Points	Goals	Record win	Player highest number of goals Aggregate	Individual	Most League appearances	Most capped player
62, Div. 3 1973–74	95, Div. 4 1962–63	11–0 v Southport Div. 4 26 December 1962	Eric Gemmell 110, 1947–54	Tom Davis 33 Div. 3(N) 1936–37	Ian Wood 488, 1966–79	Albert Gray 9, Wales 1924–27

Ground	Capacity & Record	League career	Honours (domestic) League	Cup
ORIENT (1881) White with two red stripes/white				
Leyton Stadium Brisbane Road Leyton London E10 5NE 110 × 80 yd	25,000 34,345 v West Ham U FA Cup 4th Rd 25 January 1964	1905 elected to Div. 2 1929–56 Div. 3(S) 1956–62 Div. 2 1962–63 Div. 1	1963–66 Div. 2 1966–70 Div. 3 1970– Div. 2	Div. 2 runners-up 1962 Div. 3 Champions 1970 Div. 3(S) Champions 1956 Runners-up 1955	FA Cup semi-finalists 1978 League Cup never past 5th Rd
OXFORD UNITED (1896) Yellow/blue				
Manor Ground Beech Road Headington Oxford 112 × 78 yd	18,000 22,730 v Preston NE FA Cup 6th Rd 29 February 1964	1962 elected to Div. 4 1965–68 Div. 3	1968–76 Div. 2 1976– Div. 3	Div. 3 Champions 1968	FA Cup never past 6th Rd League Cup never past 5th Rd
PETERBOROUGH UNITED (1923) Blue-white stripes/blue				
London Road Ground Peterborough PE2 8AL 112 × 76 yd	30,000 30,096 v Swansea T FA Cup 5th Rd 20 February 1965	1960 elected to Div. 4 1961–68 Div. 3 1968 demoted for financial irregularities	1968–74 Div. 4 1974–79 Div. 3 1979– Div. 4	Div. 4 Champions 1961, 1974	FA Cup never past 6th Rd League Cup semi-finalists 1966
PLYMOUTH ARGYLE (1886) Green/white				
Home Park Plymouth Devon 112 × 75 yd	40,000 43,596 v Aston Villa Div. 2 10 October 1936	1920 (founder member of Div. 3) 1921–30 Div. 3(S) 1930–50 Div. 2 1950–52 Div. 3(S) 1952–56 Div. 2 1956–58 Div. 3(S)	1958–59 Div. 3 1959–68 Div. 2 1968–75 Div. 3 1975–77 Div. 2 1977– Div. 3	Div. 3(S) Champions 1930, 1952 Runners-up 1922, 1923, 1924, 1925, 1926, 1927 Div. 3 Champions 1959 Runners-up 1975	FA Cup never past 5th Rd League Cup semi-finalists 1965, 1974
PORTSMOUTH (1898) Blue/white				
Fratton Park Frogmore Road Portsmouth PO8 8RA 116 × 73 yd	46,000 51,385 v Derby Co FA Cup 6th Rd 26 February 1949	1920 (founder member of Div. 3) 1921–24 Div. 3(S) 1924–27 Div. 2 1927–59 Div. 1 1959–61 Div. 2	1961–62 Div. 3 1962–76 Div. 2 1976–78 Div. 3 1978– Div. 4	Div. 1 Champions 1949, 1950 Div. 2 runners-up 1927 Div. 3(S) Champions 1924 Div. 3 Champions 1962	FA Cup winners 1939 Runners-up 1929, 1934 League Cup never past 5th Rd

Most League Points	Goals	Record win	Player highest number of goals		Most League appearances	Most capped player
			Aggregate	Individual		
						ORIENT
66, Div. 3(S) 1955–56	106, Div. 3(S) 1955–56	9–2 v Aldershot Div. 3(S) 10 February 1934 Chester League Cup 3rd Rd 15 October 1962	Tom Johnston 121, 1956–58, 1959–61	Tom Johnston 35 Div. 2 1957–58	Peter Allen 430, 1965–78	Tony Grealish 8, Eire 1976–79
						OXFORD UNITED
61, Div. 4 1964–65	87, Div. 4 1964–65	7–1 v Barrow Div. 4 19 December 1964	Graham Atkinson 73, 1962–73	Colin Booth 23 Div. 4 1964–65	John Shuker 480, 1962–77	David Roberts 6, Wales 1973–74
						PETERBOROUGH UNITED
66, Div. 4 1960–61	134, Div. 4 1960–61	8–1 v Oldham Athletic Div. 4 26 November 1969	Jim Hall 120, 1967–75	Terry Bly 52 Div. 4 1960–61	Tommy Robson 421, 1968–79	Ollie Conmy 5, Eire 1965–69
						PLYMOUTH ARGYLE
68, Div. 3(S) 1929–30	107, Div. 3(S) 1925–26, 1951–52	8–1 v Millwall Div. 2 16 January 1932	Sammy Black 180, 1924–38	Jack Cock 32 Div. 3(S) 1925–26	Sammy Black 470, 1924–38	Moses Russell 20, Wales 1920–28
						PORTSMOUTH
65, Div. 3 1961–62	87, Div. 3(S) 1923–24 Div. 2 1926–27 Div. 3 1961–62	9–1 v Notts County Div. 2 9 April 1927	Peter Harris 194, 1946–60	Billy Haines 40 Div. 2 1926–27	Jimmy Dickinson 764, 1946–65	Jimmy Dickinson 48, England 1949–56

Ground	Capacity & Record	League career	Honours (domestic) League	Cup

PORT VALE (1876) White/black

Vale Park Burslem Stoke-on-Trent 116 × 76 yd	35,000 50,000 v Aston Villa FA Cup 5th Rd 20 February 1960	1892 (founder member of Div. 2) 1896 failed re-election 1898 re-elected 1907 resigned 1919 returned in October and took over the fixtures of Leeds City 1929–30 Div. 3(N)	1930–36 Div. 2 1936–38 Div. 3(N) 1938–52 Div. 3(S) 1952–54 Div. 3(N) 1954–57 Div. 2 1957–58 Div. 3(S) 1958–59 Div. 4 1959–65 Div. 3 1965–70 Div. 4 1970–78 Div. 3 1978– Div. 4	Div. 3(N) Champions 1930, 1954 Runners-up 1953 Div. 4 Champions 1959	FA Cup semi-finalists 1954 League Cup never past 2nd Rd

PRESTON NORTH END (1881) White/white

Deepdale Preston PR1 6RU 112 × 78 yd	38,000 42,684 v Arsenal Div. 1 23 April 1938	1888 (founder member of League) 1901–04 Div. 2 1904–12 Div. 1 1912–13 Div. 2 1913–14 Div. 1 1914–15 Div. 2 1919–25 Div. 1 1925–34 Div. 2	1934–49 Div. 1 1949–51 Div. 2 1951–61 Div. 1 1961–70 Div. 2 1970–71 Div. 3 1971–74 Div. 2 1974–78 Div. 3 1978– Div. 2	Div. 1 Champions 1889, 1890 Runners-up 1891, 1892, 1893, 1906, 1953, 1958 Div. 2 Champions 1904, 1913, 1951 Runners-up 1915, 1934 Div. 3 Champions 1971	FA Cup winners 1889, 1938 Runners-up 1888, 1922, 1937, 1954, 1964 League Cup never past 4th Rd

QUEEN'S PARK RANGERS (1885) Blue-white hoops/white

South Africa Road London W12 7PA 112 × 72 yd	30,000 35,353 v Leeds U Div. 1 28 April 1974	1920 (founder member of Div. 3) 1921–48 Div. 3(S) 1948–52 Div. 2 1952–58 Div. 3(S) 1958–67 Div. 3	1967–68 Div. 2 1968–69 Div. 1 1969–73 Div. 2 1973–79 Div. 1 1979– Div. 2	Div. 1 runners-up 1976 Div. 2 runners-up 1968, 1973 Div. 3(S) Champions 1948 Runners-up 1947 Div. 3 Champions 1967	FA Cup never past 6th Rd or equivalent League Cup winners 1967

READING (1871) Blue-white hoops/white

Elm Park Norfolk Reading 112 × 77 yd	27,200 33,042 v Brentford FA Cup 5th Rd 19 February 1927	1920 (founder member of Div. 3) 1921–26 Div. 3(S) 1926–31 Div. 2 1931–58 Div. 3(S)	1958–71 Div. 3 1971–76 Div. 4 1976–77 Div. 3 1977–79 Div. 4 1979– Div. 3	Div. 3(S) Champions 1926 Runners-up 1932, 1935, 1949, 1952 Div. 4 Champions 1979	FA Cup semi-finalists 1927 League Cup never past 4th Rd

ROCHDALE (1907) Blue/white

Spotland Willbutts Lane Rochdale 113 × 75 yd	28,000 24,231 v Notts Co FA Cup 2nd Rd 10 December 1949	1921 elected to Div. 3(N) 1958–59 Div. 3 1959–69 Div. 4	1969–74 Div. 3 1974– Div. 4	Div. 3(N) runners-up 1924, 1927	FA Cup never past 4th Rd League Cup runners-up 1962

Most League Points	Goals	Record win	Player highest number of goals Aggregate	Individual	Most League appearances	Most capped player
						PORT VALE
69, Div. 3(N) 1953–54	110, Div. 4 1958–59	9–1 v Chesterfield Div. 2 24 September 1932	Wilf Kirkham 154, 1923–29, 1931–33	Wilf Kirkham 38 Div. 2 1926–27	Roy Sproson 761, 1950–72	Sammy Morgan 7, N Ireland 1972–73
						PRESTON NORTH END
61, Div. 3 1970–71	100, Div. 2 1927–28 Div. 1 1957–58	26–0 v Hyde FA Cup 1st series 1st Rd 15 October 1887	Tom Finney 187, 1946–60	Ted Harper 37 Div. 2 1932–33	Alan Kelly 447, 1961–75	Tom Finney 76, England 1946–58
						QUEEN'S PARK RANGERS
67, Div. 3 1966–67	111, Div. 3 1961–62	9–2 v Tranmere Rovers Div. 3 3 December 1960	George Goddard 172, 1926–34	George Goddard 37 Div. 3(S) 1929–30	Tony Ingham 519, 1950–63	Don Givens 21, Eire 1973–78
						READING
65, Div. 4 1978–79	112, Div. 3(S) 1951–52	10–2 v Crystal Palace Div. 3(S) 4 September 1946	Ronnie Blackman 156, 1947–54	Ronnie Blackman 39 Div. 3(S) 1951–52	Dick Spiers 453, 1955–70	Pat McConnell 8, N Ireland 1925–28
						ROCHDALE
62, Div. 3(N) 1923–24	105, Div. 3(N) 1926–27	8–1 v Chesterfield Div. 3(N) 18 December 1926	Albert Whitehurst 117, 1923–28	Albert Whitehurst 44 Div. 3(N) 1926–27	Graham Smith 317, 1966–74	None

Ground	Capacity & Record	League career		Honours (domestic) League	Cup

ROTHERHAM UNITED (1884) Red, white sleeves/white

Ground	Capacity & Record	League career		Honours (domestic) League	Cup
Millmoor Ground Rotherham 115 × 76 yd	22,000 25,000 v Sheffield U Div. 2 13 December 1952 and Sheffield W Div. 2 26 January 1952	1893 elected to Div. 2 1896 failed re-election 1919 re-elected to Div. 2	1923–51 Div. 3(N) 1951–68 Div. 2 1968–73 Div. 3 1973–75 Div. 4 1975– Div. 3	Div. 3(N) Champions 1951 Runners-up 1947, 1948, 1949	FA Cup never past 5th Rd League Cup runners-up 1961

SCUNTHORPE UNITED (1904) Red/red

Ground	Capacity & Record	League career		Honours (domestic) League	Cup
Old Show Ground Scunthorpe South Humberside 112 × 78 yd	27,000 23,935 v Portsmouth FA Cup 4th Rd 30 January 1954	1950 elected to Div. 3(N) 1958–64 Div. 2 1964–68 Div. 3	1968–72 Div. 4 1972–73 Div. 3 1973– Div. 4	Div. 3(N) Champions 1958	FA Cup never past 5th Rd League Cup never past 3rd Rd

SHEFFIELD UNITED (1889) Red, white and thin black stripes/black

Ground	Capacity & Record	League career		Honours (domestic) League	Cup
Bramall Lane Ground Sheffield S2 4SU 117 × 75 yd	49,000 68,287 v Leeds U FA Cup 5th Rd 15 February 1936	1892 elected to Div. 2 1893–1934 Div. 1 1934–39 Div. 2 1946–49 Div. 1 1949–53 Div. 2 1953–56 Div. 1	1956–61 Div. 2 1961–68 Div. 1 1968–71 Div. 2 1971–76 Div. 1 1976–79 Div. 2 1979– Div. 3	Div. 1 Champions 1898 Runners-up 1897, 1900 Div. 2 Champions 1953 Runners-up 1893 1939, 1961, 1971	FA Cup winners 1899, 1902, 1915, 1925 Runners-up 1901, 1936 League Cup never past 5th Rd

SHEFFIELD WEDNESDAY (1867) Blue-white stripes/blue

Ground	Capacity & Record	League career		Honours (domestic) League	Cup
Hillsborough Sheffield S6 1SW 115 × 75 yd	55,000 72,841 v Manchester C FA Cup 5th Rd 17 February 1934	1892 elected to Div. 1 1899–1900 Div. 2 1900–20 Div. 1 1920–26 Div. 2 1926–37 Div. 1 1937–50 Div. 2 1950–51 Div. 1	1951–52 Div. 2 1952–55 Div. 1 1955–56 Div. 2 1956–58 Div. 1 1958–59 Div. 2 1959–70 Div. 1 1970–75 Div. 2 1975– Div. 3	Div. 1 Champions 1903, 1904, 1929, 1930 Runners-up 1961 Div. 2 Champions 1900, 1926, 1952, 1956, 1959 Runners-up 1950	FA Cup winners 1896, 1907, 1935 Runners-up 1890, 1966 League Cup never past 4th Rd

SHREWSBURY TOWN (1886) Blue/blue

Ground	Capacity & Record	League career		Honours (domestic) League	Cup
Gay Meadow Shrewsbury 116 × 76 yd	18,000 18,917 v Walsall Div. 3 26 April 1961	1950 elected to Div. 3(N) 1951–58 Div. 3(S) 1958–59 Div. 4	1959–74 Div. 3 1974–75 Div. 4 1975–79 Div. 3 1979– Div. 2	Div. 3 Champions 1979 Div. 4 runners-up 1975	FA Cup never past 6th Rd League Cup semi-finalists 1961

SOUTHAMPTON (1885) Red-white stripes/black

Ground	Capacity & Record	League career		Honours (domestic) League	Cup
The Dell Milton Road Southampton SO9 4XX 110 × 72 yd	26,000 31,044 v Manchester U Div. 1 8 October 1969	1920 (founder member of Div. 3) 1921–22 Div. 3(S) 1922–53 Div. 2 1953–58 Div. 3(S) 1958–60 Div. 3	1960–66 Div. 2 1966–74 Div. 1 1974–78 Div. 2 1978– Div. 1	Div. 2 runners-up 1966, 1978 Div. 3(S) Champions 1922 Runners-up 1921 Div. 3 Champions 1960	FA Cup winners 1976 Runners-up 1900, 1902 League Cup runners-up 1979

Most League Points	Goals	Record win	Player highest number of goals		Most League appearances	Most capped player
			Aggregate	Individual		

ROTHERHAM UNITED

| 71, Div. 3(N) 1950–51 | 114, Div. 3(N) 1946–47 | 8–0 v Oldham Athletic Div. 3(N) 26 May 1947 | Gladstone Guest 130, 1946–56 | Wally Ardron 38 Div. 3(N) 1946–47 | Danny Williams 459, 1946–62 | Harold Millership 6, Wales 1920–21 |

SCUNTHORPE UNITED

| 66, Div. 3(N) 1957–58 | 88, Div. 3(N) 1957–58 | 9–0 v Boston United FA Cup 1st Rd 21 November 1953 | Barrie Thomas 92, 1959–62, 1964–66 | Barrie Thomas 31 Div. 2 1961–62 | Jack Brownsword 600, 1950–65 | None |

SHEFFIELD UNITED

| 60, Div. 2 1952–53 | 102, Div. 1 1925–26 | 11–2 v Cardiff City Div. 1 1 January 1926 | Harry Johnson 205, 1919–30 | Jimmy Dunne 41 Div. 1 1930–31 | Joe Shaw 629, 1948–66 | Billy Gillespie 25, N Ireland 1913–30 |

SHEFFIELD WEDNESDAY

| 62, Div. 2 1958–59 | 106, Div. 2 1958–59 | 12–0 v Halliwell FA Cup 1st Rd 17 January 1891 | Andy Wilson 200, 1900–20 | Derek Dooley 46 Div. 2 1951–52 | Andy Wilson 502, 1900–20 | Ron Springett 33, England 1959–66 |

SHREWSBURY TOWN

| 62, Div. 4 1974–75 | 101, Div. 4 1958–59 | 7–0 v Swindon Town Div. 3(S) 1954–55 | Arthur Rowley 152, 1958–65 | Arthur Rowley 38 Div. 4 1958–59 | Joe Wallace 329, 1954–63 | Jimmy McLaughlin 5, N Ireland 1961–63 |

SOUTHAMPTON

| 61, Div. 3(S) 1921–22 Div. 3 1959–60 | 112, Div. 3(S) 1957–58 | 11–0 v Northampton Town Southern League 28 December 1901 | Terry Paine 160, 1956–74 | Derek Reeves 39 Div. 3 1959–60 | Terry Paine 713, 1956–74 | Mike Channon 45, England 1972–77 |

Ground	Capacity & Record	League career	Honours (domestic) League	Cup

SOUTHEND UNITED (1906) Blue/white

Roots Hall Ground	35,000	1920 (founder	1966–72 Div. 4	Div. 4 runners-up	FA Cup never
Victoria Avenue	31,036 v	member of Div. 3)	1972–76 Div. 3	1972, 1978	past 5th Rd
Southend-on-Sea	Liverpool	1921–58 Div. 3(S)	1976–78 Div. 4		League Cup
SS2 6NQ	FA Cup 3rd Rd	1958–66 Div. 3	1978– Div. 3		never past
110 × 74 yd	10 January 1979				3rd Rd

STOCKPORT COUNTY (1883) White/blue

Edgeley Park	24,904	1900 elected	1922–26 Div. 2	Div. 3(N)	FA Cup never
Stockport	27,833 v	to Div. 2	1926–37 Div. 3(N)	Champions	past 5th Rd
Cheshire	Liverpool	1904 failed	1937–38 Div. 2	1922, 1937	League Cup
SK3 9DD	FA Cup 5th Rd	re-election	1938–58 Div. 3(N)	Runners-up	never past
110 × 75 yd	11 February 1950	1905 re-elected	1958–59 Div. 3	1929, 1930	4th Rd
		to Div. 2	1959–67 Div. 4	Div. 4 Champions	
		1905–21 Div. 2	1967–70 Div. 3	1967	
		1921–22 Div. 3(N)	1970– Div. 4		

STOKE CITY (1863) Red-white stripes/white

Victoria Ground	40,000	1888 (founder	1922–23 Div. 1	Div. 2 Champions	FA Cup
Stoke-on-Trent	51,380 v	member of	1923–26 Div. 2	1933, 1963	semi-finalists
116 × 75 yd	Arsenal Div. 1	League)	1926–27 Div. 3(N)	Runners-up 1922	1899, 1971, 1972
	29 March 1937	1890 not re-elected	1927–33 Div. 2	Div. 3(N)	League Cup
		1891 re-elected	1933–53 Div. 1	Champions 1927	winners 1972
		1907–08 Div. 2	1953–63 Div. 2		
		1908 resigned for	1963–77 Div. 1		
		financial reasons	1977–79 Div. 2		
		1919 re-elected	1979– Div. 1		
		to Div. 2			

SUNDERLAND (1879) Red-white stripes/black

Roker Park	47,000	1890 elected	1970–76 Div. 2	Div. 1 Champions	FA Cup winners
Sunderland	75,118 v	to Div. 1	1976–77 Div. 1	1892, 1893, 1895,	1937, 1973
112 × 72 yd	Derby Co	1958–64 Div. 2	1977– Div. 2	1902, 1913, 1936	Runners-up 1913
	FA Cup 6th Rd	1964–70 Div. 1		Runners-up	League Cup
	replay			1894, 1898, 1901,	semi-finalists
	8 March 1933			1923, 1935	1963
				Div. 2 Champions	
				1976	
				Runners-up 1964	

SWANSEA CITY (1900) White/white

Vetch Field	35,000	1920 (founder	1965–67 Div. 3	Div. 3 runners-up	FA Cup
Swansea	32,796 v	member of Div. 3)	1967–70 Div. 4	1979	semi-finalists
110 × 70 yd	Arsenal	1921–25 Div. 3(S)	1970–73 Div. 3	Div. 3(S)	1926, 1964
	FA Cup 4th Rd	1925–47 Div. 2	1973–78 Div. 4	Champions	League Cup
	17 February 1968	1947–49 Div. 3(S)	1978–79 Div. 3	1925, 1949	never past
		1949–65 Div. 2	1979– Div. 2		5th Rd

Most League Points	Goals	Record win	Player highest number of goals		Most League appearances	Most capped player
			Aggregate	Individual		

SOUTHEND UNITED

Most League Points	Goals	Record win	Aggregate	Individual	Most League appearances	Most capped player
60, Div. 4 1971–72 Div. 4 1977–78	92, Div. 3(S) 1950–51	10–1 v Golders Green FA Cup 1st Rd 24 November 1934 Brentwood FA Cup 2nd Rd 7 December 1968	Roy Hollis 122, 1953–60	Jim Shankly 31 Div. 3(S) 1928–29 Sammy McCrory 31 Div. 3(S) 1957–58	Sandy Anderson 451, 1950–63	George Mackenzie 9, Eire 1937–39

STOCKPORT COUNTY

Most League Points	Goals	Record win	Aggregate	Individual	Most League appearances	Most capped player
64, Div. 4 1966–67	115, Div. 3(N) 1933–34	13–0 v Halifax Town Div. 3(N) 6 January 1934	Jackie Connor 132, 1951–56	Alf Lythgoe 46 Div. 3(N) 1933–34	Bob Murray 465, 1952–63	Harry Hardy 1, England 1924

STOKE CITY

Most League Points	Goals	Record win	Aggregate	Individual	Most League appearances	Most capped player
63, Div. 3(N) 1926–27	92, Div. 3(N) 1926–27	10–3 v West Bromwich Albion Div. 1 4 February 1937	Freddie Steele 142, 1934–49	Freddie Steele 33 Div. 1 1936–37	Eric Skeels 506, 1958–76	Gordon Banks 35, England 1967–72

SUNDERLAND

Most League Points	Goals	Record win	Aggregate	Individual	Most League appearances	Most capped player
61, Div. 2 1963–64	109, Div. 1 1935–36	11–1 v Fairfield FA Cup 1st Rd 1894–95	Charlie Buchan 209, 1911–25	Dave Halliday 43 Div. 1 1928–29	Jim Montgomery 537, 1962–77	Billy Bingham 33, N Ireland 1951–58 Martin Harvey 33, N Ireland 1961–71

SWANSEA CITY

Most League Points	Goals	Record win	Aggregate	Individual	Most League appearances	Most capped player
62, Div. 3(S) 1948–49	90, Div. 2 1956–57	8–0 v Hartlepool United Div. 4 1 April 1978	Ivor Allchurch 166, 1949–58, 1965–68	Cyril Pearce 35 Div. 2 1931–32	Wilfred Milne 585, 1919–37	Ivor Allchurch 42, Wales 1950–58

Ground	Capacity & Record	League career		Honours (domestic) League	Cup

SWINDON TOWN (1881) Red/white

| County Ground
Swindon
Wiltshire
114 × 72 yd | 28,000
32,000 v
Arsenal
FA Cup 3rd Rd
15 January 1972 | 1920 (founder
member of Div. 3)
1921–58 Div. 3(S)
1958–63 Div. 3
1963–65 Div. 2 | 1965–69 Div. 3
1969–74 Div. 2
1974–   Div. 3 | Div. 3 runners-up
1963, 1969 | FA Cup
semi-finalists
1910, 1912
League Cup
winners 1969 |

TORQUAY UNITED (1898) White with blue and yellow trim/white

| Plainmoor Ground
Torquay
Devon
TQ1 3PS
112 × 74 yd | 22,000
21,908 v
Huddersfield T
FA Cup 4th Rd
29 January 1955 | 1927 elected to
Div. 3(S)
1958–60 Div. 4
1960–62 Div. 3 | 1962–66 Div. 4
1966–72 Div. 3
1972–   Div. 4 | Div. 3(S)
runners-up 1957 | FA Cup never
past 4th Rd
League Cup
never past
3rd Rd |

TOTTENHAM HOTSPUR (1882) White/blue

| 748 High Road
Tottenham
London N17
110 × 73 yd | 52,000
75,038 v
Sunderland
FA Cup 6th Rd
5 March 1938 | 1908 elected
to Div. 2
1909–15 Div. 1
1919–20 Div. 2
1920–28 Div. 1
1928–33 Div. 2 | 1933–35 Div. 1
1935–50 Div. 2
1950–77 Div. 1
1977–78 Div. 2
1978–   Div. 1 | Div. 1 Champions
1951, 1961
Runners-up 1922,
1952, 1957, 1963
Div. 2 Champions
1920, 1950
Runners-up
1909, 1933 | FA Cup winners
1901, 1921, 1961,
1962, 1967
League Cup
winners
1971, 1973 |

TRANMERE ROVERS (1883) White/blue

| Prenton Park
Prenton Road West
Birkenhead
112 × 74 yd | 25,000
24,242 v
Stoke City
FA Cup 4th Rd
5 February 1972 | 1921 (founder
member of
Div. 3(N))
1938–39 Div. 2
1946–58 Div. 3(N)
1958–61 Div. 3 | 1961–67 Div. 4
1967–75 Div. 3
1975–76 Div. 4
1976–79 Div. 3
1979–   Div. 4 | Div. 3(N)
Champions 1938 | FA Cup never
past 5th Rd
League Cup
never past
4th Rd |

WALSALL (1888) Red/white

| Fellows Park
Walsall
113 × 73 yd | 24,100
25,453 v
Newcastle U
Div. 2
29 August 1961 | 1892 elected
to Div. 2
1895 failed
re-election
1896–1901 Div. 2
1901 failed
re-election
1921 (founder
member of
Div. 3(N)) | 1927–31 Div. 3(S)
1931–36 Div. 3(N)
1936–58 Div. 3(S)
1958–60 Div. 4
1960–61 Div. 3
1961–63 Div. 2
1963–79 Div. 3
1979–   Div. 4 | Div. 4 Champions
1960
Div. 3 runners-up
1961 | FA Cup never
past 5th Rd
League Cup
never past
4th Rd |

WATFORD (1891) Yellow/red

| Vicarage Road
Watford
WD1 8ER
113 × 73 yd | 36,500
34,099 v
Manchester U
FA Cup 4th Rd
3 February 1969 | 1920 (founder
member of Div. 3)
1921–58 Div. 3(S)
1958–60 Div. 4
1960–69 Div. 3 | 1969–72 Div. 2
1972–75 Div. 3
1975–78 Div. 4
1978–79 Div. 3
1979–   Div. 2 | Div. 3 Champions
1969
Div. 4 Champions
1978 | FA Cup
semi-finalists
1970
League Cup
semi-finalists
1979 |

Most League Points	Goals	Record win	Player highest number of goals		Most League appearances	Most capped player
			Aggregate	Individual		
						SWINDON TOWN
64, Div. 3 1968–69	100, Div. 3(S) 1926–27	10–1 v Farnham United Breweries FA Cup 1st Rd 28 November 1925	Harry Morris 216, 1926–33	Harry Morris 47 Div. 3(S) 1926–27	John Trollope 756, 1960–79	Rod Thomas 30, Wales 1967–73
						TORQUAY UNITED
60, Div. 4 1959–60	89, Div. 3(S) 1956–57	9–0 v Swindon Town Div. 3(S) 8 March 1952	Sammy Collins 204, 1948–58	Sammy Collins 40 Div. 3(S) 1955–56	Dennis Lewis 443, 1947–59	None
						TOTTENHAM HOTSPUR
70, Div. 2 1919–20	115, Div. 1 1960–61	13–2 v Crewe Alexandra FA Cup 4th Rd replay 3 February 1960	Jimmy Greaves 220, 1961–70	Jimmy Greaves 37 Div. 1 1962–63	Pat Jennings 472, 1964–77	Pat Jennings 66, N Ireland 1964–77
						TRANMERE ROVERS
60, Div. 4 1964–65	111, Div. 3(N) 1930–31	13–4 v Oldham Athletic Div. 3(N) 26 December 1935	Bunny Bell 104, 1931–36	Bunny Bell 35 Div. 3(N) 1933–34	Harold Bell 595, 1946–64	Albert Gray 3, Wales 1931
						WALSALL
65, Div. 4 1959–60	102, Div. 4 1959–60	10–0 v Darwen Div. 2 4 March 1899	Tony Richards 184, 1954–63 Colin Taylor 184, 1958–73	Gilbert Alsop 40 Div. 3(N) 1933–34, 1934–35	Colin Taylor 459, 1958–63, 1964–68, 1969–73	Mick Kearns 15, Eire 1973–79
						WATFORD
71, Div. 4 1977–78	92, Div. 4 1959–60	10–1 v Lowestoft Town FA Cup 1st Rd 27 November 1926	Tom Barnett 144, 1928–39	Cliff Holton 42 Div. 4 1959–60	Duncan Welbourne 411, 1963–74	Frank Hoddinott 2, Wales 1921 Pat Jennings 2, N Ireland 1964

Ground	Capacity & Record	League career		Honours (domestic) League	Cup

WEST BROMWICH ALBION (1879) Blue-white stripes/white

The Hawthorns West Bromwich B71 4LF 115 × 75 yd	44,000 64,815 v Arsenal FA Cup 6th Rd 6 March 1937	1888 (founder member of League) 1901–02 Div. 2 1902–04 Div. 1 1904–11 Div. 2 1911–27 Div. 1	1927–31 Div. 2 1931–38 Div. 1 1938–49 Div. 2 1949–73 Div. 1 1973–76 Div. 2 1976– Div. 1	Div. 1 Champions 1920 Runners-up 1925, 1954 Div. 2 Champions 1902, 1911 Runners-up 1931, 1949	FA Cup winners 1888, 1892, 1931, 1954, 1968 Runners-up 1886, 1887, 1895, 1912, 1935 League Cup winners 1966 Runners-up 1967, 1970

WEST HAM UNITED (1900) Claret with blue yoke/white

Boleyn Ground Green Street Upton Park London E13 110 × 72 yd	41,000 42,322 v Tottenham H Div. 1 17 October 1970	1919 elected to Div. 2 1923–32 Div. 1 1932–58 Div. 2	1958–78 Div. 1 1978– Div. 2	Div. 2 Champions 1958 Runners-up 1923	FA Cup winners 1964, 1975 Runners-up 1923 League Cup runners-up 1966

WIGAN ATHLETIC (1932) Blue-white stripes/blue

Springfield Park Wigan 117 × 73 yd	30,000 27,500 v Hereford U FA Cup 2nd Rd 12 December 1953	1978 elected to Div. 4		Highest placing 6th Div. 4 1979	FA Cup never past 3rd Rd League Cup never past 2nd Rd

WIMBLEDON (1889) Yellow and blue/blue

Plough Lane Ground Durnsford Wimbledon London SW19	15,000 18,000 v HMS Victory FA Amateur Cup 1932–33	1977 elected to Div. 4 1979– Div. 3		Promoted to Div. 3 1979	FA Cup never past 4th Rd League Cup never past 2nd Rd

WOLVERHAMPTON WANDERERS (1877) Gold/black

Molineux Grounds Wolverhampton WV1 4QR 115 × 72 yd	43,000 61,315 v Liverpool FA Cup 5th Rd 11 February 1939	1888 (founder member of League) 1906–23 Div. 2 1923–24 Div. 3(N) 1924–32 Div. 2	1932–65 Div. 1 1965–67 Div. 2 1967–76 Div. 1 1976–77 Div. 2 1977– Div. 1	Div. 1 Champions 1954, 1958, 1959 Runners up 1938, 1939, 1950, 1955, 1960 Div. 2 Champions 1932, 1977 Runners-up 1967 Div. 3(N) Champions 1924	FA Cup winners 1893, 1908, 1949, 1960 Runners-up 1889, 1896, 1921, 1939 League Cup winners 1974

WREXHAM (1873) Red/white

Racecourse Ground Mold Road Wrexham 117 × 75 yd	28,000 34,445 v Manchester U FA Cup 4th Rd 26 January 1957	1921 (founder member of Div. 3(N)) 1958–60 Div. 3 1960–62 Div. 4	1962–64 Div. 3 1964–70 Div. 4 1970–78 Div. 3 1978– Div. 2	Div. 3(N) runners-up 1933 Div. 4 runners-up 1970	FA Cup never past 6th Rd League Cup never past 5th Rd

YORK CITY (1922) White with maroon 'Y' on front/white

Bootham Crescent York 115 × 75 yd	17,000 28,123 v Huddersfield T FA Cup 5th Rd 5 March 1938	1929 elected to Div. 3(N) 1958–59 Div. 4 1959–60 Div. 3 1960–65 Div. 4 1965–66 Div. 3	1966–71 Div. 4 1971–74 Div. 3 1974–76 Div. 2 1976–77 Div. 3 1977– Div. 4	Highest placing 15th Div. 2 1975	FA Cup semi-finalists 1955 League Cup never past 5th Rd

Most League Points	Goals	Record win	Player highest number of goals		Most League appearances	Most capped player
			Aggregate	Individual		
WEST BROMWICH ALBION						
60, Div. 1 1919–20	105, Div. 2 1929–30	12–0 v Darwen Div. 1 4 April 1892	Tony Brown 215, 1963–79	William Richardson 39 Div. 1 1935–36	Tony Brown 558, 1963–79	Stuart Williams 33, Wales 1954–62
WEST HAM UNITED						
57, Div. 2 1957–58	101, Div. 2 1957–58	8–0 v Rotherham United Div. 2 8 March 1958 Sunderland Div. 1 19 October 1968	Vic Watson 306, 1920–35	Vic Watson 41 Div. 1 1929–30	Bobby Moore 544, 1958–74	Bobby Moore 108, England 1962–73
WIGAN ATHLETIC						
55, Div. 4 1978–79	63, Div. 4 1978–79	3–0 v Reading Div. 4 18 November 1978 Rochdale Div. 4 13 September 1978	Peter Houghton 13, 1978–79	Peter Houghton 13, Div. 4 1978–79	Tommy Gore, Ian Purdie & Jeff Wright, 46, 1978–79	None
WIMBLEDON						
61, Div. 4 1978–79	78, Div. 4 1978–79	6–1 v Torquay United Div. 4 28 February 1979	John Leslie 32, 1977–79	Alan Cork 22, Div. 4 1978–79	John Leslie 86, 1977–79	None
WOLVERHAMPTON WANDERERS						
64, Div. 1 1957–58	115, Div. 2 1931–32	14–0 v Crosswell's Brewery FA Cup 2nd Rd 1886–87	Bill Hartill 164, 1928–35	Dennis Westcott 37 Div. 1 1946–47	Billy Wright 491, 1946–59	Billy Wright 105, England 1946–59
WREXHAM						
61, Div. 4 1969–70 Div. 3 1977–78	106, Div. 3(N) 1932–33	10–1 v Hartlepool United Div. 4 3 March 1962	Tom Bamford 175, 1928–34	Tom Bamford 44 Div. 3(N) 1933–34	Arfon Griffiths 592, 1959–61 1962–79	Horace Blow 22, Wales 1899–1910
YORK CITY						
62, Div. 4 1964–65	92, Div. 3(N) 1954–55	9–1 v Southport Div. 3(N) 2 February 1957	Norman Wilkinson 125, 1954–66	Bill Fenton 31 Div. 3(N) 1951–52 Arthur Bottom 31 Div. 3(N) 1955–56	Barry Jackson 481, 1958–70	Peter Scott 5, N Ireland 1976–78

F.A. CUP POTPOURRI

F.A. Cup winners

Since the Second World War only one non-league club has reached the fourth round of the F.A. Cup and then defeated a Division One side. Yeovil Town beat Sunderland on 29 January 1949. At the end of full-time the score was 1–1 and extra time was played if necessary in those days to restrict excess travelling and loss of working days. Yeovil had taken the lead through Alec Stock, their player-manager, while Jackie Robinson equalised for Sunderland. The winning goal came tragically for Len Shackleton, whose attempted overhead kick presented Ray Wright with the ball. Eric Bryant scored for Yeovil from his pass. In the fifth round Yeovil lost 8–0 away to Manchester United.

Blyth Spartans were the first non-league club to reach the fifth round of the F.A. Cup and then force a replay since the Football League was expanded to 86 clubs in 1921 when they achieved this feat in 1977–78. Their victims from the first round were: Burscough (H) 1–0, Chesterfield (H)

Len Shackleton the Sunderland inside-forward experienced an example of the vageries of 'giant-killing' when he played against Yeovil in the F.A. Cup.

Year	Winners	Runners-up
1872	¹Wanderers 1	Royal Engineers 0
1873	²Wanderers 2	Oxford University 0
1874	¹Oxford University 2	Royal Engineers 0
1875	¹Royal Engineers 2	Old Etonians 0
	(Replay after 1–1 draw, Kennington Oval, 3,000)	
1876	³Wanderers 3	Old Etonians 0
	(Replay after 0–0 draw Kennington Oval, 3,000)	
1877	⁴Wanderers 2	Oxford University 0
	(After extra time)	
1878	⁵Wanderers 3	Royal Engineers 1
1879	¹Old Etonians 1	Clapham R 0
1880	¹Clapham R 1	Oxford University 0
1881	¹Old Carthusians 3	Old Etonians 0
1882	²Old Etonians 1	Blackburn R 0
1883	¹Blackburn Olympic 2	Old Etonians 1
	(After extra time)	
1884	¹Blackburn R 2	Queen's P, Glasgow 1
1885	²Blackburn R 2	Queen's P, Glasgow 0
1886	³Blackburn R 2	West Bromwich A 0
	(Replay after 0–0 draw, Kennington Oval, 15,000)	
1887	¹Aston Villa 2	West Bromwich A 0
1888	¹West Bromwich A 2	Preston NE 1
1889	¹Preston NE 3	Wolverhampton W 0
1890	⁴Blackburn R 6	Sheffield W 1
1891	⁵Blackburn R 3	Notts Co 1
1892	²West Bromwich A 3	Aston Villa 0
1893	¹Wolverhampton W 1	Everton 0
1894	¹Notts Co 4	Bolton W 1
1895	²Aston Villa 1	West Bromwich A 0
1896	¹Sheffield W 2	Wolverhampton W 1
1897	³Aston Villa 3	Everton 2
1898	¹Nottingham F 3	Derby Co 1
1899	¹Sheffield U 4	Derby Co 1
1900	¹Bury 4	Southampton 0
1901	¹Tottenham H 3	Sheffield U 1
	(Replay after 2–2 draw, Crystal Palace, 110,820)	
1902	²Sheffield U 2	Southampton 1
	(Replay after 1–1 draw, Crystal Palace, 76,914)	
1903	²Bury 6	Derby Co 0
1904	¹Manchester C 1	Bolton W 0
1905	⁴Aston Villa 2	Newcastle U 0
1906	¹Everton 1	Newcastle U 0
1907	²Sheffield W 2	Everton 1
1908	³Wolverhampton W 3	Newcastle U 1
1909	¹Manchester U 1	Bristol C 0
1910	¹Newcastle U 2	Barnsley 0
	(Replay after 1–1 draw, Crystal Palace, 77,747)	
1911	¹Bradford C 1	Newcastle U 0
	(Replay after 0–0 draw, Crystal Palace, 69,098)	
1912	¹Barnsley 1	West Bromwich A 0
	(After extra time)	(Replay after 0–0 draw, Crystal
1913	⁵Aston Villa 1	Sunderland 0
1914	¹Burnley 1	Liverpool 0
1915	³Sheffield U 3	Chelsea 0
1920	⁶Aston Villa 1	Huddersfield 0
	(After extra time)	
1921	²Tottenham H 1	Wolverhampton W 0
1922	¹Huddersfield 1	Preston NE 0
1923	¹Bolton W 2	West Ham U 0
1924	²Newcastle U 2	Aston Villa 0
1925	⁴Sheffield U 1	Cardiff C 0
1926	²Bolton W 1	Manchester C 0
1927	¹Cardiff C 1	Arsenal 0

Venue	Attendance	Facts and Feats
Kennington Oval	2,000	First injury : Lt Cresswell breaks his collar bone after ten minutes but carries on.
Lillie Bridge	3,000	The Dark Blues dispense with their goalkeeper after the first goal by The Wanderers.
Kennington Oval	2,000	Conquerors of The Wanderers, Oxford had four England internationals in their side.
Kennington Oval	3,000	The Chatham Sappers thus completed 20 matches that season without losing one of them.
Kennington Oval	3,500	The Heron brothers become the only pair to win cup medals and international honours.
Kennington Oval	3,000	More revenge for The Wanderers against their well beaten undergraduate opposition.
Kennington Oval	4,500	C. H. R. Wollaston wins his fifth medal ; Wanderers return the trophy to the Association.
Kennington Oval	5,000	Despite a marathon quarter-final with Darwen, the Old Boys' stamina lasts out the better.
Kennington Oval	6,000	Lloyd Jones scores the only goal and Oxford play their last ever F.A. Cup tie.
Kennington Oval	4,500	Charterhouse has its finest moment and they are the first team to show any real teamwork.
Kennington Oval	6,500	Hon. A. F. Kinnaird achieves his fifth winners' medal but the era of the amateur is to pass.
Kennington Oval	8,000	The winners are the first team to train for the match ; they go away to Blackpool.
Kennington Oval	4,000	Two goals disallowed upset the Scots who are used to a different 'offside' interpretation.
Kennington Oval	12,500	The first five figure attendance and invasion of the South by fans travelling from the North.
Derby	12,000	Rovers receive a silver shield for their third consecutive victory in the final.
Kennington Oval	15,500	A disputed first goal claimed to be offside is the issue in the first all-Midlands derby.
Kennington Oval	19,000	Albion become the first winners with an all-English side ; Billy Bassett at 18 makes both goals.
Kennington Oval	22,000	The first League and Cup double. Preston do not concede a goal during their cup run.
Kennington Oval	20,000	William Townley is the first to record a hat-trick in the biggest final win to date.
Kennington Oval	23,000	James Forrest wins his fifth medal to emulate the feat of Wollaston and Hon. A. F. Kinnaird.
Kennington Oval	25,000	Crossbar and goal nets are featured for the first time in the second all-Midlands final.
Fallowfield, Manchester	45,000	Cup fever is reflected in the crowd bursting in and surrounding the touchlines in play.
Everton	37,000	The first winners from the Second Division and James Logan scores a hat-trick for them.
Crystal Palace	42,560	John Devey gets a final touch in Villa's revenge and the goal comes in 40 seconds.
Crystal Palace	48,836	Yorkshire's first taste of cup glory and a new cup ; the first is stolen on 11 September 1895.
Crystal Palace	65,891	Aston Villa become the second side in history to achieve the League and Cup double.
Crystal Palace	62,017	Forest had lost 5–0 to Derby a week before winning this final of near neighbours.
Crystal Palace	73,833	With broken ribs and a ruptured side United back Harry Thickett plays in 50 yards of bandages.
Crystal Palace	68,945	The Shakers on their way to living up to the nickname that has remained ever since.
Bolton	20,470	Last non-league side to win the cup ; Alex Brown scores in every round, 15 goals in all.
Crystal Palace	33,068	The goal area, penalty area and penalty spot were features to take a familiar place.
Crystal Palace	63,102	Bury concede no goals in their run and record the biggest margin of cup final victory.
Crystal Palace	61,374	A goal by Welshman Billy Meredith is enough to win this first all-Lancashire final.
Crystal Palace	101,117	Twenty year old 'Happy' Harry Hampton scores in the third minute and again after 75.
Crystal Palace	75,609	Newcastle field ten players with cup final experience but their Palace hoodoo stays.
Crystal Palace	84,584	Everton have ten with similar experience but Wednesday win with four minutes remaining.
Crystal Palace	74,967	Second Division winners. The four men with 'H' score : Rev. Hunt, Hedley, Harrison and Howie.
Crystal Palace	71,401	Meredith collects his second cup-winners medal – for the other Mancunian team.
Everton	69,000	Albert Shepherd scores twice in the replay, one of them from the first recorded final penalty.
Old Trafford	58,000	City with a record eight Scots win a new trophy costing 50 guineas and made in Bradford.
Bramall Lane Palace, 54,556)	38,555	Barnsley make it a record for a Second Division side : their second final in three years.
Crystal Palace	120,081	Record attendance for a match involving the chief League championship challengers.
Crystal Palace	72,778	King George V becomes the first reigning monarch to attend the final of the F.A. Cup.
Old Trafford	49,557	War-time game known as 'The Khaki Cup Final' with the crowd packed with servicemen.
Stamford Bridge	50,018	The only goal comes off the neck of Billy Kirton from a corner, but it is just as valid.
Stamford Bridge	72,805	Cloudburst during the game turns the pitch into a quagmire but the classic Spurs win well.
Stamford Bridge	53,000	Billy Smith scores the winning goal from a penalty ; the first decisive spot kick.
Wembley	126,047	Wembley's initial occasion and an invasion by the crowd estimated at around 200,000.
Wembley	91,695	Drama reserved for the last ninety seconds during which Newcastle score both goals.
Wembley	91,763	Keeping goal for Sheffield, Charlie Sutcliffe, youngest brother of Bolton's 1894 'keeper.
Wembley	91,447	Bolton with ten men possessing previous final experience score through David Jack.
Wembley	91,206	The cup goes out of England for the first and only time, a tragic mistake by goalkeeper Lewis.

Jackie Milburn is one of a select number of players who have gone through an entire F.A. Cup season by scoring in every round of the competition. (Colorsport)

F.A. CUP FINAL TABLE CONTINUED

Year	Winners	Runners-up
1928	[6]Blackburn R 3	Huddersfield T 1
1929	[3]Bolton W 2	Portsmouth 0
1930	[1]Arsenal 2	Huddersfield T 0
1931	[3]West Bromwich A [2]	Birmingham 1
1932	[3]Newcastle U 2	Arsenal 1
1933	[2]Everton 3	Manchester C 0
1934	[2]Manchester C 2	Portsmouth 1
1935	[3]Sheffield W 4	West Bromwich A 2
1936	[2]Arsenal 1	Sheffield U 0
1937	[1]Sunderland 3	Preston NE 1
1938	[2]Preston NE 1	Huddersfield T 0
	(After extra time)	
1939	[1]Portsmouth 4	Wolverhampton W 1
1946	[1]Derby Co 4	Charlton Ath 1
	(After extra time)	
1947	[1]Charlton Ath 1	Burnley 0
	(After extra time)	
1948	[2]Manchester U 4	Blackpool 2
1949	[3]Wolverhampton W 3	Leicester C 1
1950	[3]Arsenal 2	Liverpool 0
1951	[4]Newcastle U 2	Blackpool 0
1952	[5]Newcastle U 1	Arsenal 0
1953	[1]Blackpool 4	Bolton W 3
1954	[4]West Bromwich A 3	Preston NE 2
1955	[6]Newcastle U 3	Manchester C 1
1956	[3]Manchester C 3	Birmingham C 1
1957	[7]Aston Villa 2	Manchester U 1
1958	[4]Bolton W 2	Manchester U 0
1959	[2]Nottingham F 2	Luton T 1
1960	[4]Wolverhampton W 3	Blackburn R 0
1961	[3]Tottenham H 2	Leicester C 0
1962	[4]Tottenham H 3	Burnley 1
1963	[3]Manchester U 3	Leicester C 1
1964	[1]West Ham U 3	Preston NE 2
1965	[1]Liverpool 2	Leeds U 1
	(After extra time)	
1966	[3]Everton 3	Sheffield W 2
1967	[5]Tottenham H 2	Chelsea 1
1968	[5]West Bromwich A 1	Everton 0
	(After extra time)	
1969	[4]Manchester C 1	Leicester C 0
1970	[1]Chelsea 2	Leeds U 1
	(Replay after 2–2 draw, after extra time, at Wembley	
1971	[4]Arsenal 2	Liverpool 1
	(After extra time)	
1972	[2]Leeds U 1	Arsenal 0
1973	[2]Sunderland 1	Leeds U 0
1974	[2]Liverpool 3	Newcastle U 0
1975	[2]West Ham U 2	Fulham 0
1976	[1]Southampton 1	Manchester U 0
1977	[4]Manchester U 2	Liverpool 1
1978	[1]Ipswich 1	Arsenal 0
1979	[5]Arsenal 3	Manchester U 2

N.B. Figures in front of name of winning team denote number of cup victories to date.

1–0, Enfield (H) 1–0, Stoke City (A) 3–2. In the fifth round they lost 1–2 to Wrexham at home after a 1–1 draw. Colchester United had 30 years earlier also reached the fifth round when still outside the League and then lost 5–0 away to Blackpool. United's previous victims had been from the first round: Banbury Spencer (H) 2–1, Wrexham (H) 1–0, Huddersfield Town (H) 1–0 and Bradford Park Avenue (H) 3–2.

The F.A. Cup has produced many outstanding individual achievements. Ted MacDougall scored nine goals in a single game for Bournemouth against Margate on 20 November 1971; Frank O'Donnell (Preston North End), Alex Brown (Tottenham Hotspur), Ellis Rimmer (Sheffield Wednesday), Jackie Milburn (Newcastle United), Stan Mortensen (Blackpool), Nat Lofthouse (Bolton Wanderers), Charlie Wayman (Preston North End), Jeff Astle (West Bromwich Albion) and Peter Osgood (Chelsea), all scored in every round of the competition in a single season.

Venue	Attendance	Facts and Feats
Wembley	92,041	First BBC final broadcast and a goal in under a minute; first loser's goal in 18 years.
Wembley	92,576	Bolton win again and a total of only 17 different players used by them in 3 finals.
Wembley	92,488	Manager Herbert Chapman of Arsenal wins at the expense of the club he formerly guided.
Wembley	92,406	A double of a rather different kind; Albion win the Cup and also win promotion.
Wembley	92,298	Arsenal become the first team to score first in the final and finish as the losers.
Wembley	92,950	The players are numbered for the first time in the final but unusually from 1 to 22.
Wembley	93,258	Fred Tilson omitted from the City side in 1933 scores twice to ensure City's victory.
Wembley	93,204	Two goals from Ellis Rimmer for Wednesday mean that the winger has scored in each round.
Wembley	93,384	Despite the discomforture of an injured knee Ted Drake is the Arsenal goalscoring hero.
Wembley	93,495	Frank O'Donnell scores in every round of the Cup for Preston but to no final avail.
Wembley	93,497	In the last minute of extra time George Mutch hits a penalty off the crossbar to seal it.
Wembley	99,370	The heavy favourites are beaten and Bert Barlow scores one of the goals against his old club.
Wembley	98,000	Charlton's John Oakes is the oldest ever cup finalist at 42; Bert Turner scores for both sides.
Wembley	99,000	The ball bursts for the second year but Chris Duffy scores with six minutes remaining.
Wembley	99,000	Eddie Shimwell becomes the first full-back to score at Wembley for Blackpool with a penalty.
Wembley	99,500	Don Revie misses the game for Leicester City because of an eve of the game nose bleed.
Wembley	100,000	Arsenal are the oldest team to play at Wembley but Reg Lewis scores twice for victory.
Wembley	100,000	Jackie Milburn scores in every round including both goals in this final triumph.
Wembley	100,000	Arsenal lose Walley Barnes with a split cartilage; Chilean George Robledo scores.
Wembley	100,000	Nat Lofthouse scores in every round but injury hit Bolton lose to a Stan Mortensen hat-trick.
Wembley	100,000	Charlie Wayman scores in every round for losers; Ronnie Allen's two include one penalty.
Wembley	100,000	A Milburn goal in 45 seconds for Newcastle's fifth Wembley win; but City's Jimmy Meadows twists his knee.
Wembley	100,000	Bert Trautmann plays the last 15 minutes in goal for Manchester City with a broken neck.
Wembley	100,000	Record seventh win for Villa but United goalkeeper Ray Wood suffers a broken collar bone.
Wembley	100,000	Stan Crowther already cup tied with Villa plays for United in post-Munich patched side.
Wembley	100,000	Roy Dwight scores for Forest, breaks his leg, then watches the game on a hospital TV set.
Wembley	100,000	Kevin Howley at 35 is the youngest Wembley referee but Rovers' Dave Whelan breaks a leg.
Wembley	100,000	Tottenham achieve the first League Championship and Cup double of the present century.
Wembley	100,000	Danny Blanchflower converts the fourth penalty awarded at Wembley nine minutes from the end.
Wembley	100,000	Winter of postponements means that the final was put back to May 25 for first time.
Wembley	100,000	Howard Kendall at 17 years 345 days becomes the youngest cup finalist for Preston.
Wembley	100,000	Gerry Byrne breaks his collar bone for Liverpool and extra time is played before victory.
Wembley	100,000	Everton recover from a two goal deficit to win and Wednesday do a loser's lap of honour.
Wembley	100,000	The first all-London final and Spurs achieve their fifth win in five final appearances.
Wembley	100,000	Jeff Astle manages to score in every round with the only goal in third minute of extra time.
Wembley	100,000	Leicester suffer their fourth Wembley defeat and follow it with relegation to Division Two.
Old Trafford 100,000)	62,078	First ever replay for a Wembley final; Peter Osgood scores in every round.
Wembley	100,000	Arsenal become the fourth side to achieve the double; Eddie Kelly the first substitute to score.
Wembley	100,000	Despite having ten players with previous cup final experience Arsenal are the losers.
Wembley	100,000	The first Second Division club to win the trophy in 42 years; Leeds' Johnny Giles 5th final.
Wembley	100,000	A record 11th final for Newcastle but it coincides with their first Wembley reverse.
Wembley	100,000	The second all-London final and both goals are scored by Alan Taylor signed in November.
Wembley	100,000	Another Second Division side are successful; it is Southampton's third time lucky.
Wembley	100,000	United manager Tommy Docherty's eighth appearance at Wembley as player or manager but first as a winner.
Wembley	100,000	A goal from Roger Osborne puts the 40th different name on the cup but he has to be taken off.
Wembley	100,000	United score twice to level in 86 and 88 minutes but Alan Sunderland seals it 60 seconds later.

The only players who ever scored Cup Final hat-tricks are Billy Townley (Blackburn Rovers), Jimmy Logan (Notts County) and Stan Mortensen (Blackpool).

Jimmy Brown, the Blackburn Rovers centre-forward in the 1880s must have been something special, for when Rovers won the Cup three seasons in a row (only the Wanderers achieved as much), he scored in each of those winning finals.

Mortensen, who was probably one of the fastest centre-forwards ever seen, once scored in 12 consecutive Cup rounds for Blackpool. Although he failed to find the net in a couple of replays he scored in every round in which Blackpool appeared from the third round in 1945–46 until the third round in 1949–50. During that period he actually scored in nine consecutive Cup ties.

Jimmy Greaves must certainly be rated among the F.A. Cup's finest goalscorers. When Tottenham Hotspur won the Cup for the second season in succession in 1961–62 he scored nine, registering in every round except the sixth against Aston Villa. When Spurs won the trophy again in 1966–67 he obtained a total of six goals, although he failed to find the net in the Final against his former club, Chelsea.

Throughout his career Greaves reached a total of 35 goals in the F.A. Cup competition proper, but even that figure, which puts him well ahead of others like Mortensen, Ronnie Allen, John Atyeo and Jack Rowley, does not match the figure achieved by Denis Law.

This Scot with the razor sharp reflexes was always a man for the big occasion. Completely unpredictable on the field he was a terror to opposing defences and one of the most exciting and entertaining players to watch, probably because he was so unorthodox. It could be argued that he was the finest inside-forward of the post-war era, maybe even of all time, but whether he was or not, one thing is certain, he scored more goals in the F.A. Cup than any other player.

Making his League debut as a 16-year-old for Huddersfield Town at Meadow Lane on Christmas Eve 1956 he spent nearly 18 years at the top. Matt Busby offered Huddersfield £10,000 for his transfer to Manchester United after spotting him in their Youth team but the offer was rejected. In March 1960 he went to Manchester City for £55,000 and became their top scorer. In July 1961 the Italian club Torino secured his transfer for £100,000 and promised a life of luxury for the shrewd Aberdonian. Italy, however, was a disaster for such a single-minded individual as Law, who was at variance with their brand of discipline, and there was no happier footballer in the world when Busby brought him back to England to United for

a new record fee of £115,000 in 1962. He proved to be a bargain for his days at Old Trafford were the most successful of his career.

In 1973 United gave him a free transfer to Manchester City and it was ironic that his last League goal was the one that sent his old club Manchester United tumbling into Division Two. The Reds needed to win at Old Trafford to retain Division One status at the end of 1973–74 but they were beaten 1–0 with Law applying the finishing touch.

In the F.A. Cup he scored a record total of 41 goals in 61 appearances (substitutions in brackets) as follows:–

DENIS LAW

		Apprs	Gls
1956–57	Huddersfield Town	5	1
1957–58	Huddersfield Town	2	1
1958–59	Huddersfield Town	1	—
1959–60	Huddersfield Town	3	1
1960–61	Manchester City	3	2
1961–62	Torino	—	—
1962–63	Manchester United	6	6
1963–64	Manchester United	6	10
1964–65	Manchester United	6	3
1965–66	Manchester United	7	6
1966–67	Manchester United	2	2
1967–68	Manchester United	1	—
1968–69	Manchester United	6	7
1969–70	Manchester United	– (2)	—
1970–71	Manchester United	2	—
1971–72	Manchester United	7	—
1972–73	Manchester United	1	—
1973–74	Manchester City	1	2
		59 (2)	41

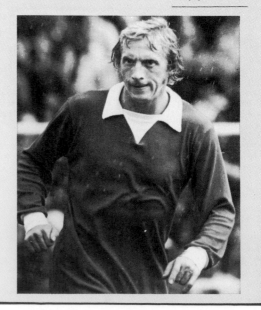

In fact Law's most outstanding Cup scoring feat is not even included in those figures because this remarkable display of sharpshooting occurred in a game which was abandoned. This was a fourth round tie at Luton on 28 January 1961, when in pouring rain, and on a pitch which was saturated even before the game began, Luton were two goals ahead in 18 minutes. Then despite the clinging mud and pools of water which made ball control so difficult, Law turned on one of the most mercurial displays of goalscoring ever seen from one individual. He scored six goals in succession to equal the record for the Competition Proper up to that time, but which has since been beaten. Imagine his chagrin when shortly after completing his second hat-trick the referee decided the pitch was too bad to continue and abandoned the game with 31 minutes remaining for play. Law, in this scintilating form, might have scored more if this game had been played out.

An astonishing footnote to this display is that Luton won the replay 3–1. Law, of course, was City's scorer.

In 1946 Vic Woodley, the former Chelsea goalkeeper, was playing with Bath City and thinking of retirement at the age of 35. Derby County had a lengthy injury list of their own goalkeepers and signed him. This was in March and he played in the semi-final and final and gained a winner's medal against Charlton Athletic. Two years earlier he had appeared at Wembley in the Football League South Cup Final for Chelsea in what must have seemed at the time his last chance of an appearance at Wembley. Woodley was capped 19 times by England.

The lowest attendance since the war in an F.A.

Cup tie between League sides is 1,763 on 18 November 1972 at Darlington for the visit of Wrexham. On the same day another first round match involving non-league sides Banbury and Barnet attracted 1,762.

The highest attendance in one season of the Football League Cup competition was 2,399,129 in the 1971–72 season. The 123 matches produced an average of 19,505 per game.

Corinthians' last two F.A. Cup ties were both against Southend United and produced two defeats. On 27 November 1937 Southend won 2–0 at White City and on 26 November 1938 in another first round tie United won 3–0 at Southend Stadium.

Norwich City share with Bradford City the odd honour of playing an F.A. Cup match without any cash receipts being taken for it. In 1915 two drawn games, 1–1 and 0–0, necessitated a third meeting. The First World War was in progress and to prevent interference with the war effort they were ordered to play the third match behind closed doors on Lincoln City's ground. Even so some 500 spectators gathered outside the ground and eventually forced their way in to see the match which Bradford won 2–0.

Manchester City scored 31 goals in the F.A. Cup during the 1925–26 season but still did not win it. They beat Corinthians 4–0 after a 3–3 draw, Huddersfield Town 4–0, Crystal Palace 11–4, Clapton Orient 6–1 and Manchester United 3–0 to reach the final where they lost by the only goal to Bolton Wanderers.

SCOTTISH LEAGUE INFORMATION

A number of teams have gone through a season of Scottish League matches with only one defeat, but the finest record in this respect, because it was achieved in Division One before the number of games was cut to below 42, was that of the **Rangers** in the 1920–21 season. In fact this was one of only three seasons in which as many as 42 matches were played in either Division of the Scottish League. Rangers' 76 points secured that season is a Scottish League record. Rangers finished 10 points more than their nearest rivals, Celtic, and 16 points more than Hearts who finished in third place. It was Rangers' third Championship win in four seasons.

Rangers' only defeat that season was inflicted on New Year's Day by Celtic, who won 2–0 at Ibrox Park. When one considers that Rangers lost only two League games the previous season (2–1 to Clydebank at Ibrox, and 1–0 at Motherwell) the tremendous superiority of a team that was beaten only three times in 84 matches is obvious.

In 1920–21 Rangers conceded only 24 goals while scoring 91. The side included outstanding Scottish Internationals like Sandy Archibald, Alan Morton, Andy Cunningham, Tommy Cairns, Billy McCandless and David Meiklejohn. Goalkeeper Willie Robb played in every game while

Cunningham and George Henderson shared the goalscoring honours with 21 each.

The Scottish Cup tie between **Inverness Thistle and Falkirk** was postponed 29 times during the winter of 1978–79 because of a snow and ice covered ground.

Third Lanark resigned from the Scottish League, Division Two at the end of the 1966–67 season having finished 11th. They were the last club to resign from the competition. Formed between 1868 and 1872 by members of the 3rd Lanark Rifle Volunteers they became Third Lanark Athletic when membership no longer required association with the military. They entered the League, Division One in 1890 and remained until relegated in 1925. Between then and their demise they had four spells in the lower division and another four

in the top division. They won the Scottish League championship in 1904 and were twice champions of Division Two, in 1931 and 1935. In addition Third Lanark won the Scottish Cup in 1889 and 1905 and finished as runners-up in 1876, 1878, 1906 and 1936. They were League Cup beaten finalists in 1960.

In 1872 they set up headquarters in a private ground in Crosshill, Glasgow and when Queen's Park moved to nearby Mount Florida, Third Lanark took over the vacated ground, renaming it Cathkin Park. For a Scottish Cup third round tie against Rangers on 27 February 1954 they had a record attendance of 45,455.

Alan Morton obtained 92 international 'caps' and medals during his career. In international matches

GLASGOW DERBY MATCHES

for Scotland he played against England 11 times, Wales 10, Ireland 9 and France once; for the Scottish League v Football League 11 and twice against the Irish League. In Victory internationals he appeared three times against England and twice against Ireland. He also played in an Inter-League Victory match against the Football League, three times for Glasgow v Sheffield and for the Rest of Scotland v Glasgow once.

His medals were as follows: Airdrie Schools Cup 2; Stirlingshire Juvenile Cup 1; Scottish Amateur League 1; Ayrshire Charity Cup 2; Belgian Relief Fund 3; Scottish Cup 3; Glasgow Cup 7; Glasgow Charity Cup 8; Scottish League Championship 9; Lord Provost's Relief Fund 1; Scotland v England (for the Scottish Engineering and Munition Workers Benevolent Association) 1.

Born Jordanhill, Glasgow his father was a coal master and Alan Morton and four brothers went into the mining industry. Alan became a mining engineer. He started his career with Queen's Park playing for them between 1913 and 1920 before joining Rangers where he remained until the end of the 1932–33 season whereupon he was taken on the Board of Directors and remained active until 1968. He died three years later.

He was a 5ft. 4in. outside-left and became known as the 'Wee Blue Devil'. He scored 115 goals in 495 games for Rangers and appeared on 31 occasions for Scotland.

Morton won 23 successive matches in the Scottish League, Division One in 1898–99 and the first four of the following season. Then they dropped a point in a 1–1 draw with Heart of Midlothian.

Celtic won 23 League, League Cup and European Cup matches in 1966–67 before being held to a 1–1 draw by St Mirren on 5 November 1966.

Rangers v. Celtic
Rangers were founded in 1873

In League matches the results at Ibrox have been (Rangers score first):

Season	Score	Season	Score	Season	Score
1890–91	1–2	1919–20	3–0	1955–56	0–0
1891–92	1–1	1920–21	0–2	1956–57	2–0
1892–93	2–2	1921–22	1–1	1957–58	2–3
1893–94	5–0	1922–23	2–0	1958–59	2–1
1894–95	1–1	1923–24	0–0	1959–60	3–1
1895–96	2–4	1924–25	4–1	1960–61	2–1
1896–97	2–0	1925–26	1–0	1961–62	2–2
1897–98	0–4	1926–27	2–1	1962–63	4–0
1898–99	4–1	1927–28	1–0	1963–64	2–1
1899–1900	3–3	1928–29	3–0	1964–65	1–0
1900–01	2–1	1929–30	1–0	1965–66	2–1
1901–02	2–2	1930–31	1–0	1966–67	2–2
1902–03	3–3	1931–32	0–0	1967–68	1–0
1903–04	0–0	1932–33	0–0	1968–69	1–0
1904–05	1–4	1933–34	2–2	1969–70	0–1
1905–06	3–2	1934–35	2–1	1970–71	1–1
1906–07	2–1	1935–36	1–2	1971–72	2–3
1907–08	0–1	1936–37	1–0	1972–73	2–1
1908–09	1–3	1937–38	3–1	1973–74	0–1
1909–10	0–0	1938–39	2–1	1974–75	3–0
1910–11	1–1	1946–47	1–1	1975–76	2–1
1911–12	3–1	1947–48	2–0		1–0
1912–13	0–1	1948–49	4–0	1976–77	0–1
1913–14	0–2	1949–50	4–0		2–2
1914–15	2–1	1950–51	1–0	1977–78	3–2
1915–16	3–0	1951–52	1–1		3–1
1916–17	0–0	1952–53	1–0	1978–79	1–1
1917–18	1–2	1953–54	1–1		1–0
1918–19	1–1	1954–55	4–1		

Left: Bobby Lennox (hooped shirt) scored for Celtic against Rangers in 1967, watched by his colleague Jimmy Johnstone (left). Lennox was still a senior choice for the Parkhead club in their 1978–79 championship winning season. (Syndication International)

Celtic v. Rangers
Celtic were founded in 1888.

In League matches the results at Parkhead have been (Celtic score first):

Season	Score	Season	Score	Season	Score
1890–91	2–2	1919–20	1–1	1955–56	0–1
1891–92	3–0	1920–21	1–2	1956–57	0–2
1892–93	3–0	1921–22	0–0	1957–58	0–1
1893–94	3–2	1922–23	1–3	1958–59	2–2
1894–95	5–3	1923–24	2–2	1959–60	0–1
1895–96	6–2	1924–25	0–1	1960–61	1–5
1896–97	1–1	1925–26	2–2	1961–62	1–1
1897–98	0–0	1926–27	0–1	1962–63	0–1
1898–99	0–4	1927–28	1–0	1963–64	0–1
1899–1900	3–2	1928–29	1–2	1964–65	3–1
1900–01	2–1	1929–30	1–2	1965–66	5–1
1901–02	2–4	1930–31	2–0	1966–67	2–0
1902–03	1–1	1931–32	1–2	1967–68	2–2
1903–04	2–2	1932–33	1–1	1968–69	2–4
1904–05	2–2	1933–34	2–2	1969–70	0–0
1905–06	1–0	1934–35	1–1	1970–71	2–0
1906–07	2–1	1935–36	3–4	1971–72	2–1
1907–08	2–1	1936–37	1–1	1972–73	3–1
1908–09	2–3	1937–38	3–0	1973–74	1–0
1909–10	1–1	1938–39	6–2	1974–75	1–2
1910–11	0–1	1946–47	2–3	1975–76	1–1
1911–12	3–0	1947–48	0–4		0–0
1912–13	3–2	1948–49	0–1	1976–77	2–2
1913–14	4–0	1949–50	1–1		1–0
1914–15	2–1	1950–51	3–2	1977–78	1–1
1915–16	2–2	1951–52	1–4		2–0
1916–17	0–0	1952–53	2–1	1978–79	3–1
1917–18	0–0	1953–54	1–0		4–2
1918–19	0–3	1954–55	2–0		

Overall record

CELTIC	49 wins
RANGERS	71 wins
DRAWN	52
TOTAL	172

Scottish Club directory

Ground	Honours League	Scottish FA Cup	League Cup

ABERDEEN (1903) Scarlet/scarlet

Pittodrie Park Aberdeen	Premier Div. runners-up 1977–78 Div. 1 Champions 1954–55 Runners-up 1910–11, 1936–37, 1955–56, 1970–71, 1971–72	Winners 1947, 1970 Runners-up 1937, 1953, 1954, 1959, 1967, 1978	Winners 1946, 1956, 1977 Runners-up 1979

AIRDRIEONIANS (1878) White/white

Broomfield Park Airdrie	Div. 1 runners-up 1922–23, 1923–24, 1924–25, 1925–26 Div. 2 Champions 1902–03, 1954–55, 1973–74 Runners-up 1900–01, 1946–47, 1949–50, 1965–66	Winners 1924 Runners-up 1975	

ALBION ROVERS (1882) Yellow/white

Cliftonhill Park Coatbridge	Div. 2 Champions 1933–34 Runners-up 1913–14, 1937–38, 1947–48	Runners-up 1920	

ALLOA (1883) Gold/black

Recreation Ground Alloa	Div. 2 Champions 1921–22 Runners-up 1938–39, 1976–77		

ARBROATH (1878) Maroon/white

Gayfield Park Arbroath	Div. 2 runners-up 1934–35, 1958–59, 1967–68, 1971–72		

AYR UNITED (1910) White/black

Somerset Park Ayr	Div. 2 Champions 1911–12, 1912–13, 1927–28, 1936–37, 1958–59, 1965–66 Runners-up 1910–11, 1955–56, 1968–69		

BERWICK RANGERS (1881) Gold/black

Shielfield Park Tweedmouth Berwick-on-Tweed	Div. 2 Champions 1978–79		

BRECHIN CITY (1906) Red/red

Glebe Park Brechin	Highest League placing 5th, Div. 2, 1958–59		

CELTIC (1888) Green, white/white

Celtic Park Glasgow SE	Prem. Div. Champions 1976–77, 1978–79 Div. 1 Champions 1892–93, 1893–94, 1895–96, 1897–98, 1904–05, 1905–06, 1906–07, 1907–08, 1908–09, 1909–10, 1913–14, 1914–15, 1915–16, 1916–17, 1918–19, 1921–22, 1925–26, 1935–36, 1937–38, 1953–54, 1965–66, 1966–67, 1967–68, 1968–69, 1969–70, 1970–71, 1971–72, 1972–73, 1973–74 Runners-up 16 times Premier Div. Runners-up 1975–76	Winners 1892, 1899, 1900, 1904, 1907, 1908, 1911, 1912, 1914, 1923, 1925, 1927, 1931, 1933, 1937, 1951, 1954, 1965, 1967, 1969, 1971, 1972, 1974, 1975, 1977 Runners-up 14 times	Winners 1957, 1958 1966, 1967, 1968, 1969, 1970, 1975 Runners-up 8 times

League career			Record win	Highest number of league goals
				ABERDEEN
1904–05 Div. 2 1905–17 Div. 1	1919–75 Div. 1	1975– Pr. Div.	13–0 v Peterhead, Scottish Cup, 1922–23	Benny Yorston, 38, 1929–30
				AIRDRIEONIANS
1894–1903 Div. 2 1903–36 Div. 1 1936–47 Div. 2 1947–48 Div. 1	1948–50 Div. 2 1950–54 Div. 1 1954–55 Div. 2 1955–65 Div. 1	1965–66 Div. 2 1966–73 Div. 1 1973–74 Div. 2 1974– Div. 1	11–1 v Falkirk, Div. 1, 1950–51	Bert Yarnall, 39, 1916–17
				ALBION ROVERS
1903–15 Div. 2 1919–23 Div. 1 1923–34 Div. 2	1934–37 Div. 1 1937–38 Div. 2 1938–39 Div. 1	1946–48 Div. 2 1948–49 Div. 1 1949– Div. 2	10–0 v Brechin City, Div. 2, 1937–38	Jim Renwick, 41, 1932–33
				ALLOA
1921–22 Div. 2 1922–23 Div. 1	1923–77 Div. 2 1977–78 Div. 1	1978– Div. 2	9–2 v Forfar, Div. 2, 1932–33	Wee Crilley, 49, 1921–22
				ARBROATH
1921–35 Div. 2 1935–39 Div. 1 1946–59 Div. 2	1959–60 Div. 1 1960–68 Div. 2 1968–69 Div. 1	1969–72 Div. 2 1972– Div 1.	36–0 v Bon Accord, Scottish Cup, 1885–86	Dave Easson, 45, 1958–59
				AYR UNITED
1897–1913 Div. 2 1913–25 Div. 1 1925–28 Div. 2 1928–36 Div. 1 1936–37 Div. 2 1937–39 Div. 1	1946–56 Div. 2 1956–57 Div. 1 1957–59 Div. 2 1959–61 Div. 1 1961–66 Div. 2 1966–67 Div. 1	1967–69 Div. 2 1969–75 Div. 1 1975–78 Pr. Div. 1978– Div. 1	11–1 v Dumbarton, League Cup, 1952–53	Jimmy Smith, 66, 1927–28
				BERWICK RANGERS
1955–79 Div. 2	1979– Div. 1		8–2 v Dundee United, 1957–58	Ken Bowron, 38, 1963–64
				BRECHIN CITY
1929–39 Div. 2	1954– Div. 2		12–1 v Thornhill, Scottish Cup, 1925–26	Willie McIntosh, 26, 1959–60
				CELTIC
1890–1975 Div. 1	1975– Pr. Div.		11–0 v Dundee, Div. 1, 1895–96	Jimmy McGrory, 50, 1935–36

Ground	Honours League	Scottish FA Cup	League Cup
CLYDE (1878) White/black			
Shawfield Stadium Glasgow C5	Div. 2 Champions 1904–05, 1951–52, 1956–57, 1961–62, 1972–73, 1977–78 Runners-up 1903–04, 1905–06, 1925–26, 1963–64	Winners 1939, 1955, 1958 Runners-up 1910, 1912, 1949	
CLYDEBANK (1965) White/white			
Kilbowie Park Clydebank	Div. 1 runners-up 1976–77 Div. 2 Champions 1975–76		
COWDENBEATH (1881) Blue/white			
Central Park Cowdenbeath	Div. 2 Champions 1913–14, 1914–15, 1938–39 Runners-up 1921–22, 1923–24, 1969–70		
DUMBARTON (1872) White/white			
Boghead Park Dumbarton	Div. 1 Champions 1890–91 (shared), 1891–92 Div. 2 Champions 1910–11, 1971–72 Runners-up 1907–08	Winners 1883 Runners-up 1881, 1882, 1887, 1891, 1897	
DUNDEE (1893) Blue/white			
Dens Park Dundee	Div. 1 Champions 1961–62, 1978–79 Runners-up 1902–03, 1906–07, 1908–09, 1948–49 Div. 2 Champions 1946–47	Winners 1910 Runners-up 1925, 1952, 1964	Winners 1952, 1953, 1974 Runners-up 1968
DUNDEE UNITED (1910) Tangerine/tangerine			
Tannadice Park Dundee	Div. 2 Champions 1924–25, 1928–29 Runners-up 1930–31, 1959–60	Runners-up 1974	
DUNFERMLINE ATHLETIC (1885) White, black/black			
East End Park Dunfermline	Div. 2 Champions 1925–26 Runners-up 1912–13, 1933–34, 1954–55, 1957–58, 1972–73, 1978–79	Winners 1961, 1968 Runners-up 1965	Runners-up 1950
EAST FIFE (1903) Gold/black			
Bayview Park Methil	Div. 2 Champions 1947–48 Runners-up 1929–30, 1970–71	Winners 1938 Runners-up 1927, 1950	Winners 1948, 1950, 1954
EAST STIRLING(SHIRE) (1881) Black, white/black			
Firs Park Falkirk	Div. 2 Champions 1931–32 Runners-up 1962–63		
FALKIRK (1876) Blue/white			
Brockville Park Falkirk	Div. 1 runners-up 1907–08, 1909–10 Div. 2 Champions 1935–36, 1969–70, 1974–75 Runners-up 1904–05, 1951–52, 1960–61	Winners 1913, 1957	Runners-up 1948

League career			Record win	Highest number of league goals
				CLYDE
1891–93 Div. 1	1951–52 Div. 2	1964–72 Div. 1	11–1 v Cowdenbeath,	Bill Boyd, 32, 1932–33
1893–94 Div. 2	1952–56 Div. 1	1972–73 Div. 2	Div. 2, 1951–52	
1894–1900 Div. 1	1956–57 Div. 2	1973–76 Div. 1		
1900–06 Div. 2	1957–61 Div. 1	1976–78 Div. 2		
1906–24 Div. 1	1961–62 Div. 2	1978– Div. 1		
1924–26 Div. 2	1962–63 Div. 1			
1926–51 Div. 1	1963–64 Div. 2			
				CLYDEBANK
1966–76 Div. 2	1977–78 Pr. Div.	1978– Div. 1	7–1 v Hamilton, Div. 2,	Joe McCallan, 27, 1976–77
1976–77 Div. 1			1971–72 and v Queen's	
			Park, Div. 2, 1970–71	
				COWDENBEATH
1905–24 Div. 2	1934–70 Div. 2	1971– Div. 2	12–0 v St Johnstone,	Willie Devlin, 40, 1925–26
1924–34 Div. 1	1970–71 Div. 1		Scottish Cup, 1927–28	
				DUMBARTON
1890–96 Div. 1	1913–22 Div. 1	1972– Div. 1	8–0 v Cowdenbeath,	Kenny Wilson, 38, 1971–72
1896–97 Div. 2	1922–54 Div. 2		Div. 2, 1963–64	
1906–13 Div. 2	1955–72 Div. 2			
				DUNDEE
1893–1917 Div. 1	1947–75 Div. 1	1979– Pr. Div.	10–0 v Alloa, Div. 2, 1946–47 and	Dave Halliday, 38, 1923–24
1919–38 Div. 1	1975–76 Pr. Div.		v Dunfermline, Div. 2, 1946–47	
1938–47 Div. 2	1976–79 Div. 1			
				DUNDEE UNITED
1910–15 Div. 2	1929–30 Div. 1	1960–75 Div. 1	14–0 v Nithsdale,	John Coyle, 41, 1955–56
1923–25 Div. 2	1930–31 Div. 2	1975– Pr. Div.	Scottish Cup, 1930–31	
1925–27 Div. 1	1931–32 Div. 1			
1927–29 Div. 2	1932–60 Div. 2			
				DUNFERMLINE
1912–15 Div. 2	1934–37 Div. 1	1958–72 Div. 1	11–2 v Stenhousemuir,	Bobby Skinner, 55, 1925–26
1921–26 Div. 2	1937–55 Div. 2	1972–73 Div. 2	Div. 2, 1930–31	
1926–28 Div. 1	1955–57 Div. 1	1973–76 Div. 1		
1928–34 Div. 2	1957–58 Div. 2	1976– Div. 2		
				EAST FIFE
1921–30 Div. 2	1948–58 Div. 1	1974–75 Div. 2	13–2 v Edinburgh City,	Henry Morris, 41, 1947–48
1930–31 Div. 1	1958–71 Div. 2	1975–78 Div. 1	Div. 2, 1937–38	
1931–48 Div. 2	1971–74 Div. 1	1978– Div. 2		
				EAST STRILING(SHIRE)
1900–15 Div. 2	1924–39 Div. 2	1963–64 Div. 1	8–2 v Brechin City, Div. 2,	Malcolm Morrison, 36, 1938–39
1921–23 Div. 2	1955–63 Div. 2	1964– Div. 2	1961–62	
				FALKIRK
1902–05 Div. 2	1952–59 Div. 1	1974–75 Div. 2	10–0 v Breadalbane,	Evelyn Morrison, 43, 1928–29
1905–35 Div. 1	1959–61 Div. 2	1975–77 Div. 1	Scottish Cup, 1922–23	
1935–36 Div. 2	1961–69 Div. 1	1977– Div. 2	and 1925–26	
1936–51 Div. 1	1969–70 Div. 2			
1951–52 Div. 2	1970–74 Div. 1			

Ground	Honours League	Scottish FA Cup	League Cup
FORFAR ATHLETIC (1884) Blue/blue			
Station Park Forfar	Highest League placing 5th, Div. 2, 1927–28		
HAMILTON ACADEMICAL (1875) Red, white/white			
Douglas Park Hamilton	Div. 2 Champions 1903–04 Runners-up 1952–53, 1964–65	Runners-up 1911, 1935	
HEART OF MIDLOTHIAN (1874) Maroon/white			
Tynecastle Park Edinburgh	Div. 1 Champions 1894–95, 1896–97, 1957–58, 1959–60 Runners-up 1893–94, 1898–99, 1903–04, 1905–06, 1914–15, 1937–38 1953–54, 1956–57, 1958–59, 1964–65, 1977–78	Winners 1891, 1896, 1901, 1906, 1956 Runners-up 1903, 1907, 1968, 1976	Winners 1955, 1959, 1960, 1963 Runners-up 1962
HIBERNIAN (1875) Green/white			
Easter Road Park Edinburgh	Div. 1 Champions 1902–03, 1947–48, 1950–51, 1951–52 Runners-up 1896–97, 1946–47, 1949–50, 1952–53, 1973–74, 1974–75 Div. 2 Champions 1893–94, 1894–95, 1932–33	Winners 1887, 1902 Runners-up 1896, 1914, 1923, 1924, 1947, 1958, 1972, 1979	Winners 1973 Runners-up 1951, 1969, 1975
KILMARNOCK (1869) White/white			
Rugby Park Kilmarnock	Div. 1 Champions 1964–65 Runners-up 1959–60, 1960–61, 1962–63, 1963–64, 1975–76, 1978–79 Div. 2 Champions 1897–98, 1898–99 Runners-up 1953–54, 1973–74	Winners 1920, 1929 Runners-up 1898, 1932, 1938, 1957, 1960	Runners-up 1953, 1961, 1963
MEADOWBANK THISTLE (1974) Amber/black			
Meadowbank Stadium Edinburgh	Highest League placing 11th, Div. 2, 1976–77		
MONTROSE (1879) Blue/blue			
Links Park Montrose	Highest League placing 3rd, Div. 1, 1975–76		
MORTON (1874) Blue, white/white			
Cappielow Park Greenock	Div. 1 Champions 1977–78 Div. 1 runners-up 1916–17 Div. 2 Champions 1949–50, 1963–64, 1966–67 Runners-up 1899–1900, 1928–29, 1936–37	Winners 1922 Runners-up 1948	Runners-up 1964
MOTHERWELL (1886) Amber/amber			
Fir Park Motherwell	Div. 1 Champions 1931–32 Runners-up 1926–27, 1929–30, 1932–33, 1933–34 Div. 2 Champions 1953–54, 1968–69 Runners-up 1894–95, 1902–03	Winners 1952 Runners-up 1931, 1933, 1939, 1951	Winners 1951 Runners-up 1955
PARTICK THISTLE (1876) Red, yellow/black			
Firhill Park Glasgow NW	Div. 1 Champions 1975–76 Div. 2 Champions 1896–97, 1899–1900, 1970–71 Runners-up 1901–02	Winners 1921 Runners-up 1930	Winners 1972 Runners-up 1954, 1957, 1959

League career			Record win	Highest number of league goals

FORFAR ATHLETIC

| 1921–25 Div. 2 | 1926–39 Div. 2 | 1949– Div. 2 | 9–1 v Stenhousemuir, Div. 2, 1968–69 | Davie Kilgour, 45, 1929–30 |

HAMILTON ACADEMICAL

1897–1906 Div. 2	1953–54 Div.1	1966–75 Div. 2	10–2 v Cowdenbeath, Div. 1, 1932–33	David Wilson, 34, 1936–37
1906–47 Div. 1	1954–65 Div. 2	1975– Div. 1		
1947–53 Div. 2	1965–66 Div.1			

HEART OF MIDLOTHIAN

| 1890–1975 Div. 1 | 1977–78 Div. 1 | 1979– Div. 1 | 15–0 v King's Park, Scottish Cup, 1936–37 | Barney Battles, 44, 1930–31 |
| 1975–77 Pr. Div. | 1978–79 Pr. Div. | | | |

HIBERNIAN

| 1893–95 Div. 2 | 1931–33 Div. 2 | 1975– Pr. Div. | 15–1 v Peebles Rovers, Scottish Cup, 1960–61 | Joe Baker, 42, 1959–60 |
| 1895–1931 Div. 1 | 1933–75 Div. 1 | | | |

KILMARNOCK

1895–99 Div. 2	1954–73 Div. 1	1976–77 Pr. Div.	11–1 v Paisley Academicals, Scottish Cup, 1929–30	Peerie Cunningham, 35, 1927–28
1899–1947 Div 1	1973–74 Div. 2	1977–79 Div. 1		
1947–54 Div. 2	1974–76 Div. 1	1979– Pr. Div.		

MEADOWBANK THISTLE

| 1974– Div. 2 | | | 4–1 v Albion Rovers, Div. 2, 1975–76 and v Forfar, League Cup, 1975–76 | Kenny Davidson and Jim Hancock, 8, 1976–77, Jim Hancock, 8, 1977–78 |

MONTROSE

| 1929–39 Div. 2 | 1975–79 Div. 1 | 1979– Div. 2 | 2–0 v Vale of Leithen, Scottish Cup, 1974–75 | Brian Third, 29, 1972–73 |
| 1955–75 Div. 2 | | | | |

MORTON

1893–1900 Div. 2	1937–38 Div. 1	1952–64 Div. 2	11–0 v Carfin Shamrock, Scottish Cup, 1886–87	Allan McGraw, 41, 1963–64
1900–27 Div. 1	1938–39 Div. 2	1964–66 Div. 1		
1927–29 Div. 2	1946–49 Div. 1	1966–67 Div. 2		
1929–33 Div. 1	1949–50 Div. 2	1967–78 Div. 1		
1933–37 Div. 2	1950–52 Div. 1	1978– Pr. Div.		

MOTHERWELL

1893–1903 Div. 2	1954–68 Div. 1	1975–79 Pr. Div.	12–1 v Dundee United, Div. 2, 1953–54	Willie MacFayden, 52, 1931–32
1903–53 Div. 1	1968–69 Div. 2	1979– Div. 1		
1953–54 Div. 2	1969–75 Div. 1			

PARTICK THISTLE

1893–97 Div. 2	1900–01 Div. 1	1970–71 Div. 2	16–0 v Royal Albert, Scottish Cup, 1930–31	Alec Hair, 41, 1926–27
1897–99 Div. 1	1901–02 Div. 2	1971–76 Div. 1		
1899–1900 Div. 2	1902–70 Div. 1	1976– Pr. Div.		

Ground	Honours League	Scottish FA Cup	League Cup

QUEEN OF THE SOUTH (1919) Blue/white

Palmerston Park Dumfries	Div. 2 Champions 1950–51 Runners-up 1932–33, 1961–62, 1974–75		

QUEEN'S PARK (1867) Black, white/white

Hampden Park Glasgow G42 9BA	Div. 2 Champions 1922–23, 1955–56	Winners 1874, 1875, 1876, 1880, 1881, 1882, 1884, 1886, 1890, 1893 Runners-up 1892, 1900 English FA Cup runners-up 1884, 1885	

RAITH ROVERS (1893) Blue/white

Stark's Park Kirkcaldy	Div. 2 Champions 1907–08, 1909–10 (shared), 1937–38, 1948–49 Runners-up 1908–09, 1926–27, 1966–67, 1975–76, 1977–78	Runners-up 1913	Runners-up 1949

RANGERS (1873) Blue/white

Ibrox Stadium Glasgow SW	Premier Div. Champions 1975–76, 1977–78 Premier Div. Runners-up 1976–77, 1978–79 Div. 1 Champions 1890–91 (shared), 1898–99, 1899–1900, 1900–01, 1901–02, 1910–11, 1911–12, 1912–13, 1917–18, 1919–20, 1920–21, 1922–23, 1923–24, 1924–25, 1926–27, 1927–28, 1928–29, 1929–30, 1930–31, 1932–33, 1933–34, 1934–35, 1936–37, 1938–39, 1946–47, 1948–49, 1949–50, 1952–53, 1955–56, 1956–57, 1958–59, 1960–61, 1962–63, 1963–64, 1974–75 Runners-up 21 times	Winners 1894, 1897, 1898, 1903, 1928, 1930, 1932, 1934, 1935, 1936, 1948, 1949, 1950, 1953, 1960, 1962, 1963, 1964, 1966, 1973, 1976, 1978, 1979 Runners-up 11 times	Winners 1947, 1949, 1961, 1962, 1964, 1965, 1971, 1976, 1978, 1979 Runners-up 5 times

ST JOHNSTONE (1884) Blue/white

Muirton Park Perth	Div. 2 Champions 1923–24, 1959–60, 1962–63 Runners-up 1931–32		Runners-up 1970

ST MIRREN (1876) Black, white/white

St Mirren Park Paisley	Div. 1 Champions 1976–77 Div. 2 Champions 1967–68 Runners-up 1935–36	Winners 1926, 1959 Runners-up 1908, 1934, 1962	Runners-up 1956

STENHOUSEMUIR (1884) Maroon/white

Ochilview Park Larbert	Highest League placing 3rd, Div. 2, 1958–59, 1960–61		

STIRLING ALBION (1945) Red/red

Annfield Park Stirling	Div. 2 Champions 1952–53, 1957–58, 1960–61, 1964–65, 1976–77 Runners-up 1948–49, 1950–51		

STRANRAER (1870) Blue/white

Stair Park Stranraer	Highest League placing 4th, Div. 2, 1960–61, 1976–77		

League career			Record win	Highest number of league goals

QUEEN OF THE SOUTH

1925–33 Div. 2	1951–59 Div. 1	1964–75 Div. 2	11–1 v Stranraer,	Jimmy Gray, 33, 1927–28
1933–50 Div. 1	1959–62 Div. 2	1975–79 Div. 1	Scottish Cup, 1931–32	
1950–51 Div. 2	1962–64 Div. 1	1979– Div. 2		

QUEEN'S PARK

1900–22 Div. 1	1923–48 Div. 1	1956–58 Div. 1	16–0 v St Peter's,	Willie Martin, 30, 1937–38
1922–23 Div. 2	1948–56 Div. 2	1958– Div. 2	Scottish Cup, 1885–86	

RAITH ROVERS

1902–10 Div. 2	1929–38 Div. 2	1967–70 Div. 1	10–1 v Coldstream,	Norman Haywood, 38, 1937–38
1910–17 Div. 1	1938–39 Div. 1	1970–76 Div. 2	Scottish Cup, 1953–54	
1919–26 Div. 1	1946–49 Div. 2	1976–77 Div. 1		
1926–27 Div. 2	1949–63 Div. 1	1977–78 Div. 2		
1927–29 Div. 1	1963–67 Div. 2	1978– Div. 1		

RANGERS

1890–1975 Div. 1	1975– Pr. Div.		14–2 v Blairgowrie,	Sam English, 44, 1931–32
			Scottish Cup, 1933–34	

ST JOHNSTONE

1911–15 Div. 2	1932–39 Div. 1	1963–75 Div. 1	8–1 v Partick Thistle,	Jimmy Benson, 36, 1931–32
1921–24 Div. 2	1946–60 Div. 2	1975–76 Pr. Div.	Scottish Cup, 1969–70	
1924–30 Div. 1	1960–62 Div. 1	1976– Div. 1		
1930–32 Div. 2	1962–63 Div. 2			

ST MIRREN

1890–1935 Div. 1	1967–68 Div. 2	1975–77 Div. 1	15–0 v Glasgow University,	Dunky Walker, 45, 1921–22
1935–36 Div. 2	1968–71 Div. 1	1977– Pr. Div.	Scottish Cup, 1959–60	
1936–67 Div. 1	1971–75 Div. 2			

STENHOUSEMUIR

1921– Div. 2			9–2 v Dundee United,	Evelyn Morrison, 29, 1927–28
			Div. 2, 1936–37	

STIRLING ALBION

1947–49 Div. 2	1953–56 Div. 1	1962–65 Div. 2	7–0 v Albion Rovers, Div. 2,	Michael Lawson, 26, 1975–76
1949–50 Div. 1	1956–58 Div. 2	1965–68 Div. 1	1947–48 ; v Montrose, Div. 2,	
1950–51 Div. 2	1958–60 Div. 1	1968–77 Div. 2	1957–58 ; v St Mirren, Div. 1,	
1951–52 Div. 1	1960–64 Div. 2	1977– Div. 1	1959–60 and v Arbroath,	
1952–53 Div. 2	1961–62 Div. 1		Div. 2, 1964–65	

STRANRAER

1955– Div. 2			7–0 v Brechin City, Div. 2,	Derek Frye, 27, 1977–78
			1964–65	

Welsh/Irish Soccer

The Football Association of Wales
The idea of forming the Welsh Football Association came following a letter written to *The Field* in January 1876 by G. A. Clay-Thomas a London domiciled Welshman. It aroused considerable interest in North Wales and before the end of the month a meeting at which the F.A. of Wales was actually formed took place at Wrexham and was reported in *The Field*:

'A meeting to discuss the project of playing an international football match between Wales and Scotland according to Association rules was held at the Wynnstay Arms Hotel, Wrexham, when a committee was appointed to make preliminary arrangements.

'Gentlemen desirous of playing in trial matches are requested to send in their names and addresses to the chairman of the Cambrian Football Association, Ruabon as early as possible.'

Though described as the Cambrian Football Association this name lasted only a few days, since the minutes of the first committee meeting at Wrexham on 2 February 1876 bore the name 'The Association of Wales'.

Irish Football Association
The match which marked the beginning of football under Association rules in Ireland came about in 1878 between two Scottish clubs. On 24 October an exhibition match was played between selected players from Queen's Park and The Caledonians at the Ulster cricket ground in Belfast under the auspices of the Ulster and Windsor Football Clubs. Queen's Park won 3–2 and the success of the venture helped towards the popularity of the game in Ireland.

British International Soccer

BRITISH INTERNATIONAL CHAMPIONSHIP
The British International Championship began when all four home countries started playing each other. Previously matches between some of them had only been regarded as friendlies. The tournament itself began in 1883–84. If countries were level on points at the top they shared the title, as goal average or goal difference did not count in determining the winner until the latter in 1978–79.

England have won the title outright on 32 occasions, Scotland 24, Wales seven and Ireland once. England have been concerned in all the 20 shared titles, Scotland 17, Wales and Ireland in five each.

In the overall record of matches between the four home countries, in addition to the friendlies played before the International Championship started, England and Wales met each other twice in qualifying matches for the 1974 World Cup, as did Scotland and Wales in the 1978 World Cup, Scotland played England as part of their Centenary in 1973 and Wales met England in their Centenary match in 1976.

England also played Ireland in the qualifying competition of the 1980 European Championship.

England v Scotland

First match	Scotland 0 England 0 30 November 1872 Glasgow
Overall record	97 matches: Scotland 38 wins, England 37, drawn 22. Goals–England 177, Scotland 164
Record win	England 9 Scotland 3 15 April 1961 Wembley
Best individual performance	Dennis Wilshaw (England) 4 goals v Scotland, 2 April 1955, Wembley
Most appearances	Billy Wright (England) 13

Wales v Scotland

First match	Scotland 4 Wales 0 25 March 1876 Glasgow
Overall record	94 matches: Scotland 56 wins, Wales 17, drawn 21. Goals: Scotland 231, Wales 106
Record win	Scotland 9 Wales 0 23 March 1878 Old Hampden

Best individual performance	Willie Paul (Scotland) 4 goals v Wales 22 March 1890, Paisley. John Madden (Scotland) 4 goals v Wales 18 March 1883, Wrexham
Most appearances	Billy Meredith (Wales) 12, Ivor Allchurch (Wales) 12

England v Wales

First match	England 2 Wales 1 18 January 1879 Kennington Oval
Overall record	92 matches: England 60 wins, Wales 12, drawn 20. Goals: England 235, Wales 84
Record win	Wales 1 England 9 16 March 1896 Cardiff
Best individual performance	Steve Bloomer (England) 5 goals v Wales, 16 March 1896, Cardiff
Most appearances	Billy Meredith (Wales) 20

Ireland v Wales

First match	Wales 7 Ireland 1 25 February 1882 Wrexham
Overall record	86 matches: Wales 40 wins, Ireland 26, drawn 20. Goals: Wales 176, Ireland 124
Record win	Wales 11, Ireland 0 3 March 1888 Wrexham
Best individual performance	Joe Bambrick (Ireland) 6 goals v Wales, 1 February 1930, Belfast
Most appearances	Billy Meredith (Wales) 16

Ireland v England

First match	England 7 Ireland 0 24 February 1883 Liverpool
Overall record	87 matches: England 68 wins, Ireland 6, drawn 13. Goals: England 302, Ireland 78
Record win	Ireland 0 England 13 18 February 1882 Belfast
Best individual performance	Willie Hall (England) 5 goals v Ireland, 16 November 1938, Old Trafford
Most appearances	Pat Jennings (Ireland) 15

Scotland v Ireland

First match	Ireland 0 Scotland 5 26 January 1884 Belfast

Overall record	84 matches: Scotland 59 wins, Ireland 13, drawn 12. Goals: Scotland 249, Ireland 76
Record win	Scotland 11 Ireland 0 23 February 1901 Hampden Park
Best individual performance	Charles Heggie (Scotland) 5 goals v Ireland, 20 March 1886, Belfast
Most appearances	Danny Blanchflower (Ireland) 13

Youngest international players

England:	Duncan Edwards (Manchester United) 18 years 183 days, left-half v Scotland, 2 April 1955
Ireland:	Norman Kernoghan (Belfast Celtic) 17 years 80 days, outside-right v Wales, 11 March 1936
Scotland:	Denis Law (Huddersfield Town) 18 years 236 days, inside-forward v Wales, 18 October 1958
Wales:	John Charles (Leeds United) 18 years 71 days, centre-half v Ireland, 8 March 1950

(There are claims that other players have been younger, but the above examples are the ones which have so far been proved satisfactorily.)

International Mosaic

Aston Villa have provided England with a total of 45 international players from Arthur Brown and Howard Vaughton (v Ireland 18 February 1882) to John Gidman. Rangers provided their first international for the Scottish team v Wales on 25 March 1876. He was Moses NcNeil. Since then their total of Scottish internationals has reached 106. Wrexham hold the record for Wales with a total of 65. They had two men, E. A. Cross and A. Davies in the very first international played by Wales, which was against Scotland on 25 March 1876. Ireland played their first international (v England) on 18 February 1882. Their side, beaten 13–0 on that occasion, included no less than five Cliftonville players, and this is the club that has since provided Ireland with a record total of 63 internationals.

The first player to appear in an international championship match while with a club in Division Three was Robert McCracken of Crystal Palace who appeared at right-half for Ireland against England at Sunderland on 23 October 1920. It was the first season the division had been in operation. Palace also supplied the first international from Division Four in its inaugural season when goalkeeper Vic Rouse played for Wales against Ireland at Belfast on 22 April 1959.

On 1 March 1926 Wales played England at Crystal Palace but had to rely on one of their players bringing a club colleague with him to complete the Welsh line-up. All that was known for certain was that the newcomer had been born in Wales. In the event Moses Russell of Plymouth Argyle brought his centre-half Jack Pullen with him for an unusual debut. Wales won 3–1.

Wales won the International Championship in the 1923–24 season, winning all three matches and conceding only one goal. Only twelve players were used with just a change at inside-right.

The record number of appearances for England in full international matches by a player from a non-League side in the period since World War I is four by Lt K. E. Hegan, a speedy winger who played for the Army and the Corinthians. His first appearance in a full international was against Belgium at Highbury on 19 March 1923. England won 6–1 and Hegan at outside-left scored twice. He also scored twice in his next international which was a 4–1 victory over France in Paris on 10 May. The following season he was chosen as outside-right against both Ireland and Belgium and it was rather surprising to find an amateur selected out of his normal position for England

FULL INTERNATIONAL RECORD

ENGLAND

Opponents	P	W	D	L	F	A
Argentina	7	3	3	1	9	6
Austria	15	8	3	4	54	25
Belgium	16	12	3	1	65	23
Bohemia	1	1	0	0	4	0
Brazil	11	1	4	6	9	18
Bulgaria	4	2	2	0	5	1
Chile	2	2	0	0	4	1
Colombia	1	1	0	0	4	0
Cyprus	2	2	0	0	6	0
Czechoslovakia	9	5	2	2	17	11
Denmark	6	5	1	0	20	7
Ecuador	1	1	0	0	2	0
Finland	5	5	0	0	22	3
France	18	13	2	3	57	24
East Germany (GDR)	3	2	1	0	6	3
West Germany	14	8	2	4	30	19
Greece	2	2	0	0	5	0
Hungary	11	6	0	5	36	26
Northern Ireland	87	68	13	6	302	78
Republic of Ireland	7	3	3	1	12	7
Italy	13	6	4	3	23	17
Luxembourg	5	5	0	0	25	3
Malta	2	2	0	0	6	0
Mexico	4	2	1	1	11	2
Netherlands (Holland)	6	3	2	1	11	5
Norway	4	4	0	0	20	2
Peru	2	1	0	1	5	4
Poland	4	1	2	1	3	4
Portugal	14	8	5	1	35	16
Rumania	4	2	2	0	4	1
Scotland	97	37	22	38	177	164
Spain	11	7	1	3	26	14
Sweden	10	6	2	2	23	13
Switzerland	12	8	2	2	33	9
USA	4	3	0	1	24	5
USSR	7	3	3	1	14	7
Uruguay	6	2	2	2	7	8
Wales	92	60	20	12	235	84
Yugoslavia	11	2	5	4	15	18
Rest of Europe	1	1	0	0	3	0
FIFA	1	0	1	0	4	4
Rest of the World	1	1	0	0	2	1
Team America*	1	1	0	0	3	1

SCOTLAND

Opponents	P	W	D	L	F	A
Argentina	2	0	1	1	2	4
Austria	13	3	3	7	17	27
Belgium	6	3	0	3	10	7
Brazil	5	0	2	3	1	5
Bulgaria	1	1	0	0	2	1
Cyprus	2	2	0	0	13	0
Chile	1	1	0	0	4	2
Czechoslovakia	10	5	1	4	18	16
Denmark	9	8	0	1	17	5
England	97	38	22	37	164	177
Finland	4	4	0	0	13	3
France	7	5	0	2	10	6
East Germany (GDR)	2	1	0	1	3	1
West Germany	9	3	4	2	16	13
Hungary	5	1	2	2	10	12
Northern Ireland	84	59	12	13	249	76
Republic of Ireland	4	2	1	1	8	3
Italy	3	1	0	2	1	6
Iran	1	0	1	0	1	1
Luxembourg	1	1	0	0	6	0
Netherlands (Holland)	7	4	1	2	11	9
Norway	8	6	1	1	27	12
Paraguay	1	0	0	1	2	3
Peru	2	1	0	1	3	3
Poland	4	1	1	2	6	7
Portugal	8	3	1	4	8	8
Rumania	2	0	2	0	2	2
Spain	6	2	2	2	13	11
Sweden	4	1	1	2	6	7
Switzerland	7	5	0	2	13	9
Turkey	1	0	0	1	2	4
Uruguay	2	0	0	2	2	10
USA	1	1	0	0	6	0
USSR	2	0	0	2	0	3
Wales	94	56	22	16	231	106
Yugoslavia	5	1	4	0	8	6
Zaire	1	1	0	0	2	0

* Not a full international.

even in those days, which underlines Hegan's ability.

K. E. (Jackie) Hegan played regularly for the Corinthians for several seasons after the First World War and was one of the outstanding players in their F.A. Cup victory over Blackburn Rovers in 1924 when they surprised the Division One side by beating them 1–0 at the Crystal Palace in the first round. He also figured in their two games with Manchester City in 1926 when the Division One team needed a replay to beat the amateurs.

However, probably the most remarkable display Hegan ever gave and so typical of the determination and enthusiasm of the amateurs of his class,

was the first replay against Millwall in 1930. Indeed this has been dubbed 'Hegan's match'.

The Corinthians had held Millwall to a 2–2 draw at the Crystal Palace and the replay at New Cross turned out to be a really tough game with the ever dangerous Hegan the target for some hefty tackles. With the score standing at 1–1 after 90 minutes, an extra half hour was played, but without further score. It was not until the players had left the field that it was discovered that Hegan had played for 50 minutes with a broken leg, his tibia having been fractured shortly before half-time! It is a mystery how he not only continued to play but also outpaced the Millwall defence with

OF THE HOME COUNTRIES

WALES

Opponents	P	W	D	L	F	A
Austria	4	1	0	3	3	6
Belgium	2	1	0	1	6	4
Brazil	5	0	0	5	3	11
Chile	1	0	0	1	0	2
Czechoslovakia	6	2	0	4	5	7
Denmark	2	1	0	1	4	3
England	92	12	20	60	84	235
Finland	2	2	0	0	4	0
France	3	0	1	2	3	9
East Germany	4	1	0	3	7	8
West Germany	5	0	3	2	3	7
Greece	2	1	0	1	4	3
Hungary	7	3	2	2	11	10
Luxembourg	2	2	0	0	8	1
Northern Ireland	86	40	20	26	176	124
Republic of Ireland	1	1	0	0	3	2
Iran	1	1	0	0	1	0
Israel	2	2	0	0	4	0
Italy	3	0	0	3	2	9
Kuwait	2	0	2	0	0	0
Malta	2	2	0	0	9	0
Mexico	2	0	1	1	2	3
Poland	2	1	0	1	2	3
Portugal	2	1	0	1	4	4
Rumania	2	0	1	1	0	2
Scotland	94	16	22	56	106	231
Spain	2	0	1	1	2	3
Sweden	1	0	1	0	0	0
Switzerland	2	1	0	1	3	6
Turkey	1	1	0	0	4	0
Rest of the UK	2	1	0	1	3	3
USSR	2	1	0	1	3	3
Yugoslavia	4	0	1	3	4	11

NORTHERN IRELAND

Opponents	P	W	D	L	F	A
Albania	2	1	1	0	5	2
Argentina	1	0	0	1	1	3
Belgium	2	1	0	1	3	2
Bulgaria	4	2	1	1	4	3
Cyprus	4	3	0	1	11	1
Czechoslovakia	2	2	0	0	3	1
Denmark	2	1	0	1	2	5
England	87	6	13	68	78	302
France	3	0	1	2	3	9
Greece	2	1	0	1	3	2
Netherlands (Holland)	5	1	2	2	4	8
Israel	2	1	1	0	4	3
Iceland	2	1	0	1	2	1
Republic of Ireland	1	0	1	0	0	0
Italy	4	1	1	2	6	7
Mexico	1	1	0	0	4	1
Norway	2	1	0	1	4	2
Poland	2	2	0	0	4	0
Portugal	4	1	3	0	6	3
Scotland	84	13	12	59	76	249
Spain	5	0	2	3	4	12
Sweden	2	1	0	1	3	2
Switzerland	2	1	0	1	2	2
Turkey	2	2	0	0	7	1
Uruguay	1	1	0	0	3	0
USSR	4	0	2	2	1	4
Wales	86	26	20	40	124	176
West Germany	5	0	1	4	6	15
Yugoslavia	2	1	0	1	1	1

some typical spirited runs down the left wing.

Incidentally without Hegan in the second replay, the Corinthians proved no match for Millwall at Stamford Bridge and were beaten 5–1.

On the following pages there is a list of international players for England, Scotland, N. Ireland and Wales who have made 50 or more appearances for their respective countries at full international level.

INTERNATIONAL APPEARANCES (ENGLAND) 50 or more		Int. Champ.	Others	Total
Bobby Moore (West Ham United)	1962–1973	30	78	108
Bobby Charlton (Manchester United)	1958–1970	32	74	106
Billy Wright (Wolverhampton Wanderers)	1946–1959	38	67	105
Tom Finney (Preston North End)	1946–1956	29	47	76
Gordon Banks (Leicester City, Stoke City)	1963–1972	23	50	73
Alan Ball (Blackpool, Everton, Arsenal)	1965–1975	20	52	72
Martin Peters (West Ham, Tottenham Hotspur)	1966–1974	19	48	67
Ray Wilson (Huddersfield Town, Everton)	1960–1968	15	48	63
Emlyn Hughes (Liverpool)	1969–	18	41	59
Jimmy Greaves (Chelsea, Tottenham Hotspur)	1959–1967	14	43	57
Johnny Haynes (Fulham)	1954–1962	16	40	56
Stanley Matthews (Stoke City, Blackpool)	1934–1956	24	30	54*

* Matthews' total would have been substantially more had the 29 war-time and Victory internationals in which he appeared been added to this total.

Emlyn Hughes of Liverpool, the 1978–79 player with more international appearances for his country than any other. (Syndication International)

Above: Tom Finney who made 76 appearances for England after the last war. (Colorsport)

Right: Billy Wright the first England player to reach 100 appearances for his country. (Colorsport)

INTERNATIONAL APPEARANCES (SCOTLAND) 50 or more		Int. Champ.	Others	Total
Kenny Dalglish (Celtic, Liverpool)	1971–	20	45	65
Denis Law (Huddersfield Town, Manchester City, Torino, Manchester United)	1958–1974	26	29	55
Billy Bremner (Leeds United)	1965–1976	19	35	54
George Young (Rangers)	1946–1957	29	24	53
INTERNATIONAL APPEARANCES (NORTHERN IRELAND) 50 or more				
Pat Jennings (Watford, Tottenham Hotspur, Arsenal)	1964–	40	40	80
Terry Neill (Arsenal, Hull City)	1961–1973	30	30	60
Danny Blanchflower (Barnsley, Aston Villa, Tottenham Hotspur)	1949–1962	37	19	56
Billy Bingham (Sunderland, Luton Town, Everton)	1951–1963	34	22	56
Jimmy McIlroy (Burnley)	1951–1965	36	19	55
Allan Hunter (Blackburn Rovers, Ipswich Town)	1969–	23	28	51
INTERNATIONAL APPEARANCES (WALES) 50 or more				
Ivor Allchurch (Swansea, Newcastle United, Cardiff City)	1950–1966	37	31	68
Cliff Jones (Swansea, Tottenham Hotspur, Fulham)	1954–1969	31	28	59

Kenny Dalglish who is the record holder for Scottish international appearances was voted Footballer of the Year in 1978–79 by the Football Writers Association.

Awards

FOOTBALLER OF THE YEAR

The Football Writers Association founded in 1947 has elected a Footballer of the Year at the end of each season since 1947–48.

Season	Int. Apps.	Winner	Club	Position	Club Lge Position	Cup Holders
1947–48	5 (Eng)	Stanley Matthews	Blackpool	Outside-right	9th	F.A. Cup R-Up
1948–49	3 (NI) 2 (Rep of Ire)	Johnny Carey	Manchester United	Full-back	2nd	—
1949–50	—	Joe Mercer	Arsenal	Wing-half	6th	FA Cup Winners
1950–51	1 (Eng)	Harry Johnston	Blackpool	Half-back	3rd	F.A. Cup R-Up
1951–52	8 (Eng)	Billy Wright	Wolverhampton Wanderers	Centre-half	16th	—
1952–53	8 (Eng)	Nat Lofthouse	Bolton Wanderers	Centre-forward	14th	F.A. Cup R-Up
1953–54	7 (Eng)	Tom Finney	Preston North End	Winger	11th	F.A. Cup R-Up
1954–55	1 (Eng)	Don Revie	Manchester City	Centre-forward	7th	F.A. Cup R-Up
1955–56	—	Bert Trautmann	Manchester City	Goalkeeper	4th	F.A. Cup Winners
1956–57	7 (Eng)	Tom Finney	Preston North End	Winger	3rd	—
1957–58	10 (NI)	Danny Blanchflower	Tottenham Hotspur	Wing-half	3rd	—
1958–59	—	Syd Owen	Luton Town	Centre-Half	17th	F.A. Cup R-Up
1959-60	1 (Eng)	Bill Slater	Wolverhampton Wanderers	Half-back	2nd	F.A. Cup Winners
1960–61	5 (NI)	Danny Blanchflower	Tottenham Hotspur	Wing-half	1st	F.A. Cup Winners
1961–62	—	Jimmy Adamson	Burnley	Wing-half	2nd	F.A. Cup R-Up
1962–63	—	Stanley Matthews	Stoke City	Outside-right	1st (Div 2)	—
1963–64	10 (Eng)	Bobby Moore	West Ham United	Half-back	14th	F.A. Cup Winners
1964–65	3 (Scot)	Bobby Collins	Leeds United	Inside-forward	2nd	F.A. Cup R-Up
1965–66	16 (Eng)	Bobby Charlton	Manchester United	Forward	4th	—
1966–67	4 (Eng)	Jackie Charlton	Leeds United	Centre-half	4th	Fairs Cup R-Up
1967–68	1 (NI)	George Best	Manchester United	Forward	2nd	Eur Cup Winners
1968–69	—	Dave Mackay	Derby County	Wing-half	1st (Div 2)	—
	—	Tony Book	Manchester City	Full-back	13th	F.A. Cup Winners
1969–70	3 (Scot)	Billy Bremner	Leeds United	Wing-half	2nd	F.A. Cup R-Up
1970–71	3 (Scot)	Frank McLintock	Arsenal	Centre-half	1st	F.A. Cup Winners
1971–72	6 (Eng)	Gordon Banks	Stoke City	Goalkeeper	17th	Lge Cup Winners
1972–73	6 (NI)	Pat Jennings	Tottenham Hotspur	Goalkeeper	8th	Lge Cup Winners
1973–74	—	Ian Callaghan	Liverpool	Winger	2nd	F.A. Cup Winners
1974–75	—	Alan Mullery	Fulham	Wing-half	9th (Div 2)	F.A. Cup R-Up
1975–76	9 (Eng)	Kevin Keegan	Liverpool	Forward	1st	U.E.F.A. Cup Winners
1976–77	7 (Eng)	Emlyn Hughes	Liverpool	Centre-half	1st	F.A. Cup R-Up; Eur Cup Winners
1977–78	5 (Scot)	Kenny Burns	Nottingham Forest	Centre-half	1st	Lge Cup Winners
1978–79	8 (Scot)	Kenny Dalglish	Liverpool	Forward	1st	—

(International appearances refer to the season in question only)

EUROPEAN FOOTBALLER OF THE YEAR

Annual award organised by France Football and selected in December by panel of journalists from various European countries who award marks to five players of their choice in order of preference.

Year	First	Second	Third
1956	Stanley Matthews (E)	Alfredo di Stefano (A)	Raymond Kopa (F)
1957	Alfredo di Stefano (A)	Billy Wright (E)	Raymond Kopa (F)
1958	Raymond Kopa (F)	Helmut Rahn (WG)	Just Fontaine (F)
1959	Alfredo di Stefano (A)	Raymond Kopa (F)	John Charles (W)
1960	Luis Suarez (Sp)	Ferenc Puskas (H)	Uwe Seeler (WG)
1961	Omar Sivori (A)	Luis Suarez (Sp)	Johnny Haynes (E)
1962	Josef Masopust (Cz)	Eusebio (Po)	Karl-Heinz Schnellinger (WG)
1963	Lev Yashin (Ru)	Gianni Rivera (I)	Jimmy Greaves (E)
1964	Denis Law (S)	Luis Suarez (Sp)	Amancio (Sp)
1965	Eusebio (Po)	Giacinto Facchetti (I)	Luis Suarez (Sp)
1966	Bobby Charlton (E)	Eusebio (Po)	Franz Beckenbauer (WG)
1967	Florian Albert (H)	Bobby Charlton (E)	Jimmy Johnstone (S)
1968	George Best (NI)	Bobby Charlton (E)	Dragan Dzajic (Y)
1969	Gianni Rivera (I)	Luigi Riva (I)	Gerd Muller (WG)
1970	Gerd Muller (WG)	Bobby Moore (E)	Luigi Riva (I)
1971	Johan Cruyff (Ho)	Sandro Mazzola (I)	George Best (NI)
1972	Franz Beckenbauer (WG)	Gerd Muller (WG)	Gunter Netzer (WG)
1973	Johan Cruyff (Ho)	Dino Zoff (I)	Gerd Muller (WG)
1974	Johan Cruyff (Ho)	Franz Beckenbauer (WG)	Kazimierz Deyna (Pl)
1975	Oleg Blokhin (Ru)	Franz Beckenbauer (WG)	Johan Cruyff (Ho)
1976	Franz Beckenbauer (WG)	Robby Rensenbrink (Ho)	Ivo Viktor (Cz)
1977	Allan Simonsen (D)	Kevin Keegan (E)	Michel Platini (F)
1978	Kevin Keegan (E)	Hans Krankl (Au)	Robby Rensenbrink (Ho)

Key to countries: A = Argentina; Au = Austria; Cz = Czechoslovakia; D = Denmark; E = England; F = France; WG = West Germany; H = Hungary; Ho = Holland; I = Italy; NI = Northern Ireland; Po = Portugal; Pl = Poland; Ru = USSR; S = Scotland; Sp = Spain; W = Wales; Y = Yugoslavia.

GOLDEN BOOT AWARD (Europe's Leading Goalscorer)

Season	First	Goals	Second	Goals	Third	Goals
1967–68	Eusebio (Benfica)	43	Antal Dunai (Ujpest Dozsa)	36	Bobby Lennox (Celtic)	32
1968–69	Petar Jekov (CSKA Sofia)	36	George Sideris (Olympiakos)	35	Helmut Kogelberger (FK Austria)	31
					Antal Dunai (Ujpest Dozsa)	31
1969–70	Gerd Muller (Bayern Munich)	38	Jan Devillet (Spora Luxembourg)	31		
			Petar Jekov (CSKA Sofia)	31		
1970–71	Josip Skoblar (Marseilles)	44	Salif Keita (St. Etienne)	42	Georges Dedes (Panionios)	28
1971–72	Gerd Muller (Bayern Munich)	40	Antonis Antoniadis (Panathinaikos)	39	Joe Harper (Aberdeen)	33
					Slobodan Santrac (OFK Belgrade)	33
					Francis Lee (Manchester City)	33
1972–73	Eusebio (Benfica)	40	Gerd Muller (Bayern Munich)	36	Petar Jekov (CSKA Sofia)	29
1973–74	Hector Yazalde (Sporting Lisbon)	46	Hans Krankl (Rapid Vienna)	36	Gerd Muller (Bayern Munich)	30
					Jupp Heynckes (Borussia Moenchengladbach)	30
					Carlos Bianchi (Reims)	30
1974–75	Dudu Georgescu (Dinamo Bucharest)	33	Hector Yazalde (Sporting Lisbon)	30		
			Ruud Geels (Ajax)	30		
			Delio Onnis (Monaco)	30		

Golden Boot Award continued.

1975–76	Sotiris Kaiafas (Omonia Nicosia)	39	Carlos Bianchi (Reims)	34	Peter Risi (Zurich)	33
1976–77	Dudu Georgescu (Dinamo Bucharest)	47	Bela Varadi (Vasas Budapest)	36	Ruud Geels (Ajax)	34
					Dieter Muller (FC Cologne)	34
1977–78	Hans Krankl (Rapid Vienna)	41	Carlos Bianchi (Paris St. Germain)	37	Ruud Geels (Ajax)	34
1978–79	Kees Kist (AZ 67 Alkmaar)	34	Thomas Mavros (AEK Athens)	31		
			Laszo Fekete (Ujpest Dozsa)	31		

Above : Joe Harper is one of only two Scots who has appeared in the list of top three scorers in Europe since the Golden Boot Award was first made. He scored 33 goals in 1971–72.

Right : Francis Lee is the only English player to appear in the Golden Boot Award since its inception in 1967–68. He scored 33 goals in the same season as Harper.

Managers

Eric Taylor was with Sheffield Wednesday from August 1929 to June 1974 graduating on the administrative staff from junior to assistant secretary and then secretary just before the war. He became manager in 1942, secretary-manager in 1945 and general manager and secretary from September 1958.

Eddie Davison was manager of Sheffield United for 20 years from June 1932 to the summer of 1952. He had served Sheffield Wednesday as a goalkeeper from 1908 to 1926 after joining them from Gateshead Town. He made one appearance for England. Before taking over as United's manager he had been in charge of Chesterfield where he later returned.

Billy Walker was appointed manager of Sheffield Wednesday in December 1933 and took up a similar position with Nottingham Forest in March 1939 after being in charge of Chelmsford for a time. He remained at Forest for 21 years until 1960 when he retired to be appointed a member of the Club Committee. His aggregate of 213 League goals from inside-left between 1919 and 1934 is still a joint Aston Villa record and he previously held the highest number of 480 League appearances for them over the same period. While at Villa he made 18 appearances for England.

Joe Smith became manager of Blackpool in 1935 after four seasons in charge of Reading. Over the next 23 years until May 1958 the club won promotion to Division One in 1937, became F.A. Cup runners-up 1948 and 1951, F.A. Cup winners in 1953 and Division One runners-up in 1955–56. As an inside-forward he had had a career of more than 20 years with Bolton Wanderers and Stockport County as well as appearing for England five times.

Jimmy Seed had just over 23 years in charge of Charlton Athletic from May 1933 to September 1956. He had also been an inside-forward with Tottenham Hotspur and Sheffield Wednesday and similarly made five appearances for England. Under his guidance Charlton won promotion in successive seasons from Division Three (Southern Section) to Division One and in their first season in that division 1936–37 they were runners-up. They also won the F.A. Cup in 1947 after finishing as runners-up the previous season.

Billy McCandless managed three Welsh teams

who achieved promotion from the Third Division: Newport County 1938–39, Cardiff City 1946–47 and Swansea Town 1948–49. He was an Irishman from Ballymena.

Herbert Chapman the first manager in the modern sense of the word. (Popperfoto)

Herbert Chapman, born Kiveton Park, Yorkshire had a modest playing career with Grimsby, Swindon, Northampton, Sheffield United, Notts County and Tottenham Hotspur, then a successful one as a manager (date joined club in brackets):

1908–09	Northampton Town (1907)	Southern League Champions
1916–17	Leeds City (1912)	Midland Section Champions
1917–18	Leeds City	Football League
1921–22	Huddersfield Town (1920)	F.A. Cup winners
1923–24	Huddersfield Town	Football League Champions
1924–25	Huddersfield Town	Football League Champions

1929–30	Arsenal (1925)	F.A. Cup winners
1930–31	Arsenal	Football League Champions
1932–33	Arsenal	Football League Champions

Investigations into financial irregularities in administration at Leeds City resulted in the Club being expelled in 1919 and the directors suspended along with Chapman. He was pardoned a year later to continue a successful career ended by his death in January 1934 when Arsenal were in the middle of emulating Huddersfield's three successive League Championships.

Jimmy Cochrane was manager of Reading for just 13 days from 31 March 1939 to 13 April 1939.

Tim Ward was appointed manager of Exeter City in March 1953 but became manager of his former club Barnsley 25 days later. His actual stay at Exeter was only seven days because he was recalled by Barnsley who still held his registration as a player.

Bill Lambton was appointed manager of Scunthorpe United on 21 April 1959 but the appointment, a verbal one, was cancelled three days later. Jimmy McIlroy was team-manager of Bolton Wanderers for 18 days during November 1970 before resigning.

Bobby Flavell spent 17 days as manager of Ayr United in December 1961 before returning in a similar capacity to St Mirren, where he had previously been coach.

George Raynor, born Wombwell, Yorkshire, a right-winger with Sheffield United, Mansfield Town, Rotherham United, Bury and Aldershot, later became the national team coach of Sweden when they won the 1948 Olympic Games competition, were runners-up in the 1958 World Cup and finished third in both the 1950 World Cup and 1952 Olympic Games competitions. His previous appointment had been as Aldershot's reserve team trainer, though he had once organised an international team in Iraq.

Andy Beattie managed eight different Football League clubs: Barrow, Stockport County, Huddersfield Town, Carlisle United, Nottingham Forest, Plymouth Argyle, Wolverhampton Wanderers, and then became general manager of Notts County in March 1967. He managed three clubs in three divisions in less than a month in 1952. He was with Stockport (Division Three, Northern Section) until appointed on 18 April by Huddersfield Town (Division One) who were relegated to Division Two on 3 May.

Major Frank Buckley was manager of seven different clubs: Norwich City, Blackpool, Wolverhampton Wanderers, Notts County, Hull City, Leeds United and Walsall, before retiring in September 1955.

The most outstanding example of a club producing a lengthy list of managers has concerned Newcastle United. There have been no fewer than 39 instances during the present century of former Newcastle players having later managed either Football League or Scottish League clubs. But no other club over the last 20 years has equalled West Ham United in producing managers.

There have been 13 who have played for the club during that time and later become managers of Football League clubs: Malcolm Allison (Plymouth Argyle, Manchester City and Crystal Palace), Jimmy Andrews (Cardiff City), John Bond (Bournemouth and Norwich City), Jimmy Bloomfield (Orient, Leicester City and Orient again), Noel Cantwell (Coventry City and Peterborough United), Trevor Hartley (Bournemouth), John Lyall (West Ham United), Malcolm Musgrove (Torquay United), Andy Nelson (Gillingham and Charlton Athletic), Frank O'Farrell (Torquay United, Leicester City, Manchester United, Cardiff City and Torquay United again), Dave Sexton (Orient, Chelsea, Queen's Park Rangers and Manchester United), and Ron Tindall (Portsmouth). In addition Jack Burkett had a short spell as caretaker-manager of Southend United in 1976.

Leeds United's managers since the formation of the club in 1920 have totalled 13 and 12 of them were born in England. The sequence has been: Arthur Fairclough, Dick Ray, Billy Hampson, Willis Edwards, Frank Buckley, Raich Carter, Jack Taylor, Bill Lambton, Don Revie, Brian Clough, Jimmy Armfield and Jimmy Adamson.

During the 1976–77 season Leeds had on their staff six men who had managed other clubs themselves. They were United's own manager Jimmy Armfield (Bolton Wanderers), plus various assistants in Maurice Lindley (Crewe Alexandra and Swindon Town), Don Howe (West Bromwich Albion), Bobby Collins (Huddersfield Town), Jimmy McAnearney (Rotherham United) and Brian Green (Rochdale).

Sam Cowan's entire career as a manager with Manchester City extended only from November

1946 to June 1947 but it was not an entirely un-
successful association because the club won the
championship of Division Two that season. He had
won a Division Two championship medal with the
club as a player in 1927–28 and also an F.A. Cup
winner's medal in 1934. He had later become
trainer to Brighton and Hove.

Cowan was said not to have kicked a football
until he was 17 years old and in the first game in
which he played to oblige some friends who were
members of a junior team he played wearing only
one football boot.

He progressed to become captain of Manchester
City and also played three times for England. On
receiving a loser's medal in the 1933 F.A. Cup
Final from King George V, he promised that he
would be back the following year to collect a
winning one and was able to keep his word.

Six player-managers have led their teams to
Football League promotions since the war when in
their first season with the clubs concerned: Raich
Carter (Hull City 1948–49), Peter Doherty (Don-
caster Rovers 1949–50), Allenby Chilton (Grimsby
Town 1955–56), Arthur Rowley (Shrewsbury
Town 1958–59), Jimmy Scoular (Bradford Park
Avenue 1960–61) and John Toshack (Swansea
City 1977–78).

Since the war there have been only two instances
of Division One clubs employing player-managers.
They were Les Allen with Queen's Park Rangers
in 1968–69 and Johnny Giles with West Bromwich
Albion in 1976–77.

Walter Galbraith, a Scot who began his career as a
left-back with Queen's Park is the only man who
since the war has managed three Football League
clubs no longer in the competition: New Brighton,
Accrington Stanley and Bradford Park Avenue.

West Bromwich Albion are the only club ever to
have won the F.A. Cup twice when they had a
manager in his first full season with the club. Vic
Buckingham achieved it first in 1953–54 season
and Alan Ashman emulated him in 1967–68.

At one time during the 1946–47 season Luton
Town's team included both Dally Duncan (player-
manager) and Frank Soo (player-coach) but neither
was in charge on the field, for centre-half Horace
Gager captained the Division Two side.

Bert Tann, Bill Dodgin and Fred Ford were
Charlton Athletic half-backs together during the
1936–37 season. During the 1960s all three of them
had spells in turn as manager of Bristol Rovers.
In the 1953–54 season Dodgin managed two

Jimmy Sirrel, manager of Notts County during the 1978–79
season. (Syndication International)

Division Two clubs within nine days when both
of them were at the bottom. He resigned the
Fulham (then last in the table) post on 22 September and on 1 October was appointed by
Brentford (who subsequently became last).

When Scottish-born Jimmy Sirrel was manager of
Brentford from 1965–69 he was the only non-
Englishman in charge of any of London's 11
Football League clubs. The others who have been
similarly placed since then have been Dublin-born
Theo Foley (when manager of Charlton Athletic)
and Northern Ireland native Terry Neill (Totten-
ham Hotspur and subsequently Arsenal).

Yorkshire born Gordon Clark has been associated
with a full team of clubs. He left Denaby United
for Manchester City as a full-back in January 1936
and as either a player, coach, manager or scout has
since been with Southend United, Waterford
(Republic of Ireland), Belfast Distillery, Hyde
United, Aldershot, West Bromwich Albion,
Sheffield Wednesday, Peterborough United,
Arsenal and Fulham.

Tommy Docherty, one of the game's wandering managers.
(Syndication International)

Lancastrian Dick Duckworth has completed over 50 years in the game listing eight clubs as a player, four as a manager and five as scout. He played for Rochdale, Oldham, Chesterfield, Southport, Chester, Rotherham United, York City and Newark; managed York City, Stockport County, Darlington and Scunthorpe United; and has scouted for Birmingham City, Sheffield United, Brighton and Hove Albion, Oxford United and Portsmouth.

When Tommy Docherty became manager of Derby County in September 1977 it was his seventh managerial appointment in Britain, though he had also held an appointment overseas and had a short period as assistant-manager with Hull City. His previous clubs as manager were: Chelsea, Rotherham United, Aston Villa, Queen's Park Rangers, Porto (Portugal), the Scottish National team and Manchester United. He returned to Q.P.R. in May 1979.

Allan Brown took his managerial appointments to six when he took over Blackpool in May 1976. His earlier positions had been at Luton Town, Torquay United, Bury, Nottingham Forest and Southport.

Joe Mercer, Bill Nicholson and Don Revie rank as the only men who ever led their teams to the Football League championship plus winning the F.A. Cup, Football League Cup and one or other of the major European cup competitions.

Nine managers have achieved the double of F.A. Cup and League Championship winning teams since the war: Tom Whittaker and Bertie Mee (both Arsenal), Matt Busby (Manchester United), Joe Mercer (Manchester City), Bill Shankly (Liverpool), Harry Catterick (Everton), Bill Nicholson (Tottenham Hotspur), Don Revie (Leeds United) and Stan Cullis (Wolverhampton Wanderers).

Only three members of England's World Cup-winning team of 1966 have had spells as Football League managers, two of them with the same club.

They were Nobby Stiles, who became manager of Preston North End in 1977–78, the club with whom Bobby Charlton had previously acted as player-manager and Bobby's elder brother Jack Charlton who took over as manager of Sheffield Wednesday after holding a similar position with Middlesbrough.

After a pair of Taylor brothers had played together as a full-back partnership with Wolverhampton Wanderers, both first became Football League club managers within eight days of each other – Frank, the younger, with Stoke City on 16 June 1952 and Jack with Queen's Park Rangers on 24 June.

No Football League club is being managed by a former referee in the competition at present but Herbert Bamlett (Manchester United and Middlesbrough), David Ashworth and Matt McQueen (Liverpool), Jimmy Jewell (Norwich City), Harry Curtis (Brentford) and Captain Albert Prince-Cox (Bristol Rovers) all formerly made a success of the role after being noted referees. The latter combined the membership of the Bristol club with promoting boxing and later running a circus during the holiday season.

Former goalkeepers who have become Football League managers have been rare and Plymouth Argyle created a situation without parallel in the Football League's entire history when they sacked former England international goalkeeper Tony Waiters and replaced him with former Queen's Park Rangers and Birmingham City goalkeeper Mike Kelly.

Managers have tended to become younger in recent years. But none was as youthful as one engaged in August 1946. Carlisle United then made Ivor Broadis (later to become an England international inside-forward) player-manager when he was 23 years old – the game's youngest such appointment.

Thus Carlisle have been responsible for both the youngest and oldest post war appointments of managers undergoing their first experience in the life because in November 1976 they engaged Dick Young, who was 57 years old at the time.

There has been only one post war instance of a club winning either the Division Three or Four championship without an official 'permanent' manager in charge. Doncaster Rovers became Division Four champions in the 1965–66 season when Jackie Bestall was acting as 'caretaker' manager.

Brentford manager Bill Dodgin used to be a Fulham and Arsenal centre-half, then Millwall's assistant manager and manager of Q.P.R. and Fulham, so he has seen service with six clubs in London. But even that still leaves him one behind current Manchester United chief Dave Sexton, appointed during 1977–78, who had spells at various levels with seven clubs in the capital.

In 1965 Tommy Docherty, when Chelsea's manager, gave a trial to 15 year old Bruce Rioch but could not sign him because the club had its maximum permitted quota of apprentice professionals. In July 1969, Docherty, as Aston Villa's manager, paid Luton Town a six-figure fee for the services of Rioch.

At Stockport at the start of the 1977–78 season, player-manager Alan Thompson was then 25 years old while County winger Mike Summerbee, previously with Manchester City Burnley and Blackpool was just under 35.

When David Steele, as Bradford Park Avenue manager, turned out in an emergency in a wartime match against Sheffield Wednesday in October 1942, his age exceeded the combined ages of three other members of the team – Billy Elliott, Johnny Downie and Geoff Walker. Steele was 49 at the time and the three youngsters were 16-year-olds.

Before World War Two there was, with one exception, no England team-manager. The exception was a last minute decision to allow a manager travelling unofficially with the F.A. party to take over charge of the team shortly before their match. This was when the Arsenal manager, Herbert Chapman, travelled to Rome with the England team which drew 1–1 with Italy on 13 May 1933. One assumes that he was also in charge for the second game of this tour – with Switzerland in Berne where they won 4–0 – but his appointment was so informal that it can practically be dismissed from any list of England team-managers.

Before the war, and indeed for several years afterwards, England teams were selected by an International Committee, and if ever anyone could be said to have been in charge of the England team it was a member of the International Committee, although he, of course, did not discuss tactics but merely concerned himself with arrangements off the field.

The first time the F.A. actually appointed a team-manager and advised him of their decision well in advance of the game for which he was to be in charge was in April 1946 when they informed

Tom Whittaker, the Arsenal trainer, that they would require his services as manager of the England team to meet Switzerland at Stamford Bridge on 11 May 1946 and France in Paris eight days later. These were Victory Internationals and England won the first game 4–1 but lost the second 2–1.

However, even this appointment was only a temporary one for the F.A. were somewhat reluctantly, it seemed, considering the appointment of a full-time manager. The man pressing for such an appointment to be made was the F.A's secretary, Stanley Rous, and he had his way in the summer of 1946 when former Manchester United half-back Walter Winterbottom was appointed director of coaching and England team manager. The first official England international game in which Winterbottom actually took charge of the team was that against Ireland in Belfast on 28 September 1946. England won 7–2. He had, however, been present a month earlier when England met Scotland at Maine Road, Manchester, in aid of the Bolton Disaster Fund.

Surprisingly enough there was considerable resistance to the appointment of an England team-manager both inside and outside the F.A., and it is true to say that during his appointment, which lasted until August 1962 when he resigned to become general secretary of the Central Council of Physical Education, he never had the power that one would expect a man in this position to be given.

The first man to be granted this power was his successor Alf Ramsey (later Sir Alfred) who was appointed in October 1962 and officially took over his new office in May 1963, though he was in charge of the team for the first time in February of that year for a European Nations Cup match in Paris against France which ended in a 5–2 defeat for England.

Goalscoring

Frank Bokas had his first-class career restricted to four seasons because of the Second World War, one with Blackpool in Division Two and three with Barnsley, the first two in that division and the last in Division Three (Northern Section). This Scot, who had begun his career with Kirkintilloch Rob Roy, was a left-half and Barnsley paid only £250 when they secured his transfer from Blackpool in 1936.

However, Bokas achieved a special place in the game's history because he did something which has eluded players with longer careers. This rare feat, especially in an important match, was to score with a throw-in. It is, of course, not permitted to score direct from a throw-in, but Bokas came as near to that as makes little difference.

The occasion was a fourth round F.A. Cup tie at Oakwell, between Barnsley and Manchester United, then one of the most successful sides in the country and heading for promotion from Division Two. It was on 22 January 1938.

This exciting match was long remembered by the crowd of nearly 36,000. The inimitable Johnny Carey put the visitors ahead, but in the 13th minute left-half Bokas equalised in a most astonishing manner. Taking a throw-in from a point in line with the edge of the penalty area, he floated the ball high into the goalmouth. Whether Tom Breen, United's Irish international goalkeeper, was surprised by the length of the throw or not, the fact was that he was caught a little too far forward, and although he got a hand to it he could not prevent it from dropping behind him under the bar for the equaliser.

The cheers echoed around Oakwell when the crowd recovered from the momentary shock of such an extraordinary solo effort and the game ended in a 2–2 draw, though Barnsley lost the replay 1–0 at Old Trafford.

The old adage that a game is never lost until it is won was proved again at Stamford Bridge in

Name	Clubs	Years	Goals	Games
Seven players have scored more than 350 goals in Football League and Scottish League games:				
Arthur Rowley	West Bromwich Albion, Leicester City, Shrewsbury Town	1946–65	434	619
Jimmy McGrory	Celtic, Clydebank	1922–38	410	408
Hughie Gallacher	Airdrieonians, Newcastle United, Chelsea, Derby County, Notts County, Grimsby Town, Gateshead	1921–39	387	541
Dixie Dean	Tranmere Rovers, Everton, Notts County	1923–39	379	437
Hugh Ferguson	Motherwell, Cardiff City, Dundee	1916–30	361	422
Jimmy Greaves	Chelsea, Tottenham Hotspur, West Ham United	1957–71	357	516
Steve Bloomer	Derby County (two spells), Middlesbrough	1892–1914	352	600

Division One on 21 December 1907, when with less than 20 minutes remaining Chelsea were leading Bury 3–1 and seemingly well set for victory. They suffered no injuries yet still lost 4–3. The referee was blamed for awarding a questionable free-kick which the Chelsea goalkeeper completely misjudged and allowed Bury to nip in and score. This was the turning point of the game.

In 1925 Chesterfield signed one of two brothers who were with Manchester City, **Jimmy Cookson.** His elder brother Sammy later went to Bradford. They were both full-backs, but in October 1925 Chesterfield, having suffered three defeats in a row and slipping to 20th in the table were desperate for a centre-forward. They decided to give Jimmy Cookson a chance in this position for the game at Tranmere and he obliged with three goals in a 4–0 victory – one of the most prolific goalscorers in Football history had been discovered.

In this first season as a centre-forward Jimmy Cookson scored 44 goals in Division Three (Northern Section) and added another 42 in his next season.

West Bromwich Albion were fortunate enough to secure his transfer in the summer of 1927, and on 17 December that year, in a 3–0 victory over South Shields, Cookson created a new Football League record by hitting his 100th goal in only his 87th League game. When he completed his career in 1939, after spells with Plymouth Argyle and Swindon Town, he had scored a total of 256 goals in 292 games, including six for West Bromwich Albion in a 6–3 victory over Blackpool in September 1927.

There were many remarkable goalscoring feats during the First World War but nothing to excel what happened in the 1915–16 season. One was Preston North End's 8–0 defeat by Manchester City at Hyde Road. This was the victory that clinched the Championship of the League's wartime Lancashire Section competition, and the hero of the match was **Private Albert Fairclough,** who was re-appearing in the side after a long absence and taking the place of his brother Peter at centre-forward. He scored five goals in succession.

Preston had difficulty in raising a team for this game and actually arrived at Manchester Station with only nine men. There they encountered some members of the Bury team, returning from

Oldham where their game had been abandoned because of snow, and obtained the club's permission to include two Bury players, Chorlton and Edwards.

Preston's difficulties did not end there, however, for just before half-time, when they were 3–0 down, they lost right-back, Threlfall, with an ankle injury.

Cartwright and Barnes opened the scoring for Manchester City before Fairclough netted the last five, four in the second half.

The finest scoring combination of this season was Chelsea. They were led by **Bobby Thomson**, a centre-forward who had only one eye, and had one of the cleverest forwards in the game's history, **Charlie Buchan**, at inside-right. These two combined together with considerable effect. On 13 November 1915, Buchan scored five goals in succession against Clapton Orient, but on 11 March 1916, Thomson scored seven in an 11–1 win against Luton Town at Stamford Bridge. On this occasion Buchan scored the other four.

Charlie Buchan. (Syndication International)

On the same day that Chelsea were defeating Luton, **Jimmy Morris** hit five goals for Preston in a 6–1 victory over Bolton Wanderers at Burnden Park, and **Jimmy McIlvenny**, making only his second appearance in the centre-forward position for Bradford City, also registered all five against Rochdale. A few weeks earlier this player had scored five when Bradford City had beaten Hull City 8–4 at Valley Parade. He had scored a hat-trick in his previous game when he was playing at left-half.

Incidentally, **Sam Stevens** scored three consecutive goals for Hull City in that 8–4 defeat.

On Good Friday 1916 Chelsea beat Arsenal 9–0 with Buchan scoring three and Thomson another five goals. These two players headed the list of goalscorers in the London Combination section of the war-time League that season with Thomson netting 39 goals in 31 games, and Buchan 38 goals in 30 appearances.

Another of the many shock results in 1915–16 took place at Herne Hill, then the home of Crystal Palace, when they beat Reading 10–1. On this occasion **Sid Sanders** scored three goals in seven minutes and went on to total six.

At the end of 1978–79 season, **Ted MacDougall** was the most prolific scoring player still active in the Football League with 248 goals in the competition. His first League club had been Liverpool but he made his League debut with York City and subsequently played for Bournemouth, Manchester United, West Ham United, Norwich City and Southampton. In November 1978 he returned to Bournemouth. Of the 92 clubs in membership of the Football League that season, he had played on the grounds of all except Swindon Town. But his appearance at Wigan Athletic's Springfield Park had been for Runcorn Reserves before he came into League football.

A Scot from Inverness, he was capped seven times by his country during his service with Norwich. MacDougall also set up the record individual score in an F.A. Cup match when he scored nine goals against Margate for Bournemouth in the first round on 20 November 1971.

Jimmy Hampson established both the individual and aggregate scoring records for Blackpool between the wars. But he might well have added to both totals. Signed in October 1927 from Nelson where he had spent two years after starting his career with Walkden Park and Little Hulton St Johns, a team in his Lancashire home town, he cost Blackpool only £2,000. A centre- or inside-forward, Hampson scored 31 goals in 32 League games in his first season for them. Blackpool escaped relegation by a point and the crowd at Bloomfield Road chaired him from the pitch.

The following season he scored 40 goals and finished as top scorer in Division Two. In 1929–30 he set up a club record with 45 goals out of the 98 registered by Blackpool in League matches and his total was not bettered by any player in the country. Blackpool also achieved 58 points and won promotion as champions of the division.

On Good Friday 1930 Oldham Athletic, one of their closest challengers, attracted a then record crowd of 23,000 to Bloomfield Road who paid £1,825. Blackpool won 3–0 and on Easter Monday at Oldham they clinched promotion by winning 2–1. Hampson even missed a penalty.

In 1930–31 he scored 32 in Division One, as his team again missed relegation by a point, and made the first of three appearances for England, scoring on his debut against Ireland in October 1930 and twice against Wales a month later.

The following season his 23 goals again helped towards yet another narrow one point escape but another 18 goals in 1932–33 could not prevent relegation. But he kept scoring goals and had the satisfaction of being selected for England again in December 1932 when Austria made their first visit to this country. Hampson scored twice in the first 25 minutes to play a significant role in a memorable 4–3 victory at Stamford Bridge.

It took Blackpool four seasons to regain their Division One status and, as runners-up in Division Two in 1936–37, Hampson collected 18 goals. Mid-way through 1937–38 in his 30th year he had added four more League goals in 19 matches bringing his total to 247 in 360 games.

On 10 January 1938 he went on a fishing trip in a small boat from Fleetwood. He was presumed drowned as his body was never recovered.

George Camsell made only nine full international appearances for England and those spread over seven years, but he succeeded in scoring in every one of them and registered a total of 18 goals. He scored four times against Belgium on 11 May 1929 in a 5–1 win and three at Stamford Bridge, Chelsea against Wales on 20 November the same year in a 6–0 success.

Camsell played for Durham Chapel, Tow Law Town, Esh Winning and Durham City before joining Middlesbrough in October 1925. He scored 346 League goals with Durham and Middlesbrough, and remained with the latter club until retiring during the Second World War. He then became in turn, the club's chief scout, coach and assistant secretary until retiring through ill-health in 1963. His total of League goals included 326 for Middlesbrough alone.

One of the most resounding Football League debuts ever made was that by **George Hilsdon,** a Londoner from the East End, soon after he was signed by Chelsea in 1906.

Hilsdon had been scoring a few goals for West Ham United reserves when he was spotted by Chelsea's player-manager, Jackie Robertson, on the look out for more talent to strengthen his side in only their second season as members of Division Two of the Football League. They had finished in third position in their first season and it was obvious that it would not take much to turn this side into a promotion-winning one. It was Hilsdon who provided that little extra.

The new centre-forward made his Football League debut on the opening day of the 1906–07 season when Glossop were visitors to Stamford Bridge. Glossop were beaten 9–2 and Hilsdon created a goalscoring record for a player making his League debut by scoring five goals.

He certainly made an impression for only six weeks later he was in the Football League side that beat the Irish League in Belfast and scored three goals in a 6–0 victory.

By the end of his first season of League football Hilsdon had scored 27 goals in 32 appearances and Chelsea won promotion to Division One. The Chelsea supporters nicknamed him 'Gatling Gun' after the rapid-firing machine gun.

In the 1919–20 season before the old Southern League was absorbed into the Football League to form the new Division Three, Millwall, or Millwall Athletic as they were then known, scored a total of 52 Southern League goals. Centre-forward **Jimmy Broad** scored 32 of these goals, which made him the highest scorer in the Southern League that season, although his team finished below half-way in the table.

Broad came from a football family. His brother Tommy was with Bristol City while Jimmy was with Oldham Athletic before joining Millwall after the First World War. They joined Stoke City together in 1921 and Jimmy helped them into Division One in 1921–22 with 25 goals in 41 games. Jimmy was later with Everton, New Brighton and Watford, while brother Tommy went to Southampton. Their father, also Jimmy, was Manchester City's trainer for many years. During the First World War Jimmy Jnr. also scored goals for Greenock Morton in the Scottish League.

On 1 December 1964, Leicester City beat Coventry City 8–1 in a fifth round, Football League Cup tie. The game was played at Coventry's Highfield Road. It not only represents the highest score in this stage of the League Cup but the biggest ever away victory in the history of the competition.

Leicester were leading 3–1 at half-time. Their scorers were Stringfellow 2, Hodgson 2, Curtis o.g., Gibson and Norman 2. Hudson scored for Coventry.

Among the spectators at this game was centre-forward **Ken Keyworth** who had just been transferred from Leicester City to Coventry City. While it did not seem as if Leicester would miss his services it must have been painfully obvious to him that his new club were desperately in need of another goalscorer. As a matter of fact he obliged with a goal for Coventry on his debut for them the following Saturday against Rotherham, but they still lost 5–3 at home. Four goals scored and 13 conceded in two successive home matches.

Tommy Lawton might well have become one of the most prolific scoring centre-forwards produced in modern times but for the Second World War. He succeeded Dixie Dean with Everton, after being transferred from Burnley at the age of 17 for £6,500 in 1936. Up to the war he had scored 66 goals in 87 games for Everton and in all matches in the period 1939–45 he scored a further 212 in matches for Everton and as a guest for Tranmere Rovers, Aldershot and Chelsea. He was transferred to Chelsea and then Notts County paid a record for a Division Three club of £20,000 for his services in 1947. He subsequently assisted Brentford and Arsenal.

His peace-time total before and after the war with six clubs was 236. He made 23 full appearances for England over the same period and scored 22 goals, while in another 23 war-time and victory internationals he amassed an impressive 25 more goals.

Hugh Kilpatrick (Hughie) Gallacher scored 387 League goals in 541 matches between 1921 and 1939. He started his career with Bellshill Athletic in his native Scotland, before joining Queen of the South in 1920 at 17 for £6 a week.

On 29 January 1921 Queens played St. Cuthbert Wanderers in a friendly at home. Gallacher, who had already become a junior international, was on trial from Bellshill. He scored four goals in a 7–0 win. In fact, in his first seven games he scored 18 goals.

At the end of the 1921–22 season he returned as a guest player in the Southern Counties Charity Cup and scored another five.

He then signed for Airdrie on 9 May while convalescing from double pneumonia. He had worked on munitions during the World War and then down the pits. His transfer to Newcastle in December 1925 cost £5,750 and he scored 13

Tommy Lawton a prolific scoring centre-forward in his day. (Popperfoto)

Hughie Gallacher a prolific-scoring Scot in English football between the two World Wars. (Colorsport)

goals in his first seven games including two on his debut. The following season his 36 goals set up a club record which has not been beaten at St. James Park.

Gallacher moved to Chelsea in May 1930 for £10,000 after a disagreement, but on his return to Newcastle on 3 September a crowd of 68,385 turned up to watch him; an attendance never beaten at the ground and this reflected his popularity which remained throughout.

He scored five goals then four on the same ground in two matches ending 7–3. He had five in succession for the Scottish League against the Irish League at Belfast on 11 November 1925 and four for Scotland against Ireland there on 23 February 1929. Some sources give Alex James' goal to him, making it five again. He had also achieved the hat-trick in a Scottish League trial at Tynecastle on 4 March 1925 and scored five out of six goals for Airdrie v Clyde in a Scottish League match at Airdrie on 29 September 1923. He had a spell of 30 goals in five matches at one time. In 20 international matches he scored 23 goals.

In 1938–39, his last full season, he scored 18 goals in 31 League games for Gateshead in the Division Three (Northern Section). And at the time his aggregate of transfer fees still represented a record though his market value had dropped alarmingly as Derby paid £3,000 for him in 1934, Notts County £2,000, Grimsby £1,000 and finally Gateshead £500.

Despite being just under 5ft. 6in., he was an outstanding centre-forward at his peak with agility, speed, control, spirit, finish and heading ability. Off the field a broken marriage and death of his baby son were early set-backs. Though generous he was restless, highly temperamental and his move to the London area accentuated his drinking problems. Often sent off and suspended, on one occasion he voluntarily left a match for five minutes to cool down.

On 11 June 1957 at the age of 54, after a variety of menial jobs, he threw himself under the Edinburgh to York express at Dead Man's Crossing at Low Fall, near his Gateshead home, on the day before he was to appear in court.

Before making his debut in the Football League Gallacher had scored 91 Scottish League goals. His total in the Football League was 296 in 430 games, a figure which puts him well ahead of any of his countrymen.

By coincidence the Scot with the second highest total of goals in the Football League until the 1978–79 season, made his debut in England during the same season as Gallacher, and also in the north-east. This was **David Halliday** who joined Sunderland from Dundee in the summer of

David Halliday a free-scoring centre forward in Scotland and England.

1925. He was quite a different style of centre-forward at six feet and powerfully built. Although he did not score as many goals as his smaller countryman, he scored them at a faster rate, and by the time he had completed his Football League career with Sunderland, Arsenal, Manchester City and Clapton Orient (going to Yeovil Town as player-manager in 1935) he had netted 244 Football League goals in 309 appearances. His 42 goals for Sunderland in 42 Division One matches in 1928–29 is still a record for the Roker Park club. Before coming south, David Halliday had scored 94 goals in the Scottish League with St. Mirren and Dundee.

John Charles joined Swansea Town's ground staff in 1945. He played only three games with the Swansea 'A' team in the 1945–46 season and none at all the following year. But he was seen by a Leeds United scout during a kickabout game in a Swansea park and was approached to join the Elland Road club. On 18 September 1947 at 16 he went to Leeds, then managed by Major Frank Buckley.

He played variously at right-back, left-half and right-half, graduating from the 'A' team to reserves and at Easter 1948 he played centre-half for the first time in a Central League game at Preston. It was at centre-half that he made his League debut at the age of 17 and on 8 March 1950 he made his debut for Wales, as their youngest international.

John Charles (centre) revealing his prowess in the air. (Popperfoto)

In the spring of 1951 he was switched to centre-forward for the first time against Manchester City and though moved back, he remained there for virtually the rest of his career. In the 1953–54 season he scored 42 League goals and later helped Leeds win promotion to Division One. In 1956–57 he had scored 38 goals in Division One and was the top scorer in the division when Juventus paid a record British fee of £65,000 for his services.

He scored 93 goals in 155 appearances for the Italian club before returning to Leeds in August 1962 but he went back to Italy three months later, joining Roma for £70,000. Back to Wales in August 1963 it was Cardiff City who obtained his signature and he ended his career as player-manager with Hereford United and then Merthyr. He made 39 appearances for Wales and scored 15 goals. His total for Leeds in two spells, Roma and Cardiff was 388 matches and 175 goals.

Bob Hatton was the leading scorer in Division Two in the 1977–78 season with 22 League goals for Blackpool. On 4 February 1978 before the match against Blackburn Rovers, he was presented with a silver salver for scoring three hat-tricks in the season. He completed his fourth that afternoon beating a club record set up by Hampson and actually scored four times in a 5–2 win over Blackburn. Blackpool were seventh in the division at the time.

During the following week Hatton suffered a hamstring injury playing squash and missed the next six matches, only one of which Blackpool won. Hatton reappeared for the last nine matches but scored in only two of them. Blackpool did not win any of these and were relegated as the third club from the bottom.

Hatton, born in Hull, had started his career with Wolverhampton Wanderers, scoring after 30 seconds of his debut against Portsmouth in 1966–67. Subsequently he played for Bolton Wanderers, Northampton Town, Carlisle United and Birmingham City and joined Luton Town in July 1978 when his total of League goals was 145.

Jimmy Jones was one of the most promising young centre-forwards in Northern Ireland and had played three times for the Irish League before his 18th birthday. He was 20 when he played for Belfast Celtic against Linfield on Boxing Day 1948 at Windsor Park. It was a rough match. One Linfield player sustained a broken ankle, and another a chest injury. At the end of the match Jones, who had been involved in the collision which led to the first injury, was attacked by a section of the crowd. He was punched, kicked and thrown over a wall and sustained a broken leg. Windsor Park was closed for a month. Jones had to have his leg re-set twice and was out of action for two years with his career apparently ended. But he fought his way back to fitness and signed for Larne. Before kicking a ball for them he was transferred to Fulham in March 1950 but the Football League refused to register him as he had received £4,000 compensation for malicious injuries in November 1949. Jones returned to Ireland and signed for Glenavon.

On 11 April 1956 Jones made his international debut for Northern Ireland against Wales. Though overweight by now he still had the distinction of scoring on his debut in a 1–1 draw. He played in the subsequent match against England which was also drawn 1–1 and made one more appearance in the following year against Wales in a goalless draw.

He continued scoring goals for Glenavon and reached a total of 583 before retiring and he even had the misfortune to break his shoulder in a motor cycle accident.

Cliff Holton scored 295 League goals in a career in the Football League which lasted from 1950 to 1968 and embraced service with Arsenal, Watford (in two spells), Northampton Town, Crystal Palace, Charlton Athletic and Leyton Orient. In the early part of his career he had been a full-back and wing-half and might well have added to his total of goals but for this fact. Yet he might not have played professional football at all.

An amateur with Oxford City he had decided to join the Royal Air Force on an eight year engagement as a flight mechanic. He passed his medical but was sent home pending the arrival of his indentures which had to be cancelled as he was an apprentice tool-maker at the time. During that time Arsenal approached him, he decided to sign, played right-back against Cambridge University in a friendly and then turned professional. Two months later he was called up for his National Service in the Army.

MAJOR RECORDS

Highest scores – Teams
First-class match
Arbroath 36 Bon Accord 0, Scottish Cup first round, 5 September 1885

International
England 13 Northern Ireland 0, 18 February 1882

F.A. Cup
Preston North End 26 Hyde United 0, first round, 15 October 1887.

Football League
Newcastle United 13 Newport County 0, Division Two, 5 October 1946
Stockport County 13 Halifax Town 0, Division Three (Northern), 6 January 1934

Scottish League
Celtic 11 Dundee 0, Division One, 26 October 1895
East Fife 13 Edinburgh City 2, Division Two, 11 December 1937

Aggregate
Tranmere Rovers 13 Oldham Athletic 4, Division Three (Northern) 26 December 1935

Most goals in a season
Football League
134 goals by Peterborough United, Division Four, 1960–61 in 46 matches

Scottish League
142 goals by Raith Rovers, Division Two, 1937–38 in 34 matches

Most goals - Individual
Match
13 goals by John Petrie for Arbroath v Bon Accord, Scottish Cup first round, 5 September 1885

Career
1,329 goals by Artur Friedenreich in Brazilian football between 1910–1930

Most League appearances
The record for Football League appearances is the 824 by Terry Paine for Southampton and Hereford United, 1957 to 1977.

ATTENDANCE RECORDS

Any match
205,000 (199,854 paid) for the Brazil v Uruguay match in the 1950 World Cup final series on 16 July 1950 at the Maracana Stadium, Rio de Janeiro.

European Cup
136,505 for the Celtic v Leeds United semifinal at Hampden Park, Glasgow, on 15 April 1970.

International
149,547 for the Scotland v England international at Hampden Park, Glasgow, on 17 April 1937.

F.A. Cup final
160,000 (estimated) for the Bolton Wanderers v West Ham United match at Wembley on 28 April 1923 (counted admissions were 126,047).

Scottish Cup final
146,433 for the Celtic v Aberdeen final at Hampden Park, Glasgow, on 24 April 1937.

Football League
Division One: Manchester United v Arsenal at Maine Road, 17 January 1948, 83,260.

Division Two: Aston Villa v Coventry City at Villa Park, 30 October 1937, 68,029.

Division Three (Southern): Cardiff City v Bristol City at Ninian Park, 7 April 1947, 51,621.

Division Three (Northern): Hull City v Rotherham United at Boothferry Park, 25 December 1948, 49,655.

Division Three: Aston Villa v Bournemouth at Villa Park, 12 February 1972, 48,110.

Division Four: Crystal Palace v Millwall at Selhurst Park, 31 March 1961, 37,774.

Scottish League: Rangers v Celtic, Ibrox Park, 2 January 1939, 118,567.

EUROPEAN SOCCER

EUROPEAN FOOTBALL CHAMPIONSHIP

The European Football Championship of 1978–80 will be finalised in the spring of 1980 with the seven group qualifiers joining the host nation Italy in a final tournament. It will be organised along the same lines as the final stages of the World Cup with two groups from countries each initially then a final and match for third and fourth place. This is a new departure from previous competitions which have produced a straight knock-out basis when the quarter-final stage has been reached. In the past also it has been a practice for only the European Championship semi-finals to be held by the host nation,

EUROPEAN FOOTBALL CHAMPIONSHIP (FORMERLY NATIONS CUP) RECORD OF COMPETING TEAMS 1958–1976

		P	W	D	L	F	A
1	USSR	38	23	7	8	68	34
2	Yugoslavia	37	19	9	9	63	40
3	Czechoslovakia	32	19	6	7	78	32

		P	W	D	L	F	A
4	Spain	32	17	9	6	61	24
5	Hungary	35	18	7	10	69	43
6	Italy	29	14	10	5	47	20
7	West Germany	24	14	8	2	53	20
8	England	26	15	6	5	50	22
9	France	32	13	8	11	65	49
10	Bulgaria	27	13	6	8	44	30
11	Holland	26	13	4	9	60	36
12	Belgium	26	12	5	9	39	40
13	Portugal	25	11	6	8	35	32
14	Rumania	27	10	8	9	51	42
15	East Germany	24	9	7	8	38	35
16	Sweden	24	9	6	9	28	33
17	Austria	23	9	4	10	43	37
18	Scotland	18	8	5	5	22	21
19	Poland	22	8	5	9	34	31
20	Wales	22	8	5	9	31	28
21	Republic of Ireland	26	8	5	13	30	46
22	Northern Ireland	22	8	4	10	26	21
23	Turkey	22	7	5	10	16	40
24	Switzerland	20	7	4	9	36	32
25	Denmark	29	6	5	18	34	62
26	Greece	19	5	6	8	24	33
27	Norway	22	3	3	16	23	55
28	Luxembourg	23	1	5	17	17	87
29	Albania	12	2	2	8	6	25
30	Iceland	8	1	3	4	6	13
31	Finland	18	0	4	14	9	41
32	Malta	14	1	1	12	6	45
33	Cyprus	18	1	0	17	5	77

EUROPEAN CHAMPIONSHIP FINALS

Season Series	Games Goals The Final Final				Attendances Overall	Average No of entries
1958–60	(10 July 1960, Paris att. 17,966) USSR (Metreveli, Ponedelnik)	(0) (1) 2	Yugoslavia (Netto o.g.)		(1) (1) 1	17
1962–64	(21 June 1964, Madrid att. 120,000) Spain (Pereda, Marcelino)	(1) 2	USSR (Khusainov)		(1) 1	29
1966–68	(8 June 1968, Rome att. 75,000) Italy (Domenghini)	(0) (1) 1	Yugoslavia (Dzajic)		(1) (1) 1	31
Replay	(10 June 1968, Rome att. 60,000) Italy (Riva, Anastasi)	(2) 2	Yugoslavia		(0) 0	
1970–72	(18 June 1972, Brussels att. 43,437) West Germany (Muller (G) 2, Wimmer)	(1) 3	USSR		(0) 0	32
1974–76	(20 June 1976, Belgrade att. 45,000) Czechoslovakia (Svehlik, Dobias) Czechoslovakia won 5–3 on penalties	(2) (2) 2	West Germany (Muller (D), Holzenbein)		(1) (2) 2	32

European Cup Records

EUROPEAN CHAMPION CLUBS CUP

Season	Games	Goals	The Final	Attendances Overall	Average
1955–56	29	127	13.6.56, Paris, 38,000 **Real Madrid (2) 4, Stade de Reims (2) 3** Di Stefano, Rial 2, Marquitos; Leblond, Templin, Hidalgo	912,000	31,450
1956–57	44	170	30.5.57, Madrid, 124,000 **Real Madrid (0) 2, Fiorentina (0) 0** Di Stefano (pen), Gento	1,786,000	40,590
1957–58	48	189	28.5.58, Brussels, 67,000 **Real Madrid (0) (2) 3, AC Milan (0) (2) 2** **(a.e.t.)** Di Stefano, Rial, Gento; Schiaffino, Grillo	1,790,000	37,290
1958–59	55	199	2.6.59, Stuttgart, 80,000 **Real Madrid (1) 2, Stade de Reims (0) 0** Mateos, Di Stefano	2,010,000	36,545
1959–60	52	218	18.5.60, Glasgow, 135,000 **Real Madrid (3) 7, Eintracht Frankfurt (1) 3** Di Stefano 3, Puskas 4; Kress, Stein 2	2,780,000	50,545
1960–61	51	166	31.3.61, Berne, 28,000 **Benfica (2) 3, Barcelona (1) 2** Aguas, Ramallets (og), Coluna; Kocsis, Czibor	1,850,000	36,274
1961–62	55	221	2.5.62, Amsterdam, 65,000 **Benfica (2) 5, Real Madrid (3) 3** Aguas, Cavem, Coluna, Eusebio 2; Puskas 3	2,135,000	45,727
1962–63	59	214	22.5.63, London, 45,000 **AC Milan (0) 2, Benfica (1) 1** Altafini 2; Eusebio	2,158,000	36,593
1963–64	61	212	27.5.64, Vienna, 74,000 **Inter Milan (1) 3, Real Madrid (0) 1** Mazzola 2, Milani; Felo	2,180,000	35,737
1964–65	62	215	28.5.65, Milan, 80,000 **Inter Milan (1) 1, Benfica (0) 0** Jair	2,577,000	41,564
1965–66	58	234	11.5.66, Brussels, 55,000 **Real Madrid (0) 2, Partizan Belgrade (1) 1** Amancio, Serena; Vasovic	2,112,000	36,431
1966–67	65	211	25.5.67, Lisbon, 56,000 **Celtic (0) 2, Inter Milan (1) 1** Gemmell, Chalmers; Mazzola (pen)	2,248,000	34,584
1967–68	60	162	29.5.68, London, 100,000 **Manchester United (0) (1) 4, Benfica (0) (1) 1 (a.e.t.)** Charlton 2, Best, Kidd; Graca	2,544,000	42,500
1968–69	52	176	28.5.69, Madrid, 50,000 **AC Milan (2) 4, Ajax (0) 1** Prati 3, Sormani; Vasovic (pen)	2,056,000	39,540
1969–70	63	202	6.5.70, Milan, 50,000 **Feyenoord (1) (1) 2, Celtic (1) (1) 1 (a.e.t.)** Israel, Kindvall; Gemmell	2,345,000	37,222
1970–71	63	210	2.6.71, London, 90,000 **Ajax (1) 2, Panathinaikos (0) 0** Van Dijk, Kapsis (og)	2,124,000	33,714
1971–72	64	175	31.5.72, Rotterdam, 67,000 **Ajax (0) 2, Inter Milan (0) 0** Cruyff 2	2,066,976	32,280
1972–73	58	160	30.5.73, Belgrade, 93,500 **Ajax (0) 1, Juventus (0) 0** Rep	1,712,277	30,000
1973–74	60	180	15.5.74, Brussels, 65,000 **Bayern Munich (0) (0) 1, Atletico Madrid (0) (0) 1 (a.e.t.)** Schwarzenbeck; Luis		
		replay:	17.5.74, Brussels, 65,000 **Bayern Munich (1) 4, Atletico Madrid (0) 0** Muller 2, Hoeness 2	1,586,852	26,448
1974–75	55	174	28.5.75, Paris, 50,000 **Bayern Munich (0) 2, Leeds United (0) 0** Roth, Muller	1,380,254	25,096
1975–76	61	202	12.5.76, Glasgow, 54,864 **Bayern Munich (0) 1, St Etienne (0) 0** Roth	1,736,087	28,460
1976–77	61	155	25.5.77, Rome, 57,000 **Liverpool (1) 3, Borussia Moenchengladbach (0) 1** McDermott, Smith, Neal (pen); Simonsen	2,010,000	34,325
1977–78	59	172	10.5.78, London, 92,000 **Liverpool (0) 1, FC Bruges (0) 0** Dalglish	1,509,471	25,584
1978–79	*		30.5.79, Munich, 57,500 **Nottingham Forest (1) 1, Malmo (0) 0** Francis	*	

*Figures not available at the time of going to press

EUROPEAN CUP-WINNERS CUP

Season	Games	Goals	The Final	Attendances Overall	Average
1960–61	18	60	1st leg, 17.5.61, Glasgow, 80,000 **Rangers (0) 0, Fiorentina (1) 2** Milan 2		
			2nd leg, 27.5.61, Florence, 50,000 **Fiorentina (1) 2, Rangers (1) 1** Milan, Hamrin; Scott	290,000	16,111
1961–62	44	174	10.5.62, Glasgow, 27,389 **Fiorentina (1) 1, Atletico Madrid (1) 1** Hamrin; Piero		
		replay:	5.9.62, Stuttgart, 45,000 **Atletico Madrid (2) 3, Fiorentina (0) 0** Jones, Mendonca, Piero	650,000	14,733
1962–63	48	169	15.5.63, Rotterdam, 25,000 **Tottenham Hotspur (2) 5, Atletico Madrid (0) 1** Greaves 2, White, Dyson 2; Collar (pen)	1,100,000	22,916
1963–64	62	202	13.5.64, Brussels, 9,000 **MTK Budapest (1) (3) 3, Sporting Lisbon (1) (3) 3 (a.e.t.)** Sandor 2, Kuti; Figueiredo 2, Dansky (og)		
		replay:	15.5.64, Antwerp, 18,000 **Sporting Lisbon (1) 1, MTK Budapest (0) 0** Mendes	1,300,000	20,967
1964–65	61	163	19.5.65, London, 100,000 **West Ham United (0) 2, Munich 1860 (0) 0** Sealey 2	1,100,000	18,032
1965–66	59	188	5.5.66, Glasgow, 41,657 **Borussia Dortmund (0) (1) 2, Liverpool (0) (1) 1 (a.e.t.)** Held, Yeats (og); Hunt	1,546,000	26,203
1966–67	61	170	31.5.67, Nuremberg, 69,480 **Bayern Munich (0) (0) 1, Rangers (0) (0) 0 (a.e.t.)** Roth	1,556,000	25,508
1967–68	64	200	23.5.68, Rotterdam, 60,000 **AC Milan (2) 2, SV Hamburg (0) 0** Hamrin 2	1,683,000	26,269
1968–69	51	157	21.5.69, Basle, 40,000 **Slovan Bratislava (3) 3, Barcelona (1) 2** Cvetler, Hrivnak, Jan Capkovic; Zaldua, Rexach	957,000	18,765
1969–70	64	179	29.4.70, Vienna, 10,000 **Manchester City (2) 2, Gornik Zabrze (0) 1** Young, Lee (pen); Ozlizlo	1,675,000	25,890
1970–71	67	203	19.5.71, Athens, 42,000 **Chelsea (0) (1) 1, Real Madrid (0) (1) 1** Osgood; Zoco		
		replay:	21.5.71, Athens, 24,000 **Chelsea (2) 2, Real Madrid (0) 1** Dempsey, Osgood; Fleitas	1,570,000	23,582
1971–72	65	186	24.5.72, Barcelona, 35,000 **Rangers (2) 3, Dynamo Moscow (0) 2** Stein, Johnston 2; Estrekov, Makovikov	1,145,211	17,615
1972–73	61	174	16.5.73, Salonika, 45,000 **AC Milan (1) 1, Leeds United (0) 0** Chiarugi	908,564	15,000
1973–74	61	169	8.5.74, Rotterdam, 5,000 **FC Magdeburg (1) 2, AC Milan (0) 0** Lanzi (og), Seguin	1,105,494	18,123
1974–75	59	177	14.5.75, Basle, 13,000 **Dynamo Kiev (2) 3, Ferencvaros (0) 0** Onischenko 2, Blokhin	1,298,850	22,014
1975–76	61	189	5.5.76, Brussels, 58,000 **Anderlecht (1) 4, West Ham United (1) 2** Rensenbrink 2 (1 pen), Van der Elst 2; Holland, Robson	1,128,962	18,508
1976–77	63	198	11.5.77, Amsterdam, 65,000 **SV Hamburg (0) 2, Anderlecht (0) 0** Volkert (pen), Magath	1,537,000	24,400
1977–78	63	179	3.5.78, Amsterdam, 48,679 **Anderlecht (3) 4, Austria/WAC (0) 0** Rensenbrink 2 (1 pen), Van Binst 2	1,161,383	18,434
1978–79	*		16.5.79, Basle, 58,000 **Barcelona (2) (2) 4, Fortuna Dusseldorf (2) (2) 3 (a.e.t.)** Sanchez, Asensi, Rexach, Kvankl, Klaus, Allofs, Seel 2	*	

FAIRS CUP/UEFA CUP

1955–58 First leg: 5.3.58, London, 45,466
London (1) 2, Barcelona (2) 2
Greaves, Langley (pen); Tejada, Martinez

Second leg: 1.5.58, Barcelona, 62,000
Barcelona (3) 6, London (0) 0
Suarez 2, Evaristo 2, Martinez, Verges

1958–60 First leg: 29.3.60, Birmingham, 40,500
Birmingham City (0) 0, Barcelona (0) 0

Second leg: 4.5.60, Barcelona, 70,000
Barcelona (2) 4, Birmingham City (0) 1
Martinez, Czibor 2, Coll; Hooper

1960–61 First leg :   27.9.61, Birmingham, 21,005
                        **Birmingham City (0) 2, AS
                        Roma (1) 2**
                        Hellawell, Orritt ; Manfredini 2
         Second leg : 11.10.61, Rome, 60,000
                        **AS Roma (0) 2, Birmingham
                        City (0) 0**
                        Farmer (og), Pestrin
1961–62 First leg :   8.9.62, Valencia, 65,000
                        Valencia 6, Barcelona 2
                        Yosu 2, Guillot 3, Nunez ; Kocsis 2
         Second leg : 12.9.62, Barcelona, 60,000
                        Barcelona 1, Valencia 1
                        Kocsis ; Guillot
1962–63 First leg :   12.6.63, Zagreb, 40,000
                        **Dynamo Zagreb (1) 1, Valencia
                        (0) 2**
                        Zambata ; Waldo, Urtiaga
         Second leg : 26.6.63, Valencia, 55,000
                        **Valencia (1) 2, Dynamo Zagreb
                        (0) 0**
                        Mano, Nunez
1963–64 Final :   Barcelona, 24.6.64, 50,000
                        **Real Zaragoza (1) 2, Valencia
                        (1) 1**
                        Villa, Marcelino ; Urtiaga
1964–65 Final :   23.6.65, Turin, 25,000
                        Ferencvaros(1)1, Juventus(0)0
                        Fenyvesi
1965–66 First leg :   14.9.66, Barcelona, 70,000
                        **Barcelona (0) 0, Real
                        Zaragoza (1) 1**
                        Canario
         Second leg : 21.9.66, Zaragoza, 70,000
                        **Real Zaragoza (1) 2,
                        Barcelona (1) 4**
                        Marcelino 2 ; Pujol 3, Zabella
1966–67 First leg :   30.8.67, Zagreb, 40,000
                        **Dynamo Zagreb (1) 2, Leeds
                        United (0) 0**
                        Cercer 2
         Second leg : 6.9.67, Leeds, 35,604
                        **Leeds United (0) 0, Dynamo
                        Zagreb (0) 0**
1967–68 First leg :   7.8.68, Leeds, 25,368
                        **Leeds United (1) 1, Ferencvaros
                        (0) 0**
                        Jones
         Second leg : 11.9.68, Budapest, 70,000
                        **Ferencvaros (0) 0, Leeds
                        United (0) 0**
1968–69 First leg :   25.5.69, Newcastle, 60,000
                        **Newcastle United (0) 3,
                        Ujpest Dozsa (0) 0**
                        Moncur 2, Scott
         Second leg : 11.6.69, Budapest, 37,000
                        **Ujpest Dozsa (2) 2,
                        Newcastle United (0) 3**
                        Bene, Gorocs ; Moncur, Arentoft,
                        Foggon
1969–70 First leg :   22.4.70, Brussels, 37,000
                        Anderlecht (2) 3, Arsenal (0) 1
                        Devrindt, Mulder 2 ; Kennedy
         Second leg : 28.4.70, London, 51,612
                        Arsenal (1) 3, Anderlecht (0) 0
                        Kelly, Radford, Sammels
1970–71 First leg :   26.5.71, Turin, 65,000
                        **Juventus (0) 0, Leeds United
                        (0) 0**
                        (game abandoned after 51 minutes)
                        28.5.71, Turin, 65,000
                        **Juventus (1) 2, Leeds United
                        (0) 2**
                        Bettega, Capello ; Madeley, Bates

         Second leg : 3.6.71, Leeds, 42,483
                        **Leeds United (1) 1, Juventus
                        (1) 1**
                        Clarke ; Anastasi
                        Leeds won on away goals rule.
1971–72 First leg :   3.5.72, Wolverhampton, 45,000
                        **Wolverhampton Wanderers
                        (0) 1, Tottenham Hotspur (0) 2**
                        McCalliog ; Chivers 2
         Second leg : 17.5.72, London, 48,000
                        **Tottenham Hotspur (1) 1,
                        Wolverhampton Wanderers (0)
                        1**
                        Mullery ; Wagstaffe
1972–73 First leg :   10.5.73, Liverpool, 41,169
                        **Liverpool (3) 3, Borussia
                        Moenchengladbach (0) 0**
                        Keegan 2, Lloyd
         Second leg : 25.5.73, Moenchengladbach,
                        35,000
                        **Borussia Moenchengladbach
                        (2) 2, Liverpool (0) 0**
                        Heynckes 2
1973–74 First leg :   21.5.74, London, 46,281
                        **Tottenham Hotspur (1) 2,
                        Feyenoord (1) 2**
                        England, Van Daele (og) ; Van
                        Hanegem, De Jong
         Second leg : 29.5.74, Rotterdam, 68,000
                        **Feyenoord (1) 2, Tottenham
                        Hotspur (0) 0**
                        Rijsbergen, Ressel
1974–75 First leg :   7.5.75, Dusseldorf, 45,000
                        **Borussia Moenchengladbach
                        (0) 0, Twente Enschede (0) 0**
         Second leg : 21.5.75, Enschede, 24,500
                        **Twente Enschede (0) 1, Borussia
                        Moenchengladbach (2) 5**
                        Drost ; Heynckes 3, Simonsen 2 (1
                        pen)
1975–76 First leg :   28.4.76, Liverpool, 56,000
                        Liverpool (0) 3, Bruges (2) 2
                        Kennedy, Case, Keegan (pen) ;
                        Lambert, Cools
         Second leg : 19.5.76, Bruges, 32,000
                        Bruges (1) 1, Liverpool (1) 1
                        Lambert (pen) ; Keegan
1976–77 First leg :   4.5.77, Turin, 75,000
                        **Juventus (1) 1, Athletic
                        Bilbao (0) 0**
                        Tardelli
         Second leg : 18.5.77, Bilbao, 43,000
                        **Athletic Bilbao (1) 2,
                        Juventus (1) 1**
                        Iruerta, Carlos ; Bettega
1977–78 First leg :   26.4.78, Bastia, 15,000
                        **Bastia (0) 0, PSV Eindhoven
                        (0) 0**
         Second leg : 9.5.78, Eindhoven, 27,000
                        **PSV Eindhoven (1) 3, Bastia
                        (0) 0**
                        Willy van der Kerkhof, Deijkers,
                        van der Kuylen
1978–79 First Leg :   9.5.79, Belgrade, 87,500
                        **Red Star Belgrade (1) 1,
                        Borussia Moenchengladbach
                        (0) 1**
                        Setic, Jurisic (og)
         Second leg : 23.5.79, Dusseldorf, 45,000
                        **Borussia Moenchengladbach
                        (1) 1, Red Star Belgrade (0) 0**
                        Simonsen

British Clubs in Europe

FOOTBALL LEAGUE CLUBS

Season	Competition	Round	Date	Opponents (Country)	Venue	Result		Scorers
ARSENAL								
1971–72	European Cup	1	15.9.71	Stromsgodset (Norway)	A	W	3-1	Simpson, Marinello, Kelly
			29.9.71		H	W	4–0	Kennedy, Radford 2, Armstrong
		2	20.10.71	Grasshoppers	A	W	2–0	Kennedy, Graham
			3.11.71	(Switzerland)	H	W	3–0	Kennedy, George, Radford
		QF	8.3.72	Ajax (Holland)	A	L	1–2	Kennedy
			22.3.72		H	L	0–1	
1963–64	Fairs Cup	1	25.9.63	Staevnet (Denmark)	A	W	7–1	Strong 3, Baker 3, MacLeod
			22.10.63		H	L	2–3	Skirton, Barnwell
		2	13.11.63	Liege (Belgium)	H	D	1–1	Anderson
			18.12.63		A	L	1–3	McCullough
1969–70	Fairs Cup	1	9.9.69	Glentoran (Northern	H	W	3–0	Graham 2, Gould
			29.9.69	Ireland)	A	L	0–1	
		2	29.10.69	Sporting Lisbon (Portugal)	A	D	0–0	
			26.11.69		H	W	3–0	Radford, Graham 2
		3	17.12.69	Rouen (France)	A	D	0–0	
			13.1.70		H	W	1–0	Sammels
		QF	11.3.70	Dynamo Bacau	A	W	2–0	Sammels, Radford
			18.3.70	(Rumania)	H	W	7–1	George 2, Sammels 2, Radford 2, Graham
		SF	8.4.70	Ajax (Holland)	H	W	3–0	George 2 (1 pen), Sammels
			15.4.70		A	L	0–1	
		F	22.4.70	Anderlecht (Belgium)	A	L	1–3	Kennedy
			28.4.70		H	W	3–0	Kelly, Radford, Sammels
1970–71	Fairs Cup	1	16.9.70	Lazio (Italy)	A	D	2–2	Radford 2
			23.9.70		H	W	2–0	Radford, Armstrong
		2	21.10.70	Sturm Graz (Austria)	A	L	0–1	
			4.11.70		H	W	2–0	Storey (pen), Kennedy
		3	2.12.70	Beveren (Belgium)	H	W	4–0	Graham, Kennedy 2, Sammels
			16.12.70		A	D	0–0	
		QF	9.3.71	FC Cologne (West	H	W	2–1	McLintock, Storey
			23.3.71	Germany) *	A	L	0–1	
1978–79	UEFA Cup	1	13.9.78	Lokomotive Leipzig (East	H	W	3–0	Stapleton 2, Sunderland
			27.9.78	Germany)	A	W	4–1	Brady, Stapleton 2, Sunderland
		2	18.10.78	Hajduk Split	A	L	1–2	Brady
			1.11.78	(Yugoslavia)	H	W	1–0	Young
		3	22.11.78	Red Star Belgrade	A	L	0–1	
			6.12.78	(Yugoslavia)	H	D	1–1	Sunderland
ASTON VILLA								
1975–76	UEFA Cup	1	17.9.75	Antwerp (Belgium)	A	L	1–4	Graydon
			1.10.75		H	L	0–1	
1977–78	UEFA Cup	1	14.9.77	Fenerbahce (Turkey)	H	W	4–0	Gray, Deehan 2, Little
			28.9.77		A	W	2–0	Deehan, Little
		2	19.10.77	Gornik Zabrze (Poland)	H	W	2–0	McNaught 2
			2.11.77		A	D	1–1	Gray
		3	23.11.77	Athletic Bilbao (Spain)	H	W	2–0	Iribar own goal, Deehan
			7.12.77		A	D	1-1	Mortimer
		QF	1.3.78	Barcelona (Spain)	H	D	2–2	McNaught, Deehan
			15.3.78		A	L	1–2	Little
BIRMINGHAM CITY								
1955–56	Fairs Cup	Gp.D	15.5.56	Inter-Milan (Italy)	A	D	0–0	
			17.4.57		H	W	2–1	Govan 2
			22.5.56	Zagreb (Yugoslavia)	A	W	1–0	Brown
			3.12.56		H	W	3–0	Orritt, Brown, Murphy
		SF	23.10.57	Barcelona (Spain)	H	W	4–3	Murphy 2, Brown, Orritt
			13.11.57		A	L	0–1	
			26.11.57		N	L	1–2	Murphy

Season	Competition	Round	Date	Opponents (Country)	Venue	Result		Scorers

BIRMINGHAM CITY continued

Season	Competition	Round	Date	Opponents (Country)	Venue	Result		Scorers
1958–60	Fairs Cup	1	14.10.58	FC Cologne (West	A	D	2–2	Neal, Hooper
			11.11.58	Germany)	H	W	2–0	Larkin, Taylor
		QF	6.5.59	Zagreb (Yugoslavia)	H	W	1–0	Larkin
			25.5.59		A	D	3–3	Larkin 2, Hooper
		SF	7.10.59	Union St Gillosie	A	W	4–2	Hooper, Gordon, Barrett, Taylor
			11.11.59	(Belgium)	H	W	4–2	Gordon 2, Larkin, Hooper
		F	29.3.60	Barcelona (Spain)	H	D	0–0	
			4.5.60		A	L	1–4	Hooper
1960–61	Fairs Cup	1	19.10.60	Ujpest Dosza (Hungary)	H	W	3–2	Gordon 2, Astall
			26.10.60		A	W	2–1	Rudd, Singer
		QF	23.11.60	Copenhagen (Denmark)	A	D	4–4	Gordon 2, Singer 2
			7.12.60		H	W	5–0	Stubbs 2, Harris, Hellawell, own goal
		SF	19.4.61	Inter-Milan (Italy)	A	W	2–1	Harris, own goal
			3.5.61		H	W	2–1	Harris 2
		F	27.9.61	AS Roma (Italy)	H	D	2–2	Hellawell, Orritt
			11.10.61		A	L	0–2	
1961–62	Fairs Cup	1		bye				
		2	15.11.61	Espanol (Spain)	A	L	2–5	Bloomfield, Harris (pen)
			7.12.61		H	W	1–0	Auld

BURNLEY

Season	Competition	Round	Date	Opponents (Country)	Venue	Result		Scorers
1960–61	European Cup	Pr		bye				
		1	16.11.60	Reims (France)	H	W	2–0	Robson, McIlroy
			30.11.60		A	L	2–3	Robson, Connelly
		QF	18.1.61	SV Hamburg (West	H	W	3–1	Pilkington 2, Robson
			15.3.61	Germany)	A	L	1–4	Harris
1966–67	Fairs Cup	1	20.9.66	Stuttgart (West Germany)	A	D	1–1	Irvine
			27.9.66		H	W	2–0	Coates, Lochhead
		2	19.10.66	Lausanne (Switzerland)	A	W	3–1	Coates, Harris, Lochhead
			25.10.66		H	W	5–0	Lochhead 3, O'Neil, Irvine
		3	18.1.67	Napoli (Italy)	H	W	3–0	Coates, Latcham, Lochhead
			8.2.67		A	D	0–0	
		QF	4.4.67	Eintracht Frankfurt	A	D	1–1	Miller
			18.4.67	(West Germany)	H	L	1–2	Miller

CARDIFF CITY

Season	Competition	Round	Date	Opponents (Country)	Venue	Result		Scorers
1964–65	Cup Winners' Cup	1	9.9.64	Esbjerg (Denmark)	A	D	0–0	
			13.10.64		H	W	1–0	King
		2	16.12.64	Sporting Lisbon (Portugal)	A	W	2–1	Farrell, Tapscott
			23.12.64		H	D	0–0	
		QF	20.1.65	Real Zaragoza (Spain)	A	D	2–2	Williams, King
			3.2.65		H	L	0–1	
1965–66	Cup Winners' Cup	1	8.9.65	Standard Liege (Belgium)	H	L	1–2	Johnston
			20.10.65		A	L	0–1	
1967–68	Cup Winners' Cup	1	20.9.67	Shamrock Rovers (Eire)	A	D	1–1	King
			4.10.67		H	W	2–0	Toshack, Brown (pen)
		2	15.11.67	NAC Breda (Holland)	A	D	1–1	King
			29.11.67		H	W	4–1	Brown, Barrie Jones, Clark, Toshack
		QF	6.3.68	Moscow Torpedo	H	W	1–0	Barrie Jones
			19.3.68	(USSR)	A	L	0–1	
			3.4.68		H	W	1–0	Dean
		SF	24.4.68	SV Hamburg (West	A	D	1–1	Dean
			1.5.68	Germany)	H	L	2–3	Dean, Harris
1968–69	Cup-Winners' Cup	1	18.9.68	Porto (Portugal)	H	D	2–2	Toshack, Bird (pen)
			2.10.68		A	L	1–2	Toshack
1969–70	Cup-Winners' Cup	1	17.9.69	Mjoendalen (Norway)	A	W	7–1	Clark 2, Toshack 2, Lea, Sutton, King
			1.10.69		H	W	5–1	King 2, Allan 3
		2	12.11.69	Goztepe Izmir (Turkey)	A	L	0–3	
			16.11.69		H	W	1–0	Bird
1970–71	Cup-Winners' Cup	1	16.9.70	Pezoporikos (Cyprus)	H	W	8–0	Toshack 2, Clark 2, Sutton, Gibson, King, Woodruff
			30.9.70		A	D	0–0	

Season	Competition	Round	Date	Opponents (Country)	Venue	Result		Scorers
CARDIFF CITY continued								
		2	21.10.70	Nantes (France)	H	W	5–1	Toshack 2, Gibson, King, Phillips
			4.11.70		A	W	2–1	Toshack, Clark
		QF	10.3.70	Real Madrid (Spain)	H	W	1–0	Clark
			24.3.71		A	L	0–2	
1971–72	Cup-Winners Cup	1	15.9.71	Dynamo Berlin (East Germany) †	A	D	1–1	Gibson
			29.9.71		H	D	1–1	Clark
1973–74	Cup-Winners' Cup	1	19.9.73	Sporting Lisbon (Portugal)	H	D	0–0	
			3.10.73		A	L	1–2	Vincent
1974–75	Cup-Winners Cup	1	18.9.74	Ferencvaros (Hungary)	A	L	0–2	
			2.10.74		H	L	1–4	Dwyer
1976–77	Cup-Winners' Cup	Pr	4.8.76	Servette (Switzerland)	H	W	1–0	Evans
			11.8.76		A	L	1–2*	Showers
		1	15.9.76	Dynamo Tbilisi (USSR)	H	W	1–0	Alston
			29.9.76		A	L	0–3	
1977–78	Cup-Winners Cup	1	14.9.77	Austria/WAC (Austria)	H	D	0–0	
			28.9.77		A	L	0–1	
CHELSEA								
1970–71	Cup-Winners' Cup	1	16.9.70	Aris Salonika (Greece)	A	D	1–1	Hutchinson
			30.9.70		H	W	5–1	Hutchinson 2, Hollins 2, Hinton
		2	21.10.70	CSKA Sofia (Bulgaria)	A	W	1–0	Baldwin
			4.11.70		H	W	1–0	Webb
		QF	10.3.71	FC Bruges (Belgium)	A	L	0–2	
			24.3.71		H	W	4–0	Houseman, Osgood 2, Baldwin
		SF	14.4.71	Manchester City (England)	H	W	1–0	Smethurst
			28.4.71		A	W	1–0	Weller
		F	19.5.71	Real Madrid (Spain)	N	D	1–1	Osgood
			21.5.71		N	W	2–1	Dempsey, Osgood
1971–72	Cup-Winners' Cup	1	15.9.71	Jeunesse Hautcharage (Luxembourg)	A	W	8–0	Osgood 3, Houseman 2, Hollins, Webb, Baldwin
			29.9.71		H	W	13–0	Osgood 5, Baldwin 3, Hollins (pen), Hudson, Webb, Houseman, Harris
		2	20.10.71	Atvidaberg (Sweden) *	A	D	0–0	
			3.11.71		H	D	1–1	Hudson
1958–59	Fairs Cup	1	30.9.58	Frem Copenhagen (Denmark)	A	W	3–1	Harrison, Greaves, Nicholas
			4.11.58		H	W	4–1	Greaves 2, Sillett (P), own goal
		QF	29.4.59	Belgrade (Yugoslavia)	H	W	1–0	Brabrook
			13.5.59		H	L	1–4	Brabrook
1965–66	Fairs Cup	1	22.9.65	AS Roma (Italy)	H	W	4–1	Venables 3, Graham
			6.10.65		A	D	0–0	
		2	17.11.65	Weiner SK (Austria)	A	L	0–1	
			1.12.65		H	W	2–0	Murray, Osgood
		3	9.2.66	AC Milan (Italy)	A	L	1–2	Graham
			16.2.66		H	W	2–1	Graham, Osgood
			2.3.66		A	D	1–1 ‡	Bridges
		QF	15.3.66	Munich 1860 (West Germany)	A	D	2–2	Tambling 2
			29.3.66		H	W	1–0	Osgood
		SF	27.4.66	Barcelona (Spain)	A	L	0–2	
			11.5.66		H	W	2–0	own goals 2
			25.5.66		A	L	0–5	
1968–69	Fairs Cup	1	18.9.68	Morton (Scotland)	H	W	5–0	Osgood, Birchenall, Cooke, Boyle, Hollins
			30.9.68		A	W	4–3	Baldwin, Birchenall, Houseman, Tambling
		2	23.10.68	DWS Amsterdam (Holland) ‡	H	D	0–0	
			30.10.68		A	D	0–0	
COVENTRY CITY								
1970–71	Fairs Cup	1	16.9.70	Trakia Plovdiv (Bulgaria)	A	W	4–1	O'Rourke 3, Martin
			30.9.70		H	W	2–0	Joicey, Blockley
		2	20.10.70	Bayern Munich (West Germany)	A	L	1–6	Hunt
			3.11.70		H	W	2–1	Martin, O'Rourke

Season	Competition	Round	Date	Opponents (Country)	Venue	Result		Scorers

DERBY COUNTY

Season	Competition	Round	Date	Opponents (Country)	Venue	Result		Scorers
1972–73	European Cup	1	13.9.72	Zeljeznicar (Yugoslavia)	H	W	2–0	McFarland, Gemmill
			27.9.72		A	W	2–1	Hinton, O'Hare
		2	25.10.72	Benfica (Portugal)	H	W	3–0	McFarland, Hector, McGovern
			8.11.72		A	D	0–0	
		QF	7.3.73	Spartak Trnava	A	D	0–0	
			21.3.73	(Czechoslovakia)	H	W	2–0	Hector 2
		SF	11.4.73	Juventus (Italy)	A	L	1–3	Hector
			25.4.73		H	D	0–0	
1975–76	European Cup	1	17.9.75	Slovan Bratislava	A	L	0–1	
			1.10.75	(Czechoslovakia)	H	W	3–0	Bourne, Lee 2
		2	22.10.75	Real Madrid (Spain)	H	W	4–1	George 3 (2 pen), Nish
			5.11.75		A	L	1–5	George
1974–75	UEFA Cup	1	18.9.74	Servette (Switzerland)	H	W	4–1	Hector 2, Daniel, Lee
			2.10.74		A	W	2–1	Lee, Hector
		2	23.10.74	Atletico Madrid (Spain)	H	D	2–2	Nish, Rioch (pen)
			6.11.74		A	D	2–2†	Rioch, Hector
		3	27.11.74	Velez (Yugoslavia)	H	W	3–1	Bourne 2, Hinton
			11.12.74		A	L	1–4	Hector
1976–77	UEFA Cup	1	15.9.76	Finn Harps (Eire)	H	W	12–0	Hector 5, James 3, George 3, Rioch
			29.9.76		A	W	4–1	Hector 2, George 2
		2	20.10.76	AEK Athens (Greece)	A	L	0–2	
			3.11.76		H	L	2–3	George, Rioch

EVERTON

Season	Competition	Round	Date	Opponents (Country)	Venue	Result		Scorers
1963–64	European Cup	1	18.9.63	Inter-Milan (Italy)	H	D	0–0	
			25.9.63		A	L	0–1	
1970–71	European Cup	1	16.9.70	Keflavik (Iceland)	H	W	6–2	Ball 3, Royle 2, Kendall
			30.9.70		A	W	3–0	Royle 2, Whittle
		2	21.10.70	Borussia Moenchenglad-	A	D	1–1	Kendall
			4.11.70	bach (West Germany)	H	D	1–1†	Morrissey
		QF	9.3.71	Panathinaikos (Greece) *	H	D	1–1	Johnson
			24.3.71		A	D	0–0	
1966–67	Cup-Winners' Cup	1	28.9.66	Aalborg (Denmark)	A	D	0–0	
			11.10.66		H	W	2–1	Morrissey, Ball
		2	9.11.66	Real Zaragoza (Spain)	A	L	0–2	
			23.11.66		H	W	1–0	Brown
1962–63	Fairs Cup	1	24.10.62	Dunfermline Athletic	H	W	1–0	Stevens
			31.10.62	(Scotland)	A	L	0–2	
1964–65	Fairs Cup	1	23.9.64	Valerengen (Norway)	A	W	5–2	Pickering 2, Harvey, Temple 2
			14.10.64		H	W	4–2	Young 2, Vernon, own goal
		2	11.11.64	Kilmarnock (Scotland)	A	W	2–0	Temple, Morrissey
			23.11.64		H	W	4–1	Harvey, Pickering 2, Young
		3	20.1.65	Manchester United	A	D	1–1	Pickering
			9.2.65	(England)	H	L	1–2	Pickering
1965–66	Fairs Cup	1	28.9.65	IFC Nuremberg (West	A	D	1–1	Harris
			12.10.65	Germany)	H	W	1–0	Gabriel
		2	3.11.65	Ujpest Dosza (Hungary)	A	L	0–3	
			16.11.65		H	W	2–1	Harris, own goal
1975–76	UEFA Cup	1	17.9.75	AC Milan (Italy)	H	D	0–0	
			1.10.75		A	L	0–1	
1978–79	UEFA Cup	1	12.9.78	Finn Harps (Eire)	A	W	5–0	Thomas, King 2, Latchford, Walsh
			26.9.78		H	W	5–0	King, Latchford, Walsh, Ross, Dobson
		2	18.10.78	Dukla Prague	H	W	2–1	Latchford, King
			1.11.78	(Czechoslovakia)	A	L	0–1	

IPSWICH TOWN

Season	Competition	Round	Date	Opponents (Country)	Venue	Result		Scorers
1962–63	European Cup	Pr	18.9.62	Floriana (Malta)	A	W	4–1	Crawford 2, Phillips 2
			25.9.62		H	W	10–0	Crawford 5, Moran 2, Phillips 2, Elsworthy
		1	14.11.62	AC Milan (Italy)	A	L	0–3	
			28.11.62		H	W	2–1	Crawford, Blackwood

Season	Competition	Round	Date	Opponents (Country)	Venue	Result		Scorers
IPSWICH TOWN continued								
1973–74	UEFA Cup	1	19.9.73	Real Madrid (Spain)	H	W	1–0	own goal
			3.10.73		A	D	0–0	
		2	24.10.73	Lazio (Italy)	H	W	4–0	Whymark 4
			7.11.73		A	L	2–4	Viljoen (pen), Johnson
		3	28.11.73	Twente Enschede	H	W	1–0	Whymark
			12.12.73	(Holland)	A	W	2–1	Morris, Hamilton
		QF	6.3.74	Lokomotive Leipzig	H	W	1–0	Beattie
			20.3.74	(East Germany) †	H	L	0–1	
1974–75	UEFA Cup	1	18.9.74	Twente Enschede	H	D	2–2	Hamilton, Talbot
			2.10.74	(Holland) *	A	D	1–1	Hamilton
1975–76	UEFA Cup	1	17.9.75	Feyenoord (Holland)	A	W	2 1	Whymark, Johnson
			1.10.75		H	W	2 0	Woods, Whymark
		2	22.10.75	FC Bruges (Belgium)	H	W	3–0	Gates, Peddelty, Austin
			5.11.75		A	L	0–4	
1977–78	UEFA Cup	1	14.9.77	Landskrona (Sweden)	A	W	1–0	Whymark
			28.9.77		H	W	5–0	Whymark 4 (1 pen), Mariner
		2	19.10.77	Las Palmas (Spain)	H	W	1–0	Gates
			2.11.77		A	D	3–3	Mariner 2, Talbot
		3	23.11.77	Barcelona (Spain)	H	W	3 -0	Gates, Whymark, Talbot
			7.12.77		A	L	0–3 †	
1978–79	Cup-Winners' Cup	1	13.9.78	AZ 67 (Holland)	A	D	0–0	
			27.9.78		H	W	2–0	Mariner, Wark (pen)
		2	18.10.78	SW Innsbruck (Austria)	H	W	1–0	Wark (pen)
			1.11.78		A	D	1- 1	Burley
		QF	7.3.79	Barcelona (Spain)	H	W	2–1	Gates 2
			21.3.79		A	L	0- 1	
LEEDS UNITED								
1969–70	European Cup	1	17.9.69	Lyn Oslo (Norway)	H	W	10–0	Jones 3, Clarke 2, Giles 2, Bremner 2, O'Grady
			1.10.69		A	W	6–0	Belfitt 2, Hibbitt 2, Jones, Lorimer
		2	12.11.69	Ferencvaros (Hungary)	H	W	3–0	Giles, Jones 2
			26.11.69		A	W	3–0	Jones 2, Lorimer
		QF	4.3.70	Standard Liege (Belgium)	A	W	1–0	Lorimer
			18.3.70		H	W	1–0	Giles (pen)
		SF	1.4.70	Celtic (Scotland)	H	L	0–1	
			15.4.70		A	L	1–2	Bremner
1974–75	European Cup	1	28.9.74	Zurich (Switzerland)	H	W	4–1	Clarke 2, Lorimer (pen), Jordan
			2.10.74		A	L	1–2	Clarke
		2	23.10.74	Ujpest Dosza (Hungary)	A	W	2–1	Lorimer, McQueen
			6.11.74		H	W	3–0	McQueen, Bremner, Yorath
		QF	5.3.75	Anderlecht (Belgium)	H	W	3–0	Jordan, McQueen, Lorimer
			19.3.75		A	W	1–0	Bremner
		SF	9.4.75	Barcelona (Spain)	H	W	2–1	Bremner, Clarke
			24.4.75		A	D	1–1	Lorimer
		F	28.5.75	Bayern Munich (West Germany)	N	L	0–2	
1972–73	Cup-Winners' Cup	1	13.9.72	Ankaragucu (Turkey)	A	D	1–1	Jordan
			28.9.72		H	W	1–0	Jones
		2	25.10.72	Carl Zeiss Jena (East Germany)	A	D	0–0	
			8.11.72		H	W	2–0	Cherry, Jones
		QF	7.3.73	Rapid Bucharest (Rumania)	H	W	5–0	Giles, Clarke, Lorimer 2, Jordan
			23.3.73		A	W	3- 1	Jones, Jordan, Bates
		SF	11.4.73	Hajduk Split (Yugoslavia)	H	W	1–0	Clarke
			25.4.73		A	D	0–0	
		F	16.5.73	AC Milan (Italy)	N	L	0–1	
1965–66	Fairs Cup	1	29.9.65	Torino (Italy)	H	W	2–1	Bremner, Peacock
			6.10.65		A	D	0–0	
		2	24.11.65	Lokomotive Leipzig (East Germany)	A	W	2–1	Lorimer, Bremner
			1.12.65		H	D	0–0	
		3	2.2.66	Valencia (Spain)	H	D	1–1	Lorimer
			16.2.66		A	W	1–0	O'Grady
		QF	2.3.66	Ujpest Dosza (Hungary)	H	W	4–1	Cooper, Bell, Storrie, Bremner
			9.3.66		A	D	1–1	Lorimer

Season	Competition	Round	Date	Opponents (Country)	Venue	Result		Scorers

LEEDS UNITED continued

Season	Competition	Round	Date	Opponents (Country)	Venue	Result		Scorers
		SF	20.4.66	Real Zaragoza (Spain)	A	L	0–1	
			27.4.66		H	W	2–1	Johanneson, Charlton
			11.5.66		N	L	1–3	Charlton
1966–67	Fairs Cup	1		bye				
		2	18.10.66	DWS Amsterdam (Holland)	A	W	3–1	Bremner, Johanneson, Greenhoff
			26.10.66		H	W	5–1	Johanneson 3, Giles, Madeley
		3	18.1.67	Valencia (Spain)	H	D	1–1	Greenhoff
			8.2.67		A	W	2–0	Giles, Lorimer
		QF	22.3.67	Bologna (Italy)	A	L	0–1	
			19.4.67		H	W	1–0‡	Giles (pen)
		SF	19.5.67	Kilmarnock (Scotland)	H	W	4–2	Belfitt 3, Giles (pen)
			24.5.67		A	D	0–0	
		F	30.8.67	Dynamo Zagreb (Yugoslavia)	A	L	0–2	
			6.9.67		H	D	0–0	
1967–68	Fairs Cup	1	3.10.67	Spora Luxembourg (Luxembourg)	A	W	9–0	Lorimer 4, Greenhoff 2, Madeley, Jones, Bremner
			17.10.67		H	W	7–0	Johanneson 3, Greenhoff 2, Cooper, Lorimer
		2	29.11.67	Partizan Belgrade (Yugoslavia)	A	W	2–1	Lorimer, Belfitt
			6.12.67		H	D	1–1	Lorimer
		3	20.12.67	Hibernian (Scotland)	H	W	1–0	Gray (E)
			10.1.68		A	D	0–0	
		QF	26.3.68	Rangers (Scotland)	A	D	0–0	
			9.4.68		H	W	2–0	Lorimer, Giles (pen)
		SF	1.5.68	Dundee (Scotland)	A	D	1–1	Madeley
			15.5.68		H	W	1–0	Gray (E)
		F	7.8.68	Ferencvaros (Hungary)	H	W	1–0	Charlton
			11.9.68		A	D	0–0	
1968–69	Fairs Cup	1	18.9.68	Standard Liege (Belgium)	A	D	0–0	
			23.10.68		H	W	3–2	Charlton, Lorimer, Bremner
		2	13.11.68	Napoli (Italy)	H	W	2–0	Charlton 2
			27.11.68		A	L	0–2‡	
		3	18.12.68	Hanover 96 (West Germany)	H	W	5–1	O'Grady, Hunter, Lorimer 2, Charlton
			4.2.69		A	W	2–1	Belfitt, Jones
		QF	5.3.69	Ujpest Dosza (Hungary)	A	L	0–1	
			19.3.69		A	L	0–2	
1970–71	Fairs Cup	1	15.9.70	Sarpsborg (Norway)	H	W	1–0	Lorimer
			29.9.70		H	W	5–0	Charlton 2, Bremner 2, Lorimer
		2	21.10.70	Dynamo Dresden (East Germany)	A	W	1–0	Lorimer
			4.11.70		A	L	1–2*	Jones
		3	2.12.70	Sparta Prague (Czechoslovakia)	H	W	6–0	Clarke, Bremner, Gray (E) 2, Charlton own goal
			9.12.70		A	W	3–2	Gray (E), Clarke, Belfitt
		QF	10.3.71	Setubal (Portugal)	H	W	2–1	Lorimer, Giles (pen)
			24.3.71		A	D	1–1	Lorimer
		SF	14.4.71	Liverpool (England)	A	W	1–0	Bremner
			28.4.71		H	D	0–0	
		F	28.5.71	Juventus (Italy)	A	D	2–2	Madeley, Bates
			3.6.71		H	D	1–1*	Clarke
1971–72	UEFA Cup	1	15.9.71	Lierse (Belgium)	A	W	2–0	Galvin, Lorimer
			29.9.71		H	L	0–4	
1973–74	UEFA Cup	1	19.9.73	Stromsgodset (Norway)	A	D	1–1	Clarke
			3.10.73		H	W	6–1	Clarke 2, Jones 2, Gray (F), Bates
		2	24.10.73	Hibernian (Scotland)	H	D	0–0	
			7.11.73		A	D	0–0†	
		3	28.11.73	Setubal (Portugal)	H	W	1–0	Cherry
			12.12.73		A	L	1–3	Liddell

N.B. Leeds met Barcelona in Spain on 22.9.71 in a match to determine who should hold the Fairs Cup trophy permanently. Barcelona, the first winners beat Leeds, the holders 2–1 (Jordan was the United scorer).

Season	Competition	Round	Date	Opponents (Country)	Venue	Result		Scorers

LEICESTER CITY

Season	Competition	Round	Date	Opponents (Country)	Venue	Result		Scorers
1961–62	Cup-Winners Cup	1	13.9.61	Glenavon (Northern	A	W	4–1	Walsh 2, Appleton, Keyworth
			27.9.61	Ireland)	H	W	3–1	Wills, Keyworth, McIlmoyle
		2	25.10.61	Atletico Madrid (Spain)	H	D	1–1	Keyworth
			15.11.61		A	L	0–2	

LIVERPOOL

Season	Competition	Round	Date	Opponents (Country)	Venue	Result		Scorers
1964–65	European Cup	Pr	17.8.64	KR Reykjavik (Iceland)	A	W	5–0	Wallace 2, Hunt 2, Chisnall
			14.9.64		H	W	6–1	Byrne, St John 2, Graham, Hunt, Stevenson
		1	25.11.64	Anderlecht (Belgium)	H	W	3–0	St John, Hunt, Yeats
			16.12.64		A	W	1–0	Hunt
		QF	10.2.65	FC Cologne (West	A	D	0–0	
			17.3.65	Germany)	H	D	0–0	
			24.3.65		N	D	2–2‡	St John, Hunt
		SF	4.5.65	Inter-Milan (Italy)	H	W	3–1	Hunt, Callaghan, St John
			12.5.65		A	L	0–3	
1966–67	European Cup	1	28.9.66	Petrolul Ploesti (Rumania)	H	W	2–0	St John, Callaghan
			12.10.66		A	L	1–3	Hunt
			19.10.66		N	W	2–0	St John, Thompson (P)
		2	7.12.66	Ajax (Holland)	A	L	1–5	Lawler
			14.12.66		H	D	2–2	Hunt 2
1973–74	European Cup	1	19.9.73	Jeunesse D'Esch	A	D	1–1	Hall.
			3.10.73	(Luxembourg)	H	W	2–0	Toshack, own goal
		2	24.10.73	Red Star Belgrade	A	L	1–2	Lawler
			6.11.73	(Yugoslavia)	H	L	1–2	Lawler
1976–77	European Cup	1	14.9.76	Crusaders (Northern	H	W	2–0	Neal (pen), Toshack
			28.9.76	Ireland)	A	W	5–0	Johnson 2, Keegan, McDermott, Heighway
		2	20.10.76	Trabzonspor (Turkey)	A	L	0–1	
			3.11.76		H	W	3–0	Heighway, Johnson, Keegan
		QF	2.3.77	St Etienne (France)	A	L	0–1	
			16.3.77		H	W	3–1	Keegan, Kennedy, Fairclough
		SF	6.4.77	Zurich (Switzerland)	A	W	3–1	Neal 2 (1 pen), Heighway
			20.4.77		H	W	3–0	Case 2, Keegan
		F	25.5.77	Borussia Moenchenglad-bach (West Germany)	N	W	3–1	McDermott, Smith, Neal (pen)
1977–78	European Cup	1		bye				
		2	19.10.77	Dynamo Dresden (East Germany)	H	W	5–1	Hansen, Case 2, Neal (pen), Kennedy
			2.11.77		A	L	1–2	Heighway
		QF	1.3.78	Benfica (Portugal)	A	W	2–1	Case, Hughes
			15.3.78		H	W	4–1	Callaghan, Dalglish, McDermott, Neal
		SF	29.3.78	Borussia Moenchenglad-bach (West Germany)	A	L	1–2	Johnson
			12.4.78		H	W	3–0	Kennedy, Dalglish, Case
		F	10.5.78	FC Bruges (Belgium)	N	W	1–0	Dalglish
1978–79	European Cup	1	13.9.78	Nottingham Forest	A	L	0–2	
			27.9.78	(England)	H	D	0–0	
1965–66	Cup-Winners' Cup	1	29.9.65	Juventus (Italy)	A	L	0–1	
			13.10.65		H	W	2–0	Lawler, Strong
		2	1.12.65	Standard Liege (Belgium)	H	W	3–1	Lawler 2, Thompson (P)
			15.12.65		A	W	2–1	Hunt, St John
		QF	1.3.66	Honved (Hungary)	A	D	0–0	
			8.3.66		H	W	2–0	Lawler, St John
		SF	14.4.66	Celtic (Scotland)	A	L	0–1	
					H	W	2–0	Lawler, St John
		F	5.5.66	Borussia Dortmund (West Germany)	N	L	1–2	Hunt
1971–72	Cup-Winners' Cup	1	15.9.71	Servette (Switzerland)	A	L	1–2	Lawler
			29.9.71		H	W	2–0	Hughes, Heighway
		2	20.10.71	Bayern Munich	H	D	0–0	
			3.11.71	(West Germany)	A	L	1–3	Evans
1974–75	Cup-Winners'	1	17.9.74	Stromsgodset (Norway)	H	W	11–0	Lindsay (pen), Boersma 2, Heighway, Thompson (P B) 2, Smith, Cormack, Hughes, Callaghan, Kennedy
			1.10.74		A	W	1–0	Kennedy

Season	Competition	Round	Date	Opponents (Country)	Venue	Result		Scorers

LIVERPOOL continued

Season	Competition	Round	Date	Opponents (Country)	Venue	Result		Scorers
		2	23.10.74	Ferencvaros (Hungary) *	H	D	1–1	Keegan
			5.11.74		A	D	0–0	
1967–68	Fairs Cup	1	19.9.67	Malmo FF (Sweden)	A	W	2–0	Hateley 2
			4.10.67		H	W	2–1	Yeats, Hunt
		2	7.11.67	Munich 1860 (West Germany)	H	W	8–0	St John, Hateley, Thompson (P), Smith (pen), Hunt 2, Callaghan 2
			14.11.67		A	L	1–2	Callaghan
		3	28.11.67	Ferencvaros (Hungary)	A	L	0–1	
			9.1.68		H	L	0–1	
1968–69	Fairs Cup	1	18.9.68	Atletico Bilbao (Spain) ‡	A	L	1–2	Hunt
			2.10.68		H	W	2–1	Lawler, Hughes
1969–70	Fairs Cup	1	16.9.69	Dundalk (Eire)	H	W	10–0	Evans 2, Smith 2, Graham 2, Lawler, Lindsay, Thompson (P) Callaghan
			30.9.69		A	W	4–0	Thompson (P) 2, Graham, Callaghan
		3	11.11.69	Setubal (Portugal) *	A	L	0–1	
			26.11.69		H	W	3–2	Smith (pen), Evans, Hunt
1970–71	Fairs Cup	1	15.9.70	Ferencvaros (Hungary)	H	W	1–0	Graham
			29.9.70		A	D	1–1	Hughes
		2	21.10.70	Dynamo Bucharest (Rumania)	H	W	3–0	Lindsay, Lawler, Hughes
			4.11.70		A	D	1–1	Boersma
		3	9.12.70	Hibernian (Scotland)	A	W	1–0	Toshack
			22.12.70		H	W	2–0	Heighway, Boersma
		QF	10.3.71	Bayern Munich (West Germany)	H	W	3–0	Evans 3
			24.3.71		A	D	1–1	Ross
		SF	14.4.71	Leeds United (England)	H	L	0–1	
			28.4.71		A	D	0–0	
1972–73	UEFA Cup	1	12.9.72	Eintracht Frankfurt (West Germany)	H	W	2–0	Keegan, Hughes
			26.9.72		A	D	0–0	
		2	24.10.72	AEK Athens (Greece)	H	W	3–0	Boersma, Cormack, Smith (pen)
			7.11.72		A	W	3–1	Hughes 2, Boersma
		3	29.11.72	Dynamo Berlin (East Germany)	A	D	0–0	
			12.12.72		H	W	3–1	Boersma, Heighway, Toshack
		QF	7.3.73	Dynamo Dresden (East Germany)	H	W	2–0	Hall, Boersma
			21.3.73		A	W	1–0	Keegan
		SF	10.4.73	Tottenham Hotspur (England)	H	W	1–0	Lindsay
			25.4.73		A	L	1–2 *	Heighway
		F	10.5.73	Borussia Moenchenglad- bach (West Germany)	H	W	3–0	Keegan 2, Lloyd
			23.5.73		A	L	2–0	
1975–76	UEFA Cup	1	17.9.75	Hibernian (Scotland)	A	L	0–1	
			30.9.75		H	W	3–1	Toshack 3
		2	22.10.75	Real Sociedad (Spain)	A	W	3–1	Heighway, Callaghan, Thompson (P B)
			4.11.75		H	W	6–0	Toshack, Kennedy 2, Fair- clough, Heighway, Neal
		3	26.11.75	Slask Wroclaw (Poland)	A	W	2–1	Kennedy, Toshack
			10.12.75		H	W	3–0	Case 3
		QF	3.3.76	Dynamo Dresden (East Germany)	A	D	0–0	
			17.3.76		H	W	2–1	Case, Keegan
		SF	30.3.76	Barcelona (Spain)	A	W	1–0	Toshack
			14.4.76		H	D	1–1	Thompson (P B)
		F	28.4.76	FC Bruges (Belgium)	H	W	3–2	Kennedy, Case, Keegan (pen)
			19.5.76		A	D	1–1	Keegan
1977–78	Super Cup	F	22.11.77	Hamburg (West Germany)	A	D	1·1	Fairclough
			6.12.77		H	W	6–0	Thompson, McDermott 3, Fairclough, Dalglish
1978–79	Super Cup	F	4.12.78	Anderlecht (Belgium)	A	L	1–3	Case
			19.12.78		H	W	2–1	Hughes, Fairclough

MANCHESTER CITY

Season	Competition	Round	Date	Opponents (Country)	Venue	Result		Scorers
1968–69	European Cup	1	18.9.68	Fenerbahce (Turkey)	H	D	0–0	
			2.10.68		A	L	1–2	Coleman
1969–70	Cup-Winners' Cup	1	17.9.69	Atletico Bilbao (Spain)	A	D	3–3	Young, Booth, own goal
			1.10.69		H	W	3–0	Oakes, Bell, Bowyer

Season	Competition	Round	Date	Opponents (Country)	Venue	Result		Scorers

MANCHESTER CITY continued

		2	12.11.69	Lierse (Belgium)	A	W	3–0	Lee 2, Bell
			26.11.69		H	W	5–0	Bell 2, Lee 2, Summerbee
		QF	4.3.70	Academica Coimbra	A	D	0–0	
			18.3.70	(Portugal)	H	W	1–0	Towers
		SF	1.4.70	Schalke 04 (West	A	L	0–1	
			15.4.70	Germany)	H	W	5–1	Young 2, Doyle, Lee, Bell
		F	29.4.70	Gornik Zabrze (Poland)	N	W	2–1	Young, Lee (pen)
1970–71	Cup-Winners' Cup	1	16.9.70	Linfield (Northern	H	W	1–0	Bell
			30.9.70	Ireland)	A	L	1–2*	Lee
		2	21.10.70	Honved (Hungary)	A	W	1–0	Lee
			4.11.70		H	W	2–0	Bell, Lee
		QF	10.3.71	Gornik Zabrze (Poland)	A	L	0–2	
			24.3.71		H	W	2–0	Mellor, Doyle
			31.3.71		N	W	3–1	Young, Booth, Lee
		SF	14.4.71	Chelsea (England)	A	L	0–1	
			28.4.71		H	L	0–1	
1972–73	UEFA Cup	1	13.9.72	Valencia (Spain)	H	D	2–2	Mellor, Marsh
			27.9.72		A	L	1–2	Marsh
1976–77	UEFA Cup	1	15.9.76	Juventus (Italy)	H	W	1–0	Kidd
			29.9.76		A	L	0–2	
1977–78	UEFA Cup	1	14.9.77	Widzew Lodz (Poland) *	H	D	2–2	Barnes, Channon
			28.9.77		A	D	0–0	
1978–79	UEFA Cup	1	13.9.78	Twente Enschede	A	D	1–1	Watson
			27.9.78	(Holland)	H	W	3–2	Kidd, Bell, own goal
		2	18.10.78	Standard Liege (Belgium)	H	W	4–0	Hartford, Kidd 2 (1 pen), Palmer
			1.11.78		A	L	0–2	
		3	23.11.78	AC Milan (Italy)	A	D	2–2	Kidd, Power
			6.12.78		H	W	3–0	Booth, Hartford, Kidd
		QF	7.3.79	Borussia Moenchenglad-	H	D	1–1	Channon
			21.3.79	bach (West Germany)	A	L	1–3	Deyna

MANCHESTER UNITED

1956–57	European Cup	Pr	12.9.56	Anderlecht (Belgium)	A	W	2–0	Viollet, Taylor (T)
			26.9.56		H	W	10–0	Viollet 4, Taylor (T) 3, Whelan 2, Berry
		1	17.10.56	Borussia Dortmund	H	W	3–2	Viollet 2, Pegg
			21.11.56	(West Germany)	A	D	0–0	
		QF	16.1.57	Altetico Bilbao (Spain)	A	L	3–5	Taylor (T), Viollet, Whelan
			6.2.57		H	W	3–0	Viollet, Taylor (T), Berry
		SF	11.4.57	Real Madrid (Spain)	A	L	1–3	Taylor (T)
			24.4.57		H	D	2–2	Taylor (T), Charlton
1957–58	European Cup	Pr	25.9.57	Shamrock Rovers (Eire)	A	W	6–0	Whelan 2, Taylor (T) 2, Berry, Pegg
			2.10.57		H	W	3–2	Viollet 2, Pegg
		1	20.11.57	Dukla Prague	H	W	3–0	Webster, Taylor (T), Pegg
			4.12.57	(Czechoslovakia)	A	L	0–1	
		QF	14.1.58	Red Star Belgrade	H	W	2–1	Charlton, Colman
			5.2.58	(Yugoslavia)	A	D	3–3	Viollet, Charlton 2
		SF	8.5.58	AC Milan (Italy)	H	W	2–1	Viollet, Taylor (E) (pen)
			14.5.58		A	L	0–4	
1965–66	European Cup	Pr	22.9.65	HJK Helsinki (Finland)	A	W	3–2	Herd, Connelly, Law
			6.10.65		H	W	6–0	Connelly 3, Best 2, Charlton
		1	17.11.65	Vorwaerts Berlin	A	W	2–0	Law, Connelly
			1.12.65	(East Germany)	H	W	3–1	Herd 3
		QF	2.2.66	Benfica (Portugal)	H	W	3–2	Herd, Law, Foulkes
			9.3.66		A	W	5–1	Best 2, Connelly, Crerand, Charlton
		SF	13.4.66	Partizan Belgrade	A	L	0–2	
			20.4.66	(Yugoslavia)	H	W	1–0	own goal
1967–68	European Cup	1	20.9.67	Hibernians (Malta)	H	W	4–0	Sadler 2, Law 2
			27.9.67		A	D	0–0	
		2	15.11.67	Sarajevo (Yugoslavia)	A	D	0–0	
			29.11.67		H	W	2–1	Aston, Best
		QF	28.2.68	Gornik Zabrze (Poland)	H	W	2–0	Kidd, own goal
			13.3.68		A	L	0–1	

Season	Competition	Round	Date	Opponents (Country)	Venue	Result		Scorers
MANCHESTER UNITED continued								
		SF	24.4.68	Real Madrid (Spain)	H	W	1–0	Best
			15.5.68		A	D	3–3	Sadler, Kidd, Foulkes
		F	29.5.68	Benfica (Portugal)	N	W	4–1	Charlton 2, Best, Kidd
1968–69	European Cup	1	18.9.68	Waterford (Eire)	A	W	3–1	Law 3
			2.10.68		H	W	7–1	Stiles, Law 4, Burns, Charlton
		2	13.11.68	Anderlecht (Belgium)	H	W	3–0	Kidd, Law 2
			27.11.68		A	L	1–3	Sartori
		QF	26.2.69	Rapid Vienna (Austria)	H	W	3–0	Best 2, Morgan
			5.3.69		A	D	0–0	
		SF	23.4.69	AC Milan (Italy)	A	L	0–2	
			15.5.69		H	W	1–0	Charlton
1963–64	Cup-Winners' Cup	1	25.9.63	Tilburg Willem II (Holland)	A	D	1–1	Herd
			15.10.63		H	W	6–1	Setters, Law 3, Charlton, Chisnall
		2	3.12.63	Tottenham Hotspur	A	L	0–2	
			10.12.63	(England)	H	W	4–1	Herd 2, Charlton 2
		QF	26.2.64	Sporting Lisbon	H	W	4–1	Law 3 (2 pens), Charlton
			18.3.64	(Portugal)	A	L	0–5	
1977–78	Cup-Winners' Cup	1	14.9.77	St. Etienne (France)	A	D	1–1	Hill
			5.10.77		H	W	2–0	Pearson, Coppell
		2	19.10.77	Porto (Portugal)	A	L	0–4	
			2.11.77		H	W	5–2	Coppell 2, own goals 2, Nicholl
1964–65	Fairs Cup	1	23.9.64	Djurgaarden (Sweden)	A	D	1–1	Herd
			27.10.64		H	W	6–1	Law 3 (1 pen), Charlton 2, Best
		2	11.11.64	Borussia Dortmund	A	W	6–1	Herd, Charlton 3, Best, Law
			2.12.64	(West Germany)	H	W	4–0	Charlton 2, Law, Connelly
		3	20.1.65	Everton (England)	H	D	1–1	Connelly
			9.2.65		A	W	2–1	Connelly, Herd
		QF	12.5.65	Strasbourg (France)	A	W	5–0	Connelly, Herd, Law 2, Charlton
			19.5.65		H	D	0–0	
		SF	31.5.65	Ferencvaros (Hungary)	H	W	3–2	Law (pen), Herd 2
			6.6.65		A	L	0–1	
			16.6.65		A	L	1–2	Connelly
1976–77	UEFA Cup	1	15.9.76	Ajax (Holland)	A	L	0–1	
			29.9.76		H	W	2–0	Macari, McIlroy
		2	20.10.76	Juventus (Italy)	H	W	1–0	Hill
			3.11.76		A	L	0–3	
NEWCASTLE UNITED								
1968–69	Fairs Cup	1	11.9.68	Feyenoord (Holland)	H	W	4–0	Scott, Robson(B), Gibb, Davies
			17.9.68		A	L	0–2	
		2	30.10.68	Sporting Lisbon	A	D	1–1	Scott
			20.11.68	(Portugal)	H	W	1–0	Robson (B)
		3	1.1.69	Real Zaragoza (Spain)	A	L	2–3	Robson (B), Davies
			15.1.69		H	W	2–1 *	Robson (B), Gibb
		QF	12.3.69	Setubal (Portugal)	H	W	5–1	Robson (B) 2, Gibb, Davies, Foggon
			26.3.69		A	L	1–3	Davies
		SF	14.5.69	Rangers (Scotland)	A	D	0–0	
			22.5.69		H	W	2–0	Scott, Sinclair
		F	29.5.69	Ujpest Dosza (Hungary)	H	W	3–0	Moncur 2, Scott
			11.6.69		A	W	3–2	Moncur, Arentoft, Foggon
1969–70	Fairs Cup	1	15.9.69	Dundee United (Scotland)	A	W	2–1	Davies 2
			1.10.69		H	W	1–0	Dyson
		2	19.11.69	Porto (Portugal)	A	D	0–0	
			26.11.69		H	W	1–0	Scott
		3	17.12.69	Southampton (England)	H	D	0–0	
			13.1.70		A	D	1–1 *	Robson (B)
		QF	11.3.70	Anderlecht (Belgium) *	A	L	0–2	
			18.3.70		H	W	3–1	Robson (B) 2, Dyson
1970–71	Fairs Cup	1	23.9.70	Inter-Milan (Italy)	A	D	1–1	Davies
			30.9.70		H	W	2–0	Moncur, Davies
		2	21.10.70	Pecs Dosza (Hungary) †	H	W	2–0	Davies 2
			4.11.70		A	L	0–2	
1977–78	UEFA Cup	1	14.9.77	Bohemians (Eire)	A	D	0–0	
			28.9.77		H	W	4–0	Gowling 2, Craig 2
		2	19.10.77	Bastia (France)	A	L	1–2	Cannell
			2.11.77		H	L	1–3	Gowling

Season	Competition	Round	Date	Opponents (Country)	Venue	Result		Scorers

NOTTINGHAM FOREST

Season	Competition	Round	Date	Opponents (Country)	Venue	Result		Scorers
1961–62	Fairs Cup	1	13.9.61	Valencia (Spain)	A	L	0–2	
			4.10.61		H	L	1–5	Cobb
1967–68	Fairs Cup	1	20.9.67	Eintracht Frankfurt	A	W	1–0	Baker
			17.10.67	(West Germany)	H	W	4–0	Baker 2, Chapman, Lyons
		2	31.10.67	Zurich (Switerland) *	H	W	2–1	Newton, Moore (pen)
			14.11.67		A	L	0–1	
1978–79	European Cup	1	13.9.78	Liverpool (England)	H	W	2–0	Birtles, Barrett
			27.9.78		A	D	0–0	
		2	18.10.78	AEK Athens (Greece)	A	W	2–1	McGovern, Birtles
			1.11.78		H	W	5–1	Needham, Woodcock, Anderson, Birtles 2
		QF	7.3.79	Grasshoppers (Switzerland)	H	W	4–1	Birtles, Robertson (pen), Gemmill, Lloyd
			21.3.79		A	D	1–1	O'Neill
		SF	11.4.79	IFC Cologne (West	H	D	3–3	Birtles, Bowyer, Robertson
			25.4.79	Germany)	A	W	1–0	Bowyer
			30.5.79	Malmo (Sweden)	N	W	1–0	Francis

QUEEN'S PARK RANGERS

Season	Competition	Round	Date	Opponents (Country)	Venue	Result		Scorers
1976–77	UEFA Cup	1	15.9.76	Brann Bergen (Norway)	H	W	4–0	Bowles 3, Masson
			29.9.76		A	W	7–0	Bowles 3, Givens 2, Thomas, Webb
		2	20.10.76	Slovan Bratislava	A	D	3–3	Bowles 2, Givens
			3.11.76	(Czechoslovakia)	H	W	5–2	Givens 3, Bowles, Clement
		3	24.11.76	IFC Cologne (West	H	W	3–0	Givens, Webb, Bowles
			7.12.76	Germany)	A	L	1–4 *	Masson
		QF	2.3.77	AEK Athens (Greece)	H	W	3–0	Francis (2 pens), Bowles
			16.3.77		A	L	0–3†	

SHEFFIELD WEDNESDAY

Season	Competition	Round	Date	Opponents (Country)	Venue	Result		Scorers
1961–62	Fairs Cup	1	12.9.61	Lyon (France)	A	L	2–4	Ellis, Young
			4.10.61		H	W	5–2	Fantham 2, Griffin, McAnearney (pen), Dobson
		2	29.11.61	AS Roma (Italy)	H	W	4–0	Fantham, Young 3
			13.12.61		A	L	0–1	
		QF	28.2.62	Barcelona (Spain)	H	W	3–2	Fantham 2, Finney
			28.3.62		A	L	0–2	
1963–64	Fairs Cup	1	25.9.63	DOS Utrecht (Holland)	A	W	4–1	Holliday, Layne, Quinn, own goal
			15.10.63		H	W	4–1	Layne 3 (1 pen), Dobson
		2	6.11.63	IFC Cologne (West	A	L	2–3	Pearson 2
			27.11.63	Germany)	H	L	1–2	Layne

SOUTHAMPTON

Season	Competition	Round	Date	Opponents (Country)	Venue	Result		Scorers
1976–77	Cup-Winners' Cup	1	15.9.76	Marseille (France)	H	W	4–0	Waldron, Channon 2 (1pen), Osgood
			29.9.76		A	L	1–2	Peach
		2	20.10.76	Carrick Rangers (Northern Ireland)	A	W	5–2	Stokes, Channon 2, McCalliog, Osgood
			3.11.76		H	W	4–1	Williams, Hayes 2, Stokes
		QF	2.3.77	Anderlecht (Belgium)	A	L	0–2	
			16.3.77		H	W	2–1	Peach (pen), MacDougall
1969–70	Fairs Cup	1	17.9.69	Rosenborg (Norway)	A	L	0–1	
			1.10.69		H	W	2–0	Davies, Paine
		2	4.11.69	Vitoria Guimaraes	A	D	3–3	Channon, Davies, Paine
			12.11.69	(Portugal)	H	W	5–1	Gabriel, Davies 2 (1 pen), Channon, own goal
		3	17.12.69	Newcastle United	A	D	0–0	
			13.1.70	(England) *	H	D	1–1	Channon
1971–72	UEFA Cup	1	15.9.71	Atletico Bilbao (Spain)	H	W	2–1	Jenkins, Channon (pen)
			29.9.71		A	L	0–2	

Season	Competition	Round	Date	Opponents (Country)	Venue	Result	Scorers
STOKE CITY							
1972–73	UEFA Cup	1	13.9.72	Kaiserslautern (West	H	W 3–1	Conroy, Hurst, Ritchie
			27.9.72	Germany)	A	L 0–4	
1974–75	UEFA Cup	1	18.9.74	Ajax (Holland) *	H	D 1–1	Smith
			2.10.74		A	D 0–0	
SUNDERLAND							
1973–74	Cup-Winners'	1	19.9.73	Vasas-Budapest	A	W 2–0	Hughes, Tueart
	Cup		3.10.73	(Hungary)	H	W 1–0	Tueart (pen)
		2	24.10.73	Sporting Lisbon	H	W 2–1	Kerr, Horswill
			7.11.73	(Portugal)	A	L 0–2	
SWANSEA CITY							
1961–62	Cup-Winners'	1	16.9.61	Motor Jena	H	D 2–2	Reynolds, Nurse (pen)
	Cup		18.10.61	(East Germany)	A	L 1–5	Reynolds
				(in Linz, Austria)			
1966–67	Cup-Winners'	1	21.9.66	Slavia Sofia (Bulgaria)	H	D 1–1	Todd
	Cup		5.10.66		A	L 0–4	
TOTTENHAM HOTSPUR							
1961–62	European Cup	Pr	13.9.61	Gornik Zabrze (Poland)	A	L 2–4	Jones, Dyson
			20.9.61		H	W 8–1	Blanchflower (pen), Jones 3, Smith 2, Dyson, White
		1	1.11.61	Feyenoord (Holland)	A	W 3–1	Dyson, Saul 2
			15.11.61		H	D 1–1	Dyson
		QF	14.2.62	Dukla Prague	A	L 0–1	
			26.2.62	(Czechoslovakia)	H	W 4–1	Smith 2, Mackay 2
		SF	21.3.62	Benfica (Portugal)	A	L 1–3	Smith
			5.4.62		H	W 2–1	Smith, Blanchflower (pen)
1962–63	Cup-Winners'	1		bye			
	Cup	2	31.10.62	Rangers (Scotland)	H	W 5–2	White, Greaves, Allen, Norman, own goal
			11.12.62		A	W 3–2	Greaves, Smith 2
		QF	5.3.63	Slovan Bratislava	A	L 0–2	
			14.3.63	(Czechoslovakia)	H	W 6–0	Mackay, Smith, Greaves 2, Jones, White
		SF	24.4.63	OFK Belgrade	A	W 2–1	White, Dyson
			1.5.63	(Yugoslavia)	H	W 3–1	Mackay, Jones, Smith
		F	15.5.63	Atletico Madrid (Spain)	N	W 5–1	Greaves 2, White, Dyson 2
1963–64	Cup-Winners'	1		exempt			
	Cup	2	3.12.63	Manchester United	H	W 2–0	Mackay, Dyson
			10.12.63	(England)	A	L 1–4	Greaves
1967–68	Cup-Winners'	1	20.9.67	Hajduk Split (Yugoslavia)	A	W 2–0	Robertson, Greaves
	Cup		27.9.67		H	W 4–3	Robertson 2, Gilzean, Venables
		2	29.11.67	Lyon (France) *	A	L 0–1	
			13.12.67		H	W 4–3	Greaves 2 (1 pen), Jones, Gilzean
1971–72	UEFA Cup	1	14.9.71	Keflavik (Iceland)	A	W 6–1	Gilzean 3, Coates, Mullery 2
			28.9.71		H	W 9–0	Chivers 3, Gilzean 2, Perryman, Coates, Knowles, Holder
		2	20.10.71	Nantes (France)	A	D 0–0	
			2.11.71		H	W 1–0	Peters
		3	8.12.71	Rapid Bucharest	H	W 3–0	Peters, Chivers 2
			15.12.71	(Rumania)	A	W 2–0	Pearce, Chivers
		QF	7.3.72	UT Arad (Rumania)	A	W 2–0	Morgan, England
			21.3.72		H	D 1–1	Gilzean
		SF	5.4.72	AC Milan (Italy)	H	W 2–1	Perryman 2
			19.4.72		A	D 1–1	Mullery
		F	3.5.72	Wolverhampton	A	W 2–1	Chivers 2
			17.5.72	Wanderers (England)	H	D 1–1	Mullery
1972–73	UEFA Cup	1	13.9.72	Lyn Oslo (Norway)	A	W 6–3	Peters, Pratt, Gilzean 2, Chivers 2
			27.9.72		H	W 6–0	Chivers 3, Coates 2, Pearce
		2	25.10.72	Olympiakos Piraeus	H	W 4–0	Pearce 2, Chivers, Coates
			8.11.72	(Greece)	A	L 0–1	

Season	Competition	Round	Date	Opponents (Country)	Venue	Result	Scorers
TOTTENHAM HOTSPUR continued							
		3	29.11.72	Red Star Belgrade	H	W 2–0	Chivers, Gilzean
			13.12.72	(Yugoslavia)	A	L 0–1	
		QF	7.3.73	Setubal (Portugal)	H	W 1–0	Evans
			21.3.73		A	L 1–2*	Chivers
		SF	10.4.73	Liverpool (England) *	A	L 0–1	
			25.4.73		H	W 2–1	Peters 2
1973–74	UEFA Cup	1	19.9.73	Grasshoppers	A	W 5–1	Chivers 2, Evans, Gilzean 2
			3.10.73	(Switzerland)	H	W 4–1	Peters 2, England, own goal
		2	24.10.73	Aberdeen (Scotland)	A	D 1–1	Coates
			7.11.73		H	W 4–1	Peters, Neighbour, McGrath 2
		3	28.11.73	Dynamo Tbilisi (USSR)	A	D 1–1	Coates
			12.12.73		H	W 5–1	McGrath, Chivers 2, Peters 2
		QF	6.3.74	IFC Cologne	A	W 2–1	McGrath, Peters
			20.3.74	(West Germany)	H	W 3–0	Chivers, Coates, Peters
		SF	10.4.74	Lokomotive Leipzig	A	W 2–1	Peters, McGrath
			24.4.74	(East Germany)	H	W 2–0	McGrath, Chivers
		F	21.5.74	Feyenoord (Holland)	H	D 2–2	England, own goal
			29.5.74		A	L 0–2	
WEST BROMWICH ALBION							
1968–69	Cup-Winners' Cup	1	18.9.68	FC Bruges (Belgium)	A	L 1–3	Hartford
			2.10.68		H	W 2–0*	Brown (T), Hartford
		2	13.11.68	Dynamo Bucharest	A	D 1–1	Hartford
			27.11.68	(Rumania)	H	W 4–0	Lovett, Astle, Brown (T) 2 (1 pen)
		QF	15.1.69	Dunfermline Athletic	A	D 0–0	
			19.2.69	(Scotland)	H	L 0–1	
1966–67	Fairs Cup	1		bye			
		2	2.11.66	DOS Utrecht (Holland)	A	D 1–1	Hope
			9.11.66		H	W 5–2	Brown (T) 3 (1 pen), Clark, Kaye
		3	2.2.67	Bologna (Italy)	A	L 0–3	
			8.3.67		H	L 1–3	Fairfax
1978–79	UEFA Cup	1	13.9.78	Galatasaray (Turkey)	A	W 3–1	Robson, Regis, Cunningham
			27.9.78		H	W 3–1	Robson, Cunningham (pen), Trewick
		2	18.10.78	Sporting Braga	A	W 2–0	Regis 2
			1.11.78	(Portugal)	H	W 1–0	Brown (A)
		3	22.11.78	Valencia (Spain)	A	D 1–1	Cunningham
			6.12.78		H	W 2–0	Brown (T) 2, (1 pen)
		QF	7.3.79	Red Star Belgrade	A	L 0–1	
			21.3.79	(Yugoslavia)	H	D 1–1	Regis
WEST HAM UNITED							
1964–65	Cup-Winners' Cup	1	23.9.64	La Gantoise (Belgium)	A	W 1–0	Boyce
			7.10.64		H	D 1–1	Byrne
		2	25.11.64	Sparta Prague	H	W 2–0	Bond, Sealey
			9.12.64	(Czechoslovakia)	A	L 1–2	Sissons
		QF	16.3.65	Lausanne (Switzerland)	A	W 2–1	Dear, Byrne
			23.3.65		H	W 4–3	Dear 2, Peters, own goal
		SF	7.4.65	Real Zaragoza (Spain)	H	W 2–1	Dear, Byrne
			28.4.65		A	D 1–1	Sissons
		F	19.5.65	Munich 1860 (West Germany)	N	W 2–0	Sealey 2
1965–66	Cup-Winners' Cup	1		bye			
		2	24.11.65	Olympiakos Piraeus	H	W 4–0	Hurst 2, Byrne, Brabrook
			1.12.65	(Greece)	A	D 2–2	Peters 2
		QF	2.3.66	Magdeburg (East Germany)	H	W 1–0	Byrne
			16.3.66		A	D 1–1	Sissons
		SF	5.4.66	Borussia Dortmund	H	L 1–2	Peters
			13.4.66	(West Germany)	A	L 1–3	Byrne
1975–76	Cup-Winners' Cup	1	17.9.75	Lahden Reipas (Finland)	A	D 2–2	Brooking, Bonds
			1.10.75		H	W 3–0	Robson (K), Holland, Jennings
		2	22.10.75	Ararat Erevan (USSR)	A	D 1–1	Taylor (A)
			5.11.75		H	W 3–1	Paddon, Robson(K), Taylor(A)

Season	Competition	Round	Date	Opponents (Country)	Venue	Result		Scorers

WEST HAM UNITED continued

		QF	3.3.76	Den Haag (Holland)	A	L	2–4	Jennings 2
			17.3.76		H	W	3–1 *	Taylor (A), Lampard, Bonds (pen)
		SF	31.3.76	Eintracht Frankfurt	A	L	1–2	Paddon
			14.4.76	(West Germany)	H	W	3–1	Brooking 2, Robson (K)
		F	5.5.76	Anderlecht (Belgium)	N	L	2–4	Holland, Robson (K)

WOLVERHAMPTON WANDERERS

1958–59	European Cup	Pr		bye				
		1	12.11.58	Schalke 04	H	D	2–2	Broadbent 2
			18.11.58	(West Germany)	A	L	1–2	Jackson
1959–60	European Cup	Pr	30.9.59	Vorwaerts (East Germany)	A	L	1–2	Broadbent
			7.10.59		H	W	2–0	Broadbent, Mason
		1	11.11.59	Red Star Belgrade	A	D	1–1	Deeley
			24.11.59	(Yugoslavia)	H	W	3–0	Murray, Mason 2
		QF	10.2.60	Barcelona (Spain)	A	L	0–4	
			2.3.60		H	L	2–5	Murray, Mason
1960–61	Cup-Winners' Cup	Pr		bye				
		QF	12.10.60	FK Austria (Austria)	A	L	0–2	
			30.11.60		H	W	5–0	Kirkham 2, Mason, Broadbent 2
		SF	29.3.61	Rangers (Scotland)	A	L	0–2	
			19.4.61		H	D	1–1	Broadbent
1971–72	UEFA Cup	1	15.9.71	Academica Coimbra	H	W	3–0	McAlle, Richards, Dougan
			29.9.71	(Portugal)	A	W	4–1	Dougan 3, McAlle
		2	20.10.71	Den Haag (Holland)	A	W	3–1	Dougan, McCalliog, Hibbitt
			3.11.71		H	W	4–0	Dougan, own goals 3
		3	24.11.71	Carl Zeiss Jena	A	W	1–0	Richards
			8.12.71	(East Germany)	H	W	3–0	Hibbitt, Dougan 2
		QF	7.3.72	Juventus (Italy)	A	D	1–1	McCalliog
			21.3.72		H	W	2–1	Hegan, Dougan
		SF	5.4.72	Ferencvaros (Hungary)	A	D	2–2	Richards, Munro
			19.4.72		H	W	2–1	Bailey, Munro
		F	3.5.72	Tottenham Hotspur	H	L	1–2	McCalliog
			17.5.72	(England)	A	D	1–1	Wagstaffe
1973–74	UEFA Cup	1	26.9.73	Belenenses (Portugal)	A	W	2–0	Richards, Dougan
			3.10.73		H	W	2–1	Eastoe, McCalliog
		2	24.10.73	Lokomotive Leipzig	A	L	0–3	
			7.11.73	(East Germany)	H	W	4–1	Kindon, Munro, Dougan, Hibbitt
1974–75	UEFA Cup	1	18.9.74	Porto (Portugal)	A	L	1–4	Bailey
			2.10.74		H	W	3–1	Bailey, Daley, Dougan

WREXHAM

1972–73	Cup-Winners' Cup	1	13.9.72	Zurich (Switzerland)	A	D	1–1	Kinsey
			27.9.72		H	W	2–1	Ashcroft, Sutton
		2	25.10.72	Hajduk Split	H	W	3–1	Tinnion, Smallman, own goal
			8.11.72	(Yugoslavia) *	A	L	0–2	
1975–76	Cup-Winners' Cup	1	17.9.75	Djurgaarden (Sweden)	H	W	2–1	Griffiths, Davis
			1.10.75		A	D	1–1	Whittle
		2	22.10.75	Stal Rzeszow (Poland)	H	W	2–0	Ashcroft 2
			5.11.75		A	D	1–1	Sutton
		QF	3.3.76	Anderlecht (Belgium)	A	L	0–1	
			17.3.76		H	D	1–1	Lee
1978–79	Cup-Winners' Cup	1	13.9.78	Rijeka (Yugoslavia)	A	L	0–3	
			27.9.78		H	W	2–0	McNeil, Cartwright

*won on away goals counting double
†won on penalties
‡won on the toss of a coin

SCOTTISH LEAGUE CLUBS

Season	Competition	Round	Date	Opponents (Country)	Venue	Result	Scorers
ABERDEEN							
1967–68	Cup-Winners'	1	6.9.67	KR Reykjavik (Iceland)	H	W 10–1	Munro 3, Storrie 2, Smith 2, McMillan, Petersen, Taylor
			13.9.67		A	W 4–1	Storrie 2, Buchan, Munro
		2	29.11.67	Standard Liege (Belgium)	A	L 0–3	
			6.12.67		H	W 2–0	Munro, Melrose
1970–71	Cup-Winners' Cup	1	16.9.70	Honved (Hungary) †	H	W 3–1	Graham, Harper, Murray (S)
			30.9.70		A	L 1–3	Murray (S)
1978–79	Cup-Winners'	1	13.9.78	Marek Stanke (Bulgaria)	A	L 2–3	Jarvie, Harper
			27.9.78		H	W 3–0	Strachan, Jarvie, Harper
		2	18.10.78	Fortuna Dusseldorf (West Germany)	A	L 0–3	
			1.11.78		H	W 2–0	McLelland, Jarvie
1968–69	Fairs Cup	1	17.9.68	Slavia Sofia (Bulgaria)	D	0–0	
			2.10.68		H	W 2–0	Robb, Taylor
		2	23.10.68	Real Zaragoza (Spain)	H	W 2–1	Forrest, Smith
			30.10.68		A	L 0–3	
1971–72	UEFA Cup	1	15.9.71	Celta Vigo (Spain)	A	W 2–0	Harper, own goal
			29.9.71		H	W 1–0	Harper
		2	27.10.71	Juventus (Italy)	A	L 0–2	
			17.11.71		H	D 1–1	Harper
1972–73	UEFA Cup	1	13.9.72	Borussia Moenchenglad-bach (West Germany)	H	L 2–3	Harper, Jarvie
			27.9.72		A	L 3–6	Harper 2, Jarvie
1973–74	UEFA Cup	1	19.9.73	Finn Harps (Eire)	H	W 4–1	Miller (R), Jarvie 2, Graham
			3.10.73		A	W 3–1	Robb, Graham, Miller (R)
		2	24.10.73	Tottenham Hotspur (England)	H	D 1–1	Hermiston (pen)
			7.11.73		A	L 1–4	Jarvie
1977-78	UEFA Cup	1	14.9.77	RWD Molenbeek (Belgium)	A	D 0–0	
			28.9.77		H	L 1–2	Jarvie
CELTIC							
1966-67	European Cup	1	28.9.66	Zurich (Switzerland)	H	W 2–0	Gemmell, McBride
			5.10.66		A	W 3–0	Gemmell 2 (1 pen), Chalmers
		2	30.11.66	Nantes (France)	A	W 3–1	McBride, Lennox, Chalmers
			7.12.66		H	W 3–1	Johnstone, Lennox, Chalmers
		QF	1.3.66	Vojvodina (Yugoslavia)	A	L 0–1	
			8.3.66		H	W 2–0	Chalmers, McNeill
		SF	12.4.67	Dukla Prague (Czechoslovakia)	H	W 3–1	Johnstone, Wallace 2
			25.4.67		A	D 0–0	
		F	25.5.67	Inter-Milan (Italy)	N	W 2–1	Gemmell, Chalmers
1967–68	European Cup	1	20.9.67	Dynamo Kiev (USSR)	H	L 1–2	Lennox
			4.10.67		A	D 1–1	Lennox
1968–69	European Cup	1	18.8.68	St Etienne (France)	A	L 0–2	
			2.10.68		H	W 4–0	Gemmell (pen), Craig, Chalmers McBride
		2	13.11.68	Red Star Belgrade (Yugoslavia)	H	W 5–1	Murdoch, Johnstone 2, Lennox, Wallace
			27.11.68		A	D 1–1	Wallace
		QF	19.2.69	AC Milan (Italy)	A	D 0–0	
			12.3.69		H	L 0–1	
1969–70	European Cup	1	17.9.69	Basle (Switzerland)	A	D 0–0	
			1.10.69		H	W 2–0	Hood, Gemmell
		2	12.11.69	Benfica (Portugal)	H	W 3–0	Gemmell, Wallace, Hood
			26.11.69		A	L 0–3 ‡	
		QF	4.3.70	Fiorentina (Italy)	H	W 3–0	Auld, Wallace, own goal
			18.3.70		A	L 0–1	
		SF	1.4.70	Leeds United (England)	A	W 1–0	Connolly
			15.4.70		H	W 2–1	Hughes, Murdoch
		F	6.5.70	Feyenoord (Holland)	N	L 1–2	Gemmell
1970–71	European Cup	1	16.9.70	KPV Kokkola (Finland)	H	W 9–0	Hood 3, Wilson 2, Hughes, McNeill, Johnstone, Davidson
			30.9.70		A	W 5–0	Wallace 2, Callaghan, Davidson, Lennox
		2	21.10.70	Waterford (Eire)	A	W 7–0	Wallace 3, Murdoch 2, Marari 2
			4.11.70		H	W 3–2	Hughes, Johnstone 2

Season	Competition	Round	Date	Opponents (Country)	Venue	Result		Scorers
CELTIC continued								
		QF	10.3.70	Ajax (Holland)	A	L	0–3	
			24.3.71		H	W	1–0	Johnstone
1971–72	European Cup	1	15.9.71	BK 1903 Copenhagen	A	L	1–2	Macari
			29.9.71	(Denmark)	H	W	3–0	Wallace 2, Callaghan
		2	20.10.71	Sliema Wanderers	H	W	5–0	Gemmell, Macari 2, Hood, Brogan
				(Malta)				
			3.11.71		A	W	2–1	Hood, Lennox
		QF	8.3.72	Ujpest Dozsa (Hungary)	A	W	2–1	Macari, own goal
			22.3.72		H	D	1–1	Macari
		SF	5.4.72	Inter-Milan (Italy) †	A	D	0–0	
			19.4.72		H	D	0–0	
1972–73	European Cup	1	13.9.72	Rosenborg (Norway)	H	W	2–1	Macari, Deans
			27.9.72		A	W	3–1	Macari, Hood, Dalglish
		2	25.10.72	Ujpest Dozsa (Hungary)	H	W	2–1	Dalglish 2
			8.11.72		A	L	0–3	
1973–74	European Cup	1	19.9.73	Turun (Finland)	A	W	6–1	Callaghan 2, Hood, Johnstone, Connelly (pen), Deans
			3.10.73		H	W	3–0	Deans, Johnstone 2
		2	24.10.73	Vejle (Denmark)	H	D	0–0	
			6.11.73		A	W	1–0	Lennox
		QF	27.2.74	Basle (Switzerland)	A	L	2–3	Wilson, Dalglish
			20.3.74		H	W	4–2	Dalglish, Deans, Callaghan, Murray
		SF	10.4.74	Atletico Madrid (Spain)	H	D	0–0	
			24.4.74		A	L	0–2	
1974–75	European Cup	1	18.9.74	Olymiakos Piraeus	H	D	1–1	Wilson
			2.10.74	(Greece)	A	L	0–2	
1977–78	European Cup	1	14.9.77	Jeunesse Esch	H	W	5–0	McDonald, Wilson, Craig 2, McLaughlin
				(Luxembourg)				
			28.9.77		A	W	6–1	Lennox 2, Edvaldsson 2, Glavin, Craig
		2	19.10.77	SW Innsbruck (Austria)	H	W	2–1	Craig, Burns
			2.11.77		A	L	0–3	
1963–64	Cup-Winners'	1	17.9.63	Basle (Switzerland)	A	W	5–1	Divers, Hughes 3, Lennox
			9.10.63		H	W	5–0	Johnstone, Divers 2, Murdoch, Chalmers
		2	4.12.63	Dynamo Zagreb	H	W	3–0	Chalmers 2, Hughes
			11.12.63	(Yugoslavia)	A	L	1–2	Murdoch
		QF	26.2.64	Slovan Bratislava	H	W	1–0	Murdoch (pen)
			4.3.64	(Czechoslovakia)	A	W	1–0	Hughes
		SF	15.4.64	MTK Budapest	H	W	3–0	Johnstone, Chalmers 2
			29.4.64	(Hungary)	A	L	0–4	
1965–66	Cup-Winners' Cup	1	29.9.65	Go Ahead Deverter	A	W	6–0	Gallahger 2, Hughes, Johnston 2, Lennox
				(Holland)				
			7.10.65		H	W	1–0	McBride
		2	3.11.65	Aarhus (Denmark)	A	W	1–0	McBride
			17.11.65		H	W	2–0	McNeill, Johnstone
		QF	12.1.66	Dynamo Kiev (USSR)	H	W	3–0	Gemmell, Murdoch 2
			26.1.66		A	D	1–1	Gemmell
		SF	14.4.66	Liverpool (England)	H	W	1–0	Lennox
			19.4.66		A	L	0–2	
1975–76	Cup-Winners' Cup	1	16.9.75	Valur Reykjavik (Iceland)	A	W	2–0	Wilson, McDonald
			1.10.75		H	W	7–0	Edvaldsson, Dalglish, McCluskey (P) (pen), Hood 2, Deans, Callaghan
		2	22.10.75	Boavista (Portugal)	A	D	0–0	
			5.11.75		H	W	3–1	Dalglish, Edvaldsson, Deans
		QF	3.3.76	Sachsenring Zwickau	H	D	1–1	Dalglish
			17.3.76	(West Germany)	A	L	0–1	
1962–63	Fairs Cup	1	26.9.62	Valencia (Spain)	A	L	2–4	Carrol 2
			24.10.62		H	D	2–2	Crerand, own goal
1964–65	Fairs Cup	1	23.9.64	Leixoes (Portugal)	A	D	1–1	Murdoch
			7.10.64		H	W	3–0	Murdoch (pen), Chalmers 2
		2	18.11.64	Barcelona (Spain)	A	L	1–3	Hughes
			2.12.64		H	D	0–0	
1976–77	UEFA Cup	1	15.9.76	Wisla Krakow (Poland)	H	D	2–2	McDonald, Dalglish
			29.9.76		A	L	0–2	

Season	Competition	Round	Date	Opponents (Country)	Venue	Result		Scorers
DUNDEE								
1962–63	European Cup	Pr	5.9.62	IFC Cologne (West Germany)	H	W	8–1	Gilzean 3, own goal, Wishart, Robertson, Smith, Penman
			26.9.62		A	L	0–4	
		1	24.10.62	Sporting Lisbon	A	L	0–1	
			31.10.62	(Portugal)	H	W	4–1	Gilzean 3, Cousin
		QF	6.3.63	Anderlecht (Belgium)	A	W	4–1	Gilzean 2, Cousin, Smith
			13.3.63		H	W	2–1	Cousin, Smith
		SF	24.4.63	AC Milan (Italy)	A	L	1–5	Cousin
			1.5.63		H	W	1–0	Gilzean
1964–65	Cup-Winners' Cup	1		bye				
		2	18.11.64	Real Zaragoza (Spain)	H	D	2–2	Murray, Houston
			8.12.64		A	L	1–2	Robertson
1967–68	Fairs Cup	1	27.9.67	DWS Amsterdam	A	L	1–2	McLean (G)
			4.10.67	(Holland)	H	W	3 0	Wilson (S), McLean 2 (1 pen)
		2	1.11.67	Liege (Belgium)	H	W	3–1	Stuart 2, Wilson (S)
			14.11.67		A	W	4–1	McLean (G) 4
		3		bye				
		QF	27.3.68	Zurich (Switzerland)	H	W	1–0	Easton
			3.4.68		A	W	1–0	Wilson (S)
		SF	1.5.68	Leeds United (England)	H	D	1–1	Wilson (R)
			15.5.68		A	L	0–2	
1971–72	UEFA Cup	1	15.9.71	Akademisk Copenhagen	H	W	4–2	Bryce 2, Wallace, Lambie
			29.9.71	(Denmark)	A	W	1–0	Duncan
		2	19.10.71	IFC Cologne (West	A	L	1–2	Kinninmouth
			3.11.71	Germany)	H	W	4–2	Duncan 3, Wilson (R)
		3	24.11.71	AC Milan (Italy)	A	L	0–3	
			8.12.71		H	W	2–0	Wallace, Duncan
1973–74	UEFA Cup	1	19.9.73	Twente Enschede	H	L	1–3	Stewart
			3.10.73	(Holland)	A	L	1–2	Johnston, Scott (J)
1974–75	UEFA Cup	1	18.9.74	RWD Molenbeek	A	L	0–1	
			2.10.74	(Belgium)	H	L	2–4	Duncan, Scott (J)
DUNDEE UNITED								
1974–75	Cup-Winners' Cup	1	18.9.74	Juil Petrosani (Rumania)	H	W	3–0	Narey, Copland, Gardner
			2.10.74		A	L	0–2	
		2	23.10.74	Bursaspor (Turkey)	H	D	0–0	
			6.10.74		A	L	0–1	
1966–67	Fairs Cup	1		bye				
		2		Barcelona (Spain)	A	W	2–1	Hainey, Seeman
			16.11.66		H	W	2–0	Mitchell, Hainey
		3	8.2.67	Juventus (Italy)	A	L	0–3	
			8.3.67		H	W	1–0	Dossing
1969–70	Fairs Cup	1	15.9.69	Newcastle United	H	L	1–2	Scott
			1.10.69	(England)	A	L	0–1	
1970–71	Fairs Cup	1	15.9.70	Grasshoppers	H	W	3–2	Reid (I), Markland, Reid (A)
			30.9.70	(Switzerland)	A	D	0–0	
		2	21.10.70	Sparta Prague	A	L	1–3	Traynor
			4.11.70	(Czechoslovakia)	H	W	1–0	Gordon
1975–76	UEFA Cup	1	23.9.75	Keflavik (Iceland)	A	W	2–0	Narey 2
			30.9.75		H	W	4–0	Hall 2, Hegarty (pen), Sturrock
		2	22.10.75	Porto (Portugal)	H	L	1–2	Rennie
			5.11.75		A	D	1–1	Hegarty
1977–78	UEFA Cup	1	14.9.77	KB Copenhagen	H	W	1–0	Sturrock
			27.9.77	(Denmark)	A	L	0–3	
1978–79	UEFA Cup	1	12.9.78	Standard Liege	A	L	0–1	
			27.9.78	(Belgium)	H	D	0–0	
DUNFERMLINE ATHLETIC								
1961–62	Cup-Winners' Cup	1	12.9.61	St Patrick's Athletic (Eire)	H	W	4–1	Melrose, Peebles, Dickson, Macdonald
			27.9.61		A	W	4–0	Peebles 2, Dickson 2
		2	25.10.61	Vardar Skoplje (Yugoslavia)	H	W	5–0	Smith, Dickson 2, Melrose, Peebles
			8.11.61		A	L	0–2	

Season	Competition	Round	Date	Opponents (Country)	Venue	Result		Scorers

DUNFERMLINE ATHLETIC continued

Season	Competition	Round	Date	Opponents (Country)	Venue	Result		Scorers
		QF	13.2.62	Ujpest Dozsa (Hungary)	A	L	3–4	Smith, Macdonald 2
			20.2.62		H	L	0–1	
1967–68	Cup-Winners' Cup	1	18.9.68	Apoel (Cyprus)	H	W	10–1	Robertson 2, Renton 2, Barry, Callaghan (W) 2, Gardner, Edwards, Callaghan (T)
			2.10.68		A	W	2–0	Gardner, Callaghan (W)
		2	13.11.68	Olympiakos Pireaeus (Greece)	H	W	4–0	Edwards 2, Fraser, Mitchell
			27.11.68		A	L	0–3	
		QF	15.1.69	West Bromwich Albion (England)	H	D	0–0	
			19.2.69		A	W	1–0	Gardner
		SF	9.4.69	Slovan Bratislava (Czechoslovakia)	H	D	1–1	Fraser
			23.4.69		A	L	0–1	
1962–63	Fairs Cup	1	24.10.62	Everton (England)	A	L	0–1	
			31.10.62		H	W	2–0	Miller, Melrose
		2	12.12.62	Valencia (Spain)	A	L	0–4	
			19.12.62		H	W	6–2	Melrose, Sinclair 2, McLean, Peebles, Smith
			6.2.63		N	L	0–1	
1964–65	Fairs Cup	1	13.10.64	Oergryte (Sweden)	H	W	4–2	McLaughlin 2, Sinclair 2
			20.10.64		A	D	0–0	
		2	17.11.64	Stuttgart (West Germany)	H	W	1–0	Callaghan (T)
			1.12.64		A	D	0–0	
		3	27.1.65	Atletico Bilbao (Spain)	A	L	0–1	
			3.3.65		H	W	1–0	Smith
			16.3.65		A	L	1–2	Smith
1965–66	Fairs Cup	1		bye				
		2	3.11.65	KB Copenhagen (Denmark)	H	W	5–0	Fleming, Paton 2, Robertson, Callaghan (T)
			17.11.65		A	W	4–2	Edwards, Paton, Fleming, Ferguson
		3	26.1.66	Spartak Brno (Czechoslovakia)	H	W	2–0	Paton, Ferguson (pen)
			16.2.66		A	D	0–0	
		QF	16.3.66	Real Zaragoza (Spain)	H	W	1–0	Paton
			20.3.66		A	L	2–4	Ferguson 2
1966–67	Fairs Cup	1	24.8.66	Frigg Oslo (Norway)	A	W	3–1	Fleming 2, Callaghan (T)
			28.9.66		H	W	3–1	Delaney 2, Callaghan (T)
		2	26.10.66	Dynamo Zagreb *	H	W	4–2	Delaney, Edwards, Ferguson 2
			11.11.66		A	L	0–2	
1969–70	Fairs Cup	1	16.9.69	Bordeaux (France)	H	W	4–0	Paton 2, Mitchell, Gardner
			30.9.69		A	L	0–2	
		2	5.11.69	Gwardia Warsaw (Poland)	A	W	2–1	McLean, Gardner
			18.11.69		A	W	1–0	Renton
		3	17.12.69	Anderlecht (Belgium) *	A	L	0–1	
			14.1.70		H	W	3–2	McLean 2, Mitchell

HEARTS

Season	Competition	Round	Date	Opponents (Country)	Venue	Result		Scorers
1958–59	European Cup	Pr	3.9.58	Standard Liege (Belgium)	A	L	1–5	Crawford
			9.9.58		H	W	2–1	Bauld 2
1960–61	European Cup	Pr	29.9.60	Benfica (Portugal)	H	L	1–2	Young
			5.10.60		A	L	0–3	
1976–77	Cup-Winners' Cup	1	15.9.76	Lokomotive Leipzig (East Germany)	A	L	0–2	
			29.9.76		H	W	5–1	Kay, Gibson 2, Brown, Busby
		2	20.10.76	SV Hamburg (West Germany)	A	L	2–4	Park, Busby
			3.11.76		H	L	1–4	Gibson
1961–62	Fairs Cup	1	27.9.61	Union St Gilloise (Belgium)	A	W	3–1	Blackwood, Davidson 2
			4.10.61		H	W	2–0	Wallace, Stenhouse
		2	6.11.61	Inter-Milan (Italy)	H	L	0–1	
			22.11.61		A	L	0–4	
1963–64	Fairs Cup	1	25.9.63	Lausanne (Switzerland)	A	D	2–2	Traynor, Ferguson
			9.10.63		H	D	2–2	Cumming, Hamilton (J)
			15.10.63		A	L	2–3	Wallace, Ferguson
1965–66	Fairs Cup	1		bye				
		2	18.10.65	Valerengen (Norway)	H	W	1–0	Wallace
			27.10.65		A	W	3–1	Kerrigan 2, Trayner
		3	12.1.66	Real Zaragoza (Spain)	H	D	3–3	Anderson, Wallace, Kerrigan
			26.1.66		A	D	2–2	Anderson, Wallace
			2.3.66		A	L	0–1	

Season	Competition	Round	Date	Opponents (Country)	Venue	Result		Scorers

HIBERNIAN

Season	Competition	Round	Date	Opponents (Country)	Venue	Result		Scorers
1955–56	European Cup	1	14.9.55	Rot-Weiss Essen	A	W	4–0	Turnbull 2, Reilly, Ormond
			12.10.55	(West Germany)	H	D	1–1	Buchanan (J)
		QF	23.11.55	Djurgaarden (Sweden)	H	W	3–1	Combe, Mulkerrin, own goal
			28.11.55		A	W	1–0	Turnbull (pen)
		SF	4.4.56	Reims (France) *	A	L	0–2	
			18.4.56		H	L	0–1	
1972–73	Cup-Winners' Cup	1	13.9.72	Sporting Lisbon	A	L	1–2	Duncan
			27.9.72	(Portugal)	H	W	6–1	Gordon 2, O'Rourke 3, own goal
		2	25.10.72	Besa (Albania)	H	W	7–1	Cropley, O'Rourke 3, Duncan 2, Brownlie
			8.11.72		A	D	1–1	Gordon
		QF	7.3.73	Hajduk Split (Yugoslavia)	H	W	4–2	Gordon 3, Duncan
			21.3.73		A	L	0–3	
1960–61	Fairs Cup	1		Lausanne (Switzerland) Lausanne withdrew				
		QF	27.12.60	Barcelona (Spain)	A	D	4–4	McLeod, Preston, Baker 2
			22.2.61		H	W	3–2	Kinloch 2 (1 pen), Baker
		SF	19.4.61	AS Roma (Italy)	H	D	2–2	Baker, McLeod
			26.4.61		A	D	3–3	Baker 2, Kinloch
			27.5.61		A	L	0–6	
1961–62	Fairs Cup	1	4.9.61	Belenenses (Portugal)	H	D	3–3	Fraser 2, Baird (pen)
			27.9.61		A	W	3–1	Baxter 2, Stevenson
		2	1.11.61	Red Star Belgrade	A	L	0–4	
			15.11.61	(Yugoslavia)	H	L	0–1	
1962–63	Fairs Cup	1	3.10.62	Stavenet (Denmark)	H	W	4–0	Byrne 2, Baker, own goal
			23.10.62		A	W	3–2	Stevenson 2, Bryne
		2	27.11.62	DOS Utrecht (Holland)	A	W	1–0	Falconer
			12.12.62		H	W	2–1	Baker, Stevenson
		QF	13.3.63	Valencia (Spain)	A	L	0–5	
			3.4.63		H	W	2–1	Preston, Baker
1965–66	Fairs Cup	1	8.9.65	Valencia (Spain)	H	W	2–0	Scott, McNamme
			12.10.65		A	L	0–2	
			3.11.65		A	L	0–3	
1967–68	Fairs Cup	1	20.9.67	Porto (Portugal)	H	W	3–0	Cormack 2, Stevenson
			4.10.67		A	L	1–3	Stanton (pen)
		2	22.11.67	Napoli (Italy)	A	L	1–4	Stein
			29.11.67		H	W	5–0	Duncan, Quinn, Cormack, Stanton, Stein
		3	20.12.67	Leeds United (England)	A	L	0–1	
			10.1.68		H	D	1–1	Stein
1968–69	Fairs Cup	1	18.9.68	Ljubljana (Yugoslavia)	A	W	3–0	Stevenson, Stein, Marinello
			2.10.68		H	W	2–1	Davis (2 pen)
		2	13.11.68	Lokomotive Leipzig	H	W	3–1	McBride 3
			20.11.68	(East Germany)	A	W	1–0	Grant
		3	18.12.68	SV Hamburg (West	A	L	0–1	
			15.1.69	Germany) *	H	W	2–1	McBride 2
1970–71	Fairs Cup	1	16.9.70	Malmo (Sweden)	H	W	6–0	McBride 3, Duncan 2, Blair
			30.9.70		A	W	3–2	Duncan, McEwan, Stanton
		2	14.10.70	Vitoria Guimmaraes	H	W	2–0	Duncan, Stanton
			28.10.70	(Portugal)	A	L	1–2	Graham
		3	9.12.70	Liverpool (England)	H	L	0–1	
			22.12.70		A	L	0–2	
1973–74	UEFA Cup	1	19.9.73	Keflavik (Iceland)	H	W	2–0	Black, Higgins
			3.10.73		A	D	1–1	Stanton
		2	24.10.73	Leeds United (England) †	A	D	0–0	
			2.10.74		H	D	0–0	
1974–75	UEFA Cup	1	18.9.74	Rosenborg (Norway)	A	W	3–2	Stanton, Gordon, Cropley
			2.10.74		H	W	9–1	Harper 2, Munro 2, Stanton 2, Cropley 2 (pens), Gordon
		2	23.10.74	Juventus (Italy)	H	L	2–4	Stanton, Cropley
			6.11.74		A	L	0–4	
1975–76	UEFA Cup	1	17.9.75	Liverpool (England)	H	W	1–0	Harper
			30.9.75		A	L	1–3	Edwards
1976–77	UEFA Cup	1	15.9.76	Sochaux (France)	H	W	1–0	Brownlie
			29.9.76		A	D	0–0	

Season	Competition	Round	Date	Opponents (Country)	Venue	Result	Scorers
HIBERNIAN continued							
		2	20.10.76	Oesters Vaxjo (Sweden)	H	W 2–0	Blackley, Brownlie (pen)
			3.11.76		A	L 1–4	Smith
1978–79	UEFA Cup	1	13.9.78	Norrkoping (Sweden)	H	W 3–2	Higgins 2, Temperley
			27.9.78		A	D 0–0	
		2	18.10.78	Strasbourg (France)	A	L 0–2	
			1.11.78		H	W 1–0	McLeod (pen)
KILMARNOCK							
1965–66	European Cup	Pr	8.9.65	Nendori Tirana (Albania)	A	D 0–0	
			29.6.65		H	W 1–0	Black
		1	17.11.65	Real Madrid (Spain)	H	D 2–2	McLean (pen), McInally
			1.12.65		A	L 1–5	McIlroy
1964–65	Fairs Cup	1	2.9.64	Eintracht Frankfurt	A	L 0–3	
			22.9.64	(West Germany)	H	W 5–1	Hamilton, McIlroy, McFadzean McInally, Sneddon
		2	11.11.64	Everton (England)	H	L 0–2	
			23.11.64		A	L 1–4	McIlroy
1966–67	Fairs Cup	1		bye			
		2	25.10.66	Antwerp (Belgium)	A	W 1–0	McInally
			2.11.66		H	W 7–2	McInally 2, Queen 2, McLean 2 Watson
		3	14.12.66	La Gantoise (Belgium)	H	W 1–0	Murray
			21.12.66		A	W 2–1	McInally, McLean
		QF	19.4.67	Lokomotive Leipzig	A	L 0–1	
			26.4.67	(East Germany)	H	W 2–0	McFadzean, McIlroy
		SF	19.5.67	Leeds United (England)	A	L 2–4	McIlroy 2
			24.5.67		H	D 0–0	
1969–70	Fairs Cup	1	16.9.69	Zurich (Switzerland)	A	L 2–3	McLean (J), Mathie
			30.9.69		H	W 3–1	McGrory, Morrison, McLean(T)
		2	19.11.69	Slavia Sofia (Bulgaria)	H	W 4–1	Mathie 2, Cook, Gilmour
			26.11.69		A	L 0–2	
		3	17.12.69	Dynamo Bacau	H	D 1–1	Mathie
			13.1.70	(Yugoslavia)	A	L 0–2	
1970–71	Fairs Cup	1	15.9.70	Coleraine (Northern	A	D 1–1	Mathie
			29.9.70	Ireland)	H	L 2–3	McLean (T), Morrison
MORTON							
1968–69	Fairs Cup	1	18.9.68	Chelsea (England)	A	L 0–5	
			30.9.68		H	L 3–4	Thorop, Mason, Taylor
PARTICK THISTLE							
1963–64	Fairs Cup	1	16.9.63	Glentoran (Northern	A	W 4–1	Hainey, Yard 2, Wright
			30.9.63	Ireland)	H	W 3–0	Smith 2, Harvey (pen)
		2	18.11.63	Spartak Brno	H	W 3–2	Yard, Harvey (pen), Ferguson
			27.11.63	(Czechoslovakia)	A	L 0–4	
1972–73	UEFA Cup	1	13.9.72	Honved (Hungary)	A	L 0–1	
			27.9.72		H	L 0–3	
RANGERS							
1956–57	European Cup	Pr		bye			
		1	24.10.56	Nice (France)	H	W 2–1	Murray, Simpson
			14.11.56		A	L 1–2	Hubbard (pen)
			28.11.56		N	L 1–3	own goal
1957–58	European Cup	Pr	4.9.57	St Etienne (France)	H	W 3–1	Kichenbrand, Scott, Simpson
			25.9.57		A	L 1–2	Wilson
		1	27.11.57	AC Milan (Italy)	H	L 1–4	Murray
			11.12.57		A	L 0–2	
1959–60	European Cup	Pr	16.9.59	Anderlecht (Belgium)	H	W 5–2	Millar, Scott, Matthew, Baird 2
			24.9.59		A	W 2–0	Matthew, McMillan
		1	11.11.59	Red Star Belgrade	H	W 4–3	McMillan, Scott, Wilson, Millar
			18.11.59	(Czechoslovakia)	A	D 1–1	Scott
		QF	9.3.60	Sparta Rotterdam	A	W 3–2	Wilson, Baird, Murray
			16.3.60	(Holland)	H	L 0–1	
			30.3.60		N	W 3–2	Baird 2, own goal

Season	Competition	Round	Date	Opponents (Country)	Venue	Result	Scorers
RANGERS continued							
		SF	13.4.60	Eintracht Frankfurt	A	L 1–6	Caldow (pen)
			5.5.60	(West Germany)	H	L 3–6	McMillan 2, Wilson
1961–62	European Cup	Pr	5.9.61	Monaco (France)	A	W 3–2	Baxter, Scott 2
			12.9.61		H	W 3–2	Christie 2, Scott
		1	15.11.61	Vorwaerts (East Germany)	A	W 2–1	Caldow (pen,) Brand
			23.11.61		H	W 4–1	McMillan 2, Henderson, own goal
		QF	7.2.62	Standard Liege (Belgium)	A	L 1–4	Wilson
			14.2.62		H	W 2–0	Brand, Caldow (pen)
1963–64	European Cup	Pr	25.9.63	Real Madrid (Spain)	H	L 0–1	
			9.10.63		A	L 0–6	
1964–65	European Cup	Pr	2.9.64	Red Star Belgrade	H	W 3–1	Brand 2, Forrest
			9.9.64	(Yugoslavia)	A	L 2–4	Greig, McKinnon
			4.11.64		N	W 3–1	Forrest 2, Brand
		1	18.11.64	Rapid Vienna (Austria)	H	W 1 0	Wilson
			8.12.64		A	W 2–0	Forrest, Wilson
		QF	17.2.65	Inter-Milan (Italy)	A	L 1–3	Forest
			3.3.65		H	W 1–0	Forrest
1975–76	European Cup	1	17.9.75	Bohemians (Eire)	H	W 4–1	Fyfe, Johnstone, O'Hara, own goal
			1.10.75		A	D 1–1	Johnstone
		2	22.10.75	St Etienne (France)	H	L 0–2	
			5.11.75		A	L 1–2	MacDonald
1976–77	European Cup	1	15.9.76	Zurich (Switzerland)	H	D 1–1	Parlane
			29.9.76		A	L 0–1	
1978–79	European Cup	1	13.9.78	Juventus (Italy)	A	L 0–1	
			27.9.78		H	W 2–0	MacDonald, Smith
		2	18.10.78	PSV Eindhoven (Holland)	H	D 0–0	
			1 11.78		A	W 3–2	MacDonald, Johnstone, Russell
		QF	6.3.79	FC Cologne (West	A	L 0–1	
			22.3.79	Germany)	H	D 1–1	McLean
1960–61	Cup-Winners' Cup	Pr	28.9.60	Ferencvaros (Hungary)	H	W 4–2	Davis, Millar 2, Brand
			12.10.60		A	L 1–2	Wilson
		QF	15.11.60	Borussia Moenchenglad-	A	W 3 0	Millar, Scott, McMillan
			30.11.60	bach (West Germany)	H	W 8–0	Baxter, Brand 3, Millar 2, Davis, own goal
		SF	29.3.61	Wolverhampton	H	W 2–0	Scott, Brand
			19.4.61	Wanderers (England)	A	D 1–1	Scott
		F	17.5.61	Fiorentina (Italy)	H	L 0–2	
			27.5.61		A	L 1–2	Scott
1962–63	Cup-Winners' Cup	1	5.9.62	Seville (Spain)	H	W 4–0	Millar 3, Brand
			26.9.62		A	L 0–2	
		2	31.10.62	Tottenham Hotspur	A	L 2–5	Brand, Millar
			11.12.62	(England)	H	L 2–3	Brand, Wilson
1966–67	Cup-Winners' Cup	1	27.9.66	Glentoran (Northern	A	D 1–1	McLean
			5.10.66	Ireland)	H	W 4–0	Johnston, Smith (D), Setterington, McLean
		2	23.11.66	Borussia Dortmund	H	W 2–1	Johansen, Smith (A)
			6.12.66	(West Germany)	A	D 0–0	
		QF	1.3.67	Real Zaragoza (Spain) ‡	H	W 2–0	Smith, Willoughby
			22.3.67		A	L 0–2	
		SF	19.4.67	Slavia Sofia (Bulgaria)	A	W 1–0	Wilson
			3.5.67		H	W 1–0	Henderson
		F	31.5.67	Bayern Munich (West Germany)	N	L 0–1	
1969–70	Cup-Winners' Cup	1	17.9.69	Steaua Bucharest	H	W 2–0	Johnston 2
			1.10.69	(Rumania)	A	D 0–0	
		2	12.11.69	Gornik Zabrze (Poland)	A	L 1–3	Persson
			26.11.69		H	L 1–3	Baxter
1971–72	Cup-Winners' Cup	1	15.9.71	Rennes (France)	A	D 1–1	Johnston
			28.9.71		H	W 1–0	MacDonald
		2	20.10.71	Sporting Lisbon	H	W 3–2	Stein 2, Henderson
			3.11.71	(Portugal)	A	L 3–4 *	Stein 2, Henderson
		QF	8.3.72	Torino (Italy)	A	D 1–1	Johnston
			22.3.72		H	W 1–0	MacDonald
		SF	5.4.72	Bayern Munich	A	D 1–1	own goal
			19.4.72	(West Germany)	H	W 2–0	Jardine, Parlane

Season	Competition	Round	Date	Opponents (Country)	Venue	Result		Scorers

RANGERS continued

Season	Competition	Round	Date	Opponents (Country)	Venue	Result		Scorers
		F	24.5.72	Dynamo Moscow (USSR)	N	W	3–2	Johnstone 2, Stein
1973–74	Cup-Winners'	1	19.9.73	Ankaragucu (Turkey)	A	W	2–0	Conn, McLean
	Cup		3.10.73		H	W	4–0	Greig 2, O'Hara, Johnstone
		2	24.10.73	Borussia Moenchenglad-	A	L	0–3	
			7.11.73	bach (West Germany)	H	W	3–2	Conn, Jackson, MacDonald
1977–78	Cup-Winners'	Pr	17.8.77	Young Boys (Switzerland)	H	W	1–0	Greig
	Cup		31.8.77		A	D	2–2	Johnstone, Smith
		1	14.9.77	Twente Enschede	H	D	0–0	
			28.9.77	(Holland)	A	L	0–3	
1967–68	Fairs Cup	1	21.9.67	Dynamo Dresden	A	D	1–1	Ferguson
			4.10.67	(East Germany)	H	W	2–1	Penman, Greig
		2	8.11.67	IFC Cologne (West	H	W	3–0	Ferguson 2, Henderson
			28.11.67	Germany)	A	L	1–3	Henderson
		3		bye				
		QF	26.3.68	Leeds United (England)	H	D	0–0	
			9.4.68		A	L	0–2	
1968–69	Fairs Cup	1	18.9.68	Vojvodina (Yugoslavia)	H	W	2–0	Greig (pen), Jardine
			2.10.68		A	L	0–1	
		2	30.10.68	Dundalk (Eire)	H	W	6–1	Henderson 2, Ferguson 2, Greig, own goal
			13.11.68		A	W	3–0	Mathieson, Stein 2
		3	11.1.69	DWS Amsterdam	A	W	2–0	Johnston, Henderson
			22.1.69	(Holland)	H	W	2–1	Smith, Stein
		QF	19.3.69	Atletico Bilbao (Spain)	H	W	4–1	Ferguson, Penman, Persson, Stein
			2.4.69		A	L	0–2	
		SF	14.5.69	Newcastle United	H	D	0–0	
			22.5.69	(England)	A	L	0–2	
1970–71	Fairs Cup	1	16.9.70	Bayern Munich	A	L	0–1	
			30.9.70	(West Germany)	H	D	1–1	Stein
1972–73	Super Cup	F	16.1.73	Ajax (Holland)	H	L	1–3	MacDonald
			24.1.73		A	L	2–3	MacDonald, Young

At the end of the 1978–79 season Rangers had played more matches in Europe of any club in the British Isles. Including two matches in the Super Cup they had played 105 times. Liverpool had played 103 including four matches in the Super Cup.

ST JOHNSTONE

Season	Competition	Round	Date	Opponents (Country)	Venue	Result		Scorers
1971–72	UEFA Cup	1	15.9.71	SV Hamburg	A	L	1–2	Pearson
			29.9.71	(West Germany)	H	W	3–0	Hall, Pearson, Whitelaw
		2	20.10.71	Vasas Budapest (Hungary)	H	W	2–0	Connolly (pen), Pearson
			2.11.71		A	L	0–1	
		3	24.11.71	Zeljeznicar (Yugoslavia)	H	W	1–0	Connolly
			8.12.71		A	L	1–5	Rooney

IRISH LEAGUE CLUBS/LEAGUE OF IRELAND CLUBS

ARDS

Season	Competition	Round	Date	Opponents (Country)	Venue	Result		Scorers
1958–59	European Cup	Pr	17.9.58	Reims (France)	H	L	1–4	Lowry
			8.10.58		A	L	2–6	Lawther, Quee
1969–70	Cup-Winners'	1	17.9.69	AS Roma (Italy)	H	D	0–0	
	Cup		1.10.69		A	L	1–3	Crothers
1974–75	Cup-Winners'	1	18.9.74	PSV Eindhoven (Holland)	A	L	0–10	
	Cup		2.10.74		H	L	1–4	Guy
1973–74	UEFA Cup	1	12.9.73	Standard Liege (Belgium)	H	W	3–2	Cathcart, McAvoy (pen), McAteer (pen)
			19.9.73		A	L	1–6	Guy

Season	Competition	Round	Date	Opponents (Country)	Venue	Result		Scorers

BALLYMENA UNITED

| 1978–79 | Cup-Winners' Cup | 1 | 13.9.78 | Beveren (Belgium) | A | L | 0–3 | |
| | | | 27.9.78 | | H | L | 0–3 | |

CARRICK RANGERS

1976–77	Cup-Winners' Cup	1	15.9.76	Aris Bonnevoie (Luxembourg)	H	W	3–1	Prenter 2, Connor
			6.10.76		A	L	1–2	Irwin
		2	20.10.76	Southampton (England)	H	L	2–5	Irwin, Prenter
			3.11.76		A	L	1–4	Reid

COLERAINE

1974–75	European Cup	1	18.11.74	Feyenoord (Holland)	A	L	0–7	
			2.10.74		H	L	1–4	Simpson
1965–66	Cup-Winners' Cup	1	2.9.65	Dynamo Kiev (USSR)	H	L	1–6	Curley
			8.9.65		A	L	0–4	
1975–76	Cup-Winners' Cup	1	16.9.75	Eintracht Frankfurt (West Germany)	A	L	1–5	Cochrane
			30.9.75		H	L	2–6	McCurdy, Cochrane
1969–70	Fairs Cup	1	17.9.69	Jeunesse D'Esch (Luxembourg)	A	L	2–3	Hunter, Murray
			1.10.69		H	W	4–0	Dickson 2, Wilson, Jennings
		2	11.11.69	Anderlecht (Belgium)	A	L	1–6	Murray
			20.11.69		H	L	3–7	Dickson 2, Irwin
1970–71	Fairs Cup	1	15.9.70	Kilmarnock (Scotland)	H	D	1–1	Mullan
			29.9.70		A	W	3–2	Dickson 3
		2	20.10.70	Sparta Rotterdam (Holland)	A	L	0–2	
			4.11.70		H	L	1–2	Jennings
1977–78	Cup-Winners' Cup	1	14.9.77	Lokomotive Leipzig (East Germany)	H	L	1–4	Tweed
					A	D	2–2	Guy 2

CRUSADERS

1973–74	European Cup	1	19.9.73	Dynamo Bucharest (Rumania)	H	L	0–1	
			3.10.73		A	L	0–11	
1976–77	European Cup	1	14.9.76	Liverpool (England)	A	L	0–2	
			28.9.76		H	L	0–5	
1967–68	Cup-Winners' Cup	1	20.9.67	Valencia (Spain)	A	L	0–4	
			11.10.67		H	L	2–4	Trainor, Magill
1968–69	Cup-Winners' Cup	1	18.9.68	Norkopping (Sweden)	H	D	2–2	Jameson, Parke
			2.10.68		A	L	1–4	McPolin

DERRY CITY

1965–66	European Cup	Pr	31.8.65	Lyn Oslo (Norway)	A	L	3–5	Wood (R), Gilbert 2
			9.9.65		H	W	5–1	Wilson 2, Crossan, Wood (R), McGeough
		1	23.11.65	Anderlecht (Belgium)	A	L	0–9	
			00.00.65		withdrew			
1964–65	Cup-Winners' Cup	1	9.9.64	Steaua Bucharest (Rumania)	A	L	0–3	
			16.9.64		H	L	0–2	

DISTILLERY

1963–64	European Cup	Pr	25.9.63	Benfica (Portugal)	H	D	3–3	John Kennedy, Hamilton, Ellison
			2.10.63		A	L	0–5	
1971–72	Cup-Winners' Cup	1	15.9.71	Barcelona (Spain)	H	L	1–3	O'Neill
			29.9.71		A	L	0–4	

GLENAVON

1957–58	European Cup	Pr	11.9.57	Aarhus (Denmark)	A	D	0–0	
			25.9.57		H	L	0–3	
1960–61	European Cup	Pr	withdrew					
1961–62	Cup-Winners' Cup	1	13.9.61	Leicester City (England)	H	L	1–4	Jones
			27.9.61		A	L	1–3	Wilson
1977–78	UEFA Cup	1	14.9.77	PSV Eindhoven (Holland)	H	L	2–6	Malone (pen), McDonald
			28.9.77		A	L	0–5	

Season	Competition	Round	Date	Opponents (Country)	Venue	Result		Scorers

GLENTORAN

Season	Competition	Round	Date	Opponents (Country)	Venue	Result		Scorers
1964–65	European Cup	Pr	16.9.64	Panathinaikos (Greece)	H	D	2–2	Turner, Thompson
			30.9.64		A	L	2–3	Turner, Pavis
1967–68	European Cup	1	13.9.67	Benfica (Portugal) *	H	D	1–1	Colrain (pen)
			4.10.67		A	D	0–0	
1968–69	European Cup	1	18.9.68	Anderlecht (Belgium)	A	L	0–3	
			2.10.68		H	D	2–2	Morrow, Johnston
1970–71	European Cup	1	16.9.70	Waterford (Eire)	H	L	1–3	Hall
			30.9.70		A	L	0–1	
1977–78	European Cup	1	15.9.77	Valur (Iceland)	A	L	0–1	
			29.9.77		H	W	2–0	Robson, Jamison
		2	19.10.77	Juventus (Italy)	H	L	0–1	
			2.11.77		A	L	0–5	
1966–67	Cup-Winners' Cup	1	27.9.66	Rangers (Scotland)	H	D	1–1	Sinclair
			5.10.66		A	L	0–4	
1973–74	Cup-Winners' Cup	1	19.9.73	Chimia Ramnicu (Rumania)	A	D	2–2	Jamison, McCreary
			3.10.73		H	W	2–0	Hamison, Craig
		2	24.10.73	Brann Bergen (Norway)	A	D	1–1	Feeney
			7.11.73		H	W	3–1	Feeney, Jamison 2
		QF	5.3.74	Borussia Moenchenglad-	H	L	0–2	
			20.3.74	bach (West Germany)	A	L	0–5	
1962–63	Fairs Cup	1	26.9.62	Real Zaragoza (Spain)	H	L	0–2	
			10.10.62		A	L	2–6	Doherty 2
1963–64	Fairs Cup	1	16.9.63	Partick Thistle (Scotland)	H	L	1–4	Thompson
			30.9.63		A	L	0–3	
1965–66	Fairs Cup	1	28.9.65	Antwerp (Belgium)	A	L	0–1	
			6.10.65		H	D	3–3	Hamilton, Thompson 2
1969–70	Fairs Cup	1	9.9.69	Arsenal (England)	A	L	0–3	
			29.9.69		H	W	1–0	Henderson
1971–72	UEFA Cup	1	14.9.71	Eintracht Brunswick	H	L	0–1	
			28.9.71	(West Germany)	A	L	1–6	McCaffrey
1975–76	UEFA Cup	1	16.9.75	Ajax (Holland)	H	L	1–6	Jamison
			1.10.75		A	L	0–8	
1976–77	UEFA Cup	1	14.9.76	Basle (Switzerland)	H	W	3–2	Feeney 2, Dickenson
			29.9.76		A	L	0–3	
1978–79	UEFA Cup	1	5.9.78	IBV Westmann (Iceland)	A	D	0–0	
			14.9.78		H	D	1–1	Caskey (W)

LINFIELD

Season	Competition	Round	Date	Opponents (Country)	Venue	Result		Scorers
1959–60	European Cup	Pr	9.9.59	Gothenburg (Sweden)	H	W	2–1	Milburn 2
			23.9.59		A	L	1–6	Dickson
1961–62	European Cup	Pr	30.8.61	Vorwaerts (East Germany)	A	L	0–3	
				withdrew				
1962–63	European Cup	Pr	5.9.62	Esbjerg (Denmark)	H	L	1–2	Dickson
			19.9.62		A	A	0–0	
1966–67	European Cup	1	7.9.66	Aris Bonnevoie	A	D	3–3	Hamilton, Pavis, Scott
			16.9.66	(Luxembourg)	A	W	6–1	Thomas 3, Scott 2, Pavis
		2	26.10.66	Valerengen (Norway)	A	W	4–1	Scott, Pavis, Thomas, Shields
			8.11.66		H	D	1–1	Thomas
		QF	1.3.67	CSKA Sofia (Bulgaria)	H	D	2–2	Hamilton, Shields
			15.3.67		A	L	0–1	
1969–70	European Cup	1	17.9.69	Red Star Belgrade	A	L	0–8	
			1.10.69	(Yugoslavia)	H	L	2–4	McGraw 2
1971–72	European Cup	1	15.9.71	Standard Liege (Belgium)	A	L	0–2	
			29.9.71		H	L	2–3	Magee, Larmour
1975–76	European Cup	1	17.9.75	PSV Eindhoven (Holland)	H	L	1–2	Malone (P)
			1.10.75		A	L	0–8	
1978–79	European Cup	1	13.9.78	Lillestrom (Norway)	H	D	0–0	
			27.9.78		A	L	0–1	
1963–64	Cup-Winners' Cup	1		bye				
		2	13.11.63	Fenerbahce (Turkey)	A	L	1–4	Dickson
			11.12.63		H	W	2–0	Craig, Ferguson
1970–71	Cup-Winners' Cup	1	16.9.70	Manchester City	A	L	0–1	
			30.9.70 *	(England) *	H	W	2–1	Millen 2
1967–68	Fairs Cup	1	19.9.67	Lolomotive Leipzig	A	L	1–5	Pavis
			4.10.67	(East Germany)	H	W	1–0	Hamilton
1968–69	Fairs Cup	1	18.9.68	Setubal (Portugal)	A	L	0–3	
			9.10.68		H	L	1–3	Scott

Season	Competition	Round	Date	Opponents (Country)	Venue	Result		Scorers

PORTADOWN

Season	Competition	Round	Date	Opponents (Country)	Venue	Result		Scorers
1962–63	Cup-Winners'	1		bye				
	Cup	2	7.11.62	OFK Belgrade	A	L	1–5	Clements
			22.11.62	(Yugoslavia)	H	W	3–2	Burke, Jones, Cush
1974–75	UEFA Cup	1	18.9.74	Valur (Iceland)	A	D	0–0	
			1.10.74		H	W	2–1	MacFaul, Morrison (pen)
		2	23.10.74	Partizan Belgrade	A	L	0–5	
			6.11.74	(Yugoslavia)	H	D	1–1	Malcolmson

ATHLONE TOWN

Season	Competition	Round	Date	Opponents (Country)	Venue	Result		Scorers
1975–76	UEFA Cup	1	18.9.75	Valerengen (Norway)	H	W	3–0	Martin, Davis 2
			1.10.75		A	D	1–1	Martin
		2	22.10.75	AC Milan (Italy)	H	D	0–0	
			5.11.75		A	L	0–3	

BOHEMIANS

Season	Competition	Round	Date	Opponents (Country)	Venue	Result		Scorers
1975–76	European Cup	1	17.9.75	Rangers (Scotland)	A	L	1–4	Flanagan
			1.10.75		H	D	1–1	O'Connor (T)
1978–79	European Cup	1	13.9.78	Omonia Nicosia (Cyprus)	A	L	1–2	O'Connor (P)
			27.9.78		H	W	1–0	Joyce
		2	18.10.78	Dynamo Dresden	H	D	0–0	
			1.11.78	(East Germany)	A	L	0–6	
1970–71	Cup-Winners'	Pr	26.8.70	Gottwaldov	H	L	1–2	Swan (pen)
	Cup		2.9.70	(Czechoslovakia)	A	D	2–2	O'Connell, Dunne
1976–77	Cup-Winners'	1	15.9.76	Esbjerg (Denmark	H	W	2–1	Ryan (B), own goal
	Cup		29.9.76		A	W	1–0	Mitten
		2	20.10.76	Slask Wroclaw (Poland)	A	L	0–3	
			3.11.76		H	L	0–1	
1972–73	UEFA Cup	1	13.9.72	IFC Cologne (West	A	L	1–2	Daly
			27.9.72	Germany)	H	L	0–3	
1974–75	UEFA Cup	1	18.9.74	SV Hamburg (West	A	L	0–3	
			2.10.74	Germany)	H	L	0–1	

CORK CELTIC

Season	Competition	Round	Date	Opponents (Country)	Venue	Result		Scorers
1974–75	European Cup	1		walkover				
		2	23.10.74	Ararat Erevan (USSR)	H	L	1–2	Tambling
			6.11.74		A	L	0–5	
1964–65	Cup-Winners'	1	30.9.64	Slavia Sofia (Bulgaria)	A	D	1–1	Leahy
	Cup		7.10.64		H	L	0–2	

CORK HIBS

Season	Competition	Round	Date	Opponents (Country)	Venue	Result		Scorers
1971–72	European Cup	1	15.9.71	Borussia Moenchenglad-	H	L	0–5	
			29.9.71	bach (West Germany)	A	L	1–2	Dennehy
1972–73	Cup-Winners'	1	10.9.72	Pezoporikos (Cyprus)	A	W	2–1	Lawson (pen), Sheehan
	Cup		13.9.72		H	W	4–1	Wallace, Lawson 2, Dennehy
		2	25.10.72	Schalke 04 (West	H	D	0–0	
			8.11.72	Germany)	A	L	0–3	
1973–74	Cup-Winners'	1	19.9.73	Banik Ostrava	A	L	0–1	
	Cup		3.10.73	(Czechoslovakia)	H	L	1–2	Humphries
1970–71	Fairs Cup	1	16.9.70	Valencia (Spain)	H	L	0–3	
			26.9.70		A	L	1–3	Wigginton

DRUMCONDRA

Season	Competition	Round	Date	Opponents (Country)	Venue	Result		Scorers
1958–59	European Cup	Pr	17.9.58	Atletico Madrid (Spain)	A	L	0–8	
			1.10.58		H	L	1–5	Fullam (pen)
1961–62	European Cup	Pr	23.8.61	IFC Nuremberg (West	A	L	0–5	
			13.9.61	Germany)	H	L	1–4	Fullam
1965–66	European Cup	Pr	15.9.65	Vorwaerts (East Germany)	H	W	1–0	Morrissey
			22.9.65		A	L	0–3	
1962–63	Fairs Cup	1	3.10.62	Odense BK 09 (Denmark)	H	W	4–1	Dixon 2, Morrissey, McCann
			17.10.62		A	L	2–4	Rice, Morrissey
		2	4.12.62	Bayern Munich (West	A	L	0–6	
			12.12.62	Germany)	H	W	1–0	Dixon
1966–67	Fairs Cup	1	21.9.66	Eintracht Frankfurt	H	L	0–2	
			5.10.66	(West Germany)	A	L	1–6	Whelan

Season	Competition	Round	Date	Opponents (Country)	Venue	Result		Scorers

DUNDALK

Season	Competition	Round	Date	Opponents (Country)	Venue	Result		Scorers
1963–64	European Cup	Pr	11.9.63	Zurich (Switzerland)	H	L	0–3	
			25.9.63		A	W	2–1	Cross, Hasty
1967–68	European Cup	1	20.9.67	Vasas Budapest (Hungary)	H	L	0–1	
			11.10.67		A	L	1–8	Hale
1976–77	European Cup	1	15.9.76	PSV Eindhoven (Holland)	H	D	1–1	McDowell
			29.9.76		A	L	0–6	
1968–69	Fairs Cup	1	11.9.68	DOS Utrecht (Holland)	A	D	1–1	Stokes
			1.10.68		H	W	2–1	Stokes, Morrissey
		2	30.10.68	Rangers (Scotland)	A	L	1–6	Murray (pen)
			13.11.68		H	L	0–3	
1969–70	Fairs Cup	1	16.9.69	Liverpool (England)	A	L	0–10	
			30.9.69		H	L	0–4	

FINN HARPS

Season	Competition	Round	Date	Opponents (Country)	Venue	Result		Scorers
1974–75	Cup-Winners' Cup	1	18.11.74	Bursaspor (Turkey)	A	L	2–4	Ferry, Bradley
					H	D	0–0	
1973–74	UEFA Cup	1	19.9.73	Aberdeen (Scotland)	A	L	1–4	Harkin
			3.10.73		H	L	1–3	Harkin
1976–77	UEFA Cup	1	15.9.76	Derby County (England)	A	L	0–12	
			29.9.76		H	L	1–4	own goal
1978–79	UEFA Cup	1	12.9.78	Everton (England)	H	L	0–5	
			26.9.78		A	L	0–5	

HOME FARM

Season	Competition	Round	Date	Opponents (Country)	Venue	Result		Scorers
1975–76	Cup-Winners' Cup	1	17.9.75	Lens (France)	H	D	1–1	Brophy
			1.10.75		A	L	0–6	

LIMERICK

Season	Competition	Round	Date	Opponents (Country)	Venue	Result		Scorers
1960–61	European Cup	Pr	31.8.60	Young Boys (Switzerland)	H	L	0–5	
			5.10.60		A	L	2–4	Lynam, O'Reilly
1965–66	Cup-Winners' Cup	1	7.10.65	CSKA Sofia (Bulgaria)	H	L	1–2	O'Connor
			13.10.65		A	L	0–2	
1971–72	Cup-Winners' Cup	1	15.9.71	Torino (Italy)	H	L	0–1	
			29.9.71		A	L	0–4	

SHAMROCK ROVERS

Season	Competition	Round	Date	Opponents (Country)	Venue	Result		Scorers
1957–58	European Cup	Pr	25.9.57	Manchester United (England)	H	L	0–6	
			2.10.57		A	L	2–3	McCann, Hamilton
1959–60	European Cup	Pr	26.8.59	Nice (France)	A	L	2–3	Hamilton, Tuohy
			23.9.59		H	D	1–1	Hennessy
1964–65	European Cup	Pr	16.9.64	Rapid Vienna (Austria)	A	L	0–3	
			30.9.64		H	L	0–2	
1962–63	Cup-Winners' Cup	1		bye				
		2	24.10.62	Botev Plovdiv (Bulgaria)	H	L	0–4	
			14.11.62		A	L	0–1	
1966–67	Cup-Winners' Cup	1	28.9.66	Spora (Luxembourg)	H	W	4–1	Fullam, Dixon, Kearin, O'Neill (pen)
			5.10.66		A	W	4–1	Kearin, Dixon 2, O'Neill
		2	9.11.66	Bayern Munich (West Germany)	H	D	1–1	Dixon
			23.11.66		A	L	2–3	Gilbert, O'Neill
1967–68	Cup-Winners' Cup	1	20.9.67	Cardiff City (Wales)	H	D	1–1	Gilbert
			4.10.67		A	L	0–2	
1968–69	Cup-Winners' Cup	1	18.9.68	Randers Freja (Denmark)	A	L	0–1	
			2.10.68		H	L	1–2	Fullam
1969–70	Cup-Winners' Cup	1	17.9.69	Schalke 04 (West Germany)	H	W	2–1	Barber 2
			1.10.69		A	L	0–3	
1978–79	Cup-Winners' Cup	1	13.9.78	Apoel Nicosia (Cyprus)	H	W	2–0	Giles, Lynex
			27.9.78		A	W	1–0	Lynex
		2	18.10.78	Banik Ostrava (Czechoslovakia)	A	L	0–3	
			1.11.78		H	L	1–3	Giles
1963–64	Fairs Cup	1	18.9.63	Valencia (Spain)	H	L	0–1	
			10.10.63		A	D	2–2	O'Neill, Mooney

Season	Competition	Round	Date	Opponents (Country)	Venue	Result		Scorers

SHAMROCK ROVERS continued

1965–66	Fairs Cup	1		bye				
		2	17.11.65	Real Zaragoza (Spain)	H	D	1–1	Tuohy
			24.11.65		A	L	1–2	Fullam

SHELBOURNE

1962–63	European Cup	Pr	19.9.62	Sporting Lisbon	H	L	0–2	
			27.9.62	(Portugal)	A	L	1–5	Hennessy
1963–64	Cup-Winners'	1	24.9.63	Barcelona (Spain)	H	L	0–2	
	Cup		15.10.63		A	L	1–3	Bohnam (pen)
1964–65	Fairs Cup	1	16.9.64	Belenenses (Portugal)	A	D	1–1	Barber
			14.10.64		H	D	0–0	
			28.10.64		N	W	2–1	Hannigan, Conroy (M)
		2	25.11.64	Atletico Madrid (Spain)	H	L	0–1	
			2.12.64		A	L	0–1	
1971–72	UEFA Cup	1	15.9.71	Vasas Budapest	A	L	0–1	
			29.9.71	(Hungary)	H	D	1–1	Murray

ST PATRICK'S ATHLETIC

1961–62	Cup-Winners'	Pr	12.9.61	Dunfermline (Scotland)	A	L	1–4	O'Rourke
	Cup		27.9.61		H	L	0–4	
1967–68	Fairs Cup	1	13.9.67	Bordeaux (France)	H	L	1–3	Hennessy
			11.10.67		A	L	3–6	Campbell 2, Ryan

WATERFORD

1966–67	European Cup	Pr	31.8.66	Vorwaerts Berlin (East	H	L	1–5	Lynch
			9.9.66	Germany)	A	L	0–6	
1968–69	European Cup	1	18.9.68	Manchester United	H	L	1–3	Matthews
			2.10.68	(England)	A	L	1–7	Casey
1969–70	European Cup	1	17.9.69	Galatasaray (Turkey)	A	L	0–2	
			1.10.69		H	L	2 3	Buck, Morley
1970–71	European Cup	1	16.9.70	Glentoran (Northern	A	W	3–1	O'Neil, McGeough, Casey
			30.9.70	Ireland)	H	W	1–0	Casey
		2	21.10.70	Celtic (Scotland)	H	L	0–7	
			4.11.70		A	L	2–3	Matthews, own goal
1972–73	European Cup	1	13.9.72	Omonia Nicosia (Cyprus)	H	W	2–1	Hale 2
			27.9.72		A	L	0–2	
1973–74	European Cup	1	19.9.73	Ujpest Doza (Hungary)	H	L	2–3	Kirby, O'Neill
			3.10.73		A	L	0–3	

European Club directory

Country	Championship wins	Cup wins	European and other honours
ALBANIA	(1945) Dinamo Tirana 14; Partizan Tirana 10; 17 Nendori 5; Vlaznia 4	(1948) Dinamo Tirana 12; Partizan Tirana 8; 17 Nendori 4; Besa 1; Vlaznia 1; Labinoti 1	None
AUSTRIA	(1912) Rapid Vienna 25; Austria/WAC (previously FK Austria and WAC) 13; Admira-Energie-Wacker (previously Sportklub Admira and Admira-Energie) 8; First Vienna 6; Tirol-Svarowski-Innsbruck (previously Wacker-Innsbruck) 5; Wiener Sportklub 3; FAC 1; Hakoah 1; Linz ASK 1; Wacker Vienna 1; WAF 1; Voest Linz 1	(1919) FK Austria 19; Rapid Vienna 9; Admira-Energie-Wacker 5; Tirol-Svarowski-Innsbruck 4; First Vienna 3; Linz ASK 1; Wacker Vienna 1; WAF 1; Wiener Sportklub 1	European Cup-Winners' Cup (runners-up) Austria/WAC 1978

Country	Championship wins	Cup wins	European and other honours
BELGIUM	(1896) Anderlecht 16 ; Union St Gilloise 11 ; Beerschot 7 ; Standard Liege 6 ; RC Brussels 6 ; FC Liege 5 ; Daring Brussels 5 ; FC Bruges 5 ; Antwerp 4 ; Lierse SK 3 ; Malines 3 ; CS Bruges 3 ; RWD Molenbeek 1	(1954) Anderlecht 5 ; Standard Liege 3 ; FC Bruges 3 ; Antwerp 1 ; Beerschot 1 ; La Gantoise 1 ; Lierse SK 1 ; Tournai 1 ; Waregem 1 ; Beveren 1	European Cup (runners-up) FC Bruges 1978 European Cup-Winners' Cup (winners) Anderlecht 1976, 1978 (runners-up) Anderlecht 1977. European Fairs Cup (runners-up) Anderlecht 1970. UEFA Cup (runners-up) FC Bruges 1976
BULGARIA	(1925) CSKA Sofia (previously CDNA) 19 ; Levski Spartak (previously Levski Sofia) 13 ; Slavia Sofia 6 ; Vladislav Varna 3 ; Lokomotiv Sofia 3 ; AS23 Sofia 1 ; Botev Plovdiv 1 ; SC Sofia 1 ; Sokol Varna 1 ; Spartak Plovdiv 1 ; Tichka Varna 1 ; Trakia Plovdiv 1 ; ZSK Sofia 1	(1946) Levski Spartak 12 ; CSKA Sofia 10 ; Slavia Sofia 5 ; Lokomotiv Sofia 2 ; Botev Plovdiv 1 ; Spartak Plovdiv 1 ; Spartak Sofia 1 ; Marek Stanke 1	None
CYPRUS	(1935) Apoel 11 ; Omonia 8 ; Anorthosis 6 ; AEL 5 ; EPA 3 ; Olympiakos 3 ; Chetin Kayal 1 ; Pezoporikos 1 ; Trast 1	(1935) Apoel 9 ; EPA 5 ; AEL 3 ; Trast 3 ; Chetin Kayal 2 ; Omonia 2 ; Apollon 2 ; Pezoporikos 2 ; Anorthosis 2 ; Paralimni 1 ; Olympiakos 1	None
CZECHOSLOVAKIA	(1926) * Sparta Prague 13 ; Slavia Prague 12 ; Dukla Prague (previously UDA) 9 ; Slovan Bratislava 6 ; Spartak Trnava 5 ; Inter-Bratislava 1 ; Spartak Hradec Kralove 1 ; Viktoria Zizkov 1 ; Banik Ostrava 1 ; Zbrojovka Brno 1	(1961) Dukla Prague 4 ; Slovan Bratislava 4 ; Spartak Trnava 3 ; Sparta Prague 3 ; Banik Ostrava 2 ; TJ Gottwaldov 1 ; Lokomotiv Kosice 1	European Cup-Winners' Cup (winners) Slovan Bratislava 1969
DENMARK	(1913) KB Copenhagen 14 ; B93 Copenhagen 9 ; AB (Akademisk) 9 ; B 1903 Copenhagen 7 ; Frem 6 ; AGF Aarhus 4 ; Esbjergs FK 4 ; Vejle BK 3 ; B 1909 Odense 2 ; Hvidovre 2 ; Koge BK 2 ; Odense BK 1	(1955) AGF Aarhus 5 ; Vejile Bk 5 ; B 1909 Odense 3 ; Randers Freja 3 ; Aalborg BK 2 ; Ebsjergs BK 2 ; Frem 1 ; KB Copenhagen 1 ; Vanlose 1	None
FINLAND	(1949) * Turun Palloseura 5 ; Kuopion Palloseura 5 ; Valkeakosken Haka 4 ; Lahden Reipas 3 ; IF Kamraterna 2 ; Kotkan TP 2 ; Helsinki JK 2 ; Turun Pyrkiva 1 ; IF Kronohagens 1 ; Helsinki PS 1 ; Ilves-Kissat 1 ; Kokkolan PV 1 ; IF Kamraterna 1 ; Vasa 1	(1955) Lahden Reipas 6 ; Valkeakosken Haka 6 ; Kotkan TP 3 ; Mikkelin 2 ; IFK Abo 1 ; Drott 1 ; Helsinki JK 1 ; Helsinki PS 1 ; Kuopion Palloseura 1 ; Pallo-Peikot 1	None
FRANCE	(1933) Saint Etienne 9 ; Stade de Reims 6 ; OGC Nice 4 ; Olympique Marseille 4 ; Nantes 4 ; Lille OSC 3 ; AS Monaco 3 ; FC Sete 2 ; Sochaux 2 ; Racing Club Paris 1 ; Roubaix-Tourcoing 1 ; Girondins Bordeaux 1	(1918) Olympique Marseille 9 ; Saint Etienne 6 ; Lille OSC 5 ; Racing Club Paris 5 ; Red Star 5 ; Olympique Lyon 3 ; CAS Generaux 2 ; AS Monaco 2 ; OGC Nice 2 ; Racing Club Strasbourg 2 ; Sedan 2 ; FC Sete 2 ; Stade de Reims 2 ; Stade Rennes 2 ; Nancy-Lorraine 2 ; AS Cannes 1 ; Club Francais 1 ; Excelsior Roubaix 1 ; Girondins Bordeaux 1 ; Le Havre 1 ; SO Montpelier 1 ; Olympique de Pantin 1 ; CA Paris 1 ; Sochaux 1 ; Toulouse 1	European Champions' Cup (runners-up) Stade de Reims 1956, 1959 ; Saint Etienne 1976 UEFA Cup (runners-up) Bastia 1978

Country	Championship wins	Cup wins	European and other honours
EAST GERMANY (GDR)	(1950) ASK Vorwaerts 6; Dynamo Dresden 5; Wismut Karl-Marx-Stadt 4; FC Magdeburg 4; Carl Zeiss Jena (previously Motor Jena) 3; Chemie Leipzig 2; Turbine Erfurt 2; Turbine Halle 1; Zwickau Horch 1; Empor Rostock 1	(1949) Carl Zeiss Jena 4; Dynamo Dresden 3; Chemie Leipzig 2; FC Magdeburg 2; Magdeburg Aufbau 2; Motor Zwickau 2; ASK Vorwaerts 2; Lokomotiv Leipzig 2; Dresden Einheit SC 1; Dresden PV 1; Dynamo Berlin 1; Halle Chemie SC 1; North Dessau Waggonworks 1; Thale EHW 1; Union East Berlin 1; Wismut Karl-Marx-Stadt 1; Sachsenring Zwickau 1	European Cup-Winners' Cup (winners) FC Magdeburg 1974
WEST GERMANY	(1903) 1 FC Nuremberg 9; Schalke 7; Bayern Munich 5; Borussia Moenchengladbach 5; VfB Leipzig 3; SpV Furth 3; SV Hamburg 3; Dorussia Dortmund 3; 1FC Cologne 3; Viktoria Berlin 2; Hertha Berlin 2; Hanover 96 2; Dresden SC 2; VfB Stuttgart 2; 1FC Kaiserslautern 2; Munich 1860 1; SV Werder Bremen 1; Union Berlin 1; FC Freibourg 1; Phoenix Karlsruhe 1; Karlsruher FV 1; Holstein Kiel 1; Fortuna Dusseldorf 1; Rapid Vienna 1; VfR Mannheim 1; Rot-Weiss Essen 1; Eintracht Frankfurt 1; Eintracht Brunswick 1	(1935) Bayern Munich 5; 1FC Nuremberg 3; Dresden SC 2; Karlsruher SC 2; Munich 1860 2; Schalke 2; VfB Stuttgart 2; Borussia Moenchengladbach 2; Eintracht Frankfurt 2; 1FC Cologne 3; SV Hamburg 2; Borussia Dortmund 1; First Vienna 1; VfB Leipzig 1; Kickers Offenbach 1; Rapid Vienna 1; Rot-Weiss Essen 1; SW Essen 1; Werder Bremen 1	World Club Champion-ship (winners) Bayern Munich 1976. European Champions' Cup (winners) Bayern Munich 1974, 1975, 1976; (runners-up) Eintracht Frankfurt 1960, Borussia Moenchengladbach 1977 European Cup-Winners' Cup (winners) Borussia Dortmund 1966, Bayern Munich 1967, SV Hamburg 1977; (runners-up) Munich (1860) 1965, SV Hamburg 1968. UEFA Cup (winners) Borussia Moenchenglad-bach 1975; (runners-up) Borussia Moenchenglad-bach 1973
GREECE	(1928) Olympiakos 20; Panathinaikos 12; AEK Athens 6; Aris Salonika 3; PAOK Salonika 1	(1932) Olympiakos 16; AEK Athens 7; Panathinaikos 6; PAOK Salonika 2; Aris Salonika 1; Ethnikos 1; Iraklis 1	European Champions' Cup (runners-up) Panathinaikos 1971
HUNGARY	(1901) Ferencvaros (previously FTC) 22; MTK-VM Budapest (previously Hungaria, Bastya, and Voros Lobogo) 18; Ujpest Dozsa 17; Vasas Budapest 6; Honved 5; Csepel 4; BTC 2; Nagyvarad 1; Vasas Gyor 1	(1901) Ferencvaros 14; MTK-VM Budapest 9; Ujpest Dozsa 4; Vasas Gyor 2; Vasas Budapest 1; Bocskai 1; Honved 1; III Ker 1; Kispesti AC 1; Soroksar 1; Szolnoki MAV 1; Diosgyor 1	European Cup-Winners Cup (runners-up) MTK Budapest 1964, Ferencvaros 1975. European Fairs Cup (winners) Ferencvaros 1965; (runners-up) Ferencvaros 1968, Ujpest Dozsa 1969
ICELAND	(1912) KR Reykjavik 20; Valur 15; IA Akranes 10; IBK Keflavik 3; Vikingur 2; IBV Vestmann 1	(1960) KR Reykjavik 7; Valur 4; IBV Vestmann 2; Fram 2; IBA Akureyri 1; Vikingur 1; IBK Keflavik 1	None
IRELAND (Republic)	(1922) Shamrock Rovers 10; Shelbourne 7; Bohemians 7; Waterford 6; Cork United 5; Drumcondra 5; Dundalk 4; St Patrick's Athletic 3; St James's Gate 2; Cork Athletic 2; Sligo Rovers 2; Limerick 1; Dolphin 1; Cork Hibernians 1; Cork Celtic 1	(1922) Shamrock Rovers 21; Drumcondra 5; Dundalk 5; Bohemians 4; Shelbourne 3; Cork Athletic 2; Cork United 2; St James's Gate 2; St Patrick's Athletic 2; Cork Hibernians 2; Alton United 1; Athlone Town 1; Cork 1; Fordsons 1; Limerick 1; Transport 1; Waterford 1; Finn Harps 1; Home Farm 1	None

Country	Championship wins	Cup wins	European and other honours
ITALY	(1898) Juventus 18 ; Inter-Milan 11 ; Genoa 9 ; AC Milan 9 ; Torino 8 ; Pro Vercelli 7 ; Bologna 7 ; Fiorentina 2 ; Casale 1 ; Novese 1 ; AS Roma 1 ; Cagliari 1 ; Lazio 1	(1922) Juventus 5 ; Torino 4 ; Fiorentina 4 ; AC Milan 4 ; Napoli 2 ; AS Roma 2 ; Bologna 2 ; Inter-Milan 2 ; Atalanta 1 ; Genoa 1 ; Lazio 1 ; Vado 1 ; Venezia 1	World Club Championship (winners) Inter-Milan 1964, 1965, AC Milan 1969. European Champions' Cup (winners) AC Milan 1963, 1969, Inter-Milan 1964, 1965 ; (runners-up) Fiorentina 1957, AC Milan 1958, Inter-Milan 1967, 1972, Juventus 1973. European Cup-Winners' Cup (winners) Fiorentina 1961, AC Milan 1968, 1973 ; (runners-up) Fiorentina 1962, AC Milan 1974. European Fairs Cup (winners) AS Roma 1961 ; (runners-up) Juventus 1965, 1971. UEFA Cup (winners) Juventus 1977
LUXEMBOURG	(1910) Jeunesse Esch 15 ; Spora Luxembourg 10 ; Stade Dudelange 10 ; US Hollerich-Bonnevoie 5 ; Fola Esch 5 ; Red Boys Differdange 5 ; US Luxembourg 3 ; Aris Bonnevoie 3 ; Sporting Luxembourg 2 ; Progres Niedercorn 2 ; Racing Luxembourg 1 ; National Schifflge 1 ; Avenir Beggen 1 ;	(1922) Red Boys Differdange 13 ; Spora Luxembourg 7 ; Jeunesse Esch 7 ; US Luxembourg 6 ; Stade Dudelange 4 ; Fola Esch 3 ; Progres Niedercorn 3 ; Alliance Dudelange 2 ; US Rumelange 2 ; Aris Bonnevoie 1 ; US Dudelange 1 ; Jeunesse Hautcharage 1 ; National Schifflge 1 ; Racing Luxembourg 1 ; SC Tetange 1	None
MALTA	(1910) Floriana 24 ; Sliema Wanderers 21 ; Valletta 10 ; Hamrun Spartans 3 ; Hibernians 3 ; St George's 1 ; KOMR 1	(1935) Sliema Wanderers 15 ; Floriana 14 ; Valletta 5 ; Hibernians 3 ; Gzira United 1 ; Melita 1	None
NETHERLANDS	(1898) Ajax Amsterdam 17 ; Feyenoord 12 ; HVV The Hague 8 ; PSV Eindhoven 7 ; Sparta Rotterdam 6 ; Go Ahead Deventer 4 ; HBS The Hague 3 ; Willem II Tilburg 3 ; RCH Haarlem 2 ; RAP 2 ; Heracles 2 ; ADO The Hague 2 ; Quick the Hague 1 ; BVV Scheidam 1 ; NAC Breda 1 ; Eindhoven 1 ; Enschede 1 ; Volewijckers Amsterdam 1 ; Limburgia 1 ; Rapid JC Haarlem 1 ; DOS Utrecht 1 ; DWS Amsterdam 1 ; Haarlem 1 ; Be Quick Groningen 1 ; SVV Scheidam 1	(1899) Ajax Amsterdam 7 ; Feyenoord 4 ; Quick The Hague 4 ; PSV Eindhoven 4 ; HEC 3 ; Sparta Rotterdam 3 ; DFC 2 ; Fortuna Geleen 2 ; Haarlem 2 ; HBS The Hague 2 ; RCH 2 ; VOC 2 ; Wageningen 2 ; Willem II Tilburg 2 ; FC Den Haag 2 ; Concordia Rotterdam 1 ; CVV 1 ; Eindhoven 1 ; HVV The Hague 1 ; Longa 1 ; Quick Njimegen 1 ; RAP 1 ; Roermond 1 ; Schoten 1 ; Velocitas Breda 1 ; Velocitas Groningen 1 ; VSV 1 ; VUC 1 ; VVV 1 ; ZFC 1 ; NAC Breda 1 ; Twente Enschede 1 ; AZ 67 1	World Club Championship (winners) Feyenoord 1970, Ajax 1972. European Champions' Cup (winners) Feyenoord 1970, Ajax 1971, 1972, 1973 ; (runners-up) Ajax 1969. UEFA Cup (winners) Feyenoord 1974 ; PSV Eindhoven 1978 ; (runners-up) Twente Enschede 1975
NORWAY	(1938) Fredrikstad 9 ; Viking Stavanger 5 ; Lillestrom 3 ; Rosenborg Trondheim 3 ; Larvik Turn 3 ; Brann Bergen 2 ; Lyn Oslo 2 ; Valerengen 1 ; Friedig 1 ; Fram 1 ; Skeid Oslo 1 ; Stromgodset Drammen 1	(1902) Odds BK Skein 11 ; Fredrikstad 9 ; Lyn Oslo 8 ; Skeid Oslo 8 ; Sarpsborgs Fk 6 ; Orn Fk Horten 4 ; Brann Bergen 4 ; Mjondalens IF 3 ; Rosenborgs BK Trondheim 3 ; Stromsgodset Drammen 3 ; Mercantile 2 ; Viking Stavanger 2 ; Grane Nordstrand 1 ; Kvik Halden 1 ; Sparta 1 ; Gjovik 1 ; Bodo-Glimt 1 ; Lillestrom 1	None

Country	Championship wins	Cup wins	European and other honours
POLAND	(1921) Ruch Chorzow 11 ; Gornik Zabrze 10 ; Wisla Krakow 6 ; Cracovia 5 ; Pogon Lwow 4 ; Legia Warsaw 4 ; Warta Poznan 2 ; Polonia Bytom 2 ; Stal Mielec 2 ; Garbarnia Krakow 1 ; Polonia Warsaw 1 ; LKS Lodz 1 ; Slask Wroclaw 1	(1951) Gornik Zabrze 6 ; Legia Warsaw 5 ; Zaglebie Sosnowiec 4 ; Ruch Chorzow 2 ; Gwardia Warsaw 1 ; LKS Lodz 1 ; Polonia Warsaw 1 ; Wisla Krakow 1 ; Stal Rzeszow 1 ; Slask Wroclaw 1	European Cup-Winners' Cup (runners-up) Gornik Zabrze 1970
PORTUGAL	(1935) * Benfica 23 ; Sporting Lisbon 14 ; FC Porto 6 ; Belenenses 1	(1939) Benfica 15 ; Sporting Lisbon 9 ; FC Porto 4 ; Belenenses 2 ; Boavista 2 ; Vitoria Setubal 2 ; Academica Coimbra 1 ; Leixoes Porto 1 ; Sporting Braga 1	European Champions' Cup (winners) Benfica 1961, 1962 ; (runners-up) Benfica 1963, 1965, 1968 European Cup-Winners' Cup (winners) Sporting Lisbon 1964
RUMANIA	(1910) Dynamo Bucharest 9 ; Steaua Bucharest (previously CCA) 9 ; Venus Bucharest 7 ; CSC Temesvar 6 ; UT Arad 6 ; Rapid Bucharest 4 ; Ripensia Temesvar 3 ; Petrolul Ploesti 3 ; Olimpia Bucharest 2 ; CAC Bucharest 2 ; Soc RA Bucharest 1 ; Prahova Ploesti 1 ; CSC Brasov 1 ; Juventus Bucharest 1 ; SSUD Resita 1 ; Craiova Bucharest 1 ; Progresul 1 ; Arges 1 ; Ploesti United 1 ; University of Craiova 1	(1934) Steaua Bucharest 12 ; Rapid Bucharest 7 ; Dynamo Bucharest 3 ; UT Arad 2 ; CSC Temesvar 2 ; Progresul 2 ; RIP Timisoara 2 ; Uni Craiova 2 ; ICO Oradeo 1 ; Metal Ochimia Resita 1 ; Petrolul Ploesti 1 ; Stinta Cluj 1 ; Stinta Timisoara 1 ; Turnu Severin 1 ; Chimia Ramnicu 1 ; Jiul Petroseni 1	None
SPAIN	(1929) Real Madrid 18 ; Barcelona 9 ; Atletico Madrid 8 ; Athletic Bilbao 6 ; Valencia 4 ; Betis 1 ; Sevilla 1	(1902) Athletic Bilbao 22 ; Barcelona 18 ; Real Madrid 13 ; Atletico Madrid 5 ; Valencia 4 ; Real Union de Irun 3 ; Seville 3 ; Espanol 2 ; Real Zaragoza 2 ; Arenas 1 ; Ciclista Sebastian 1 ; Racing de Irun 1 ; Vizcaya Bilbao 1 ; Real Betis 1	European Champions' Cup (winners) Real Madrid 1956, 1957, 1958, 1959, 1960, 1966 ; (runners-up) Real Madrid 1962, 1964, Barcelona 1961, Atletico Madrid 1974. World Club Championship (winners) Real Madrid 1960, Atletico Madrid 1974. European Cup-Winners' Cup (winners) Atletico Madrid 1962 ; (runners-up) Atletico Madrid 1963, Barcelona 1969, Real Madrid 1971. European Fairs Cup (winners) Barcelona 1958, 1960, 1966 ; Valencia 1962, 1963, Zaragoza 1964 ; (runners-up) Barcelona 1962, Valencia 1964, Zaragoza 1966. UEFA Cup (runners-up) Athletic Bilbao 1977
SWEDEN	(1896) Malmo FF 14 ; Oergryte IS Gothenburg 13 ; IFK Norrkoping 11 ; Djurgaarden 8 ; AIK Stockholm 8 ; IFK Gothenburg 7 ; GAIS Gothenburg 6 ; IF Halsingborg 5 ; Boras IF Elfsborg 4 ; Atvidaberg 2 ; IFK Ekilstund 1 ; IF Gavle Brynas 1 ; IF Gothenburg Fassbergs 1 ; Norrkoping IK Sleipner 1 ; Oester Vaxjo 1 ; Halmstad 1	(1941) Malmo FF 9 ; IFK Norrkoping 3 ; AIK Stockholm 3 ; Atvidaberg 2 ; GAIS Gothenburg 1 ; IFK Halsingborg 1 ; Raa 1 ; Landskrona 1 ; Oster Vaxjo 1	None

Country	Championship wins	Cup wins	European and other honours
SWITZERLAND	(1898) Grasshoppers 17 ; Servette 13 ; Young Boys Berne 10 ; FC Zurich 8 ; Lausanne 7 ; FC Basle 7 ; La Chaux- de-Fonds 3 ; FC Lugano 3 ; Winterthur 3 ; FC Aarau 2 ; FC Anglo-Americans 1 ; St Gallen 1 ; FC Bruhl 1 ; Cantonal-Neuchatel 1 ; Biel 1 ; Bellinzona 1 ; FC Etoile la Chaux de Fonds 1	(1926) Grasshoppers 13 ; La Chaux-de- Fonds 6 ; Lausanne 6 ; FC Basle 5 ; FC Zurich 5 ; Young Boys Berne 5 ; Servette 4 ; FC Lugano 2 ; FC Sion 2 ; FC Granges 1 ; Lucerne 1 ; St Gallen 1 ; Urania Geneva 1 ; Young Fellows Zurich 1	None
TURKEY	(1960) Fenerbahce 8 ; Galatasaray 5 ; Besiktas 3 ; Trabzonspor 2	(1963) Galatasaray 6 ; Goztepe Izmir 2 ; Fenerbahce 2 ; Trabzonspor 2 Altay Izmir 1 ; Ankaragucu 1 ; Eskisehirspor 1 ; Besiktas 1 ;	None

EUROPEAN GOALSCORERS
1955-56 to 1978-79

Name	Club	International for
Alfredo di Stefano	Real Madrid	Argentina, Colombia and Spain
Eusebio da Silva	Benfica	Portugal
Gerd Muller	Bayern Munich	West Germany
Ferenc Puskas	Honved and Real Madrid	Hungary and Spain
Francisco Gento	Real Madrid	Spain
Jose Augusto	Benfica	Portugal
Jose Altafini	AC Milan and Juventus	Brazil and Italy
Paul Van Himst	Anderlecht	Belgium
Amancio Amaro	Real Madrid	Spain
Jose Torres	Benfica	Portugal
Johan Cruyff	Ajax and Barcelona	Holland
Bora Kostic	Red Star Belgrade	Yugoslavia
Jose Aguas	Benfica	Portugal
Jozef Adamec	Dukla Prague and Spartak Trnava	Czechoslovakia
Wlodzimierz Lubanski	Gornik Zabrze	Poland
Sandro Mazzola	Internazionale Milan	Italy
Jose Pirri	Real Madrid	Spain
Ferenc Bene	Ujpest Dozsa	Hungary
Denis Law	Manchester United	Scotland
Hector Rial	Real Madrid	Spain

Country	Championship wins	Cup wins	European and other honours
USSR	(1936) Dynamo Moscow 11 ; Spartak Moscow 9 ; Dynamo Kiev 8 ; CSKA Moscow 6 ; Torpedo Moscow 3 ; Dynamo Tbilisi 1 ; Saria Voroshilovgrad 1 ; Ararat Erevan 1	(1936) Spartak Moscow 9 ; Torpedo Moscow 5 ; Dynamo Moscow 5 ; CSKA Moscow 4 ; Dynamo Kiev 4 ; Donets Shaktyor 2 ; Lokomotiv Moscow 2 ; Ararat Erevan 2 ; Karpaty Lvov 1 ; Zenit Leningrad 1 ; Dynamo Tbilisi 1	European Cup-Winners' Cup (winners) Dynamo Kiev 1975 ; (runners-up) Dynamo Moscow 1972
YUGOSLAVIA	(1923) Red Star Belgrade 12 ; Hajduk Split 8 ; Partizan Belgrade 8 ; Gradjanski Zagreb 5 ; BSK Belgrade 5 ; Dynamo Zagreb 3 ; Jugoslovija Belgrade 2 ; Concordia Zagreb 2 ; HASK Zagreb 1 ; Vojvodina Novi Sad 1 ; FC Sarajevo 1 ; Zeljeznicar 1	(1947) Red Star Belgrade 9 ; Hajduk Split 6 ; Dynamo Zagreb 6 ; Partizan 4 ; BSK Belgrade 2 ; OFK Belgrade 2 ; Vardar Skoplje 1 ; Rijeka 1	European Champions' Cup (runners-up) Partizan Belgrade 1966. European Fairs Cup (winners) Dynamo Zagreb 1967 ; (runners-up) Dynamo Zagreb 1963

Real Madrid players have dominated scoring in the European Cup and it is interesting to note that during the 1978–79 season one Real player, José Pirri, was still active in their Championship-winning team. The leading goalscorer in the 1978–79 European Cup was Claudio Sulser of the Swiss club Grasshoppers, with 11 goals.

Total Goals	55–56	56–57	57–58	58–59	59–60	60–61	61–62	62–63	63–64	64–65	65–66	66–67	67–68	68–69	69–70	70–71	71–72	72–73	73–74	74–75	75–76	76–77	77–78	78–79
49	5	7	10	6	8	–	7	1	5															
46							5	6	4	8	7	–	6	1	4	–	2	2	1					
36																		11	9	6	5	5		
36		1	–	2	12	–	7	–	7	2	5													
31	1	1	3	1	2	1	2	1	3	5	3	–	5	–	3									
25							7	5	1	–	5	4	–	1	2									
24			2	–	14	4												3	1					
20								1	–	1	4	6	5				1	–	2					
19									3	5	5	–	4	1			1							
19											9	3	–	2	5									
18												3	1	6	–	1	4	3						
18		5	9	–	1	1				2														
18						11	6	1																
16							3	4					4	3						2				
16								1	2	–	3	4					1	5						
16								7	3	1	3						2							
16												3	1	3	4	1						3	1	
15																		3	6	1	3	2		
14											3	–	2	9										
14	5	2	4	2	1																			

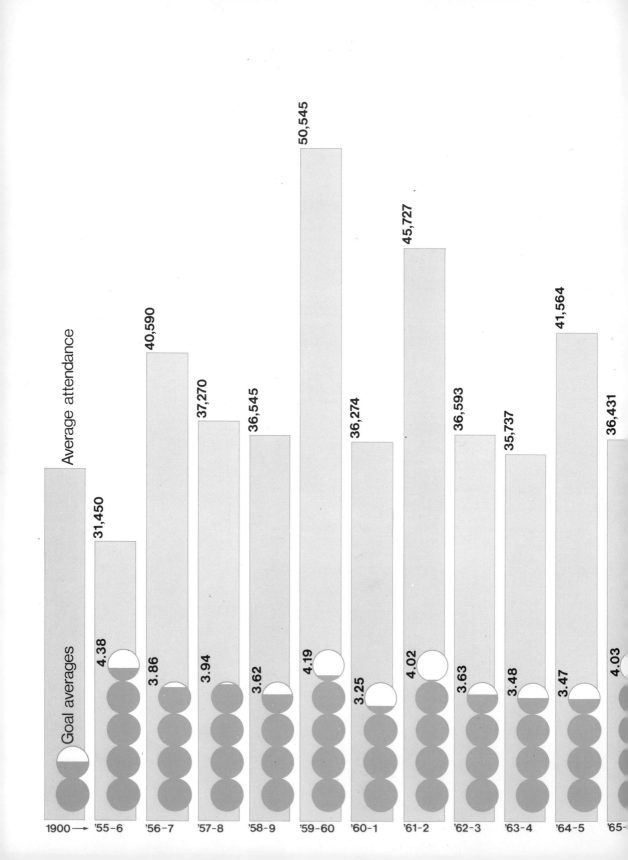

Average attendance

Goal averages

50,545

45,727

41,564

40,590

37,270

36,545

36,274

36,593

35,737

36,431

31,450

4.38   3.86   3.94   3.62   4.19   3.25   4.02   3.63   3.48   3.47   4.03

1900 →   '55-6   '56-7   '57-8   '58-9   '59-60   '60-1   '61-2   '62-3   '63-4   '64-5   '65

EUROPEAN CUP
1955-56 to 1977-78

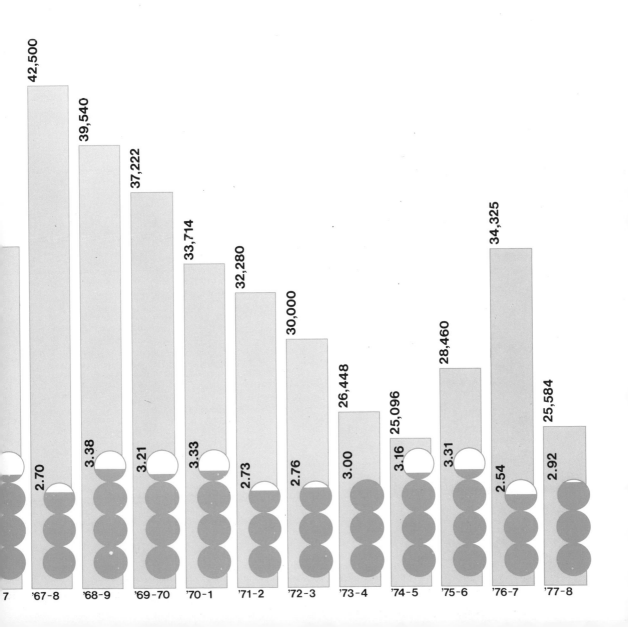

42,500

39,540

37,222

33,714

32,280

30,000

26,448

25,096

28,460

34,325

25,584

7

'67-8   2.70

'68-9   3.38

'69-70   3.21

'70-1   3.33

'71-2   2.73

'72-3   2.76

'73-4   3.00

'74-5   3.16

'75-6   3.31

'76-7   2.54

'77-8   2.92

European Survey 1978/9

	Champions Matches Points	Clubs in Division	Most wins	Fewest Defeats	Most Goals
ALBANIA	Partizan 26 36	14	Partizan 14	Partizan, 17 Nendori 4	17 Nendori 41
AUSTRIA	Austria/WAC 36 55	10	Austria/WAC 25	Austria/WAC 6	Austria/WAC 88
BELGIUM	Beveren 34 49	18	Anderlecht 21	Beveren 4	Anderlecht 76
BULGARIA	Levski Spartak 30 43	16	Levski 18	CSKA Sofia 4	Levski 54
CYPRUS	Omonia 30 45	16	Apoel 20	Omonia 3	Omonia 66
CZECHOSLOVAKIA	Dukla Prague 30 41	16	Dukla 18	Banik Ostrava 5	Dukla 65
DENMARK	Vejle 30 44	16	Vejle 19	Vejle 5	Vejle 64
ENGLAND	Liverpool 42 68	22	Liverpool 30	Nottm. Forest 3	Liverpool 85
FINLAND	HJK Helsinki 22 33	12	HJK 13	HJK, KPT 2	P. Turku 57
FRANCE	Strasbourg 38 56	20	St. Etienne 24	Strasbourg 4	Nantes 85
EAST GERMANY	Dynamo Berlin 26 46	14	Dyn. Berlin 21	Dyn. Berlin 1	Dyn. Berlin 75
WEST GERMANY	Hamburg 34 49	18	Hamburg 21	Hamburg, Stuttgart 6	Hamburg 78
GREECE	AEK Athens 34 56	18	Olympiakos 26	AEK Athens 3	AEK Athens 90
HUNGARY	Ujpest Dozsa 34 52	18	Ujpest 21	Ujpest 3	Ujpest 84
ICELAND	Valur 18 35	10	Valur 17	Valur Nil	IA Akranes 47
N. IRELAND	Linfield 22 34	12	Linfield 14	Linfield 2	Ards 47
REP. OF IRELAND	Dundalk 30 45	16	Dundalk 19	Dundalk 4	Drogheda 60
ITALY	AC Milan 30 44	16	AC Milan 17	Perugia Nil	AC Milan 46
LIECHTENSTEIN	No National League; clubs play in Switzerland Regional Leagues				
LUXEMBOURG	Red Boys 22 34	12	Red Boys 14	Progres N. 1	Progres N. 61
MALTA	Hibernians¶ 6 11	11			
NETHERLANDS	Ajax 34 54	18	Ajax 24	Feyenoord 2	Ajax 93
NORWAY	Start Kr. 22 33	12	Start 13	Start, Lillestrom 2	Brann 52
POLAND	Ruch Chorzow 30 39	16	Ruch 16	Widzew Lodz 5	Ruch 44
PORTUGAL	Porto 30 50	16	Benfica 23	Porto 1	Benfica 75
RUMANIA	Arges Pitesti 34 45	18	Arges 20	Arges, Dinamo 9	Steaua 57
SCOTLAND	Celtic 36 48	10	Celtic 21	Celtic, Rangers, Aberdeen 9	Celtic 61
SPAIN	Real Madrid 34 47	18	Real Sociedad 18	Real Madrid 3	Barcelona 69
SWEDEN	Oster Vaxjo 26 38	14	Oster 15	Oster 3	Oster 46
SWITZERLAND	Servette †	12			
TURKEY	Trabzonspor 30 42	16	Galatasaray 17	Trabzonspor 1	Galatasaray 47
USSR	Dynamo Tbilisi 30 42	16	D. Tbilisi 17	D. Tbilisi 5	D. Tbilisi 45
WALES	No National League; 4 Welsh clubs play in Football League: Cardiff City, Newport County, Swansea City, Wrexham				
YUGOSLAVIA	Hajduk Split 34 50	18	D. Zagreb 21	Hajduk 4	D. Zagreb 67

*Clubs are allowed points for only 8 drawn matches in a season
†Wrexham qualified for the Cup Winners Cup because Shrewsbury as an English club were ineligible
‡No comparisons relevant; top six clubs from championship play off for title with 10 additional matches
¶The final championship in two groups; group A with 4 teams and group B (relegation) with 6 teams

Fewest Conceded	Most Drawn	Average Goals per Game	Top Scorer	Cup Final Result	
Partizan, Flamurtari 20	Dinamo, Lokomotiva 13	2.13	Murati (Partizan), Dibra (17 Nendori) 14	Winners: Villaznia	ALBANIA
Rapid 40	Graz Ak 15	2.77	Schachner (Austria/ WAC) 24	SW Innsbruck v Admira/ Wacker 1–0, 1–1	AUSTRIA
Beveren 24	Waregem 15	2.71	Albert (Beveren) 28	Beerschot 1 FC Bruges 0	BELGIUM
Lokomotiv Sofia 22	CSKA Sofia 12	2.60	Gotchev (Levski) 19	Levski Spartak 4 Beroe 1	BULGARIA
Omonia 17	AEL 16	2.28	Kaiafas (Omonia)	Winners: Apoel	CYPRUS
Banik 12	Spartak Trnava 13	2.71	Nehoda (Dukla) 17	Lokomotiv Kosice 2 Banik Ostrava 1	CZECHO- SLOVAKIA
Esbjerg, B1903 32	Slagelse 10	3.00	Eriksen (Odense) 22	Frem v Esbjerg 1–1, 1–1, 1–1 (a.e.t.), Frem w. 5–4 on penalties	DENMARK
Liverpool 16	Norwich City 23	2.63	Worthington (Bolton W.) 24	Arsenal 3 Manchester U. 2	ENGLAND
KPT 15	Reipas, Prykiva 9	2.80	Ismail (HJK) 20	Reipas Lahden v KPT 1–1, 3–1	FINLAND
Strasbourg 28	Lille 18	3.00	Bianchi (Paris St. Germain) 27	Nantes 4 Auxerre 1 (a.e.t.)	FRANCE
Dyn. Berlin 16	Dyn. Dresden 9	3.05	Streich (Magdeburg) 23	Magdeburg 1 Dynamo Berlin 0	EAST GERMANY
Hamburg 32	Bochum, Eintracht Brunswick 13	3.14	Klaus Allofs (For. Dussel.) 22	Fortuna Dusseldorf 1 Hertha Berlin 0 (a.e.t.)	WEST GERMANY
PAOK Salonika 23	Kastoria 11	2.58	Mavros (AEK Athens) 31	Panionios 3 AEK Athens 1	GREECE
Raba ETO 33	PMSC, Csepel 15	2.88	Fekete (Ujpest) 31	Raba ETO 1 Ferencvaros 0	HUNGARY
Valur 8	Throttur, Hafnafirdi 6	3.10	Petursson (IA Akranes)	IA Akranes 1 Valur 0	ICELAND
Linfield 21	Glentoran Crusaders, Bangor 8	3.10	Platt (Cliftonville) 29	Cliftonville 3 Portadown 2	N. IRELAND
Bohemians 21	Cork A. Shelbourne 9	2.91	Delamere (Dundalk) 17**	Dundalk 1 Waterford 0	REP. OF IRELAND
Perugia 15	Perugia 19	1.89	Giordano (Lazio) 19	Juventus 2 Palermo 1 (a.e.t.)	ITALY
					LIECHENSTEIN
Red Boys 19	Avenir Beggen 10	3.29	May (Progres N.) 18	Red Boys 4 Aris 1 (a.e.t.)	LUXEMBOURG
				Sliema 2 Floriana 1	MALTA
Feyenoord 19	PEC Zwolle 18	2.85	Kist (AZ 67)	Ajax 3 Twente 0 after 1–1 draw (a.e.t.)	NETHERLANDS
Start 13	Lillestrom Strinkjer 9	3.27	Lundquist (Skeid) 19	Lillestrom 2 Brann 1	NORWAY
Zaglebie Sos 25	Zaglebie Sos 15	2.18	Kmiecik (Wisla) 17	Arka Gdynia 2 Wisla Krakow 1	POLAND
Porto 19	Varzim, Estoril 10	2.60	Gomes (Porto) 27	Boavista 1 Sporting Lisbon 0 after 1–1 draw	PORTUGAL
Uni. Craiova 25	Dinamo Iassy 9	2.47	Radu (Arges) 22	Steaua 3 Sportul 0	RUMANIA
Rangers 35	Aberdeen 14	2.68	Ritchie (Morton) 22	Rangers 3 Hibernian 2 (a.e.t.) after 2 draws 0–0	SCOTLAND
Gijon 35	Real Madrid 15	2.68	Krankl (Barcelona) 29	Valencia 2 Real Madrid 0	SPAIN
Malmo 15	Halmstad 11	2.59	Berggren (Djurgaarden) 19	Malmo 2 Kalmar 0	SWEDEN
		3.04	Risi (Zurich) 16	Servette 1 Young Boys 1 (a.e.t.) Replay, Servette 3 Young Boys 2	SWITZERLAND
Trabzonspor 7	Trabzonspor 16	2.02	Ozer (Adanaspor) 15	Fenerbahce 2 Altay Izmir 0 after 2–1 win 1st leg by Altay	TURKEY
Dynamo Kiev 20	Torpedo Moscow 11*	2.33	Yartzev (Spartak) (Moscow) 19	Dynamo Kiev 2 Schactjor Donozk 1	USSR
				†Shrewsbury T 1 Wrexham 0 after 1–1 first leg at Wrexham	WALES
Hajduk 28	• Radnicki, Osijek 13	2.47	Savic (Red Star) 24	Rijeka 2 Partizan 1 after 0–0 draw 1st leg	YUGOSLAVIA

*Includes 2 goals for Sligo Rovers

WORLD SOCCER

Super Cup

Glasgow Rangers manager Willie Waddell approached Ajax to play in a friendly at Ibrox Park as part of the club's centenary celebrations in 1973. At the time Rangers were holders of the European Cup Winners Cup and Ajax the European Cup champions.

The Dutch newspaper *De Telegraaf* suggested a new cup for a fixture on a home and away basis and the tag Super Cup was attached to it. However UEFA said that they did not approve of such a competition and stated that only friendlies could be played.

On 16 January 1973 Ajax won 3–1 at Ibrox against Rangers and the colours of all the clubs that the Scottish club had played in Europe were paraded round the ground before the game. The return in Amsterdam on 24 January was also won 3–2 by Ajax but so successful were the matches that within a year official approval had been given for what was hoped would be an annual event.

1973 Ajax (Holland) beat Rangers (Scotland) 3–1, 3–2
1974 Ajax (Holland) beat AC Milan (Italy) 0–1, 6–0
1975 Dynamo Kiev (USSR) beat Bayern Munich (West Germany) 1–0, 2–0
1976 Anderlecht (Belgium) beat Bayern Munich (West Germany) 4–1, 1–2
1977 Liverpool (England) beat Hamburg SV (West Germany) 1–1, 6–0
1978 Anderlecht (Belgium) beat Liverpool (England) 3–1, 1–2

World Club Championship

year
1960 Real Madrid (Spain) beat Penarol (Uruguay) 0–0, 5–1
1961 Penarol (Uruguay) beat Benfica (Portugal) 0–1, 5–0, 2–1
1962 Santos (Brazil) beat Benfica (Portugal) 3–2, 5–2
1963 Santos (Brazil) beat AC Milan (Italy) 2–4, 4–2, 1–0
1964 Inter-Milan (Italy) beat Independiente (Argentina) 0–1, 2–0, 1–0
1965 Inter-Milan (Italy) beat Independiente (Argentina) 3–0, 0–0
1966 Penarol (Uruguay) beat Real Madrid (Spain) 2–0, 2–0
1967 Racing Club (Argentina) beat Celtic (Scotland) 0–1, 2–1, 1–0
1968 Estudiantes (Argentina) beat Manchester United (England) 1–0, 1–1
1969 AC Milan (Italy) beat Estudiantes (Argentina) 3–0, 1–2
1970 Feyenoord (Holland) beat Estudiantes (Argentina) 2–2, 1–0
1971 Nacional (Uruguay) beat Panathinaikos (Greece) 1–1, 2–1
1972 Ajax (Holland) beat Independiente (Argentina) 1–1, 3–0
1973 Independiente (Argentina) beat Juventus (Italy) 1–0
1974 Atletico Madrid (Spain) beat Independiente (Argentina) 0–1, 2–0
1975 Independiente (Argentina) and Bayern Munich (West Germany) could not agree on dates
1976 Bayern Munich (West Germany) beat Cruzeiro (Brazil) 2–0, 0–0
1977 Boca Juniors (Argentina) beat Borussia Moenchengladbach (West Germany) 2–2, 3–0

World Cup

The 11th World Cup final tournament was held in Argentina in June 1978 in five cities and on six grounds. Cordoba, Mendoza, Rosario and Mar del Plata provided one venue each while two were used in the capital of Buenos Aires at the River Plate and Velez Sarsfield stadiums.

Brazil is the only country to have appeared in all 11 final stages and of the 16 teams in 1978 only Iran and Tunisia had never previously reached the finals, thus becoming the 46th and 47th different countries to achieve this honour.

The World Cup trophy itself is now the second in the lifetime of the competition. The first was named after Jules Rimet, the late Honorary President of FIFA from 1921 to 1954. Brazil won this cup outright in 1970.

A new trophy of solid gold 36cm high known as the FIFA World Cup and designed by an Italian from an entry of some 53 submitted for selection was used in 1974 for the first time.

Of the five previous different winners of the competition: Brazil, Italy, West Germany, Uruguay and England, only the last two named did not qualify in 1978.

Argentina became the sixth winners, beating Holland 3–1 after extra-time.

WORLD CUP WINNERS ANALYSIS (Final tournaments)

Uruguay (1930), Italy (1938) and Brazil (1970) have been the only winners with 100% records in one final series. They are also three of the four countries who have won the competition more than once, along with West Germany who have been the highest scorers in one tournament. They scored 25 in six matches (1954) which produced the highest average of 4.16 goals per game. England had the best defensive record in 1966 with only three goals conceded in six matches.

Year	Winners	Matches			Goals		Players	Appearances (goals)
		P	W	D	L	F	A	used	
1930	**Uruguay**	4	4	0	0	15	3	15	Ballesteros, Nasazzi, Cea (5), Andrade (J), Fernandez, Gestido, Iriarte (2) 4 each; Dorado (2), Macsheroni, Scarone (1) 3 each; Castro (2), Anselmo (3) 2 each; Tejera, Urdinaran, Petrone 1 each.

Final: Uruguay 4 Argentina 2   90,000 Montevideo

Italy, 1934 World Cup champions, pose in Rome.
(Popperfoto)

| 1934 | **Italy** | 5 | 4 | 1 | 0 | 12 | 3 | 17 | Combi, Allmandi, Monti, Meazza (2), Orsi (3) 5 each; Monzeglio, Bertolini, Schiavio (4), Ferrari (2), Guaita (1) 4 each; Ferraris IV 3; Pizziolo 2; Rosetta, Guarisi, Castellazzi, Borel, Demaria 1 each. |

Final: Italy 2 Czechoslovakia 1   50,000 Rome
(after extra time)

| 1938 | **Italy** | 4 | 4 | 0 | 0 | 11 | 5 | 14 | Olivieri, Rava, Serantoni, Andreolo, Locatelli, Meazza (1), Piolo (5), Ferrari (1) 4 each; Foni, Biavati, Colaussi (4) 3 each; Monzeglio, Pasinati, Ferraris II 1 each. |

Final: Italy 4 Hungary 2   45,000 Paris

| 1950 | **Uruguay** | 4 | 3 | 1 | 0 | 15 | 5 | 14 | Gonzales (M), Tejera, Valera (1), Andrade (R), Ghiggia (4), Perez, Miguez (4), Schiaffino (5) 4 each; Maspoli, Vidal (1) 3 each; Gonzales (W), Gambetta 2 each; Paz, Moran 1 each. |

Deciding match: Uruguay 2 Brazil 1   199,850 Rio de Janeiro

| 1954 | **West Germany** | 6 | 5 | 0 | 1 | 25 | 14 | 18 | Eckel, Walter (F) (3) 6 each; Turek, Kohlmeyer, Posipal, Mai, Morlock (6), Walter (O) (4), Schafer (4) 5 each; Liebrich, Rahn (4) 4 each; Laband 3; Klodt (1), Bauer 2 each; Herrmann (1), Mebus, Kwaitowski, Pfaff (1) 1 each. (own goal 1). |

Final: West Germany 3 Hungary 2   60,000 Berne

The deciding match in the 1950 World Cup finals watched by a world record crowd. Uruguay beat Brazil 2–1. (Popperfoto)

1970 World Cup Final and Carlos Alberto holds the Jules Rimet Trophy aloft after Brazil's victory over Italy. (Syndication International)

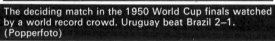

Year	Winners	Matches				Goals		Players used	Appearances (Goals)
		P	W	D	L	F	A		
1958	**Brazil**	6	5	1	0	16	4	16	Gilmar, Nilton Santos (1), Bellini, Orlando, Didi (1), Zagalo (1), 6 each; De Sordi 5; Vava (5), Zito, Garrincha, Pele (6), 4 each; Mazzola (2) 3; Dino, Joel 2 each; Djalma Santos, Dida 1 each.

Final: Brazil 5 Sweden 2   49,737 Stockholm

1962	**Brazil**	6	5	1	0	14	5	12	Gilmar, Djalma Santos, Mauro, Zozimo, Nilton Santos, Zito (1), Didi, Garrincha (4), Vara (4), Zagalo (1), 6 each; Amarildo (3) 4; Pele (1) 2.

Final: Brazil 3 Czechoslovakia 1   68,679 Santiago

1966	**England**	6	5	1	0	11	3	15	Banks, Cohen, Wilson, Stiles, Charlton (J), Moore, Charlton (R) (3), Hunt (3), 6 each; Peters (1) 5; Ball 4; Greaves, Hurst (4) 3; Paine, Callaghan, Connelly 1 each.

Final: England 4 West Germany 2   93,802 Wembley (after extra time)

1970	**Brazil**	6	6	0	0	19	7	15	Felix, Carlos Alberto (1), Piazza, Brito, Clodoaldo (1), Jairzinho (7), Tostao (2), Pele (4), 6 each: Everaldo, Rivelino (3) 5; Gerson (1) 4; Paulo Cesar 2+2 subs; Marco Antonio 1+1 sub; Roberto 2 subs; Fontana 1; Edu 1 sub.

Final: Brazil 4 Italy 1   107,412 Mexico City

1974	**West Germany**	7	6	0	1	13	4	18	Maier, Vogts, Breitner (3), Schwarzenbeck, Beckenbauer, Muller (4), Overath (2), 7 each; Hoeness (1) 6+1 sub; Grabowski (1) 5+ 1 sub; Holzenbein 4+2 subs; Bonhof (1) 4; Cullmann (1) 3; Flohe 1+2 subs; Heynckes, Herzog 2 each; Wimmer 1+1 sub; Netzer, Hottges 1 sub each.

Final: West Germany 2 Holland 1   77,833 Munich

1978	**Argentina**	7	5	1	1	15	4	17	Fillol, Luis Galvan, Olguin, Passarella (1) Tarantini (1), Gallego, Kempes (6) 7 each; Ardiles 6; Bertoni 5+1 sub; Ortiz 4+2 subs; (2) Luque (4) 5; Houseman (1) 3+3 subs; Valencia 4; Larrosa 1+1 sub; Alonso 3 subs; Villa 2 subs; Oviedo 1 sub.

Final: Argentina 3 Holland 1   77,000 Buenos Aires (after extra time)

England playing Italy in the Olympic Stadium in Rome, one of the grounds to be used in the final stages of the European Championships in 1980. (All Sport/Don Morley)

Above: Sepp Maier the West German goalkeeper who has remained a first choice for Bayern Munich and his country at the age of 35. (Syndication International)

Left: Italy (blue shirts) and Brazil in the beaten semi-finalists match in the 1978 World Cup in Argentina. (Syndication International)

Above: Peru (white shirts) playing
Poland in the 1978 World Cup in
Argentina. (Syndication International)

Right: Ally MacLeod left his position as
Scottish team manager following the
World Cup finals in Argentina to become
first Ayr United's manager then that of
Motherwell. (Syndication International)

Ticker-tape welcomes for the Argentina side were regular features in the 1978 finals.
insets: a parachutist makes a spectacular arrival. Security guards leave nothing to chance. Cesar Luis Menotti, Argentina's manager. (Syndication International)

Left: Joe Jordan (blue shirt) beats Holland's goalkeeper Jan Jongbloed in the match which restored some pride to Scotland in the 1978 World Cup. (Syndication International)

Right: An Italian supporter in Argentina, advertising the Latin culinary arts. (Synidcation International)

Below: One of the majorettes who decorated the 1978 World Cup finals in Argentina. (Syndication International)

Below right: Rain-soaked fans in Argentina with their enthusiasm scarcely dampened. (Syndication International)

Daniel Passarella, Argentina's Captain, holds the cup aloft after his side's triumph in the 11th World Cup. (Syndication International)

WORLD CUP APPEARANCES

Antonio Carbajal (Mexico) is the only player to have appeared in five World Cup final tournaments. He kept goal for Mexico in 1950, 1954, 1958, 1962 and 1966, with 11 appearances in all.

Uwe Seeler (West Germany) established a record of appearances in World Cup final tournaments by making a total of 21 appearances in 1958, 1962, 1966 and 1970 as a centre-forward.

Pele (Brazil) is the only player to have been with three World Cup winning teams, though he missed the final of the 1962 competition because of injury. He made four appearances in the 1958 final tournament, two in 1962 before injury and six in 1970. He also appeared in two matches in 1966 for a total of 14 appearances in all.

Mario Zagalo is the only man who has won a World Cup winners medal and managed a World Cup winning team. He played in the 1958 and 1962 World Cup winning teams of Brazil and was manager when they achieved their third success in 1970.

GOALSCORING

The record margin of victory in a World Cup final tournament is nine clear goals; in 1954: Hungary 9 South Korea 0 and in 1974: Yugoslavia 9 Zaire 0. The record scoreline in any World Cup match is West Germany 12 Cyprus 0 in a qualifying match on 21 May 1969.

Just Fontaine (France) scored a record 13 goals in six matches of the 1958 World Cup final tournament. **Gerd Muller** (West Germany) scored 10 goals in 1970 and four in 1974 for the highest aggregate of 14 goals. **Fontaine** and **Jairzinho** (Brazil) are the only two players to have scored in every match in a final series, as Jairzinho scored seven goals in six matches in 1970.

Including World Cup qualifying matches in the 1970 series, **Muller** scored a total of 19 goals with nine coming from six preliminary games and ten in the final stages.

Pele is the third highest scorer in World Cup final tournaments, having registered 12 goals in his four competitions.

Geoff Hurst (England) is the only player to have scored a hat-trick in a final when he registered three of his side's goals in their 4–2 win over West Germany in 1966.

The first player to score as many as four goals in any World Cup match was **Paddy Moore** who registered all the Republic of Ireland's goals in the 4–4 draw with Belgium in Dublin during a World Cup qualifying match on 25 February 1934.

Robbie Rensenbrink (Holland) scored the 1,000th goal in World Cup finals when he converted a penalty against Scotland in the 1978 tournament.

The first goal scored in the World Cup was credited to **Louis Laurent** for France against Mexico on 13 July 1930 in Montevideo. France won 4–1. With the time difference the news reached France on Bastille Day, 14 July.

The fastest goal scored in a World Cup final tournament was probably attributed to **Olle Nyberg** of Sweden against Hungary on 16 June 1938 in Paris, after approximately 30 seconds of play. **Bernard Lacombe** scored for France against Italy in 31 seconds during the 1978 tournament.

Vava (real name Edwaldo Izidio Neto) of Brazil is the only player to have scored in successive World Cup finals. He did so against Sweden in 1958 (scoring twice) and against Czechoslovakia in 1962. **Pele** is the only other to score in two finals, twice in Sweden in 1958 and once against Italy in 1970.

Leading World Cup scorers (**final tournament**)

Year	Name	Country	Goals
1930	Guillermo Stabile	Argentina	8
1934	Angelo Schiavio	Italy	4
	Oldrich Nejedly	Czechoslovakia	4
	Edmund Conen	Germany	4
1938	Leonidas da Silva	Brazil	8
1950	Ademir	Brazil	7
1954	Sandor Kocsis	Hungary	11
1958	Just Fontaine	France	13
1962	Drazen Jerkovic	Yugoslavia	5
1966	Eusebio	Portugal	9
1970	Gerd Muller	West Germany	10
1974	Grzegorz Lato	Poland	7
1978	Mario Kempes	Argentina	6

The record invididual score in a World Cup final tournament is four goals, a feat which has been achieved on eight occasions:

Name	For	Against
Gustav Wetterstroem	Sweden	v Cuba 1938
Leonidas da Silva	Brazil	v Poland 1938
Ernest Willimowski	Poland	v Brazil 1938
Ademir	Brazil	v Sweden 1950

Juan Schiaffino	Uruguay v Bolivia 1950
Sandor Kocsis	Hungary v W. Germany 1954
Just Fontaine	France v W. Germany 1958
Eusebio	Portugal v North Korea 1966

World Cup endurance

Helmut Schoen who retired as West Germany's team manager after the 1978 World Cup finals was the most successful international coach. In 1966 his team finished runners-up in the World Cup, were third in 1970 and became European Championship winners in 1972. They won the World Cup in 1974 and were runners-up in the European Championship in 1976. Schoen had been in charge for 14 years.

Making his 100th international appearance for Poland, Kazimierz Deyna had a penalty kick saved by the Argentine goalkeeper Ubaldo Fillol in the 1978 tournament.

The longest period that a goalkeeper has kept his charge intact during a World Cup final tournament is 475 minutes. Josef 'Sepp' Maier of West Germany conceded a penalty to Holland in the first minute of the 1974 World Cup Final itself and was not beaten again until Holland scored against him in the 1978 tournament.

Eusebio of Benfica and Portugal (Syndication International)

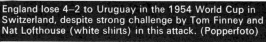

England lose 4–2 to Uruguay in the 1954 World Cup in
Switzerland, despite strong challenge by Tom Finney and
Nat Lofthouse (white shirts) in this attack. (Popperfoto)

A scramble in the Russian goalmouth during the 1966
World Cup semi-final between West Germany and the
USSR (dark shirts). (Syndication International)

Uruguay v Holland in the 1974 World Cup and Johan
Neeskens the Dutch midfield player is tackled by
Uruguay's Juan Masnik (right).

Johnny Rep (Holland) heads towards goal for Holland in
the 1978 World Cup Final watched by Daniel Passarella
(left) and Americo Gallego of Argentina. (Syndication
International)

1930–1978 World Cup Attendances and Goals

Year	Venue	Attendances	Average	Matches	Goals	Average
1930	Uruguay	434,500	24,139	18	70	3.88
1934	Italy	395,000	23,235	17	70	4.11
1938	France	483,000	26,833	18	84	4.66
1950	Brazil	1,337,000	60,772	22	88	4.00
1954	Switzerland	943,000	36,270	26	140	5.38
1958	Sweden	868,000	24,800	35	126	3.60
1962	Chile	776,000	24,250	32	89	2.78
1966	England	1,614,677	50,458	32	89	2.78
1970	Mexico	1,673,975	52,312	32	95	2.96
1974	West Germany	1,774,022	46,685	38	97	2.55
1978	Argentina	1,610,215	42,374	38	102	2.68

Summary of Matches in World Cup Finals
1930-78

		P	W	D	L	F	A
1.	Brazil	52	33	10	9	119	56
2.	West Germany*	47	28	9	10	110	68
3.	Italy	36	20	6	10	62	40
4.	Uruguay	29	14	5	10	57	39
5.	Argentina	29	14	5	10	55	43
6.	Hungary	26	13	2	11	73	42
7.	Sweden	28	11	6	11	48	46
8.	England	24	10	6	8	34	28
9.	Yugoslavia	25	10	5	10	45	34
10.	USSR	19	10	3	6	30	21
11.	Holland (Netherlands)	16	8	3	5	32	19
12.	Poland	14	9	1	4	27	17
13.	Austria	18	9	1	8	33	36
14.	Czechoslovakia	22	8	3	11	32	36
15.	France	20	8	1	11	43	38
16.	Chile	18	7	3	8	23	24
17.	Spain	18	7	3	8	22	25
18.	Switzerland	18	5	2	11	28	44
19.	Portugal	6	5	0	1	17	8
20.	Mexico	24	3	4	17	21	62
21.	Peru	12	4	1	7	17	25
22.	Scotland	11	2	4	5	12	21
23.	East Germany (GDR)	6	2	2	2	5	5
24.	Paraguay	7	2	2	3	12	19
25.	United States of America	7	3	0	4	12	21
26.	Wales	5	1	3	1	4	4
27.	Northern Ireland	5	2	1	2	6	10
28.	Rumania	8	2	1	5	12	17
29.	Bulgaria	12	0	4	8	9	29
30.	Tunisia	3	1	1	1	3	2
31.	North Korea	4	1	1	2	5	9
32.	Cuba	3	1	1	1	5	12
33.	Belgium	9	1	1	7	12	25
34.	Turkey	3	1	0	2	10	11
35.	Israel	3	0	2	1	1	3
36.	Morocco	3	0	1	2	2	6
37.	Australia	3	0	1	2	0	5
38.	Iran	3	0	1	2	2	8
39.	Colombia	3	0	1	2	5	11
40.	Norway	1	0	0	1	1	2
41.	Egypt	1	0	0	1	2	4
42.	Dutch East Indies	1	0	0	1	0	6
43.	El Salvador	3	0	0	3	0	9
44.	South Korea	2	0	0	2	0	16
45.	Haiti	3	0	0	3	2	14
46.	Zaire	3	0	0	3	0	14
47.	Bolivia	3	0	0	3	0	16

* including Germany 1934-1938

World Cup
FINAL SERIES 1930–1978 (PARTICIPATING COUNTRIES & RESULTS)

	1930	1934	1938	1950	1954
ARGENTINA	France 1–0 Mexico 6–3 Chile 3–1 USA 6–1 (SF) Uruguay 2–4 (2nd)	Sweden 2–3			
AUSTRALIA					
AUSTRIA		France 3–2 Hungary 2–1 Italy 0–1 (SF) Germany 2–3 (4th)			Scotland 1–0 Czechoslovakia 5–0 Switzerland 7–5 West Germany 1–6 (SF) Uruguay 3–1 (3rd)
BELGIUM	USA 0–3 Paraguay 0–1	Germany 2–5	France 1–3		England 4–4 Italy 1–4
BOLIVIA	Yugoslavia 0–4 Brazil 0–4			Uruguay 0–8	
BRAZIL	Yugoslavia 1–2 Bolivia 4–0	Spain 1–3	Poland 6–5 Czechoslovakia 1–1 Czechoslovakia (r) 2–1 Italy 1–2 (SF) Sweden 4–2 (3rd)	Mexico 4–0 Switzerland 2–2 Yugoslavia 2–0 Sweden 7–1 Spain 6–1 Uruguay 1–2 (2nd)	Mexico 5–0 Yugoslavia 1–1 Hungary 2–4
BULGARIA					
CHILE	Mexico 3–0 France 1–0 Argentina 1–3			England 0–2 Spain 0–2 USA 5–2	
COLOMBIA					
CUBA			Rumania 3–3 Rumania (r) 2–1 Sweden 0–8		

Key: W=Winners; 2nd=Runners up; 3rd=Won match for third place; 4th=Lost match for third place; SF=Semi final; p o=play-off; r=replay

1958	1962	1966	1970	1974	1978	
						ARGENTINA
West Germany 1–3	Bulgaria 1–0	Spain 2–1		Poland 2–3	Hungary 2–1	
Northern Ireland 3–1	England 1–3	West Germany 0–0		Italy 1–1	France 2–1	
Czechoslovakia 1–6	Hungary 0–0	Switzerland 2–0		Haiti 4–1	Italy 0–1	
		England 0–1		Netherlands 0–4	Poland 2–0	
				Brazil 1–2	Brazil 0–0	
				East Germany 1–1	Peru 6–0	
					Netherlands 3–1 (W)	
						AUSTRALIA
				East Germany 0–2		
				West Germany 0–3		
				Chile 0–0		
						AUSTRIA
Brazil 0–3					Spain 2–1	
USSR 0–2					Sweden 1–0	
England 2–2					Brazil 0–1	
					Netherlands 1–5	
					Italy 0–1	
					West Germany 3–2	
						BELGIUM
			El Salvador 3–0			
			USSR 1–4			
			Mexico 0–1			
						BOLIVIA
						BRAZIL
Austria 3–0	Mexico 2–0	Bulgaria 2–0	Czechoslovakia 4–1	Yugoslavia 0–0	Sweden 1–1	
England 0–0	Czechoslovakia 0–0	Hungary 1–3	England 1–0	Scotland 0–0	Spain 0–0	
USSR 2–0	Spain 2–1	Portugal 1–3	Rumania 3–2	Zaire 3–0	Austria 1–0	
Wales 1–0	England 3–1		Peru 4–2	East Germany 1–0	Peru 3–0	
France 5–2	Chile 4–2		Uruguay 3–1	Argentina 2–1	Argentina 0–0	
Sweden 5–2 (W)	Czechoslovakia 3–1 (W)		Italy 4–1 (W)	Netherlands 0–2	Poland 3–1	
				Poland 0–1 (4th)	Italy 2–1 (3rd)	
						BULGARIA
	Argentina 0–1	Brazil 0–2	Peru 2–3	Sweden 0–0		
	Hungary 1–6	Portugal 0–3	West Germany 2–5	Uruguay 1–1		
	England 0–0	Hungary 1–3	Morocco 1–1	Netherlands 1–4		
						CHILE
	Switzerland 3–1	Italy 0–2		West Germany 0–1		
	Italy 2–0	North Korea 1–1		East Germany 1–1		
	West Germany 0–2	USSR 1–2		Australia 0–0		
	USSR 2–1					
	Brazil 2–4 (SF)					
	Yugoslavia 1–0 (3rd)					
						COLOMBIA
	Uruguay 1–2					
	USSR 4–4					
	Yugoslavia 0–5					
						CUBA

	1930	1934	1938	1950	1954
CZECHOSLOVAKIA		Rumania 2–1 Switzerland 3–2 Germany 3–1 Italy 1–2 (2nd)	Netherlands 3–0 Brazil 1–1 Brazil (r) 1–2		Uruguay 0–2 Austria 0–5
DUTCH EAST INDIES			Hungary 0–6		
EAST GERMANY (GDR)					
EGYPT		Hungary 2–4			
ENGLAND				Chile 2–0 USA 0–1 Spain 0–1	Belgium 4–4 Switzerland 2–0 Uruguay 2–4
EL SALVADOR					
FRANCE	Mexico 4–1 Argentina 0–1 Chile 0–1	Austria 2–3	Belgium 3–1 Italy 1–3		Yugoslavia 0–1 Mexico 3–2
GERMANY		Belgium 5–2 Sweden 2–1 Czechoslovakia 1–3 (SF) Austria 3–2 (3rd)	Switzerland 1–1 Switzerland (r) 2–4		
HAITI					
HUNGARY		Egypt 4–2 Austria 1–2	Dutch East Indies 6–0 Switzerland 2–0 Sweden 5–1 Italy 2–4		South Korea 9–0 West Germany 8–3 Brazil 4–2 Uruguay 4–2 West Germany 2–3 (2nd)
IRAN					
ISRAEL					

	1958	1962	1966	1970	1974	1978
CZECHOSLOVAKIA	Northern Ireland 0–1; West Germany 2–2; Argentina 6–1; North Ireland 1–2 (p-o)	Spain 1–0; Brazil 0–0; Mexico 1–3; Hungary 1–0; Yugoslavia 3–1; Brazil 1–3 (2nd)		Brazil 1–4; Rumania 1–2; England 0–1		
DUTCH EAST INDIES						
EAST GERMANY (GDR)					Australia 2–0; Chile 1–1; West Germany 1–0; Brazil 0–1; Netherlands 0–2; Argentina 1–1	
EGYPT						
ENGLAND	USSR 2–2; Brazil 0–0; Austria 2–2; USSR 0–1 (p-o)	Hungary 1–2; Argentina 3–1; Bulgaria 0–0; Brazil 1–3	Uruguay 0–0; Mexico 2–0; France 2–0; Argentina 1–0; Portugal 2–1; West Germany 4–2 (W)	Rumania 1–0; Brazil 0–1; Czechoslovakia 1–0; West Germany 2–3		
EL SALVADOR				Belgium 0–3; Mexico 0–4; USSR 0–2		
FRANCE	Paraguay 7–3; Yugoslavia 2–3; Scotland 2–1; Northern Ireland 4–0; Brazil 2–5 (SF); West Germany 6–3 (3rd)		Mexico 1–1; Uruguay 1–2; England 0–2			Italy 1–2; Argentina 1–2; Hungary 3–1
GERMANY						
HAITI					Italy 1–3; Poland 0–7; Argentina 1–4	
HUNGARY	Wales 1–1; Sweden 1–2; Mexico 4–0; Wales 1–2 (p-o)	England 2–1; Bulgaria 6–1; Argentina 0–0; Czechoslovakia 0–1	Portugal 1–3; Brazil 3–1; Bulgaria 3–1; USSR 1–2			Argentina 1–2; Italy 1–3; France 1–3
IRAN						Netherlands 0–3; Scotland 1–1; Peru 1–4
ISRAEL				Uruguay 0–2; Sweden 1–1; Italy 0–0		

	1930	1934	1938	1950	1954
ITALY		USA 7–1 Spain 1–1 Spain (r) 1–0 Austria 1–0 Czechoslovakia 2–1 (W)	Norway 2–1 France 3–1 Brazil 2–1 Hungary 4–2 (W)	Sweden 2–3 Paraguay 2–0	Switzerland 1–2 Belgium 4–1 Switzerland 1–4 (p-o)
SOUTH KOREA					Hungary 0–9 Turkey 0–7
MEXICO	France 1–4 Chile 0–3 Argentina 3–6			Brazil 0–4 Yugoslavia 1–4 Switzerland 1–2	Brazil 0–5 France 2–3
MOROCCO					
NETHERLANDS (HOLLAND)		Switzerland 2–3	Czechoslovakia 0–3		
NORTHERN IRELAND					
NORTH KOREA					
NORWAY			Italy 1–2		
PARAGUAY	USA 0–3 Belgium 1–0			Sweden 2–2 Italy 0–2	
PERU	Rumania 1–3 Uruguay 0–1				
POLAND			Brazil 5–6		

1958	1962	1966	1970	1974	1978
					ITALY
	West Germany 0–0	Chile 2–0	Sweden 1–0	Haiti 3–1	France 2–1
	Chile 0–2	USSR 0–1	Uruguay 0–0	Argentina 1–1	Hungary 3–1
	Switzerland 3–0	North Korea 0–1	Israel 0–0	Poland 1–2	Argentina 1–0
			Mexico 4–1		West Germany 0–0
			West Germany 4–3		Austria 1–0
			Brazil 1–4 (2nd)		Netherlands 1–2
					Brazil 1–2 (4th)
					SOUTH KOREA
					MEXICO
Sweden 0–3	Brazil 0–2	France 1–1	USSR 0–0		Tunisia 1–3
Wales 1–1	Spain 0–1	England 0–2	El Salvador 4–0		West Germany 0–6
Hungary 0–4	Czechoslovakia 3–1	Uruguay 0–0	Belgium 1–0		Poland 1–3
			Italy 1–4		
					MOROCCO
			West Germany 1–2		
			Peru 0–3		
			Bulgaria 1–1		
					NETHERLANDS (HOLLAND)
			Uruguay 2–0	Iran 3–0	
			Sweden 0–0	Peru 0–0	
			Bulgaria 4–1	Scotland 2–3	
			Argentina 4–0	Austria 5–1	
			East Germany 2–0	West Germany 2–2	
			Brazil 2–0	Italy 2–1	
			West Germany 1–2 (2nd)	Argentina 1–3 (2nd)	
					NORTHERN IRELAND
Czechoslovakia 1–0					
Argentina 1–3					
West Germany 2–2					
Czechoslovakia 2–1 (p-o)					
France 0–4					
					NORTH KOREA
		USSR 0–3			
		Chile 1–1			
		Italy 1–0			
		Portugal 3–5			
					NORWAY
					PARAGUAY
France 3–7					
Scotland 3–2					
Yugoslavia 3–3					
					PERU
			Bulgaria 3–2		Scotland 3–1
			Morocco 3–0		Netherlands 0–0
			West Germany 1–3		Iran 4–1
			Brazil 2–4		Brazil 0–3
					Poland 0–1
					Argentina 0–6
					POLAND
			Argentina 3–2		West Germany 0–0
			Haiti 7–0		Tunisia 1–0
			Italy 2–1		Mexico 3–1
			Sweden 1–0		Argentina 0–2
			Yugoslavia 2–1		Peru 1–0
			West Germany 0–1		Brazil 1–3
			Brazil 1–0 (3rd)		

	1930	1934	1938	1950	1954
PORTUGAL					
RUMANIA	Peru 3–1 Uruguay 0–4	Czechoslovakia 1–2	Cuba 3–3 Cuba (r) 1–2		
SCOTLAND					Austria 0–1 Uruguay 0–7
SPAIN		Brazil 3–1 Italy 1–1 Italy (r) 0–1		USA 3–1 Chile 2–0 England 1–0 Uruguay 2–2 Brazil 1–6 Sweden 1–3 (4th)	
SWEDEN		Argentina 3–2 Germany 1–2	Cuba 8–0 Hungary 1–5 Brazil 2–4 (4th)	Italy 3–2 Paraguay 2–2 Brazil 1–7 Uruguay 2–3 Spain 3–1 (3rd)	
SWITZERLAND		Netherlands 3–2 Czechoslovakia 2–3	Germany 1–1 Germany (r) 4–2 Hungary 0–2	Yugoslavia 0–3 Brazil 2–2 Mexico 2–1	England 0–2 Italy 2–1 Italy 4–1 (p-o) Austria 5–7
TUNISIA					
TURKEY					West Germany 1–4 South Korea 7–0 West Germany 2–7 (p-o)
UNITED STATES of AMERICA	Belgium 3–0 Paraguay 3–0 Argentina 1–6 (SF)	Italy 1–7		Spain 1–3 England 1–0 Chile 2–5	
URUGUAY	Peru 1–0 Rumania 4–0 Yugoslavia 6–1 (SF) Argentina 4–2 (W)			Bolivia 8–0 Spain 2–2 Sweden 3–2 Brazil 2–1 (W)	Czechoslovakia 2–0 Scotland 7–0 England 4–2 Hungary 2–4 (SF) Austria 1–3 (4th)

1958	1962	1966	1970	1974	1978

PORTUGAL

		Hungary 3–1			
		Bulgaria 3–0			
		Brazil 3–1			
		North Korea 5–3			
		England 1–2 (SF)			
		USSR 2–1 (3rd)			

RUMANIA

			England 0–1		
			Czechoslovakia 2–1		
			Brazil 2–3		

SCOTLAND

Yugoslavia 1–1				Zaire 2–0	Peru 1–3
Paraguay 2–3				Brazil 0–0	Iran 1–1
France 1–2				Yugoslavia 1–1	Netherlands 3–2

SPAIN

	Czechoslovakia 0–1	Argentina 1–2			Austria 1–2
	Mexico 1–0	Switzerland 2–1			Brazil 0–0
	Brazil 1–2	West Germany 1–2			Sweden 1–0

SWEDEN

Mexico 3–0			Italy 0–1	Bulgaria 0–0	Brazil 1–1
Hungary 2–1			Israel 1–1	Netherlands 0–0	Austria 0–1
Wales 0–0			Uruguay 1–0	Uruguay 3–0	Spain 0–1
USSR 2–0				Poland 0–1	
West Germany 3–1				West Germany 2–4	
Brazil 2–5 (2nd)				Yugoslavia 2–1	

SWITZERLAND

	Chile 1–3	West Germany 0–5			
	West Germany 1–2	Spain 1–2			
	Italy 0–3	Argentina 0–2			

TUNISIA

					Mexico 3–1
					Poland 0–1
					West Germany 0–0

TURKEY

UNITED STATES of AMERICA

URUGUAY

	Colombia 2–1	England 0–0	Israel 2–0	Netherlands 0–2	
	Yugoslavia 1–3	France 2–1	Italy 0–0	Bulgaria 1–1	
	USSR 1–2	Mexico 0–0	Sweden 0–1	Sweden 0–3	
		West Germany 0–4	USSR 1–0		
			Brazil 1–3 (SF)		
			West Germany 0–1 (4th)		

	1930	1934	1938	1950	1954
USSR					
WALES					
WEST GERMANY				Turkey 4–1 Hungary 3–8 Turkey 7–2 (p-o) Yugoslavia 2-0 Austria 6–1 Hungary 3–2 (W)	
YUGOSLAVIA	Brazil 2–1 Bolivia 4–0 Uruguay 1–6 (SF)			Switzerland 3–0 Mexico 4–1 Brazil 0–2	France 1–0 Brazil 1–1 West Germany 0–2
ZAIRE					

1958	1962	1966	1970	1974	1978	
						USSR
England 2–2	Yugoslavia 2–0	North Korea 3–0	Mexico 0–0			
Austria 2–0	Colombia 4–4	Italy 1–0	Belgium 4–1			
Brazil 0–2	Uruguay 2–1	Chile 2–1	El Salvador 2–0			
England 1–0 (p-o)	Chile 1–2	Hungary 2–1	Uruguay 0–1			
Sweden 0–2		West Germany 1–2 (SF)				
		Portugal 1–2 (4th)				
						WALES
Hungary 1–1						
Mexico 1–1						
Sweden 0–0						
Hungary 2–1 (p-o)						
Brazil 0–1						
						WEST GERMANY
Argentina 3–1	Italy 0–0	Switzerland 5–0	Morocco 2–1	Chile 1–0	Poland 0–0	
Czechoslovakia 2–2	Switzerland 2–1	Argentina 0–0	Bulgaria 5–2	Australia 3–0	Mexico 6–0	
Northern Ireland 2–2	Chile 2–0	Spain 2–1	Peru 3–1	East Germany 0–1	Tunisia 0–0	
Yugoslavia 1–0	Yugoslavia 0–1	Uruguay 4–0	England 3–2	Yugoslavia 2–0	Italy 0–0	
Sweden 1–3 (SF)		USSR 2–1	Italy 3–4 (SF)	Sweden 4–2	Netherlands 2–2	
France 3–6 (4th)		England 2–4 (2nd)	Uruguay 1–0 (3rd)	Poland 1–0	Austria 2–3	
				Netherlands 2 -1 (W)		
						YUGOSLAVIA
Scotland 1–1	USSR 0–2			Brazil 0–0		
France 3–2	Uruguay 3–1			Zaire 9–0		
Paraguay 3–3	Colombia 5–0			Scotland 1–1		
West Germany 0–1	West Germany 1–0			West Germany 0–2		
	Czechoslovakia 1–3 (SF)			Poland 1–2		
	Chile 0–1 (4th)			Sweden 1–2		
						ZAIRE
				Scotland 0–2		
				Yugoslavia 0–9		
				Brazil 0–3		

Left: Zaire goalkeeper Kazadi in action during the 1974 World Cup in West Germany. (Syndication International)

Roberto Bettega evades the outstretched tackle of Berti Vogts (white shirt) in Italy's World Cup match with West Germany in the 1978 final tournament. (Syndication International)

GROWTH OF FIFA

INTERRUPTED MEMBERSHIPS:
ENGLAND   1905–20; 1924–28; 1946
SCOTLAND   1910–20; 1924–28; 1946
WALES   1910–20; 1924–28; 1946
N. IRELAND   1911–20; 1924–28; 1946
GERMANY   1904–45; 1950
JAPAN   1929–45; 1950

*VIETNAM NOW ONE COUNTRY
†MOZAMBIQUE ENTERED 1978

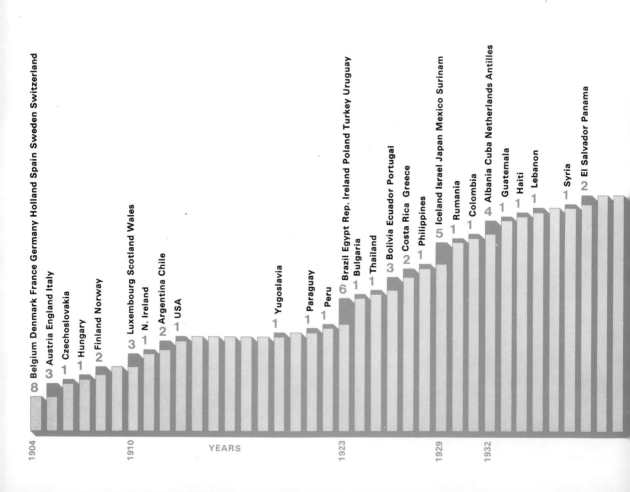

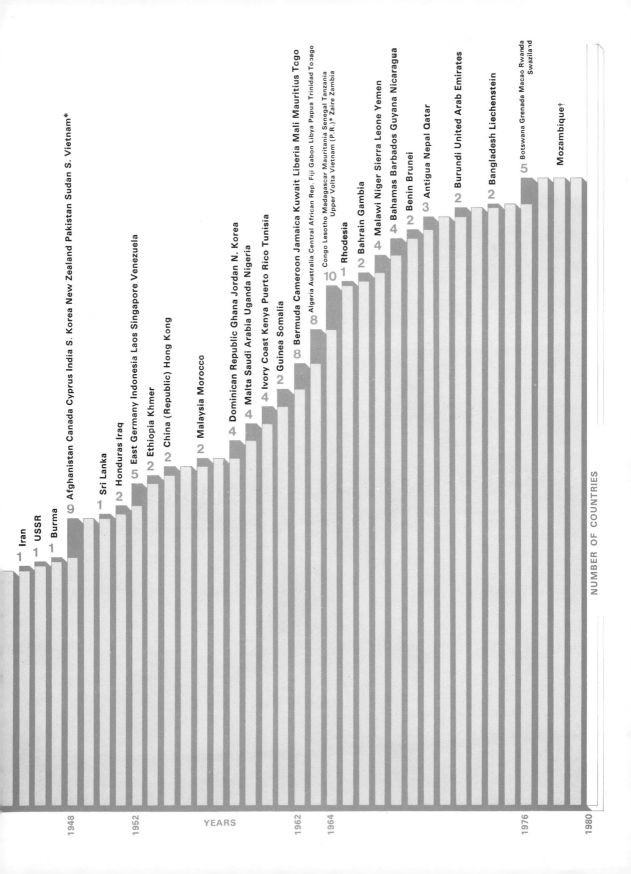

Iran 1
USSR 1
Burma 1
Afghanistan Canada Cyprus India S. Korea New Zealand Pakistan Sudan S. Vietnam* 9
Sri Lanka 1
Honduras Iraq 2
East Germany Indonesia Laos Singapore Venezuela 5
Ethiopia Khmer 2
China (Republic) Hong Kong 2
Malaysia Morocco 2
Dominican Republic Ghana Jordan N. Korea 4
Malta Saudi Arabia Uganda Nigeria 4
Ivory Coast Kenya Puerto Rico Tunisia 4
Guinea Somalia 2
Bermuda Cameroon Jamaica Kuwait Liberia Mali Mauritius Togo 8
Algeria Australia Central African Rep. Fiji Gabon Libya Papua Trinidad Tobago 8
Congo Lesotho Madagascar Mauritania Senegal Tanzania Upper Volta Vietnam (P.R.)* Zaire Zambia 10
Rhodesia 1
Bahrain Gambia 2
Malawi Niger Sierra Leone Yemen 4
Bahamas Barbados Guyana Nicaragua 4
Benin Brunei 2
Antigua Nepal Qatar 3
Burundi United Arab Emirates 2
Bangladesh Liechenstein 2
Botswana Grenada Macao Rwanda Swaziland 5
Mozambique†

YEARS

1948   1952   1962   1964   1976   1980

NUMBER OF COUNTRIES

World Soccer Competitions

Detailed background information on all the following cup competitions appears on pages 21 and 22 of the 1st Edition of *The Guinness Book of Soccer Facts and Feats.*

Mitropa Cup
1927	Sparta Prague (Czechoslovakia)
1928	Ferencvaros (Hungary)
1929	Ujpest Dozsa (Hungary)
1930	Rapid Vienna (Austria)
1931	First Vienna (Austria)
1932	Bologna (Italy)
1933	FK Austria (Austria)
1934	Bologna (Italy)
1935	Sparta Prague (Czechoslovakia)
1936	FK Austria (Austria)
1937	Ferencvaros (Hungary)
1938	Slavia Prague (Czechoslovakia)
1939	Ujpest Dozsa (Hungary)
1951	Rapid Vienna (Austria)
1955	Voros Lobogo (Hungary)
1956	Vasas Budapest (Hungary)
1957	Vasas Budapest (Hungary)
1959	Honved (Hungary)
1960	not completed
1961	Bologna (Italy)
1962	Vasas Budapest (Hungary)
1963	MTK Budapest (Hungary)
1964	Sparta Prague (Czechoslovakia)
1965	Vasas Budapest (Hungary)
1966	Fiorentina (Italy)
1967	Spartak Trnava (Czechoslovakia)
1968	Red Star Belgrade (Yugoslavia)
1969	Inter Bratislava (Czechoslovakia)
1970	Vasas Budapest (Hungary)
1971	Celik Zenica (Yugoslavia)
1972	Celik Zenica (Yugoslavia)
1973	Tatabanya (Hungary)
1974	Tatabanya (Hungary)
1975	SW Innsbruck (Austria)
1976	SW Innsbruck (Austria)
1977	Vojvodina (Yugoslavia)
1978	Partizan Belgrade (Yugoslavia)

Asian Champion Clubs Cup
1967	Hapoel Tel Aviv (Israel)
1968	not played
1969	Maccabi Tel Aviv (Israel)
1970	Tai Teheran (Iran)
1971	Maccabi Tel Aviv (Israel)
1972–78	not played

World Military Championships
1950	Italy
1951	Italy
1952	Greece
1953	Belgium
1954	Belgium
1955	Turkey
1956	Italy
1957	France
1958	Portugal
1959	Italy
1960	Belgium
1961	not played, Turkey and Greece refused to meet
1962	Greece
1963	Greece
1964	France
1965	Spain
1966	Turkey
1967	Turkey
1968	Greece
1969	Greece
1970	not played
1971	not played
1972	Iraq
1973	Italy
1974–75	West Germany
1976–77	Iraq

Competition spread over two years from 1974.

African Cup Winners Cup
1975	Tonnerre Yaounde (Cameroun)
1976	Shooting Stars Club (Nigeria)
1977	Enugu Rangers (Nigeria)

African Champion Clubs Cup
1964	Oryx, Douala (Cameroun)
1966	Stade d'Abidjan (Iveroy Coast)
1967	T.P. Mazembre (Zaire)
1968	T.P. Mazembe (Zaire)
1969	Ismaili (Egypt)
1970	Kotoko (Ghana)
1971	Canon, Yaounde (Cameroun)
1972	Hafia, Conakry (Guinea)
1973	Vita Club, Kinshasa (Zaire)
1974	C.A.R.A., Brazzaville (Congo)
1975	Hafia, Conakry (Guinea)
1976	Mouloudia Chaabia Alger (Algeria)
1977	Hafia, Conakry (Guinea)
1978	Canon, Yaounde (Cameroun)

Name	Champions	Cup Winners
Ivory Coast	Africa Sports	Alliance Bouake
Lesotho	Matlama	—
Libya	El Tahaddy	Medina
Madagascar	Corps Enseignant	Majunga
Malawi	Hardware	Sucoma
Mauritania	Chebab Riyadi	Espoirs
Morocco	W. A. Casablanca	W.A. Casablanca
Niger	Olympic	Zumunta
Nigeria	Rangers, Enugu	Shooting Stars
Somalia	Horsed	LL.PP.
Sudan	Merreick	Hilal
Tanzania	—	N.A.Y.
Togo	—	Edan Club
Tunisia	C.S. Sfaxien	—
Uganda	Kampala City	Simba
Upper Volta	Silures	Kadiogo
Zaire	Vita Club	—
Zambia	Green Buffalos	Mufulira

Inter-American Cup

1969 Estudiantes de la Plata (Argentina)
1972 Nacional (Uruguay)
1973 Independiente (Argentina)
1974 Independiente (Argentina)
1974 Independiente (Argentina)
1976 Independicnte (Argentina)
1977 America (Mexico)

Concacaf Championship (Central America)

1967 Alianza (El Salvador)
1968 Toluca (Mexico)
1969 Cruz Azul (Mexico)
1970 Three Zones:
    Cruz Azul (Mexico) in North
    Saprissa (Costa Rica) in Central
    Transvaal (Surinam) in Caribbean
1971 Cruz Azul (Mexico)
1972 Olimpia (Honduras)
1973 Transvaal (Surinam)
1974–75 Municipal (Guatemala)
1975–76 Atletico Espanol (Mexico)
1976–77 America (Mexico)

Organised on similar lines to the European Footballer of the Year, the African equivalent was first voted on in 1970 and Salif Keita of Mali was the winner. Since then the holders of the title have been: Ibrahim Sunday (Ghana) 1971, Cherif Souleymane (Guinea) 1972, Bwanga Tschimen (Zaire) 1973, Paul Moukila (Congo) 1974, Ahmed Faras (Morocco), 1975, Roger Milla (Cameroon) 1976, Tarak Dhiab (Tunisia) in 1977 and Abdoul Razak (Ghana) in 1978.

AUSTRALIA

A national league was started in Australia in 1977 with a guaranteed sponsorship from Philips Industries for three years. Fourteen teams competed and on the same principle as the North American Soccer League, guest players from Europe appeared for clubs during the season.

AFRICA

Africa has the largest membership of the six Confederations belonging to FIFA. Some of the winners of domestic championships and cups in various African countries for 1978 were:

Name	Champions	Cup Winners
Algeria	M.P. Alger	C.M. Belcourt
Cameroun	Canon, Yaounde	Caiman
Central Africa	Stade Central	Sodiam
Congo	I.T. Brazzaville	Inter-Club
Egypt	El Ahly	Zamalek
Ethiopia	Medr Babur	Saint George
Gabon	V.C. Mongougou	Football Club 105
Gambia	Wallidan	—
Ghana		
Guinea	Hafia, Conakry	Horeya Athletic

NORTH AMERICA

New York Cosmos retained their North American Soccer League title in 1978 beating Tampa Bay Rowdies 3–1 in the Soccer Bowl 78 before a crowd of 74,901 at their home ground at Giants Stadium, East Rutherford, New Jersey. It was their third NASL title following their successes in 1972 and 1977.

Of 22 players from the champions New York Cosmos seven were from the USA, three each from England and Canada, two each from Brazil, Italy and Yugoslavia and one from Angola, Turkey and West Germany.

After the end of the 1978 season three NASL clubs undertook tours outside North America: New York Cosmos, Washington Diplomats and Detroit Express. After their Soccer Bowl success, Cosmos staged three home friendlies the first of which attracted 50,757 for a 2–2 draw at the Giants Stadium in New Jersey against World Cup All-Stars.

Cosmos had the assistance of Johan Cruyff in this match and the visitors were coached by Argentina manager Cesar Luis Menotti who in 1968 played for New York Generals.

Cosmos lost 3–1 to Atletico Madrid and then

In a survey of players who played regularly in the 1978 NASL season there were most from England. Nationalities were as follows:

England 129; United States of America 101; Canada 33; Yugoslavia 32; Scotland 30; West Germany 12; Ireland 11; South Africa 9; Northern Ireland 6; Argentina 4; Bermuda 4; Brazil 4; Holland 4; Spain 3; Wales 3; Hungary 2; Italy 2; Poland 2; Portugal 2; Trinidad 2; Angola, Barbados, Costa Rica, Cyprus, Denmark, Finland, Ghana, Greece, Haiti, Iran, Israel, Nigeria, Peru, Turkey and Uruguay 1 each.

North American Soccer League—winners
1967	Oakland Clippers (National Professional Soccer League)
1968	Atlanta Chiefs
1969	Kansas City Spurs
1970	Rochester Lancers
1971	Dallas Tornado
1972	New York Cosmos
1973	Philadelphia Atoms
1974	Los Angeles Aztecs
1975	Tampa Bay Rowdies
1976	Toronto Metro-Croatia
1977	New York Cosmos
1978	New York Cosmos

drew 2–2 with Boca Juniors in the first leg of the Cosmos Invitational Americas Cup. They then played in West Germany, Italy, England, Spain Greece, Yugoslavia and Turkey before a short rest then off to Ecuador, Argentina, Bolivia and Brazil. While in Argentina they lost 4–2 to Boca in the second leg of their cup competition.

The Diplomats played in the 8th President's Cup in South Korea reaching the final before losing 6–2 to the South Korean national eleven. Detroit toured Austria, Kuwait and Switzerland.

The NASL's 13th season produced no new teams but two from 1978 switched addresses with the Oakland Stompers becoming the Edmonton Drillers and the Colorado Caribous changing to Atlanta Chiefs.

NASL Attendances 1978 season
(based on 15 home matches in regular schedule)

Team	Total	Average
New York Cosmos	717,842	47,856
Minnesota Kicks	463,903	30,926
Seattle Sounders	338,677	22,578
Tampa Bay Rowdies	271,846	18,123
Vancouver Whitecaps	236,046	15,736
San Jose Earthquakes	214,217	14,281
Detroit Express	182,906	12,193
Oakland Stompers	178,941	11,929
New England Tea Men	177,882	11,858
Portland Timbers	177,049	11,803
Tulsa Roughnecks	169,057	11,270
California Surf	157,569	11,171
Washington Diplomats	161,741	10,782
Fort Lauderdale Strikers	157,188	10,479
Memphis Rogues	142,775	9,518
Los Angeles Aztecs	138,526	9,235
Dallas Tornado	134,714	8,980
Philadelphia Fury	124,199	8,279
Colorado Caribous	111,266	7,417
Rochester Lancers	101,402	6,760
Toronto Metros-Croatia	93,501	6,233
Houston Hurricane	87,085	5,805
San Diego Sockers	79,848	5,323
Chicago Sting	62,819	4,187

Cosmos were watched by a total of 318,905 for six games in the play offs in addition to these figures. Their 15 away matches in the regular schedule attracted 328,028 for an average of 21,869 as well.

SOUTH AMERICA

South American Cup (Libertadores Cup)
Boca Juniors retained the Libertadores Cup by beating Deportivo Cali (Colombia) 4–0 on aggregate in November 1978. It was the 12th time that an Argentine club had won in 19 tournaments. The first leg in Cali was drawn 0–0 with Boca winning in Buenos Aires by four clear goals.

Previous winners
1960	Penarol (Uruguay)
1961	Penarol
1962	Santos (Brazil)
1963	Santos
1964	Independiente (Argentina)
1965	Independiente
1966	Penarol
1967	Racing (Argentina)
1968	Estudiantes (Argentina)
1969	Estudiantes
1970	Estudiantes
1971	Nacional (Uruguay)
1972	Independiente
1973	Independiente
1974	Independiente
1975	Independiente
1976	Cruzeiro (Brazil)
1977	Boca Juniors (Argentina)

Fernando Morena scored 60 goals for Penarol in League matches during 1978. He achieved this feat in three competitions namely the First Division Championship, Major League and Liguilla, the latter being a competition for top clubs in Uruguay to determine their entry in the South American Cup. It was the sixth successive season that Morena had finished as top scorer in Uruguay.

He had made his debut for the Uruguayan club River Plate (not to be confused with its Argentine namesake) in 1968 at 15 in the First Division. In 1973 he was transferred to Poland, though River Plate retained 75 per cent of his value in case of further transfer and Morena himself would collect 20 per cent of any fee.

In his first season for Penarol he scored 23 League goals, 27 in 1974 and 34 the following year to equal the Uruguayan record. At the start of the 1976 season he had scored 280 goals in his professional career.

Morena played for Uruguay in the 1974 World Cup finals but the following year in a South American Championship match against Colombia he missed two penalties and said he would never play again for his country. He later relented over the decision.

Educated at a Catholic school he studied for two years afterwards to become a notary public and speaks English and French. So dedicated to the game was he that on the day of his marriage he went through a ceremony at the registrar's office with Maria Luce, had lunch with her, played for Penarol in the afternoon and then attended his church wedding in the evening.

The previous scoring record in Uruguay had been held by Pedro Young who scored 34 goals in 1933. In Argentina the record is also 60 goals by Hector Scotta in 1975.

Artur Coimbra Antunes (Zico) established a new scoring record in the Rio de Janeiro 'Carioca' League of Brazil in 1979 by scoring his 245th goal for Flamengo. The previous record had been held by the club's forward Edvaldo Alves Santa Rosa (Dida) with 244 goals between 1953 and 1964. Earlier still Leonidas da Silva had scored 210 goals for Flamengo between 1936 and 1941. Zico had started his career with the club in 1971.

Elias Figueroa of Chile won the title of South American Footballer of the Year for the third time in succession in 1976. Previous winners of the award were Tostao (Brazil) 1971, Teofilo Cubillas (Peru) 1972, Pele (Brazil) 1973. Zico (Brazil) won in 1977 and Mario Kempes (Argentina) in 1978.

SOUTH AMERICAN DIRECTORY
up to and including 1978

Country	Championship wins
Argentina (1893–)	Boca Juniors 17 ; Racing Club 15 ; River Plate 15 ; Alumni 9 ; Independiente 9 ; San Lorenzo 8 ; Huracan 5 ; Lomas 5 ; Belgrano 3 ; Estudiantes de la Plata 2 ; Porteno 2 ; Estudiantil Porteno 2 ; Quilmes 2 ; Dock Sud 1 ; Chacarita Juniors 1 ; Lomas Academicals 1 ; English High School 1 ; Gimnasia y Esgrima La Plata 1 ; Sportivo Barracas 1 ; Newell's Old Boys 1. (National League 1967–) : Boca Juniors 3 ; Independiente 3 ; Rosario Central 2 ; San Lorenzo 2 ; Velez Sarsfield 1 ; River Plate 1.
Bolivia (1914–)*	The Strongest 18 ; Bolivar 10 ; Jorge Wilsterman 6 ; Deportivo Municipal 4 ; Litoral 3 ; Universitario 3 ; Always Ready 2 ; Chaco Petrolero 2 ; Colegio Militar 1 ; Oriente Petrolero 1 ; Nimbles Sport 1 ; Deportivo Militar 1 ; Nimbles Rail 1 ; Ayacucho 1 ; Ferroviario 1 ; Guabira 1.
Brazil	(Rio League 1906–) : Fluminense 22 ; Flamengo 19 ; Vasco de Gama 14 ; Botafogo 12 ; America 7 ; Bangu 2 ; San Christavao 1 ; Paysandu 1. (Sao Paulo League 1902–) : *SE Palmeiras 18 ; Corinthians 18 ; Santos 13 ; Sao Paulo 11 ; Paulistano 8 ; SP Athletic 4 ; AA des Palmeiras 3 ; Portuguesa 3 ; Sao Bento 2 ; Germania 2 ; Americano 2 ; Internacional 1. *formerly Palestra Italia (National Championships 1971–) : Palmeiras 2 ; Internacional Porto Alegre 2 ; Atletico Mineiro 1 ; Vasco da Gama 1 ; Sao Paulo 1 ; Guarani 1.
Chile (1933–)	Colo Colo 11 ; Universidad de Chile 7 ; Union Espanola 5 ; Magallanes 4 ; Audax Italiano 4 ; Universidad Catolica 4 ; Everton 3 ; Wanderers (Valpariso) 2 ; Palestino 2 ; Santiago Morning 1 ; Green Cross 1 ; Hauchipato 1 ; Union San Felipe 1

Country	Championship wins
Colombia (1948–)	Millionarios 11 ; Independiente Santa Fe 6 ; Deportivo Cali 5 ; Independiente Medellin 2 ; Nacional Medellin 2 ; Deportes Caldas 1 ; Atletico Nacional 1 ; Atletico Quindio 1 ; Union Magdalena 1 ; Junior Barranquilla 1.
Ecuador (1957–)	Nacional 5, Barcelona 4 ; Emelec 4 ; Liga Deportiva Universitaria 3 ; Everest 2 ; Deportivo Quito 2.
Paraguay (1906–)*	Olimpia 25 ; Cerro Porteno 19 ; Libertad 8 ; Guarani 7 ; Nacional 6 ; Sporting Luqueno 2 ; Presidente Hayes 1. (National Championship 1976–) : Olimpia 1.
Peru (1928–)	Alianza 16 ; Universitario 14 ; Sport Boys 5 ; Sporting Cristal 5 ; Deportivo Municipal 4 ; Atletico Chalaco 2 ; Mariscal Sucre 2 ; Union Huaral 1 ; Defensor Lima 1.
Uruguay (1900–)	Penarol 34 ; Nacional 32 : River Plate 4 ; Montevideo Wanderers 3 ; Defensor 1 ; Rampla Juniors 1. (Major League 1975–) : Nacional 4 ; Penarol 1.
Venezuela (1956–)	Deportivo Italia 5 ; Portuguesa 5 ; Deportivo Portugues 3 ; Deportivo Galicia 3 ; Valencia 2 ; Lasalle 1 ; Tiquire Aragua 1 ; Celta Deportivo 1 ; Lara 1 ; Union Deportiva Canarias 1.

Top left : Rivelino who played for Brazil in the 1970, 1974 and 1978 World Cup finals. (Syndication International)
Bottom left : Jairzinho who scored in every match for Brazil in the 1970 World Cup finals. (Syndication International)
Far right : Gerson (centre) is mobbed after Brazil's 1970 World Cup success. (Syndication International)

*Results not complete at the time of going to press

SOUTH AMERICAN CHAMPIONSHIP

An attempt was made in 1979 to interest countries in South America in organising the South American Championship on an annual basis with the ten countries playing each other home and away in midweek during the normal League season. Brazil were the prime movers in this and another idea was to eventually include Mexico and the United States of America in the project.

Apart from cup tournaments involving isolated countries in South America, the only competitive matches in this Continent have involved the World Cup qualifying series every four years. A list of some of the more important cups is included in the first edition of the *Guinness Book of Soccer Facts and Feats*.

Year	Country, Venue	Teams	Matches	Goals	Champions	Pts
1916	Argentina, Buenos Aires	4	6	18	Uruguay	5
1917	Uruguay, Montevideo	4	6	21	Uruguay	6
1919	Brazil, Rio de Janeiro (1)	4	7	26	Brazil	7
1920	Chile, Valparaiso	4	6	16	Uruguay	5
1921	Argentina, Buenos Aires	4	6	14	Argentina	6
1922	Brazil, Rio de Janeiro (2)	5	11	23	Brazil	7
1923	Uruguay, Montevideo	4	6	18	Uruguay	6
1924	Uruguay, Montevideo	4	6	15	Uruguay	5
1925	Argentina, Buenos Aires (3)	3	6	26	Argentina	7
1926	Chile, Santiago de Chile	5	10	55	Uruguay	8
1927	Peru, Lima	4	6	37	Argentina	6
1929	Argentina, Buenos Aires	4	6	23	Argentina	6
1935	Peru, Lima*	4	6	18	Uruguay	6
1937	Argentina, Buenos Aires (4)	6	16	68	Argentina	10
1939	Peru, Lima	5	10	47	Peru	8
1941	Chile, Santiago de Chile*	5	10	32	Argentina	8
1942	Uruguay, Montevideo (5)	7	21	81	Uruguay	12
1945	Chile, Santiago de Chile*	7	21	89	Argentina	11
1946	Argentina, Buenos Aires*	6	15	61	Argentina	10
1947	Ecuador, Guayaquil	8	28	102	Argentina	13
1949	Brazil, Rio de Janeiro (6)	8	29	130	Brazil	14
1953	Peru, Lima (7)	7	21	67	Paraguay	10
1955	Chile, Santiago de Chile	6	15	73	Argentina	9
1956	Uruguay, Montevideo*	6	15	38	Uruguay	9
1957	Peru, Lima	7	21	101	Argentina	10
1959	Argentina, Buenos Aires	7	21	86	Argentina	11
1959	Ecuador, Guayaquil*	5	20	39	Uruquay	7
1963	Bolivia, La Paz & Cochabamba	7	21	91	Bolivia	11
1967	Uruguay, Montevideo	6	15	49	Uruguay	9
1975	(Reorganised on home and away basis)	10	25	79	Peru	N/A

*extraordinary tournaments

1 : play-off : Brazil 1   Uruguay 0
2 : play-off : Brazil 3   Paraguay 1 ; Uruguay withdrew
3 : two legs were played (home and away)
4 : play-off : Argentina 2   Brazil 0
5 : Chile withdrew
6 : play-off : Brazil 7   Paraguay 0
7 : play-off : Paraguay 3   Brazil 2 (organised by the Paraguayan Football League)

OUTSTANDING INTERNATIONAL PLAYERS

A century of international appearances

The following players have appeared in 100 or more matches for their countries:

Name	Country	From	To	Total
Franz Beckenbauer	West Germany	1965	1977	103
Jozsef Bozsik	Hungary	1947	1962	100
Bobby Charlton	England	1958	1970	106
Hector Chumpitaz	Peru	1963		120*
Gylmar	Brazil	1953	1969	100
Bobby Moore	England	1962	1973	108
Bjorn Nordqvist	Sweden	1963		115*
Pele	Brazil	1957	1971	111
Leonel Sanchez	Chile	1955	1967	104
Thorbjorn Svenssen	Norway	1947	1961	105
Djalma Santos	Brazil	1952	1968	100
Rivelino	Brazil	1968		120*
Billy Wright	England	1946	1959	105
Attouga	Tunisia	1963		109*
Kazimierz Deyna	Poland	1968	1978	102

* Still adding to total in 1979.

Billy Wright (Wolverhampton Wanderers and England)

105 international appearances 1946-1959

Billy Wright

Date	Venue	Opponents	Result	Scored
1946				
28 Sep	Belfast	N. Ireland	W 7–2	
30 Sep	Dublin	R. of Ireland	W 1–0	
13 Nov	Manchester	Wales	W 3–0	
27 Nov	Huddersfield	Holland	W 8–2	
1947				
12 Apr	Wembley	Scotland	D 1–1	
3 May	Highbury	France	W 3–0	
18 May	Zurich	Switzerland	L 0–1	
25 May	Lisbon	Portugal	W 10–0	
21 Sep	Brussels	Belgium	W 5–2	
18 Oct	Cardiff	Wales	W 3–0	
5 Nov	Liverpool	N. Ireland	D 2–2	
19 Nov	Highbury	Sweden	W 4–2	
1948				
10 Apr	Glasgow	Scotland	W 2–0	
16 May	Turin	Italy	W 4–0	
26 Sep	Copenhagen	Denmark	D 0–0	
9 Oct	Belfast	N. Ireland	W 6–2	
10 Nov	Birmingham	Wales	W 1–0	
2 Dec	Highbury	Switzerland	W 6–0	
1949				
9 Apr	Wembley	Scotland	L 1–3	
13 May	Stockholm	Sweden	L 1–3	
18 May	Oslo	Norway	W 4–1	
22 May	Paris	France	W 3–1	1 g
21 Sep	Liverpool	R. of Ireland	L 0–2	
15 Oct	Cardiff	Wales	W 4–1	
16 Nov	Manchester	N. Ireland	W 9–2	
30 Nov	Tottenham	Italy	W 2–0	1 g
1950				
15 Apr	Glasgow	Scotland	W 1–0	
14 May	Lisbon	Portugal	W 5–3	
18 May	Brussels	Belgium	W 4–1	
25 Jun	Rio de Janeiro	Chile (WC)	W 2–0	
29 Jun	Belo Horizonte	USA (WC)	L 0–1	
2 July	Rio de Janeiro	Spain (WC)	L 0–1	
7 Oct	Belfast	N. Ireland	W 4–1	1 g
1951				
14 Apr	Wembley	Scotland	L 2–3	
9 May	Wembley	Argentina	W 2–1	
3 Oct	Highbury	France	D 2–2	
20 Oct	Cardiff	Wales	D 1–1	
14 Nov	Birmingham	N. Ireland	W 2–0	
28 Nov	Wembley	Austria	D 2–2	
1952				
5 Apr	Glasgow	Scotland	W 2–1	
18 May	Florence	Italy	D 1–1	
25 May	Vienna	Austria	W 3–2	
28 May	Zurich	Switzerland	W 3–0	
4 Oct	Belfast	N. Ireland	D 2–2	
12 Nov	Wembley	Wales	W 5–2	
26 Nov	Wembley	Belgium	W 5–0	
1953				
18 Apr	Wembley	Scotland	D 2–2	
17 May	Buenos Aires	Argentina	D 0–0	

24 May	Santiago	Chile	W 2–1
31 May	Montevideo	Uruguay	L 1–2
8 Jun	New York	USA	W 6–3
10 Oct	Cardiff	Wales	W 4–1
21 Oct	Wembley	FIFA	D 4–4
11 Nov	Liverpool	N. Ireland	W 3–1
25 Nov	Wembley	Hungary	L 3–6

1954

3 Apr	Glasgow	Scotland	W 4–2
16 May	Belgrade	Yugoslavia	L 0–1
23 May	Budapest	Hungary	L 1–7
17 Jun	Basle	Belgium (WC)	D 4–4
20 Jun	Berne	Switzerland (WC)	W 2–0
26 Jun	Basle	Uruguay (WC)	L 2–4
2 Oct	Belfast	N. Ireland	W 2–0
10 Nov	Wembley	Wales	W 3–2
1 Dec	Wembley	W. Germany	W 3–1

1955

2 Apr	Wembley	Scotland	W 7–2
15 May	Paris	France	L 0–1
18 May	Madrid	Spain	D 1–1
22 May	Oporto	Portugal	L 1–3
2 Oct	Copenhagen	Denmark	W 5–1
22 Oct	Cardiff	Wales	L 1–2
2 Nov	Wembley	N. Ireland	W 3–0
30 Nov	Wembley	Spain	W 4–1

1956

14 Apr	Glasgow	Scotland	D 1–1
9 May	Wembley	Brazil	W 4–2
16 May	Stockholm	Sweden	D 0–0
20 May	Helsinki	Finland	W 5–1
26 May	Berlin	W. Germany	W 3–1
6 Oct	Belfast	N. Ireland	D 1–1
14 Nov	Wembley	Wales	W 3–1
28 Nov	Wembley	Yugoslavia	W 3–0
5 Dec	Wolverhampton	Denmark	W 5–2

1957

6 Apr	Wembley	Scotland	W 2–1
8 May	Wembley	R. of Ireland	W 5–1
15 May	Copenhagen	Denmark	W 4–1
19 May	Dublin	R. of Ireland	D 1–1
19 Oct	Cardiff	Wales	W 4–0
6 Nov	Wembley	N. Ireland	L 2–3
27 Nov	Wembley	France	W 4–0

1958

19 Apr	Glasgow	Scotland	W 4–0
7 May	Wembley	Portugal	W 2–1
11 May	Belgrade	Yugoslavia	L 0–5
18 May	Moscow	USSR	D 1–1
8 Jun	Gothenburg	USSR (WC)	D 2–2
11 Jun	Gothenburg	Brazil (WC)	D 0–0
15 Jun	Boras	Austria (WC)	D 2–2
17 Jun	Gothenburg	USSR (WC)	L 0–1
4 Oct	Belfast	N. Ireland	D 3–3
22 Oct	Wembley	USSR	W 5–0
26 Nov	Birmingham	Wales	D 2–2

1959

11 Apr	Wembley	Scotland	W 1–0
6 May	Wembley	Italy	D 2–2
13 May	Rio de Janeiro	Brazil	L 0–2
17 May	Lima	Peru	L 1–4
24 May	Mexico City	Mexico	L 1–2
28 May	Los Angeles	USA	W 8–1

Wright captained England for the first time against Northern Ireland in October 1948 and remained captain until his last appearance against the USA in May 1959 which was his 90th game as captain. He played in all but three of England's first 108 international matches after the Second World War and his last 70 appearances from the match against France in October 1951 were successive ones. Originally a wing-half he moved to centre-half against Switzerland in June 1954 and remained there.

Gylmar dos Santos Neves
(Corinthians, Santos and Brazil)

100 international appearances 1953–1969

Date	Venue	Opponents	Result
1953			
1 Mar	Lima	Bolivia (sub)	W 8–1
1955			
20 Sept	Sao Paulo	Chile	W 2–1
17 Nov	Sao Paulo	Paraguay	D 2–2
1956			
10 Jan	Montevideo	Uruguay	D 0–0
24 Jan	Montevideo	Chile	L 1–4
29 Jan	Montevideo	Paraguay	D 0–0
1 Feb	Montevideo	Peru	W 2–1
5 Feb	Montevideo	Argentina	W 1–0
8 Apr	Lisbon	Portugal	W 1–0
11 Apr	Zurich	Switzerland	D 1–1
15 Apr	Vienna	Austria	W 3–2
21 Apr	Prague	Czechoslovakia	D 0–0
25 Apr	Milan	Italy	L 0–3
1 May	Istanbul	Turkey	W 1–0
9 May	Wembley	England	L 2–4
1 Jul	Rio de Janeiro	Italy	W 2–0
8 Jul	Buenos Aires	Argentina	D 0–0
5 Aug	Rio de Janeiro	Czechoslovakia	L 0–1
8 Aug	Sao Paulo	Czechoslovakia	W 4–1
1957			
13 Mar	Lima	Chile	W 4–2
21 Mar	Lima	Ecuador	W 7–1
23 Mar	Lima	Colombia	W 9–0
28 Mar	Lima	Uruguay	L 2–3
31 Mar	Lima	Peru	W 1–0
3 Apr	Lima	Argentina	L 0–3
13 Apr	Lima	Peru	D 1–1
21 Apr	Rio de Janeiro	Peru	W 1–0
10 Jul	Sao Paulo	Argentina	W 2–0
4 May	Rio de Janeiro	Paraguay	W 5–1
7 May	Sao Paulo	Paraguay	D 0–0
18 May	Sao Paulo	Bulgaria	W 3–1
29 May	Florence	Florentina	W 4–0
8 Jun	Uddevalla	Austria (WC)	W 3–0
11 Jun	Gothenburg	England (WC)	D 0–0
15 Jun	Gothenburg	USSR (WC)	W 2–0
19 Jun	Gothenburg	Wales (WC)	W 1–0
24 Jun	Stockholm	France (WC)	W 5–2
29 Jun	Stockholm	Sweden (WC)	W 5–2
1959			
26 Mar	Buenos Aires	Uruguay (sub)	W 3–1
29 Mar	Buenos Aires	Paraguay	W 4–1
4 Apr	Buenos Aires	Argentina	D 1–1
13 May	Rio de Janeiro	England	W 2–0
17 Sep	Rio de Janeiro	Chile	W 7–0
20 Sep	Sao Paulo	Chile	W 1–0

Gylmar who made a century of appearances for Brazil in goal. (Popperfoto)

1960

29 Apr	Cairo	UAR	W 5–0
1 May	Alexandria	UAR	W 3–1
6 May	Cairo	UAR	W 3–0
8 May	Malmo	Malmo FF	W 7–1
10 May	Copenhagen	Denmark	W 4–3
12 May	Milan	Internationale	D 2–2
16 May	Lisbon	Sporting Lisbon	W 4–0
25 May	Buenos Aires	Argentina	L 2–4
29 May	Buenos Aires	Argentina	W 2–0
29 Jun	Rio de Janeiro	Chile	W 4–0
3 Jul	Asuncion	Paraguay	W 2–1
9 Jul	Montevideo	Uruguay	L 0–1
12 Jul	Rio de Janeiro	Argentina	W 5–1

1961

30 Apr	Asuncion	Paraguay	W 2–0
3 May	Asuncion	Paraguay	W 3–2
7 May	Santiago	Chile	W 2–1
11 May	Santiago	Chile	W 1–0
29 Jun	Rio de Janeiro	Paraguay	W 3 -2

1962

21 Apr	Rio de Janeiro	Paraguay	W 6–0
6 May	Sao Paulo	Portugal	W 2–1
9 May	Rio de Janeiro	Portugal	W 1–0
12 May	Rio de Janeiro	Wales	W 3–1
16 May	Sao Paulo	Wales	W 3–1
30 May	Vina del Mar	Mexico (WC)	W 2–0
2 Jun	Vina del Mar	Czechoslovakia (WC)	D 0–0
6 Jun	Vina del Mar	Spain (WC)	W 2–1
10 Jun	Vina del Mar	England (WC)	W 3–1
13 Jun	Santiago	Chile (WC)	W 4–2
17 Jun	Santiago	Czechoslovakia (WC)	W 3–1

1963

13 Apr	Sao Paulo	Argentina	L 2–3
16 Apr	Rio de Janeiro	Argentina	W 4–1
21 Apr	Lisbon	Portugal	L 0–1
24 Apr	Brussels	Belgium	L 1–5
28 Apr	Paris	France	W 3–2
2 May	Amsterdam	Holland	L 0–1
5 May	Hamburg	W. Germany	W 2–1
8 May	Wembley	England	D 1–1
12 May	Milan	Italy	L 0–3
17 May	Cairo	UAR	W 1–0
19 May	Tel Aviv	Israel	W 5–0
22 May	Berlin	W. Germany	W 3–0

1964

30 May	Rio de Janeiro	England	W 5–1
3 Jun	Sao Paulo	Argentina	L 0–3
7 Jun	Rio de Janeiro	Portugal	W 4–1

1966

1 May	Rio de Janeiro	Gaucho Selection	W 2–0
14 May	Rio de Janeiro	Wales	W 3–1
19 May	Rio de Janeiro	Chile	W 1–0
4 Jun	Sao Paulo	Peru	W 4–0
12 Jun	Rio de Janeiro	Czechoslovakia	W 2–1
21 Jun	Madrid	Atletico Madrid	W 5–3
25 Jun	Hampden Park	Scotland	D 1–1
30 Jun	Gothenburg	Sweden	W 3–2
12 Jul	Goodison Park	Bulgaria (WC)	W 2–0
15 Jul	Goodison Park	Hungary (WC)	L 1–3

1968

28 Jul	Asuncion	Paraguay	L 0–1

1969

12 Jun	Rio de Janeiro	England	W 2–1

Bobby Charlton (Manchester United and England)
106 international appearances 1958–1970

Date	Venue	Opponents	Result	Scored
1958				
19 Apr	Glasgow	Scotland	W 4–0	1 g
7 May	Wembley	Portugal	W 2–1	2 g
11 May	Belgrade	Yugoslavia	L 0–5	
4 Oct	Belfast	N. Ireland	D 3–3	2 g
22 Oct	Wembley	USSR	W 5–0	1 g pen
26 Nov	Birmingham	Wales	D 2–2	
1959				
11 Apr	Wembley	Scotland	W 1–0	1 g
6 May	Wembley	Italy	D 2–2	1 g
13 May	Rio de Janeiro	Brazil	L 0–2	
17 May	Lima	Peru	L 1–4	
24 May	Mexico City	Mexico	L 1–2	
28 May	Los Angeles	USA	W 8–1	3 g
17 Oct	Cardiff	Wales	D 1–1	
28 Oct	Wembley	Sweden	L 2–3	1 g
1960				
19 Apr	Glasgow	Scotland	D 1–1	1 g pen

Bobby Charlton (Syndication International)

11 May	Wembley	Yugoslavia	D 3–3	
15 May	Madrid	Spain	L 0–3	
22 May	Budapest	Hungary	L 0–2	
8 Oct	Belfast	N. Ireland	W 5–2	1 g
19 Oct	Luxembourg	Luxembourg	W 9–0	3 g
26 Oct	Wembley	Spain	W 4–2	
23 Nov	Wembley	Wales	W 5–1	1 g

1961

15 Apr	Wembley	Scotland	W 9–3	
10 May	Wembley	Mexico	W 8–0	3 g
21 May	Lisbon	Portugal	D 1–1	
24 May	Rome	Italy	W 3–2	
27 May	Vienna	Austria	L 1–3	
28 Sep	Highbury	Luxembourg	W 4–1	2 g
14 Oct	Cardiff	Wales	D 1–1	
25 Oct	Wembley	Portugal	W 2–0	
22 Nov	Wembley	N. Ireland	D 1–1	1 g

1962

4 Apr	Wembley	Austria	W 3–1	
14 Apr	Glasgow	Scotland	L 0–2	
9 May	Wembley	Switzerland	W 3–1	
20 May	Lima	Peru	W 4–0	
31 May	Rancagua	Hungary (WC)	L 1–2	
2 Jun	Rancagua	Argentina (WC)	W 3–1	1 g
7 Jun	Rancagua	Bulgaria (WC)	D 0–0	
10 Jun	Vina del Mar	Brazil (WC)	L 1–3	

1963

27 Feb	Paris	France	L 2–5	
6 Apr	Wembley	Scotland	L 1–2	
8 May	Wembley	Brazil	D 1–1	
20 May	Bratislava	Czechoslovakia	W 4–2	1 g
2 Jun	Leipzig	GDR	W 2–1	1 g
5 Jun	Basle	Switzerland	W 8–1	3 g
12 Oct	Cardiff	Wales	W 4–0	1 g
23 Oct	Wembley	Rest of the World	W 2–1	
20 Nov	Wembley	N. Ireland	W 8–3	

1964

11 Apr	Glasgow	Scotland	L 0–1	
6 May	Wembley	Uruguay	W 2–1	
17 May	Lisbon	Portugal	W 4–3	1 g
24 May	Dublin	R. of Ireland	W 3–1	
27 May	New York	USA (sub)	W 10–0	1 g
30 May	Rio de Janeiro	Brazil	L 1–5	
6 Jun	Rio de Janeiro	Argentina	L 0–1	
3 Oct	Belfast	N. Ireland	W 4–3	
9 Dec	Amsterdam	Holland	D 1–1	

1965

10 Apr	Wembley	Scotland	D	2–2	1 g
2 Oct	Cardiff	Wales	D	0–0	
20 Oct	Wembley	Austria	L	2–3	1 g
10 Nov	Wembley	N. Ireland	W	2–1	
8 Dec	Madrid	Spain	W	2–0	

1966

23 Feb	Wembley	W. Germany	W	1–0	
2 Apr	Glasgow	Scotland	W	4–3	1 g
4 May	Wembley	Yugoslavia	W	2–0	1 g
26 Jun	Helsinki	Finland	W	3–0	
29 Jun	Oslo	Norway	W	6–1	
5 Jul	Chorzow	Poland	W	1–0	
11 Jul	Wembley	Uruguay (WC)	D	0–0	
16 Jul	Wembley	Mexico (WC)	W	2–0	1 g
20 Jul	Wembley	France (WC)	W	2–0	
23 Jul	Wembley	Argentina (WC)	W	1–0	
26 Jul	Wembley	Portugal (WC)	W	2–1	2 g
30 Jul	Wembley	W. Germany (WC)	W	4–2	
22 Oct	Belfast	N. Ireland	W	2–0	
2 Nov	Wembley	Czechoslovakia	D	0–0	
16 Nov	Wembley	Wales	W	5–1	1 g

1967

15 Apr	Wembley	Scotland	L	2–3	
21 Oct	Cardiff	Wales	W	3–0	1 g
22 Nov	Wembley	N. Ireland	W	2–0	1 g
6 Dec	Wembley	USSR	D	2–2	

1968

24 Feb	Glasgow	Scotland	D	1–1	
3 Apr	Wembley	Spain	W	1–0	1 g
8 May	Madrid	Spain	W	2–1	
22 May	Wembley	Sweden	W	3–1	1 g
5 Jun	Florence	Yugoslavia (EC)	L	0–1	
8 Jun	Rome	USSR (EC)	W	2–0	1 g
6 Nov	Bucharest	Rumania	D	0–0	
11 Dec	Wembley	Bulgaria	D	1–1	

1969

15 Jan	Wembley	Rumania	D	1–1	
3 May	Belfast	N. Ireland	W	3–1	
7 May	Wembley	Wales	W	2–1	1 g
10 May	Wembley	Scotland	W	4–1	
1 Jun	Mexico City	Mexico	D	0–0	
12 Jun	Rio de Janeiro	Brazil	L	1–2	
5 Nov	Amsterdam	Holland	W	1–0	
10 Dec	Wembley	Portugal	W	1–0	

1970

14 Jan	Wembley	Holland	D	0–0	
18 Apr	Cardiff	Wales	D	1–1	
21 Apr	Wembley	N. Ireland	W	3–1	1 g
20 May	Bogota	Colombia	W	4–0	1 g
24 May	Quito	Ecuador	W	2–0	
2 Jun	Guadalajara	Rumania (WC)	W	1–0	
7 Jun	Guadalajara	Brazil (WC)	L	0–1	
11 Jun	Guadalajara	Czechoslovakia (WC)	W	1–0	
14 Jun	Leon	West Germany (WC)	L	2–3	

Charlton established two records for England between 1958 and 1970 with 106 appearances and 49 goals. Bobby Moore eventually overtook his number of appearances. Forty of Charlton's goals came in his first 73 appearances.

(WC) = World Cup. (EC) = European Championship.

Gerd Muller

Gerd Muller wrote to Bayern Munich President Wilhelm Neudecker asking for his release from the club on 29 January 1979. He had previously announced his intention to retire at the end of the 1978–79 season, but a combination of factors including a row with Bayern trainer Pal Csernai, the club's erratic form and an offer from the North American Soccer League club Fort Lauderdale Strikers decided him upon this course of action.

His last three matches in Bayern's side were undistinguished for him and he played without conviction. In the second of these against Eintracht Frankfurt he was even withdrawn eight minutes before the end for the first time in his career. Thus he was unable to add to the 365 Bundesliga goals which he had scored against 31 different teams over the period of Bayern's association with the West German Bundesliga from 1965–66:

Hamburg SV	27
Kaiserslautern	23
MSV Duisburg	22
Rot-Weiss Essen	20
Eintracht Frankfurt	19
Rot-Weiss Oberhausen	18
Hannover 96	18
Werder Bremen	18
Schalke 04	18
Hertha Berlin	17
Eintracht Brunswick	17
IFC Cologne	15
VfB Stuttgart	14
Borussia Dortmund	14
Borussia Moenchengladbach	14
VfL Bochum	13
Kickers Offenbach	12
Fortuna Dusseldorf	11
Alemannia Aachen	7
Tennis Borussia	7
Karlsruher SC	6
IFC Saarbrucken	6
TSV Munich 1860	5
IFC Nuremberg	4
FC St. Pauli	4
Borussia Neunkirchen	4
Arminia Bielefeld	4
Fortuna Cologne	3
Wuppertal	2
Bayer Uerdingen	2
Tasmania Berlin	1

Born in the Bavarian village of Zinsen he had to leave school at 15 when his father died and he worked in the weaving trade. On Sundays he played for TSV Nordlingen and 46 goals in two

Gerd Muller of Bayern Munich. (Syndication International)

Cup Winners Cup	20
Fairs Cup	7
Super Cup	3
World Club Championship	1
Total	628

During Muller's service with Bayern they won four Bundesliga championships, four West German Cups, three European Cups, one Cup Winners Cup and one World Championship for clubs. Muller was European Footballer of the Year in 1970.

Johan Cruyff

On 7 November 1978 in the Ajax Stadium, Amsterdam, Johan Cruyff appeared in his official farewell match, wearing the colours of his original club Ajax against Bayern Munich the West German club which had emulated the Dutch team's achievement of three successive European Cup victories. At the end of the game the score was Ajax 0 Bayern 8 and instead of bouquets, only cushions were thrown onto the pitch by the disappointed crowd.

Cruyff's last competitive match had been in the Spanish League for Barcelona against Valencia at Nou Camp, Barcelona before a crowd of 90,000 on 7 May 1978. He did not score but made the one goal of the game for the Brazilian, Bio. In five seasons Cruyff had played 238 matches at competitive and friendly level after his £922,300 transfer from Ajax in September 1963. He had scored 47 League goals for Barcelona.

Cruyff also had a few games as a guest player for New York Cosmos including a friendly against Chelsea at Stamford Bridge.

Though his goalscoring achievements were not phenomenal since his entire career in Holland and Spain produced only 234 League goals, this slightly built, lanky Dutchman was probably the most outstanding forward produced by the country of his origin and one of Europe's most accomplished as well. Sharp reactions, excellent control, speed, acceleration and the ability to change direction instantly made him a difficult proposition for defenders to combat.

Born in the poor quarter of Amsterdam in 1947 his connections with Ajax were close. In fact his mother worked at the ground as a cleaner. He joined the club while still a schoolboy and made his senior debut as a 17 year old in the 1964–65 season. That season he scored four League goals and the following term as a regular player he had 16 in the League in helping Ajax to the championship and Cup. In the next seven seasons he took his total to 187 in the League as Ajax won six championships and four Dutch Cup titles altogether.

seasons had convinced Bayern's President that Muller was a prospect, but coach Tshik Cajkovski the former Yugoslavian international wing-half had a different view. His comment on Muller was: 'Do you want me to put a bear among my race-horses?'

But Muller replied with 35 goals for Bayern in the South Regional League and promotion to the Bundesliga at the end of it. Standing barely 5ft 8in, this chunky, thick-legged centre-forward had a low centre of gravity, fine balance and an agile sense of anticipation. It helped to make him one of the most dangerous players in the penalty area.

His total of goals in senior matches including one in his only Under-23 international appearance against Rumania in 1966 which has been previously overlooked underlined his prowess as a marksman:

West German Bundesliga	365
Regional League South and play-offs	39
West Germany	68
Under-23	1
West German Cup	76
League Cup	12
European Cup	36

Johan Cruyff the Ajax, Barcelona and Dutch international forward. (Colorsport)

Cruyff was a key figure in the club's three successive European Cup winning teams between 1971 and 1973, while in both years he became European Footballer of the Year.

His former manager Rinus Michels had left in 1971 to take over as boss of Barcelona and after protracted negotiations secured Cruyff's signature for a world record fee for one player of £922,300 with some £400,000 going to Cruyff himself as one of the best paid professional sportsmen in the world.

Cruyff won his third European Player award in 1974 after captaining Holland in the World Cup in which they finished as runners-up in Munich. Though he also helped Holland to qualify for the 1978 World Cup he kept his word that he would not play in the finals in Argentina and retired from all football until after speculation that his business interests were going badly he signed for Los Angeles Aztecs in May, 1979.

His international career had been erratic after his first full appearance against Hungary in 1966 at 19, as evidenced by his experience in only his second game against Czechoslovakia.

Against the Czechs he was involved in a stormy argument with the East German referee Rudi Glockner and sent off apparently for striking the official. Film later made it clear that it had been a gesture rather than a blow and the Dutch Federation suspended him from the national team for a year, later commuted to six months, though it was ten months before he was back in the side against East Germany.

His rather demonstrative temperament which sought argument as a safety valve landed him in trouble with referees resulting in many cautions and a few dismissals but in his early days he also often retaliated against uncompromising opponents, nonplussed by his talents. He made 48 appearances for Holland and scored 34 goals.

MISCELLANY

The **first coloured player** to appear with a Football League club was Arthur Wharton who originally made his mark in the sporting world as a sprinter, both amateur and professional. He won the AAA 100 Yards Championship in 1886 and 1887 and in the former year equalled the then World Record with a time of 10.0 seconds. He subsequently turned to professional football and during the 1890s appeared with Preston North End, Rotherham Town, Sheffield United and back to Rotherham for a second spell. Wharton, a half-caste, unfortunately chose a bad time to join Sheffield United in 1894, for with the giant Billy Foulke in such great form he got little opportunity of establishing himself as a goalkeeper in their League side and returned to Rotherham after only one season.

Robert or 'Rabbi' Howell, born in a caravan at

Darkie Wharton the famous sprinter and one of the earliest coloured footballers in this country. (By permission of the British Library)

Wincobank, Sheffield, is the **only gypsy to have played for England**. Although only 5ft 5¼in (1.66m) in height he was a tireless wing-half. Surprisingly enough, considering his lack of stature, he was generally a centre-half while with Ecclesfield and Rotherham Swifts, and it was Sheffield United who converted him into a wing-half when he joined them in 1890. He became a member of one of the most famous, as well as the smallest, half-back lines of the 1890s, Howell, Morren and Needham, each being under 5ft 5½in tall. It was this vital combination that did so much to enable Sheffield United to win the Football League Championship in the 1897–98 season. While with Sheffield United, Howell played for England against Ireland in 1895 and made his second international appearance against Scotland in 1899 when he was with Liverpool. He had moved to Liverpool in April 1898 and scored a goal for them on his debut in a 4–0 victory over Aston Villa.

After playing regularly for Sheffield United and Liverpool he joined Preston North End in 1901. There his career was ended by injury late in 1903.

George Latham, who began his Football League career with Liverpool in the 1904–05 season and made 10 international appearances for Wales, had two surprises late in his career. In January 1913 he travelled to Belfast as trainer of the Welsh international side for the game against Ireland but was called into the team at the last moment as right-half. Owing to the refusal of a number of clubs to allow their players to take part in this Saturday international, Wales had to call upon five players not originally selected. However, they won 1–0 with a goal in the first five minutes headed by Roberts from a Meredith centre.

Latham's second surprise came long after he had given up playing and was Cardiff City's trainer. On 2 January 1922 he stepped into the breach when Cardiff found themselves a man short for a Division One game at Blackburn. He began this game at inside-right and finished at outside-right. Cardiff won 3–1. This was 14 years after he made what he had assumed to be his last Division One appearance for Liverpool.

Jimmy Delaney won Scottish, English, Northern Ireland and Republic of Ireland cup medals over a period of 19 years: with Celtic 1937, Manchester United 1948, and Derry City 1954, all winners, and Cork Athletic 1956 as runners-up.

Jimmy Delaney who had a unique experience in an assortment of cup finals in the British Isles. (Syndication International)

Redfern Froggatt of Sheffield Wednesday whose ups and downs had little harmful effect on his career with the club.

Redfern Froggatt, a goalscoring inside-forward of Sheffield Wednesday, experienced four promotion seasons with Sheffield Wednesday from Division Two in 1949–50, 1951–52, 1955–56 and 1958–59, and suffered relegation with them from Division One three times in 1950–51, 1954–55 and 1957–58. It little affected his distinguished career with the club who he had joined from Sheffield YMCA as a professional in July 1942 and left for Stalybridge Celtic in May 1962 after 433 League appearances and 140 goals not including war-time matches. He made four international appearances for England.

When **Alec Mackay** signed for Southport on 12 September 1933 he had already been with six clubs in four divisions and was only 13 days past his 20th birthday. His five previous clubs had been Wolverhampton Wanderers, Hull City, Newcastle United, Bolton Wanderers and Bournemouth.

On 14 April 1956 **Mickey Stewart,** who had been playing cricket for England in the West Indies, flew to Middlesbrough to appear in the Amateur Cup Final replay for Corinthian Casuals against Bishop Auckland. He arrived five minutes too late for the kick-off. Casuals were beaten 4–1. Their scorer was Gerry Citron who had been their marksman at Wembley in the original match and was to have dropped out for Stewart. Already capped for the England amateur eleven that season,

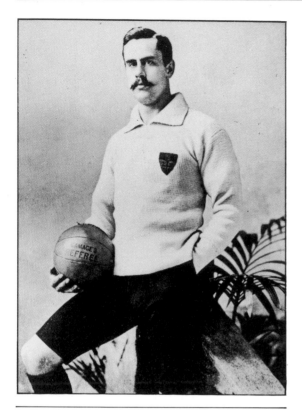

William Robert Moon, a goalkeeper who should have had a long reach.

Stewart turned professional with Charlton Athletic later in the year.

A doughty Welshman is considered to have been the first international player strong enough to kick the ball past the Moon. The occasion was an international between England and Wales at Crewe on 4 February 1888. England won 5–1 but Jack Doughty scored on William Robert Moon's debut in goal for England.

Howard Vaughton, who was at inside-left in Aston Villa's 1887 F.A. Cup Final team, became a director of the Birmingham firm which manufactured the second F.A. Cup trophy in 1896 after the first had been stolen.

George Ramsay, a Scot who had various associations with Aston Villa (he was captain from 1876 to 1880 and secretary-manager from 1884 to 1926) lost his first job in Birmingham because of his keenness to play for Aston Villa. Not all employers were keen on their employees playing the game in those days and Ramsay's employer, a Mr. Izonn,

an iron merchant in Stafford Street, was completely against it. After two warnings he dismissed Ramsay when he discovered the young Scot was continuing to turn out for the Villa.

Aston Villa once chartered a special train just to take their captain, Archie Hunter, to Nottingham. He was an amateur and his employer would never let him leave early for matches. In fact, in his early days he had played under an assumed name to avoid trouble at work. Hunter was the first Villa player to receive the F.A. Cup in 1887 in which he had scored the winning goal. He died prematurely at the age of 35 in 1894.

David McLean was a centre-forward who joined Sheffield Wednesday from Preston North End in February 1911 and scored 88 goals in League matches in four and a half seasons. He scored four goals in a match on four occasions and three 12 times. He was leading goalscorer in Division One in the 1912–13 season with 30 goals, then a club record, and the previous season had been joint leading marksman in Division One with 25. He made one international appearance for Scotland. He had started his career with Celtic in 1907 and, after leaving Wednesday, played for Third Lanark, Rangers, Bradford Park Avenue and Dundee before finishing his career with Forfar Athletic, scoring 13 goals in 1926–27 and 20 in 1927–28. In all he scored 346 League goals.

In two of their F.A. Cup finals, Preston North End fielded amateur goalkeepers. Dr. Mills-Roberts kept goal in 1889 and James Mitchell in 1922.

Billy Gray played outside-right for Orient Reserves against Chelsea reserves on the morning of 27 December 1948 and for Orient v Port Vale in Division Three (Southern Section) in the afternoon. On Christmas Day 1940 Tommy Lawton played for Everton v Liverpool in the morning and 'guested' for Tranmere v Crewe in the afternoon.

On 9 September 1916 2nd Lt. Donald Bell, a Bradford Park Avenue back, became the only Football League professional in history to win the **V.C.,** awarded posthumously 'for most conspicuous bravery' on the Somme.

It is believed that Fred J. S. Le May, an outside-right who made his Division Three (Southern Section) debut for Thames in October 1930 was the **smallest player** ever to appear regularly for a Football League club. His brother, Leslie, was also on the books of the same club as an amateur wing-half, but he was somewhat taller than Fred who stood just 5ft (1.53m) high and weighed just 8 stone (51kg). The two Le May's were Londoners but only Fred appeared in the Football League.

This outside-right remained with Thames during the first of their two seasons in the League and at the end of season 1930–31 moved to Watford where he made another three League appearances to add to his 33 with Thames.

His brief Football League career ended the following season after making ten Division Three (Southern Section) appearances with a struggling Clapton Orient side.

One of the smallest pairs of wingers ever fielded by a Division One side were Fanny Walden from Wellingborough and Sammy Brooks from Brierley Hill who played together in a few matches for Tottenham Hotspur between 1922 and 1924. They were both 5ft 2½in (1.59m) in height. Brooks did not have as many chances with Spurs at this period because of the form of Jimmy Dimmock on the left-wing, but he had previously played many games for Wolves stretching back to before the First World War. After leaving White Hart Lane he appeared with Southend United and Blackpool.

Walden was capped for England and is reckoned to have been the smallest player to achieve that distinction. He had made his reputation with Northampton Town before the First World War in the Southern League and returned to that club to round off his Football League career in 1926–27.

None of the players mentioned was the smallest man ever to appear in a Football League match for that distinction belonged to a referee, Jimmy Talks of Lincoln. Remarkably enough this fellow stood only 4ft 9½in (1.46m) tall, but he was a Southern League referee for several seasons before the First World War, when that competition was the most important outside the Football League, and he came onto the list of referees for the senior competition in 1914.

Conversely the **tallest player** ever to have appeared regularly in the Football League was the Notts County goalkeeper, Albert Iremonger. Regularly is the operative word here for this giant goalkeeper, who stood 6ft 5¼in (1.96m) in his socks, once enjoyed a run of 233 consecutive Football League appearances for the County. This was from 1907 until October 1912 when he was suspended after it was alleged that he had been discourteous to the referee when that official abandoned a game at Tottenham because of fog. County were leading by two goals at the time and Iremonger was renowned for speaking his mind.

Born at Wilford in 1884 he made his debut for Notts County against Sheffield Wednesday on April Fool's Day 1905. But he was certainly no fool, indeed, he is reckoned among the most accomplished goalkeepers ever seen in the League despite the fact that he was never capped by England. He was good enough to make 564 League appearances for Notts County up to 1926 when Lincoln City took him for another season of 36 League appearances. Naturally enough he was an ever-present when County ran away with the championship of Division Two in 1913–14. In his spare time Iremonger was a Scottish dialect comedian, an accent he picked up while playing cricket in Scotland, mostly for Aberdeen.

Although tall he generally kept his weight down to around 13½ stone (86kg) which was not much more than half the weight of the **heaviest player** ever to appear in the Football League when that player was at his top weight. This was another goalkeeper, Billy Foulke, who spent most of his career with Sheffield United.

This character was born at Dawley, Shropshire in 1874 but taken to his grandparents' home at Blackwell, Derbyshire, when only a few weeks old. He graduated to Sheffield United from Blackwell Colliery in 1894 when he weighed nearly 19 stone (120kg). As he stood around 6ft 2in (1.88m) tall

'Fatty' Foulke the Chelsea goalkeeper

he was an impossible figure. He took size 12 boots and wore 24 inch collars. He broke the cross-bar when swinging on it and could fist a ball further than many players could kick it.

Despite his size 'Fatty' Foulke was not a joke as a goalkeeper. At his best, before he put on so much more weight and reached around 25 stone (159kg), he was good enough to be capped for England in 1897. The following season, when he missed only one game, he helped United win the League Championship. This was followed by an F.A. Cup winners' medal a year later, and he collected another winners' medal in 1902 as well as a finalists' medal in 1901.

Foulke was rather temperamental and on one occasion he grabbed the opposing centre-forward and stood him on his head. On other occasions players had been known to lock themselves in their dressing room to keep out of his way. After 11 seasons with United he became one of the first players signed by the newly formed Chelsea club in May 1905, but he only stayed for a season before ending his League career with Bradford City. One of the favourite stories they used to recall at Chelsea about 'little Willie' was that he once sat down at the dinner table early and before his colleagues arrived he had eaten food intended for the whole team.

Mention has been made of the diminutive Fred Le May but he was not the **lightest player** to appear regularly in the Football League. That distinction has been claimed by Barnsley's little inside-right of the first two seasons of their League career, Walter Hepworth, who was reported to weigh only 7st 5lbs (45kg). He first played for Barnsley in 1896, and when they were elected to Division Two in 1898 he made 25 appearances and scored nine goals in their initial season. The following season he dropped out of the side and only played three games.

Campbell Cameron Buchanan who made his senior debut for Wolverhampton Wanderers v West Bromwich Albion on 26 September 1942 at the age of 14, later played in the Football League for Bournemouth and Norwich City. At the end of the 1959–60 season he retired as player-manager of Barnstaple Town. He was, however, persuaded to re-sign the following season and scored in an F.A. Cup tie against Bideford Town.

There have been many older players than **Ronnie Rooke** in Division One but what was different about this centre-forward was that in the 1947–48 season when he was 36 years of age, he not only led Arsenal to the Football League Championship but was top scorer in Division One.

In fact Arsenal were revitalised by two veterans that season, for in the space of a couple of weeks during the previous campaign, when they were struggling to avoid relegation, they signed two players who were thinking about retiring – Rooke and Joe Mercer. Mercer proved the ideal captain while Rooke provided the fire-power.

Born at Guildford in 1911 Rooke had made his League debut with Crystal Palace in 1934 and joined Fulham two years later. The war had absorbed the best of this player's active years and he was not even sure of a first-team place with Fulham when Arsenal signed him to get them out of trouble in 1946. In the Championship-winning campaign Rooke, remembered for his powerful bandy legs and his shirt sleeves flapping around his wrists, scored over 33 Division One goals, including four in an 8–0 win over Grimsby Town and three in a 7–0 victory over Middlesbrough. He played in every game, usually at centre-forward, but sometimes moving to inside-left to make way for Reg Lewis who was second highest scorer with 14. Rooke also scored another six goals during that season on visits to the continent – two against Racing Club de Paris (Arsenal lost 4–3), two against Benfica (won 4–0), one v F.C. Porto (lost 3–2), and one v Liege Selection (won 2–1).

On Wednesday 21 April 1909, Nottingham Forest defeated Leicester Fosse 12–0 at Nottingham to equal the Division One scoring record. Despite the fact that Leicester were bottom of the table and booked for relegation rumour was rife that **bribery and corruption** was involved.

Only the previous year Leicester's goalkeeper, H. P. Bailey, had kept goal for England in five internationals, and yet here he was conceding 12 goals against a side that had not been especially noted for its goalscoring prowess that season. Forest's scorers in this debacle were Spouncer (3), Hooper (3), West (3), Morris (2) and Hughes.

This scandalous talk was so persistent that the Football League decided to hold an enquiry at Leicester at which several witnesses were called including goalkeeper Bailey, the referee John Howcroft, a linesman and several other independent witnesses.

At the end of their investigations the Committee issued a statement that they were 'unanimously of the opinion that the game was played and conducted in a proper manner and that there was neither corruption, collusion, nor anything to suggest that the game had not been properly fought out'.

What had occurred, however, was that the bulk

of the Fosse players had attended the wedding of one of their former colleagues, R. F. Turner, who had only recently been transferred to Everton, and although this wedding had taken place two days before the match in question, their celebrations had continued until the Tuesday night.

It must have been quite a celebration for as the committee so politely put it, this had accounted for the indifferent form of a number of Fosse players, while all the witnesses agreed that the Forest were in remarkably good form!

Incidentally, R. F. Turner had already been fined for asking the Everton club for £100 towards the cost of his furniture.

On 18 January 1913, there was a larger than usual attendance at Swansea for their Southern League, Division Two game with Mardy, for the visiting team included one of the legendary inside-forwards of the 19th century, **John Goodall.** He had made his Football League debut for Preston North End more than 25 years earlier and was manager of Mardy at this time. Goodall was only five months short of his 50th birthday when he decided to play at Swansea. However, Mardy lost 1–0.

There was a tragedy at Highbury on 19 February 1916. Former England international full-back **Bobby Benson** died in the dressing room following his exertions on the field during a game against Reading.

Benson, who was then 33 years of age, had not played in a match for nearly 12 months, but had been working anything up to 17 hours a day in the Royal Artillery munitions factory.

He went to the match as a spectator with his wife and father-in-law, but when Arsenal were a man short he agreed to play although obviously out of condition and having put on a great deal of weight. After about an hour's play he felt so ill that he had to leave the field and he died shortly afterwards, having burst a blood vessel.

The first time **two London clubs** met in a Division One match a new **record attendance** was created in the Football League. This was when 65,000 were present at Stamford Bridge when Chelsea played hosts to Woolwich Arsenal, on Saturday 9 November 1907.

As it was the King's birthday the Royal Arsenal Works at Woolwich was closed and this enabled many more Arsenal supporters to go to Stamford Bridge where Chelsea won 2–1. As the *Athletic News* recorded 'this marked an epoch in the annals of Metropolitan football'.

On 27 December 1909 the League attendance record was raised to 68,000 on the same ground when the previous season's champions, Newcastle United, provided the opposition and Chelsea won 2–1.

To place these attendances in perspective it should be noted that the first 100,000 crowd for a football match (110,820 to be precise) had seen Tottenham Hotspur draw 2–2 with Sheffield United at the Crystal Palace in the F.A. Cup Final of 1901.

In 1971 a proposal to change the name of **Bury** to Manchester North End was found to be unpopular with the majority of supporters of the Gigg Lane club. A local reporter voiced the opinion of many when he said there was a real danger of the club being referred to as Manchester Dead End.

Before they were elected to Division Three (Northern Division) in 1928, **Carlisle United** had three different home grounds. The first, Milholme Bank, the second, Devonshire Park. They left the latter ground to take up their present headquarters at Brunton Park in 1910. The last Carlisle player to score on the old Devonshire Park ground was Billy Blyth and he was the first to score a goal at Brunton Park.

On 31 October 1978 Lincoln City transferred goalkeeper Chris Turner back to Sheffield Wednesday, the club from whom he had been on loan for 25 days. The same day they obtained the temporary transfer of Ian Turner a goalkeeper from Southampton.

Brentford fielded an unchanged team in twenty successive Division Three (Southern Section) matches from 2 November 1929 until 15 March 1930. Of the 19 players called upon that season four appeared in all 42 League games, three others missed only one match each and another was absent only twice. That season Brentford won all 21 of their home matches but could only finish second in the League, seven points behind Plymouth Argyle.

The heaviest defeat suffered by a Football League Club still in membership in 1978–79, on making their first appearance in the competition, was 7–1, a score by which Crewe Alexandra lost away to Burton Swifts on 3 September 1892 in Division Two. After four seasons Crewe were not re-elected and did not return to the League until the formation of the Third Division (Northern Section) in 1921. But Burton Swifts left in similar circumstances in 1901 and did not return.

Tony Brown (West Bromwich Albion) who added the club's aggregate goalscoring record to his list of record appearances during 1978–79. (Colorsport)

On 13 January 1979 Ron Atkinson celebrated the first anniversary of his appointment as manager of **West Bromwich Albion** by seeing his club go to the top of Division One for the first time since 1954, after they had drawn 1–1 at Norwich. That match also established a new club record of 18 games without defeat. During these twelve months Albion had reached the F.A. semi-finals for the 18th time, a record for the competition and the club's individual scoring aggregate, previously held by Ronnie Allen with 205 goals, was over-hauled by Tony Brown, who in the 1976–77 season had also overtaken Jesse Pennington's club record of 455 League appearances. Albion were also celebrating their centenary year.

Of the 92 clubs in membership of the Football League in the 1978–79 season ten had not had a player who had gained full international honours while with them. They were Cambridge United, Colchester United, Darlington, Halifax Town, Mansfield Town, Rochdale, Scunthorpe United, Torquay United, Wigan Athletic and Wimbledon.

Middlesbrough and Wimbledon are the only two clubs in current membership of the Football League who have won the F.A. Amateur Cup under their present titles. Middlesbrough achieved their success on two occasions in 1895 and 1898 during a period in the Northern League when they had reverted to amateur status between 1892 and 1899. Wimbledon won it in 1963 when members of the Isthmian League.

Southport, then members of Division Three (Northern Section) transferred two goalkeepers to Division One clubs within three weeks of each other. Joe Rutherford went to Aston Villa on 28 February 1939 and Harry Smith to Middlesbrough on 20 March.

On 22 December 1894 Grimsby Town made the mistake of taking a Christmas excursion train for their journey to Rotherham where they were due to play a Division Two game, kicking off at 2.15 pm. They actually arrived at Rotherham station shortly before 3 pm, and as a result the game was nearly an hour late getting under way. Bad light prevented it from being completed with Grimsby leading 1–0.
    The Management Committee ordered the game to be replayed with Grimsby paying their own expenses and Rotherham Town taking both gates. Grimsby also suffered the disappointment of losing the replay 3–2.

In the second round of the Football League War

Cup in the 1940–41 season, Barnsley were drawn at home in the first leg to Grimsby Town. The score was 1–1. In the second leg it was 2–2 after 90 minutes so extra time was played, with the result being no further score. The League ruling was that if after extra time it was still a draw then the match had to continue until someone did score.

After a further 50 minutes with both teams looking very tired the referee, Flying Officer McKenzie, was called away on urgent R.A.F. duties and he consequently stopped the match. The League decided that there was insufficient time for a third meeting and awarded the match to Barnsley because they had finished in a higher league position in the North League than Grimsby had in their section.

In the 1937–38 season Preston North End's 64 goals in Division One matches were divided between nine Scots and one Englishman. The nine from north of the border were responsible for 60 of them, while Dickie Watmough managed the other four.

The last match played by Leeds City was against Wolverhampton Wanderers on 4 October 1919 at Molineux. The team travelled overnight by open motor charabanc owing to a railway strike. They won 4–2. Nine days later the club, its four directors and manager were suspended because of financial irregularities during the First World War. Burslem Port Vale were elected to the Football League in City's place.

During the 1960–61 season Altrincham in the Cheshire League were worried by falling attendances. In an attempt to stimulate interest, they arranged for free admission at their game with Tranmere Rovers' reserves. Only 400 turned up, which was less than their previous home fixture when everyone had to pay to enter.

Swansea Town (later City) protested to the Football League when the fixture list was compiled for the 1935–36 season compelling them to travel from Plymouth on Good Friday to Newcastle the following day to compete two Division Two matches. The League paid for first-class sleeping berths for the club. Swansea won 2–1 against Plymouth Argyle but the next day they were beaten 2–0 by Newcastle. Between the two games they travelled about 400 miles.

Lincoln City are the only Football League Club to have experienced three spells outside the competition. Elected to Division Two in 1892 they failed to gain re-election in 1908, returned the following year but failed to gain re-admission in 1911. After only one season outside they came back but were thrown out again in 1920. However, their secretary at the time, J. H. Strawson, was one of the prime movers behind the formation of a new Division Three (Northern Section) of which Lincoln became founder members in 1921.

When Blackburn Rovers met Sheffield United on 29 October 1932 at Ewood Park, the game began in pouring rain and a driving wind. It was soon obvious that it might have to be abandoned as pools of water emerged all over the ground. At half-time Rovers were leading 3–0 but many of the players were freezing and exhausted, and although given a complete change of kit during the interval, it was still anticipated that the referee would not resume the second half.

Surprisingly enough he did, but it was not long before a number of players left the field to seek resuscitation. Mercifully the referee called a halt while he discussed the situation with his linesmen, by which time most of the players had retired to the dressing room. The referee then announced that the game would be halted for 10 minutes to give the players a chance to recover and there was intense discussion in the respective dressing rooms.

The players had been off for 20 minutes before it was decided that the game should be completed, but at that very moment the referee himself collapsed from exhaustion and was unable to resume. The final minutes were played out with the senior linesman acting as referee and with only eight United players on the field. Still Blackburn failed to increase their 3–0 half-time lead.

On the same day Chelsea were playing at Blackpool in a Division One match. There was a blizzard blowing across the ground and torrential rain falling. One after another several Chelsea players collapsed or staggered back to the dressing-room until only six of them remained at the end of a match won 4–0 by Blackpool.

First-class cricket has generally been more renowned for families than football, so some of the comparatively smaller number of families who have become involved in the winter game are worth mentioning.

George Milburn was a member of one of the most extensive of such families. He was involved in an unusual match at Chesterfield in June 1947 when the home side beat Sheffield Wednesday 4–2 in a Division Two game. That was the season of one of the worst winters in League history and the programme had to be extended to 14 June. Chesterfield were fighting to finish high enough

Jackie Milburn, uncle and cousin to four other footballing Milburns' and two Charltons'. (Popperfoto)

pair of full-backs over a period of eight years until George was transferred to Chesterfield in 1937. Another younger brother, Jim, also played full-back for Leeds in later years, making his debut in 1939 and his last appearance in the League for them was in 1952 when he moved to Bradford.

Leeds were thus able to call upon at least one member of this Ashington family over a period of 24 years. At one period before the war the entire Leeds rearguard were members of the same family, for besides the brothers Milburn at full-back there was their brother-in-law Jim Potts in goal.

The fourth Milburn brother, Stanley, made his League debut with Chesterfield in 1946–47 and did not make his final League appearance until 1965 when he was with Rochdale, having also played for Leicester City for a spell in between. This means that the League careers of the four Milburn brothers extended over a period of 37 years.

The story of this family's contribution to the game does not end there, because, of course, their cousin, Jackie Milburn, was one of England's fastest centre-forwards of the post-war era and scored 178 League goals for Newcastle United from 1946 to 1957.

The Second World War restricted the number of appearances the Milburn family could have made, but as it was, the four brothers and their cousin totalled 1,892 matches in peace-time League games.

There have been two post-war instances of uncle and nephew both having filled the same position in the England team in British International Championship matches. Jackie Milburn and his nephew, Bobby Charlton, did so at centre-forward; Colin Grainger and his nephew, Edwin Holliday, at outside-left.

Bobby Charlton holds three Manchester United club records: with 198 goals the highest number of League goals in aggregate; 606 League appearances between 1956–73 and making 106 appearances for England. He also scored a record 49 goals for his country. Later he managed and played for Preston North End.

His brother Jack Charlton, established a record of 629 League appearances for Leeds United as a centre-half between 1953 and 1973. Later he became manager of Middlesbrough and Sheffield Wednesday. The Charlton brothers appeared together in the same England team on 28 occasions between 1964 and 1970 including the 1966 World Cup Final.

The **Keetley family of Derby** was one of the best-known footballing families in the country between the two World Wars. Nine brothers all became professionals: Bill, Albert, Arthur, John, Joe, Tom, Frank, Charlie and Harold, while two

to qualify for the talent money in fourth position while Sheffield Wednesday were ending one of the most nerve racking seasons in their history by narrowly escaping relegation to Division Three. Wednesday were leading 2–1 that afternoon, but then Milburn, the Chesterfield full-back, earned himself a place in the record books by scoring three penalties in some 20 minutes and his side finished as 4–2 winners. They also secured fourth position that season and the players duly collected their talent money.

By the time that George had performed this feat he was a veteran for he had made his debut in the 1928–29 season with Leeds United. He was subsequently joined by brother Jack as the United's others, Lawrence and Sid, also played the game as amateurs. Most of these brothers were goal-scoring forwards and the leading scorer among them was Tom, a centre-forward who appeared in the Football League with Bradford, Doncaster Rovers, Notts County and Lincoln City, scoring 282 goals in 366 League games. He once scored six goals for Doncaster against Ashington on 16 February 1929.

Dick Ray as a Football League club manager signed professionally five of these brothers. In the 1920s he recruited Tom, Harold, Joe and Frank for Doncaster Rovers and, later, Charlie for Leeds United.

One of Tom's most notable scoring achievements was to score a hat-trick in each of three consecutive games for Notts County in 1931 v Plymouth Argyle, 10 October, won 4–3; v Manchester United, 24 October, draw 3–3; and v Chesterfield, 7 November, won 4–1. That season Tom scored a total of 28 goals in Division Two and would have achieved more but for the fact that a dislocated shoulder put him out of the side for nearly two months. The previous season he had scored 39 League goals for the County which was one less than his best League season of 1928–29 when he reached 40 for Doncaster Rovers.

Five of the Keetley brothers appeared in the Football League during the 1920s and 1930s and it is interesting to recall that in February 1926 Joe, Tom and Harold played in the same Doncaster Rovers team, while in the following season another combination of the family, Frank, Tom and Harold, played together in the same Rovers team on more than one occasion. In that season of 1926–27 the Keetley family scored 49 goals for the Rovers in Division Three (Northern Section).

These were not the only highlights of the various careers of the brothers. Frank scored six goals in 21 minutes for Lincoln City against Halifax Town on 16 January 1932 and Tom set up a club record of 39 League goals for Notts County in the 1930–31 season. Between 1923 and 1929 he had scored 180 goals alone for Doncaster.

Five **Wallbanks** brothers had professional careers with Football League clubs: James Wallbanks with Barnsley, Northampton Town, Portsmouth, Millwall and Reading 1929–47; John with Barnsley, Chester and Bradford 1929–35; Fred with Bradford City, West Ham United and Nottingham Forest 1932–36; Harold with Fulham 1946–48 and Horace with Grimsby Town and Luton Town 1946–48 as well.

There have been numerous occasions when brothers have played alongside each other. But **two pairs of brothers in the same international side** are rarer. It happened on three occasions for Wales, firstly on 20 April 1955 when Len and Ivor Allchurch and John and Mel Charles played against Ireland at Windsor Park, Belfast; then similarly against Israel at Tel Aviv on 15 January 1958 and Brazil at Rio de Janeiro on 12 May 1962.

The only instance in Football League history when three brothers were ever-present throughout a single season for each of three different clubs occurred in the 1970–71 season when the brothers **Worthington**, Frank with Huddersfield Town, David with Grimsby Town and Bob with Notts County, did not miss a League game with their respective clubs.

Their father used to play for Halifax Town and Manchester United, and was employed on Bradford City's secretarial staff. But it was not an unique example. **Joe Edelston** was a Hull City half-back, then manager of Reading, whose war-time secretary was daughter Kathleen, and later Maurice, Joe's son, played for and acted as Reading's secretary.

The Fulham manager in the 1978–79 season was **Bobby Campbell**, born into a Liverpool family large enough to turn out an entire 'team'. He is one of 12 children. But few can match former Derby County and England winger, Sammy Crooks, who was one of a family of 17.

Jimmy Melia who played midfield for Liverpool, Wolverhampton Wanderers, Southampton, Aldershot and Crewe Alexandra, was the fifth of a family of 11 whose father was a Liverpool bookmaker. **Frank Blunstone** was also fifth of a family of 13 (eight boys and five girls) whose father was a Crewe ticket collector.

Players who, since the war, have emulated their fathers in becoming full internationals, have been: Jimmy Blair (Blackpool) and Ronnie Simpson (Celtic) for Scotland, George Eastham (Arsenal) for England and Barry Hole (Cardiff City) and Cliff Jones (Spurs) for Wales. Barney Battles (Hearts), Jimmy Gibson (Aston Villa) and John McMenemy (Motherwell), all for Scotland, did so before the war.

The **Eastham** pair established the first example of father and son becoming English internationals and then Football League managers. George senior played for England as a Bolton Wanderer and later managed Accrington Stanley. George junior became manager of Stoke City after a playing career with Ards, Newcastle United,

Arsenal and Stoke. He also played 19 times for England at inside forward. The Easthams also played together for Ards in the Irish League during 1954–55.

Like father, like son, certainly applies remarkably to goalkeepers. Trevor Swinburne (Carlisle United) and Ian Hesford (Blackpool), were active during the 1978–79 season. The fathers of both preceded them in League football, also as goalkeepers.

The **Thompson** trio provided the only instance on record of father and two sons all keeping goal in the Football League: George with York City and Southampton; George junior with Preston and Carlisle; and Desmond (Scunthorpe United and York City).

Half-back Vic Crowe (Aston Villa) and Crystal Palace goalkeeper Vic Rouse both played for their native Wales in international matches. Crowe

Gary Owen, son of a former Rugby League playing father. (Syndication International)

made 16 appearances between 1959 and 1963, Rouse played one match in 1959. But the fathers of both were Englishmen who preceded them as Football League professionals.

West Bromwich Albion's Gary Owen capped for the first time at Under-21 level by England during the 1976–77 season is a son of a former Rugby League player. Internationals Emlyn Hughes (Liverpool) and John Mahoney (Middlesbrough) respectively of England and Wales, also turned to the rival code from that of their fathers.

Fred Everiss joined West Bromwich Albion as an office boy and was later secretary for 46 years from 1902 to 1948. He then went on to the Board of Directors. He was succeeded as secretary by his brother-in-law, Ephriam Smith, who had himself joined the club in 1906 and held the position until 1960. His son, Alan, joined the club straight from school 44 years ago and has been secretary for the last 19 years.

Fred Price and Clifford Price, his uncle, formed a left-wing partnership with Southampton in Division Two in the 1924–25 season. Billy Charlton (forward) and Jim Maidment (goalkeeper), his nephew, played in the same Newport County team in the 1920s.

Instances in Football League history of **brothers scoring for different sides** in the same match are rare. One occasion it did happen was at Molineux on 17 February 1975. Ken Hibbitt gave Wolves a 22nd-minute lead, but elder brother Terry replied for Newcastle United with a 56-minute equaliser which also saved a point.

Amos and Frank Moss were Aston Villa half-back clubmates from May 1938 to May 1956 and that 18-year spell ranks as the longest there has ever been in which two brothers were together as players with the same Football League Club.

When Harry Beacock of Scunthorpe refereed a Division Two match between Doncaster Rovers and Rotherham United on 29 December 1951, his brother Frank was one of the linesmen. It was the only postwar case of two brothers having been among the appointed officials to control a Football League fixture.

The oddest pairing of its kind of modern times arose on 29 September 1970. In a Division Two match there was the unique case of the substitutes called upon by the rival teams being brother strikers. Martin Busby went on for Queen's Park

The Futcher twins, Paul and Ron who were with Manchester City in 1978–79 after earlier service together at Luton Town and Chester. (Syndication International)

Liam Brady, youngest and most successful of the three footballing Brady brothers. (Syndication International)

Rangers, and his younger brother Vic performed a similar role for Luton Town.

The **Brady** trio rank as the only known case of three brothers born in the Republic of Ireland having become Football League professionals. Defenders Ray and Pat Brady used to be colleagues at Millwall and younger brother Liam, a midfield player, has become an Arsenal regular as well as playing for his country.

A 'double' that amounted to, probably, a million-to-one chance came up on 22 October 1955 when the **Rowley brothers** both completed a career aggregate of 200 Football League goals on the same day in Division Two away matches: younger brother Arthur with Leicester City at Fulham and Jack with Plymouth Argyle at Barnsley. Both reached 200 after the respective intervals when Arthur beat Jack to this milestone by just 12 minutes.

Signings of **twin brothers** by Football League clubs are more commonplace than one probably imagines. Robert and Graham Palin, recruited by Bolton Wanderers on schoolboy forms during the 1977–78 season, were the 20th set to be acquired by a League club since the war.

Four sets of twin brothers have been seen together on the same side in Football League post-war matches: Alfred and John Willie Stephens (Swindon Town), David and Peter Jackson (Wrexham, Tranmere Rovers and Bradford City), Ian and Roger Morgan (Queen's Park Rangers) and Paul and Ron Futcher (Chester, Luton Town and Manchester City).

On 2 November 1973, Russell Allen was in a Tranmere Rovers team which won a Division Three match by 3–0 against Walsall, whose manager was his father, Ronnie Allen, who lost his managerial position shortly afterwards.

Bob Walker played with Bradford City and Bradford Park Avenue in turn before World War Two and his son Geoffrey did so later. It was the only time that both father and son have played in the Football League for two clubs in the same city.

Football League club managers who have added their own sons to their playing staffs in recent years have included Peter Jackson (with Bradford City), John Bond (Norwich City), Tony Waddington (Stoke City), John Neal (Wrexham), Charlie Mitten (Newcastle United), Lawrie McMenemy (Southampton) and Tom McAnearney (Aldershot).

Harry Wait was Walsall's first choice goalkeeper in 1936 while his son Harry Wait Jnr kept goal for the reserves. In 1961 Harry Hough signed by Bradford Park Avenue from Barnsley was the reserve goalkeeper while his son Haydn was between the posts in the 'A' side.

Bert Turner and Dai Astley were club mates, brothers-in-law and internationals for the same country. They were together at Charlton Athletic before the war and also appeared for Wales.

On 5 May 1951 at Edgeley Park, Stockport, there occurred something that is probably unique in Football League history – a **father and his son appeared together in the same team.**

They were Alec Herd and son David, playing inside-right and inside-left respectively for Stockport County against Hartlepool United. David even obliged by scoring a goal in his side's 2–0 victory.

Alec Herd had scored his first League goal for Hamilton Academicals way back in the 1928–29 season and had established his reputation as an inside or centre-forward during 15 years with Manchester City, collecting both F.A. Cup winners' and League Championship medals.

David Herd, when playing for Stockport, achieved the unique experience of appearing in the same team as his father. (Colorsport)

Son David's professional career was almost as long for after four seasons with Stockport he had seven with Arsenal and the same number with Manchester United before rounding off his League career with a couple of seasons in Stoke City colours. He did rather better than his father by collecting one Cup winners' medal and two League Championship medals with Manchester United. He also made five appearances for Scotland.

Ralph Banks was left-back in the defeated Bolton Wanderers team in the 1953 F.A. Cup final against Blackpool. His brother Tom was Bolton's left-back in the 1958 final when Wanderers beat Manchester United.

On 31 August 1953 for their Division Three (Northern Section) match against Port Vale, Barrow fielded brothers Jack Keen (left-half), Alan Keen (inside-left) and Herbert Keen (outside-left).

Hubert Pearson was West Bromwich Albion's goalkeeper in the 1912 F.A. Cup Final when he won a runners-up medal. In 1931 his son Harold kept goal for West Bromwich when they won the trophy.

The first ex-professional player to be presented by the Football League with a long service medal to commemorate 21 years of club managership in 1922 was a Scotsman, **David Calderhead.** He had been capped for his country as a centre-half against Ireland in 1889 when with Queen of the South, and won an F.A. Cup medal with Notts County in 1894. In 1907, when they won promotion to Division One, Chelsea appointed him as manager. Calderhead remained in charge at Stamford Bridge for 26 years until his retirement in 1933.

James Commins became manager of Southport in February 1929, of Barrow in November 1930, of Southport again in March 1933 and of Barrow once more in June 1945.

In February 1927 Herbert Chapman, the Arsenal manager, sacked George Hardy, his chief coach, for shouting tactical instructions from the touch-line during a match.

Bill Lambton started the 1958–59 season as Leeds United's trainer, was appointed manager in December only to resign the following March. The same month he became Scunthorpe's trainer-coach and in April was promoted to manager.

There have been two attempts in the past to restrict the spiral of **transfer fees.**

Following the move of Alf Common to Middlesbrough in February 1905 for the first £1,000 transfer in football history, the F.A. decided to give the clubs nearly three years' notice of a new rule which would take effect on 1 January 1908 stating that 'no club shall be entitled to pay or receive any transfer fee or other payment exceeding £350 upon or in respect of the transfer of any player.'

The rule proved impossible to administer, however, and after only three months it was dropped. Clubs were paying above the limit for a particular player but spreading the fee over one or two other worthless signings.

Fees continued to rise and midway through 1922 when the record was somewhere in the region of £5,000 the Football League decided to try to do something about it. Remarkably enough the club that put the proposition this time was Arsenal, who were soon to become the leaders in the transfer market. However, they proposed that the maximum transfer fee should be £1,650. On this occasion, however, and probably remembering how impossible it had been in the past to enforce any limit, the proposition was lost.

In January 1979 the Football League transfer record was broken by West Bromwich Albion signing Middlesbrough's forward David Mills for £516,720. Mills had made his debut for Middlesbrough on the last day of the 1968–69 season when he came on as a substitute against Birmingham City.

Mills actual transfer fee was reported by the Middlesbrough club to have been £482,222 without the levies.

On the 14 February 1979 Trevor Francis' transfer from Birmingham City to Nottingham Forest was registered by the Football League. The fee involved was in excess of £1 million and Birmingham put the transfer fee alone at £975,000.

Phil Parkes the Queen's Park Rangers goalkeeper was transferred to West Ham United for £565,000 on 22 February 1979. Again West Ham quoted the figure at £527,000 including levies, £475,000 nett.

At the start of the 1977–78 season, Middlesbrough, who had been the first club to pay as much as £1,000 for a player when they signed Alf Common from Sunderland in 1905, were the only Division One club who had not paid a six figure fee for a player. But on 1 September they paid £135,000 to Wrexham for centre-forward Billy Ashcroft.

Autographs of the many guest players who assisted Aldershot Football Club during the Second World War. (Brian Bramley)

After Burnley had beaten Gainsborough Trinity 4–1 in a second round F.A. Cup tie at Turf Moor on 1 February 1913 they signed their opponents defence en bloc.

Despite their defeat the Gainsborough rearguard had evidently pleased the Burnley management, for they signed all three before they had left the ground and included them the following Saturday in their side which drew a Division Two game 2–2 away to Bristol City. The trio were goalkeeper Ronald Sewell and full-backs Sam Gunton and Cliff Jones.

The autographed roll of honour of some of the many famous guest players who assisted Aldershot Football Club during the 1939–46 period of **World War Two** hangs in the Members Club and includes some interesting names. Among them is Matt Busby who as Scotland's captain never actually played for Aldershot. The day he was due to turn out the England captain was also available and Busby stood down! Another curious entry is that of an England Test Cricketer of pre-war vintage who did not play either.

Jimmy Greenhoff was transferred in the middle of a Cup Final. He played for Leeds United in the first leg of the Fairs Cup Final against Ferencvaros in August 1968, but before the second leg he had been transferred to Birmingham City.

The **transfer** of players in the Football League after the second Thursday in March in each season is controlled by the Management Committee of the League. Players transferred after this date are not able to play for their new club in League matches unless permission is received.

Stanley Burton played in the 1939 F.A. Cup Final for Wolverhampton Wanderers on 29 April and was transferred to West Ham United the following Thursday. Two days later he made his debut for his new club in a Division Two match.

Frank Laycock, a Barrow forward, was called off the field during a Division Three (Northern Section) match with Rotherham County in order to sign transfer forms to take him to Nelson. It was on 16 March 1925, the last day of the season for unrestricted transfers.

In July Charlie Buchan was transferred from Sunderland to Arsenal for £2,000 when he was nearly 34 years of age. The deal included a proviso that Sunderland should be paid an extra £100 for each goal Buchan scored in his first season. He scored 21.

In 1905 Small Heath (later Birmingham) offered centre-forward Bob McRoberts to Chelsea at £100

Jimmy Greenhoff Manchester United (who was transferred in the middle of a Cup Final when with Leeds) is the elder brother of the club's defender or midfield player Brian. (Syndication International)

and for another £240 they were willing to part with inside-forwards Jimmy Windridge and Jimmy Robertson, the fees only to be paid if Chelsea were elected to the Football League, otherwise they were free.

Manchester United persuaded Stockport County to allow amateur wing-half Hughie McLenahan to join them in 1927 in exchange for three freezers of ice cream. United scout Louis Rocca arranged for these to be given to the County club to raise club funds at their bazaar. McLenahan turned professional with United.

Long term contracts are not the preserve of modern times. In 1892 Fred Spiksley, an outside-left, was signed by Sheffield Wednesday from Gainsborough Trinity and given a three year contract. An outside-left, he won an F.A. Cup winners medal in 1896, a League Championship medal in 1902–03, his last season with the club, and made seven appearances for England in internationals.

Billy Williamson, an inside-forward with Rangers just after the Second World War, had a remarkable Scottish F.A. Cup record. In seasons 1947–48 and 1948–49 he made only two appearances in the Cup and both of these were in the Final.

In the 1947–48 season Williamson was not even selected for the Final, at least not originally. However, the game with Morton, a side struggling to avoid relegation, ended in a draw 1–1 after extra time and Williamson was called upon to make his initial Scottish Cup appearance in the replay. This time Rangers won 1–0 and the scorer was none other than Williamson himself. More than that, his goal has gone down in history as one of the finest ever seen in a Scottish Cup final as he hurtled in horizontally to steer a Rutherford cross into the corner of the net with only five minutes remaining. The following season Rangers again

Alfie Conn, one of only three Scottish players believed to have played for both Celtic and Rangers. (Colorsport)

went through to the Final, but without Williamson. They were opposed by Clyde and, as in the previous campaign, he was called upon to make his initial Cup appearance against them. Rangers won 4–1 with Clyde conceding two penalties and Williamson was again among the scorers, although, of course, this time his goal was not decisive.

In view of these two events, the following season was just as remarkable for Rangers again went through to the Final, and with replays they needed seven games to reach there. This time Williamson played in every one of these games yet when they lined up for the Final against East Fife, Williamson was absent. Rangers won 3–0.

Towards the end of the 1915–16 season there was such a pile up of fixtures in the Scottish League that Celtic played **two League games in one day,** 16 April 1916. They beat Raith Rovers 6–0 at Celtic Park and in the evening travelled to Fir Park where they defeated Motherwell 3–1.

When Alfie Conn was transferred from Tottenham Hotspur to Celtic in March 1977 he became only the third to **play for both Rangers and Celtic.** Conn had started his career with Rangers. Previously Alec Bennett, a right-winger, had joined Rangers from Celtic in 1908 and remained with them ten years. Inside-forward George Livingstone had been with Hearts, Sunderland, Celtic, Liverpool and Manchester City when he was among a number of City players suspended in 1906. He then went to Rangers for two years before joining Manchester United.

East Fife are the only Scottish League club to have won the Scottish Cup and Scottish League Cup while members of Division Two. They won the Scottish Cup in the 1937–38 season and the League Cup for the first time in 1947–48. In the former season they also established their record score, 13–2 against Edinburgh City, and in the latter Henry Morris set up an individual club scoring record with 41 goals.

In the 1964–65 season the East Stirlingshire club was moved from Firs Park, Falkirk, to New Kilbowie Park, Clydebank by the brothers Charles and Jack Steedman and the club renamed East Stirling-Clydebank. It was not a successful venture and a court order compelled the club to be moved back to Falkirk at the end of that season.

One of the earliest but by no means the first **strike** on record among professional footballers took place in the Celtic Cup on 28 November 1896. It could be more aptly termed a 'revolt'.

Celtic were already in difficulties with a number of their players on the injured list when shortly before their game with Hibernian at Parkhead, three of their team refused to play. They were Barney Battles, Johnny Divers and Peter Meechan. Their behaviour was described by the *Athletic News* correspondent as 'insubordination as serious as it was childish,' but apparently they made a stand because of criticism they had received in a local newspaper about the foulness of their play at Cathkin Park and had asked that the reporter who had written the article be banned from the Press Box.

The Celtic Committee promised that they would consult the Editor of the offending newspaper but, of course, nothing definite could be done at such short notice, and so Celtic had to take the field with very much of a scratch team and only 10 men.

Surprisingly enough they more than held their own against the Hibs in the first half, and when Celtic completed their team after the interval, having rushed Tom Dunbar over from Hampden where he had been taking part in a reserve-team game, they actually went ahead 15 minutes from time. Hibs, however, covered their embarrassment by equalising with only three minutes to spare.

A great deal of publicity was given to this revolt without much sympathy being shown for the players concerned. The Committee decided that the trio should be punished by reducing their wages to 2s 6d (12½p) per week for the remainder of the season.

Most strikes have, naturally enough, concerned wages, and with many football clubs being often close to the bread line, players have sometimes had to make a stand to actually get any wages at all.

Such an event occurred at Walsall on 29 December 1894 when Walsall Town Swifts were due to play Newcastle United in a Division Two match. In fact, because of the home players refusal to take the field before they were paid their wages, the game kicked off 10 minutes late and as a consequence, it had to be abandoned before full-time because of bad light. Newcastle were leading 3–2 and, naturally enough, considered that they should not be compelled to return to Walsall for a replay. The League Management Committee agreed with them and ordered the result to stand.

Lincoln City's players also went on strike when the club had no money to pay them in February 1923, but fortunately this dispute was soon settled.

There have been many other similar problems over the year, the most recent being in March 1975 when the Stockport County players threatened to strike unless they received their wages on time.

In the close season of 1922, with industrial wages tumbling all around, the Football League decided to cut players' maximum wages from £9 to £8 per week during the playing season. The Players' Union held a number of meetings and threatened to strike, but before the new season had begun most players had realised that they could not escape the general drop in wages and accepted the cut.

Chris Ball, inside-right of Walsall, was twice sent off in corresponding matches against Crewe in March 1932 and March 1933 by referee Bert Mee (Mansfield). And one of the fastest sending offs in history was at Hull in a Third Division (Northern Section) game with Wrexham on Christmas Day 1936. Ambrose Brown, inside-right of Wrexham, was dismissed after only 20 seconds by the same official.

In the 1893–94 season only two amateur clubs, Middlesbrough and Reading, reached the first round of the F.A. Cup competition proper, and while Middlesbrough were beaten 4–0 by Newton Heath (Manchester United), Reading suffered one of the biggest defeats in F.A. Cup history by losing 18–0 against Preston North End.

Reading were said to be composed entirely of railwaymen and biscuit factory workers, and Preston were 'miles ahead of their opponents in scientific knowledge of the game'.

Preston included their trainer, former England international, John Barton, at inside right for this game, and Nick Ross, one of the most outstanding full-backs of the 19th century, returned to the side although he had barely recovered from influenza. In fact, when it came on to rain during the second half, he retired from the game. It subsequently transpired that he was suffering from tuberculosis and he died less than seven months later at the age of 31.

Preston's goalkeeper against Reading was the great Welsh international Jimmy Trainor, and in this game he was reported to have handled the ball only twice. He wore a mackintosh for most of the time.

Although playing against a gale of wind, Preston were leading 7–0 at half-time, and even after being reduced to 10 men, the Northern side scored a further eight goals. The unfortunate Reading goalkeeper on this occasion was H. J. Manners.

FOOTBALL LEAGUE'S FOREIGN LEGION 1978-79

Name	Country	Position	Signed by	Date
Osvaldo C. Ardiles	Argentina	Midfield	Tottenham Hotspur	21 July
Julio Ricardo Villa	Argentina	Midfield	Tottenham Hotspur	21 July
Alejandro Sabella	Argentina	Midfield	Sheffield United	15 August
Arnoldus J. H. Muhren	Holland	Midfield	Ipswich Town	19 August
Ivan Golac	Yugoslavia	Defender	Southampton (non-c) (as contract player)	22 August 13 November
Alberto C. Tarantini	Argentina	Defender	Birmingham City	12 October
Kazimierz Deyna	Poland	Midfield	Manchester City	23 November
Franciscus J. Thijssen	Holland	Midfield	Ipswich Town	14 February
Petar Borota	Yugoslavia	Goalkeeper	Chelsea	
Bozo Jankovic	Yugoslavia	Forward	Middlesbrough	24 February
Geert Meijer	Holland	Forward	Bristol City	29 March
Pertti Jantunen	Finland	Midfield	Bristol City	29 March
Tadeusz Nowak	Poland	Midfield	Bolton Wanderers	29 March

Alberto Tarantini. (Syndication International)

Alex Sabella. (Syndication International)

Petar Borota. (Syndication International)

Arnold Muhren. (Syndication International)

Before the Second World War a number of **foreign players** appeared in the Football League from various countries including Denmark, Egypt, Germany, Holland and Italy. One of the most notable was Nils Middleboe, a Danish-born half-back and one of four footballing brothers. He had played for his country in the 1908 and 1912 Olympic tournaments winning a silver medal both times before joining Chelsea, after coming to this country on business in the 1913–14 season. He played for Denmark again in the 1920 Olympics and left Chelsea in 1921 to become an outstanding coach with his first club KB Copenhagen.

Osvaldo Ardiles. (Syndication International)

Ricardo Villa. (Syndication International)

Ivan Golac. (Syndication International)

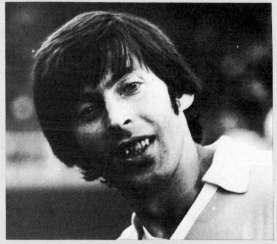
Kazimierz Deyna. (Syndication International)

The worst day in F.A. Cup history for players being sent off was 9 January 1915 in the first round at a time when clubs from Division One and Two were included in this stage of the competition.

At the match between Everton and Barnsley at Goodison Park three players were sent off and another collapsed before the end.

The notorious Frank Barson, who was probably sent off or suspended more often than any players in League history, was right-half for Barnsley on this occasion, and he was ordered off along with the Everton winger, George Harrison, after these two had been involved in an incident just as Harrison centred for Everton to open the scoring. Everton's inside-right, Bobby Parker, was also sent off later in the game, and when, shortly before the end, Joe Clennell had to be assisted off with an injury, the home side finished the game with only eight men. However, they still won 3–0.

Two men, one from either side, were also sent off that afternoon in the Millwall v Clapton Orient and Middlesbrough v Goole Town games, and a Grimsby Town player was also ordered off in their tie with Northampton Town.

The longest third round in the history of the F.A. Cup lasted 66 days during the 1962–63 season. It started on 5 January 1963 and was completed on 11 March. Ties were spread over 22 different playing days, there were 261 postponements and 16 of the 32 ties were called off ten or more times due to adverse weather conditions varying from frost, snow, ice, thawing rain and mud, to power-cuts.

The worst affected was Birmingham v Bury which stretched through 14 postponements, one abandonment and a replay, making 16 attempts before it was decided, while Lincoln v Coventry was postponed 15 times.

Only three ties were played on the original date and the highest number of third round matches completed in one day was five on two consecutive days, 6 and 7 March.

In the days when the gap between amateur and professional football was smaller, Mr. N. Lane 'Pa' Jackson, founder of the Corinthians and a leading administrator in this country, persuaded one of the Sheriffs of London, Thomas Dewar, later Lord Dewar, to present a trophy to be competed for annually between the best amateur and the best professional club, the proceeds after expenses to go to charity. Thus there came into being in 1897 the **Sheriff of London Charity Shield.**

The first teams to compete for this new trophy

G. O. Smith one of the early 'giants' among England international centre-forwards.

were the Corinthians and the League Champions, Sheffield United. In fact the Corinthians, who had hitherto refused to play in any competition, had to alter their rules to enable them to compete for this prize.

In a hard fought match at the Crystal Palace neither side was able to score so a replay was arranged on the same ground three weeks later. This also ended in a 1–1 draw and the two clubs became joint holders.

The same result happened the following season when Aston Villa and Queen's Park played a goal-less draw. With the travelling involved a replay was not considered and so they became joint holders.

The Corinthians were the first side to actually win the trophy in 1899–1900 when they beat Aston Villa 2–1, the winning goal coming through G. O. Smith, with 12 minutes left for play.

The competition continued for seven more seasons, the professionals winning all but one of them (when the Corinthians beat Bury 10–3), but was abandoned in 1907 at the time of the 'split' between the leading amateur clubs and the F.A.

The modern counterpart of this competition is the **F.A. Charity Shield** which was first competed for in 1908 with the leading amateurs meeting the leading professionals in seven of the first 16 matches before it generally settled into an annual game between the League Champions and the F.A. Cup winners. The old Sheriff of London Shield was again played for on one occasion on behalf of the National Playing Fields Association in April 1931 when Arsenal beat the Corinthians 5–3 at Highbury.

The Division One trophy is the League Championship Cup but shields are awarded for winning the other three divisions. In 1924 Huddersfield Town discovered that the names of three previous winners of the Football League championship: Sunderland 1912–13, Blackburn Rovers 1913–14 and Everton 1914–15 had been omitted from the inscription.

Substitutes were introduced in Football League matches during 1965–66 season. One substitute per team was allowed in case of injury only. The first substitute used was Keith Peacock of Charlton Athletic at Bolton on 21 August 1965.

Of the 2,028 Football League matches played that season there were 772 instances of the substitute being used. A total of 519 were made in the second half of matches. In Division Three there were 223 substitutions in 552 matches, 196 out of 552 in Division Four, while 182 were used in 462 Division Two matches and only 170 in the same number of Division One matches. The following season one substitute per team was allowed in Football League, League Cup and F.A. Cup matches for any reason.

Robert Smith, a Welsh born referee who was employed as a railway shunter, had refereed only five Football League matches when he was appointed to control the Scotland v Ireland international at Hampden Park on 5 November 1952.

When Pegasus played Bishop Auckland in the 1951 F.A. Amateur Cup Final at Wembley there was a crowd of 100,000, the first six figure attendance for this match in the history of the competition. In December 1960 a friendly between the same two clubs was arranged for the White City Stadium and there were 327 spectators present.

The **trainer's dug-out** alongside the touch-line is something taken for granted nowadays. It is certainly an improvement on the old-fashioned idea of an uncovered bench at ground level which usually meant that the respective trainers were completely exposed to the elements. The idea for it was supposed to be first attributed to the former Scottish international Donald Colman who returned to Aberdeen as trainer in 1931. The first trainers' dug-out was constructed at Pittodrie, while the first Football League club to take up the idea is thought to have been Everton.

Jack Southwood's benefit match at Ewood Park, Blackburn between Rovers and Darwen on 31 October 1892 was watched by a crowd of 6,000 under the illuminations of Wells' Light, the 6,000 candle power Gramere lights on scaffolds. The teams played with a white ball. Rovers won 2–0.

In January 1927 the B.B.C. used a midweek F.A. Cup tie at Crystal Palace between Corinthians and Newcastle United to try out several Fleet Street journalists to broadcast live commentaries on the match.

Grounds damaged by **German bombing** action during the Second World War were Arsenal, Birmingham City, Charlton Athletic, Manchester United, Sheffield United, Fulham, Sunderland, Leicester City, Notts County, West Ham United, Clapton Orient, Millwall, Plymouth Argyle and New Brighton.

It is every footballer's ambition to play at Wembley but in 1930 nine of **Clapton Orient's** players each had the unique distinction of playing two Football League games on the hallowed turf, while another four of their players plus the 22 of the teams they met could each claim to have played one League game there.

In the 1930–31 season the Orient were playing at Lea Bridge Road Speedway ground and visiting clubs were continually complaining that there was far too little space between the touch-lines and the cinder speedway track.

Consequently the Football League stepped in and gave the football club two weeks (subsequently extended by a week) to add a yard of turf along either touch-line or they would be refused permission to continue to play League games on the ground. As the pitch was already the minimum width and the Speedway company refused to move from their position, the club was forced to seek help from elsewhere.

Both Leyton F.C. and Walthamstow Avenue were approached with the idea of sub-letting their ground but they refused. Then the Orient Board hit upon the idea of approaching the Wembley

Stadium Company who agreed for the Orient to play there subject to the Company being paid a guaranteed amount.

So it was that on 22 November 1930 Clapton Orient met Brentford at Wembley, and despite the bad weather, a crowd of 10,300 turned up to witness this Division Three (Southern Section) match.

The Orient club wondered if they had not made a good move, especially as they had beaten Brentford 3–0, and although the Speedway Company then agreed to the club's request and laid an extra yard of turf down each touch-line, Orient were in no hurry to return to the Lea Bridge ground.

On Thursday 4 December they met Luton Town in a replayed F.A. Cup tie at Highbury rather than Lea Bridge, and two days later they returned to Wembley for another Division Three game against Southend United whom they defeated 3–1.

This time, however, the attendance was only around 2,500. Obviously the local derby element had boosted their previous Wembley gate. The receipts of about £100 were not enough to cover the guarantee to the Wembley Company, and so it was back to Lea Bridge Speedway for Clapton Orient, at least for another seven years.

On 18 September 1917 Ibrox Park, the home of Glasgow Rangers, was used to stage a Royal investiture. King George V travelled north to present medals and decorations.

Two native born Chesterfield players provided a unique family link with their local Football League club when **Arthur Machent** joined them in November 1927 and his younger brother Stanley was signed in November 1947, almost 20 years to the day.

Blackpool's right flank in attack against Leicester City in August 1960 was formed by **Stanley Matthews** (then 45) and **Leslie Lea** (17). Matthews had already seen eleven years of active Football League service when Lea was born.

David Steele managed two clubs simultaneously in September 1943. Already manager of Bradford

Park Avenue he was appointed by Huddersfield Town and remained in the dual role until Bradford engaged a successor. Three inside-lefts completed an aggregate service of 64 years with Sheffield United as well as an unbroken sequence of more than 45 years. **Billy Gillespie** occupied the berth from 1911 to 1932, **Jack Pickering** from 1925 to 1948 and **Jimmy Hagan** from 1938 to 1958.

Bert Sproston was chosen at right-back for Tottenham Hotspur against Manchester City in a Division Two match at Maine Road on 5 November 1938 and his name was printed in the match programme. But he was then transferred to City and turned out for them against Spurs on the day of the game.

Sam Bartram of Charlton Athletic who had a rather interesting sequence of Wembley appearances. (Colorsport)

On **10 March 1956** Sam Bartram made his 613th and last appearance in goal for Charlton Athletic; Leeds United suffered their first home defeat in 34 League matches; Southport's unbeaten run of 19 games in Division Three (Northern Section), including seven away wins, ended at Wrexham and Arthur Rowley (Leicester City) scored his 200th goal in League and Cup matches. Bartram's total was made up of 582 League games and 31 in the F.A. Cup.

Sam Bartram played in goal in four successive cup finals at Wembley. In the final of the Football League South Cup he played for Charlton Athletic against Chelsea in 1944 and for Millwall as a guest player against Chelsea again in the same final a year later. In the F.A. Cup final he was Charlton's goalkeeper against Derby County in 1946 and Burnley in 1947.

Chester drew 22 of their 46 Division Three matches in 1977–78. They drew eight at home, 14 away. In the 1976 close season **Sunderland** manager Bob Stokoe banned his forward Roy Greenwood from sitting for the official team photograph because he was growing a beard at the time.

Willie Maley and his brother Tom were in the Celtic team which won the Scottish Cup in 1892. They had been among the founder players in 1888 and Willie later became manager and secretary remaining in charge of the club's affairs for 50 years. He died in 1958 at 89. He had played twice for Scotland at right-half.

One of the most **strenuous soccer tours** ever undertaken by a team must have been that by the **Canadians** who visited the British Isles in the autumn of 1888.

As the Canadians have never been highly rated in the Football world little has been written about this tour but it did, in fact, include an 'international' against Scotland, at the Exhibition Grounds, Glasgow, which the home side won 4–0.

When one considers the speed of travel in those days and the number of games played, the 17 soccer enthusiasts from across the Atlantic must have been really exhausted long before the end of their two months stay, and it is a wonder that they were able to win any games at all. As a matter of fact, however, they won 10 and drew 5 of their 24 matches.

The Canadians began this tour at a cracking pace by playing no less than eight games in the first two weeks. They kicked off with a 6–2 victory over County Antrim in Belfast, and after winning two more and drawing another game in Ireland they crossed over to Scotland where they held Rangers to a 1–1 draw at Ibrox on the Saturday, and then proceeded to beat Abercorn (Monday), and lost to Queen's Park (Tuesday) and Ayr (Thursday). This was followed on the Saturday with a 3–0 victory over Heart of Midlothian.

Their defeat by Scotland followed on the Wednesday before they moved into England and surprisingly beat Sunderland 3–0 on Saturday.

The following week they beat both Middlesbrough and Lincoln City but were held to a draw by Sheffield on Monday of the first week in October.

That should be enough to indicate what a hectic tour this was. Remarkably, in their final encounter which was against one of the most powerful amateur sides in the country, The Swifts, including a number of internationals, the visitors were only beaten 1–0. The Prince of Wales attended this match at Kennington Oval.

They made a second tour in 1891 (the side included a number of players from the United States), but this was not as hectic, as it was spread over four months. This time they played 49 matches, winning 11 and drawing 10.

This tour was possibly more significant because the Canadians played 'internationals' against all four of the home countries. They lost all of them, 5–2 to Ireland in Belfast, 5–1 to Scotland in Glasgow, 2–1 to Wales at Wrexham and 6–1 to England at Kennington Oval.

They actually played another game against Wales, but this was abandoned with the score at 1–1. What happened was that the visitors took exception to the Welsh equaliser and retired from the match.

Probably the finest victory achieved by the Canadians on this tour was in defeating Stoke 2–1. This was only two days after holding Burnley to a 2–2 draw. Both home clubs were members of the Football League. Their heaviest defeat was one of 9–0 by Wolverhampton Wanderers.

The Anatomy of a Footballing Country

The member nations of the world governing body FIFA are mapped out on the following four pages, presenting basic information from each of them. From the details included some kind of picture of the statistical strength of the respective countries can be drawn. As an example of a more in depth look at these figures, Argentina the 1978 World Cup winners are featured below in the anatomy of a footballing country. FIFA celebrated its 75th anniversary in May 1979 so it is appropriate that this survey should be included in this edition.

The new FIFA House in Zurich, a modern and functional administrative building completed at the end of 1978, is the third headquarters of the organisation in this Swiss city. Originally a modest apartment at Bahnhofstrasse 77 was rented from 1932–1954 and was succeeded by the FIFA House at Hitzigweg II, the former Dewald residence purchased in 1954.

Diego Maradona the 18-year-old Argentine international midfield player who was first capped in 1977 at 16 but held back from the 1978 World Cup final squad. (Glasgow Herald)

ARGENTINA (Population 25,500,000)

Number of clubs affiliated	direct	88		
	indirect	2,625		
			Total	2,713
Teams taking part in championships or competitions				
	General	5,713		
	Youth	9,015		
			Total	14,728
Players registered	Professional	2,650		
	Non-amateur	61,320		
	Amateur	72,455		
	Youth	163,470		
			Total	299,895
Registered Referees	Superior	867		
	Average	1,530		
	Beginners	875		
			Total	3,272

FIFA COUNTRIES

Country	C	T	P	R
SENEGAL	75	123	3503	134
BARBADOS	82	66	950	73
GRENADA	15	15	200	15
PUERTO RICO	66	236	3200	105
DOMINICAN REPUBLIC	72	309	10165	25
CANADA	1300	7900	118872	987
*CUBA	70	714	12900	160
*NICARAGUA	31	8	160	14
HONDURAS	452	450	11550	423
GUATEMALA	1611	1962	43516	265
NETHERLANDS (ANTILLES)	85	105	3820	70
*PANAMA	No information available			
COLOMBIA	3685	5910	152050	2040
GUYANA	103	126	1665	36
BRAZIL	5436	18369	112755	1266
CHILE	5615	13620	324422	5520
*URUGUAY	970	970	101550	140
*TRINIDAD AND TOBAGO	132	132	3590	147
*ANTIGUA	42	42	644	31
BERMUDA	32	48	1712	37
HAITI	40	25	3480	41
BAHAMAS	20	31	620	12
JAMAICA	266	244	45200	122
USA	—	1696	325000	4900
MEXICO	77	105000	2752075	5031
EL SALVADOR	782	620	16396	463
*COSTA RICA	431	421	12429	126
VENEZUELA	988	1735	35047	361
ECUADOR	170	300	12300	120
*PERU	6158	6958	139360	2316
*BOLIVIA	305	320	11789	202
ARGENTINA	2713	14728	299895	3272
*PARAGUAY	742	—	110000	600
MALI	128	18	54	102
*UPPER VOLTA	55	60	35	72
*GAMBIA	39	39	850	27

Countries marked * have not provided information since the previous survey

West Hemisphere

Country	C	T	R	P
*MAURITANIA	59	64	43	1930
*PORTUGAL	880	224	1150	40815
FRANCE	18285	52000	14907	1194189
REPUBLIC OF IRELAND	2914	2928	490	54596
SCOTLAND	4074	7100	1540	109000
ENGLAND	37715	36904	9500	1505000
NORWAY	3100	6790	2000	124000
DENMARK	1453	7400	1800	208000
LUXEMBOURG	209	532	271	15730
SWITZERLAND	1382	7314	3255	146188
MALTA	231	362	67	7460
ALGERIA	780	2607	1098	58567
MOROCCO	274	704	1000	16735
*CONGO	141	130	70	4230
*NIGERIA	326	723	809	80190
*TOGO	144	144	85	4340
*UPPER VOLTA	55	60	72	3510
*SIERRA LEONE	—	104	640	8120
*LIBERIA	No information available			
ICELAND	67	427	273	13856
SPAIN	5578	5578	5305	202574
NORTHERN IRELAND	740	875	352	17685
WALES	1640	2100	990	43650
BELGIUM	3275	14400	5546	279420
SWEDEN	3220	6011	6100	152548
NETHERLANDS (HOLLAND)	7635	54048	13828	964215
LIECHTENSTEIN	7	60	11	1200
ITALY	21845	22132	13449	833564
TUNISIA	172	344	523	14314
*NIGER	45	—	100	—
CAMEROON	200	264	448	9328
*GABON	275	275	128	8086
BENIN PR	31	19	61	5165
GHANA	300	216	304	5002
*IVORY COAST	78	105	60	3255
GUINEA	306	84	138	9108

Country	C	T	R	P
ISRAEL	544	548	500	23500
LEBANON	105	141	84	8125
BULGARIA	3923	5737	3108	117280
GREECE	1762	1762	1560	91020
HUNGARY	2440	5326	4660	138461
CZECHOSLOVAKIA	6776	26847	6550	352227
GERMANY, FEDERAL REPUBLIC	17549	115145	40000	3611431
ALBANIA	42	215	265	4730
LIBYA	89	148	149	2941
*SUDAN	750	771	555	36840
*CENTRAL AFRICA	256	283	92	7200
RWANDA	No information available			
*BURUNDI	132	53	125	3930
BOTSWANA	No information available			
*RHODESIA	605	420	250	11684
*MALAWI	58	52	31	744
KENYA	351	270	148	7820
FINLAND	900	2437	2500	44330
RUMANIA	5453	5577	6573	179987
YUGOSLAVIA	4289	4289	6541	172225
POLAND	5334	11343	7160	234052
GERMAN DEMOCRATIC REPUBLIC	4981	25043	18087	557055
AUSTRIA	2041	6466	1935	255125
CYPRUS	41	57	94	12000
EGYPT, ARAB REPUBLIC	168	178	371	11695
*YEMEN	—	36	40	1700
*UGANDA	400	720	178	1582
ZAIRE	2400	2200	1875	52627
*ZAMBIA	20	280	290	4100
LESOTHO	88	98	70	2076
SWAZILAND	No information available			
*TANZANIA	—	51	76	—
JORDAN	22	56	27	2280
SYRIA	102	—	209	30600
*TURKEY	1432	1540	1821	43229
MADAGASCAR	775	310	207	23536
ETHIOPIA	305	320	1405	13425

Countries marked * have not provided information since the previous survey

East Hemisphere

IRAQ
C 155
T 74
R 404
P 1700

KUWAIT
C 14
T 28
R 51
P 1638

*AFGHANISTAN
C 30
T 150
R 230
P 3300

*NEPAL
C 33
T 45
R 21
P 700

*BURMA
C 550
T 550
R 1312
P 14000

SINGAPORE
C 172
T 70
R 152
P 8000

*VIETNAM, NORTH
C 55
T 800
R 181
P 16000

HONG KONG
C 72
T 184
R 162
P 3804

KOREA, NORTH
C 85
T 68
R 597
P 1707

*KOREA, SOUTH
C 476
T 113
R 50
P 2047

*KHMER
C 30
T 32
R 42
P 650

PHILIPPINES
C 420
T 820
R 184
P 16800

*BRUNEI
C 22
T 25
R 14
P 83

*PAPUA-NEW GUINEA
C 320
T 368
R 140
P 5700

AUSTRALIA
C 6514
T 14266
R 2110
P 214000

SRI LANKA
C 600
T 114
R 347
P 18825

*PAKISTAN
C 576
T 43
R 295
P 13000

UNITED ARAB EMIRATES
C 20
T 40
R 45
P 1162

SAUDI ARABIA
C 96
T 150
R 117
P 7600

*SOMALIA
C 16
T 29
R 37
P 816

*IRAN
C 422
T 1986
R 163
P 43300

BAHRAIN
C 30
T 62
R 54
P 2110

BANGLADESH
C 1162
T 50
R 375
P 25684

USSR
C 50664
T 164
R 136380
P 4505000

*LAOS
C 93
T 152
R 86
P 2812

MACAO
C 120
T 70
R —
P 2000

CHINA, REPUBLIC
C 36
T 842
R 365
P 16569

JAPAN
C 19840
T 19840
R 5100
P 297600

THAILAND
C 145
T 185
R 127
P 9000

*VIETNAM, SOUTH
C 58
T 58
R 70
P 1148

MALAYSIA
C 320
T 29
R 316
P 7839

FIJI
C 140
T 36
R 120
P 21500

INDONESIA
C 2880
T 468
R 457
P 97000

NEW ZEALAND
C 312
T 3049
R 500
P 41698

INDIA
C 1949
T 1949
R 3601
P 53110

MAURITIUS
C 397
T 397
R 37
P 22500

QATAR
C 8
T 14
R 36
P 1200

Index

Other Guinness

Superlatives Titles

Season Ending	Champions	Matches	Points	Home W	D	L	F	A	Pts
1931	ARSENAL	42	66	14	5	2	67	27	33
1932	EVERTON	42	56	18	0	3	84	30	36
1933	ARSENAL	42	58	14	3	4	70	27	31
1934	ARSENAL	42	59	15	4	2	45	19	34
1935	ARSENAL	42	58	15	4	2	74	17	34
1936	SUNDERLAND	42	56	17	2	2	71	33	36
1937	MANCHESTER CITY	42	57	15	5	1	56	22	35
1938	ARSENAL	42	52	15	4	2	52	16	34
1939	EVERTON	42	59	17	3	1	60	18	37
No National competition 1940, 1941, 1942, 1943, 1944, 1945 or 1946 regional leagues in opera										
1947	LIVERPOOL	42	57	13	3	5	42	24	29
1948	ARSENAL	42	52	15	3	3	56	15	33
1949	PORTSMOUTH	42	58	18	3	0	52	12	39
1950	PORTSMOUTH	42	56	12	7	2	44	15	31
1951	TOTTENHAM HOTSPUR	42	60	17	2	2	54	21	36
1952	MANCHESTER UNITED	42	57	15	3	3	55	21	33
1953	ARSENAL	42	54	15	3	3	60	30	33
1954	WOLVERHAMPTON WANDERERS	42	57	16	1	4	61	25	33
1955	CHELSEA	42	52	11	5	5	43	29	27
1956	MANCHESTER UNITED	42	60	18	3	0	51	20	39
1957	MANCHESTER UNITED	42	64	14	4	3	55	25	32
1958	WOLVERHAMPTON WANDERERS	42	64	17	3	1	60	21	37
1959	WOLVERHAMPTON WANDERERS	42	61	15	3	3	68	19	33
1960	BURNLEY	42	55	15	2	4	52	28	32
1961	TOTTENHAM HOTSPUR	42	66	15	3	3	65	28	33
1962	IPSWICH TOWN	42	56	17	2	2	58	28	36
1963	EVERTON	42	61	14	7	0	48	17	35
1964	LIVERPOOL	42	57	16	0	5	60	18	32
1965	MANCHESTER UNITED	42	61	16	4	1	52	13	36
1966	LIVERPOOL	42	61	17	2	2	52	15	36
1967	MANCHESTER UNITED	42	60	17	4	0	51	13	38
1968	MANCHESTER CITY	42	58	17	2	2	52	16	36
1969	LEEDS UNITED	42	67	18	3	0	41	9	39
1970	EVERTON	42	66	17	3	1	46	19	37
1971	ARSENAL	42	65	18	3	0	41	6	39
1972	DERBY COUNTY	42	58	16	4	1	43	10	36
1973	LIVERPOOL	42	60	17	3	1	45	19	37
1974	LEEDS UNITED	42	62	12	8	1	38	18	32
1975	DERBY COUNTY	42	53	14	4	3	41	18	32
1976	LIVERPOOL	42	60	14	5	2	41	21	33
1977	LIVERPOOL	42	57	18	3	0	47	11	39
1978	NOTTINGHAM FOREST	42	64	15	6	0	37	8	36
1979	LIVERPOOL	42	68	19	2	0	51	4	40